RACISM AND CULTURAL DIVERSITY

Michel
Thanks for being a ray
of happiness and fun.
Hope this book will
challenge you.

MJ

RACISM AND CULTURAL DIVERSITY

Cultivating Racial Harmony through Counselling, Group Analysis, and Psychotherapy

M. J. Maher

Foreword by Ian Parker

KARNAC

Reproduction of lines from "This Be The Verse" by Philip Larkin, reprinted with kind permission of the publisher, Faber and Faber Ltd, from *Collected Poems* by Philip Larkin.

First published in 2012 by
Karnac Books Ltd
118 Finchley Road
London NW3 5HT

British Library Cataloguing in Publication Data

A C.I.P. for this book is available from the British Library

ISBN-13: 978-1-85575-630-4

Typeset by Vikatan Publishing Solutions (P) Ltd., Chennai, India

Printed in Great Britain

www.karnacbooks.com

This book is dedicated to Seamus and Maureen Maher, whose nurturing and holding roots have sustained this multicultural family tree. Thank you for being present and available to the whole family in its entire extension, and what an extension it is! Thank you also for the birth of my best friend—Garrett John Brendan Maher.

Inspiration
This book was inspired by the memory of the indomitable courage and spirit of independence shown by my late father, Titus Samuel Kadhlela Mubika, my late mother, Ethel Kamwemba Mubika, my late brothers Sam Titus Zondie Mubika and Major Obediah John Mhiko Mubika, also known as Comrade Blackson Shungu. Their spirit and voices accompany and guide me through every day of my life.

"I have fought against white domination and I have fought against black domination. I have cherished the ideal of a democratic and free society in which all persons live together in harmony and with equal opportunities. It is an ideal which I hope to live for and achieve, but if needs be, it is an ideal for which I am prepared to die."

—Nelson Mandela, cited in Allen (2005, p. xvii)

CONTENTS

PART III: CAN PSYCHOTHERAPY PENETRATE BEYOND
SKIN COLOUR? TRAINEE COUNSELLORS' RESPONSES
TO QUESTIONS OF SKIN COLOUR

PART IV: PERSONAL DEVELOPMENT

ACKNOWLEDGEMENTS

My sincere gratitude to David Muggleston, Amy Manchershaw, my supervisor Professor Ian Parker and my editor John Allen, all of whom upheld and guided this ship as it struggled through troubled waters to reach its destination. Without their support and belief in this project the vessel would have capsized.

The book contains drawings and images which illustrate my thinking and the cultural concepts I wanted to put across without words. Many thanks to Georgia Manchershaw for the title illustrations and animal drawings; Kiara Thembile Maher for the Black History illustrations; Karen Mpo Zinaka and Bryan Themba Maher for helping in realizing these concepts artistically and creatively; and Jim Wellsman for the front cover photo.

Much appreciation to my analytic family for giving birth to the group analyst that I am today—Cynthia Rogers, Dr Harold Behr, Linda Anderson, Sheila Mackintosh Millard, Tony Ashton, Stephen Cogill, Sue Einhorn, Nick Tanna, Dr Keith Hyde, Dr Jim Wilson, Dr Malcolm Pines, Dr Peter Hollis, Marion deLandemeter, Christine Thornton, Nick Barwick, Chris Powell, Sally King, Ian Simpson, Marcus Page, Tim Thomas, Steve Paddock, Sheila Ritchie, Bonnie Gold and the ever-available beavers—Sue Stevenson and Bethan Marreiros.

Many thanks to the staff and students at Manchester Metropolotan University—my Personal Development Group, in particular Sam Ndoro, Alex Hamlin, Leanne Mundin and our tutors Dr Paul Duckett and Kevin Rowley.

At North East Surrey College of Technology (NECOT), where I did my Introductory to Counselling Skills, Diploma in Psychodynamic Counselling and BA (Hons) in Counselling I would like to thank Brian Maxwell, Philippa Evans and Dr Anastasios Gaitanidis and all the students and staff with whom I studied.

Thanks to all the people I worked with in the two therapeutic communities, particularly Lyston Knight, Steph Murray, Dr Fred Roach, Brenda West, Kamla Lansing, Peter Bryan, Josephine Hamilton, Heidi and Dr David.

To everyone at Westminster Pastoral Foundation Therapy (WPF Therapy)—staff and trainees, particularly those who so willingly offered their time to participate in the research with such honesty and enthusiasm, I am grateful for the time and energy you put into the project, making a heavy task seem so light and enjoyable.

I would also like to express my thanks to all the patients/clients/residents/service users who have always been a great source of learning as we travelled together in the jungle of the unknown and learnt to play rugby—holding and running with the ball, that is, working through the presenting challenges when the desired preference was volley ball or tennis—the games of butting away difficulties and responsibilities. It has been a two-way learning experience. I thank all those who gave their consent to allow me to reflect on our work together which I hope will benefit others.

To my family and friends;—the Maher—Derek and Lydia, Billy, Richard and Dolly; the Mubika, Kamwemba, Zinaka, Ovidiu Tamas, Cole, Okpokiri, Marowa, Mutandiro, Machivenyika, Mupenzeni, Tsvakai, Musoni, Chigova, Nomvete, Tsomondo, Laura Czerniewicz, Rick, Jacque and Francis de Satge; Father John Bliss, Dr John and Anne Stephens, Patricia and Ngoni Kudenga; Joyce Chivizhe-Madzivire, Peter Vincent Speyer, Dhun Manchershaw, Dr Matina Sotrilli-Harding, Terri Barnes, James Kilgore, Tony, Sally and Naomi Poyser, Margarate Hondoyenzomba, Mabel Sikhosana, Marion Gow, David and Marjorie Samudzimu—*ndinotenda nemoyo wangu wose* (I thank you with all my heart). To all those who might feel left out I say, "*Kutenda kwakitsi kurimumoyo*"—the gratitude of a cat is in its heart. You know how grateful I am.

ABOUT THE AUTHOR

M. J. Maher was born in Zimbabwe. She obtained her teacher training from Mutare Teachers' College and taught at Chitsere Government School in Mbare, Harare. As a teacher, she also worked for the Ministry of Education as a manuscript evaluator for the Curriculum Development Unit and also as a school radio lessons script writer for Audio Visual Service. She left teaching to be an editor for Zimbabwe Publishing House. In 1988 MJ came to the United Kingdom to train as a psychiatric nurse, subsequently training as a group analyst. She worked for National Health Service (NHS) for twenty-three years as a psychiatric nurse and a group psychotherapist facilitating therapy groups and staff groups. MJ has extensive experience of working in therapeutic communities for residents with a diagnosis of Personality Disorder and of Drug and Alcohol Addiction. Currently she offers individual, couple and group psychotherapy in her private practice and also facilitates carers' groups and experiential groups for trainee counsellors.

FOREWORD

by Professor Ian Parker

It is not merely a historical curiosity that one of Freud's favourite jokes for more than thirty years after first airing, usually prompted when a patient did not appear at the appointed hour, was to say "twelve o'clock and no negro". The saying was derived from the caption for a cartoon in a newspaper in 1886 that showed a yawning lion waiting for lunch. This joke, when read alongside Freud's more well-known comment that women's sexuality was a "dark continent", draws attention to the intertwinement of sex and race in psychoanalysis. The issue here is not only how blacks and women are constituted within psychoanalytic discourse, but also how psychoanalysis itself emerges as a practice that is both normalizing and pathologized, itself pathologized.

Psychoanalysis in the West, particularly in the English-speaking world, has been a predominantly white profession, and it is against that background that liberal multiculturalist agonizing about the racism of dominant practice and mistaken attempts to adapt psychoanalysis for "other" cultures have developed. This is also despite, or precisely because, psychoanalysis has often been marked as a Jewish science, something not wholly white. At the same time, psychoanalysis from the beginning, and as a function of its cultural composition as well as its interest in the secret tangles of childhood intimacy, was viewed as in some ways feminine, and this image of therapeutic work today as stereotypically feminine marks it as a domain which questions masculine reserve, and not only when analysts aim to hystericize the analysand.

It is possible, then, to interpret Freud's comments as symptomatic of the peculiar feminization and racialization of psychoanalysis; to refer to his patients as his "negroes", as he was wont to do, was to speak within chains of signification that he did not control. So, in Freud's borrowed joke, the analyst is, perhaps, the strong lion rather than being the feminized Jew, a strong lion who will master the analysand opening themselves up as a vulnerable needy patient rather being a "negro" as stereotypically hyper-masculine threat to the civilizing process. And there are limits to what psychoanalysis can do to change that; speaking on the impossibility of changing the world through analysing individuals—against "individual therapy" as a remedy for "the whole of humanity"—Freud remarked that this was akin to "the white-washing of a negro". Analysands, whether white or not, man or not, still speak within a conceptual frame that is stereotypically white (though ambivalently and complexly so) and feminine (though also riven with contradictions).

It is against that background that we must read this impressive book. It draws on psychoanalytic concepts that have been used to describe the relationship between mother and child in order to conceptualize the formation of identity, and it explains the relevance of these concepts to questions of race and racism. There is a bridging across from the psychotherapeutic context to qualitative research, and links are made with approaches to subjectivity in psychoanalysis. This is also "action research", for it aims to change the world at the same time as it interprets it. You might sometimes ask yourself if the arguments in this book are too exaggerated, but if we look back at the history of psychoanalysis we will see that it is a history of grotesque exaggerations of prejudices about different categories of human being. Here, at least, we have some response to those prejudices and a serious attempt to change the psychoanalytic world and the social context in which it took shape.

INTRODUCTION

In April of 2010 I spoke to Sir Richard Bowlby concerning his father's formulation of the Attachment Theory. He described how John Bowlby was motivated by the pain of losing his nanny and explained how pain can motivate one into a deeper way of thinking, and even though nobody at that time understood the underlying concepts, it was out of this experience that the Attachment Theory was born.

I connected strongly to this way of thinking after realizing that my reaction to the racism I experienced was highly influenced by my early life experiences with my attachment figures. The first part of this book might be perceived as whinging about institutional racism, discrimination and victimization but I hoped that whinging would get the pain out of my system and leave me better equipped to address the underlying issues in a more constructive manner. Like John Bowlby, my painful experience allowed me to reach a deeper understanding.

It is impossible to talk about racism without considering Attachment Theory, because the root of racism is connected to one's primary and secondary attachment figures in early childhood, where our attachment style is mapped out for us. Thus, how one experiences racism and reacts to it is determined by previous family experiences, some of which we replay in our adult relationships. For those whose experience of broken attachments crosses over various lines—race, colour, faith, etc.—this book is possibly the first to use Attachment Theory as a theoretical framework for understanding racism and shows how this is possible within this specific context.

Part One narrates my experiences of institutional racism and victimization, and clearly demonstrates Bowlby's characteristics of attachment:

- *Proximity maintenance*—desiring to be with the people with whom I had formed an attachment;
- *Separation distress*—being sent away and not allowed any contact with colleagues for a year;
- *Safe haven*—seeking comfort from the training institution I joined when I first arrived in the United Kingdom;
- *Secure base*—continually running back to the institution at which I trained, as it provided me with the comfort and emotional security to heal.

The book is divided into four parts:

Part One

The concepts of Attachment Theory are interwoven with the racial experiences throughout Part One, which also reflects on my three Employment Tribunal cases. Each case focuses on one specific aspect:

The First Employment Tribunal contrasts how the legal system and group analysis deal with conflict, and discusses the psychological processes one goes through during, and after, such a case.

The Second Employment Tribunal focuses on difficulties of unfair treatment by people of the same race or culture, and how that could be experienced as a betrayal and lead to individual regression. It examines the impact of such regression and how past and present need to be separated for the individual to function. This section also addresses the impact of victimization, including how an individual could be blacklisted to the extent of being unable to find employment.

The Third Employment Tribunal reflects on being a witness to discrimination and the impact of failure to react for fear of victimization. This case focuses on the shame and guilt of the witness and the consequences of eventual action, which led to immediate suspension and being investigated for fraud.

Part Two

Part Two majors on demonstrating some of the struggles between Blacks and Whites when working together in group analysis. This section follows my journey as a Black trainee group analyst in a predominantly White institution, facilitating groups of White clients while experiencing institutional racism at work. The tense feelings evoked threatened my training and contaminated my relationships with the different groups of Whites. The struggle I went through to stay on the course is explored, and analysing these events gives some interesting insights.

I work with the theme of abandonment in trying to understand the processes and dynamics that take place in analytic groups, drawing on the parallel processes which took place in my training groups and in my own therapy group. I reflect on early abandonment experiences and how they influence reaction to abandonment, separation and loss. I chose this theme because I lost my mother and two brothers during my training, and thus was able to explore the impact this had on my group.

Part Three

Part Three, carried out with trainee counsellors, is a research: *Can psychotherapy penetrate beyond skin colour*? I look at the history of skin colour and discuss the grounding theories necessary for working with racism, including Bowlby's Attachment Theory, Melanie Klein's paranoid-schizoid position, depressive position and splitting, Winnicott's Hate in Countertransference and Bollas' concept of extractive introjection. I also discuss the Minority Identity Development Model and the White Identity Development Model, linking them closely to the impact of racism, slavery, and colonization, and reflecting on cultural diversity. The research raises interesting and challenging issues for training and clinical practice.

Part Four

Part Four reflects on the process of personal development I went through while carrying out the research and working with my Personal Development Group of students at Manchester Metropolitan University. It looks at the prejudices I brought to the group and how

I had to work them through in order to obtain my optimum from the group. I discuss different learning styles and show how the group was set up and facilitated, and how I adapted to student culture as a Black Zimbabwean married woman to become the group analyst I am today.

PART I

RACIAL DISCRIMINATION: A CRY IN THE WILDERNESS?

INTRODUCTION

The Trade Union Congress's *"Root Out Racism" hotline: Exposing Racism at Work* (2000) received 439 calls from ethnic minority people complaining about institutional racism at work. These calls were made between Monday 19th and Friday 23rd June 2000, a five-day period from which I chose the following information because at that time I was also complaining about institutional racism at my work place. The following details show the groups I belong to and one comparator for each group:

1. Among the 439 callers the Black (Afro-Caribbean) were highest with fifty-three percent calls, followed by Asians with twenty-six percent calls.
2. Analysing the callers' occupations, I belonged to two categories: the professional was highest with twenty percent and the associate professional and technical (which included nurses) were fourth with twelve percent calls.
3. Concerning the type of employer, the public administration, health, and education had the highest with sixty-three percent calls followed by manufacturing, retail, hotel and catering, transport communications, with nine percent each.

4. Looking at the regions, London had the highest with sixty-two percent, followed by the southeast region with twenty-two percent.

I belong to four groups with the highest number of callers (ethnicity, profession, type of employer, and region). Is it any wonder that I also ended up complaining about institutional racism, racial discrimination, and victimization?

The American Psychiatric Association (July 2006) "recognises that racism and racial discrimination adversely affect mental health by diminishing the victim's self-image, confidence and optimal mental functioning ... attempts should be made to eliminate racism and racial discrimination by fostering a respectful appreciation of multicultural-ism and diversity".

The Trade Union Congress report states that the callers complained of suffering personal pain and anguish and seeing their job prospects blighted by institutional racism. They complained about being deliber-ately isolated at work; ignored, victimized, or sacked. They described how racism changed them—for example, they experienced feelings of self-loathing, self-destruction, and acquired an inferiority complex. Racism caused health problems such as physical illnesses, often resulting in long periods of sick leave due to stress, depression, and anxiety. The following are some of the manifestations of racism at work as experienced by these callers:

- being refused references, leaving jobs due to undue pressure;
- not being informed about training, overtime, or promotion opportunities;
- procedures not being clear, or being unfair or arbitrary;
- feeling unfairly monitored;
- being denied or consistently overlooked for promotion even though well qualified;
- being downgraded;
- feeling that they had to suffer in silence or risk being publicly iso-lated, and
- being labelled "troublemaker" or "having a chip on their shoulder" after making a complaint.

Some of these callers are the people we meet in our consulting rooms seeking psychotherapy to deal with the impact of the racism they experience. The fact that 439 people called within just five days begs us to take racism seriously. The aim of this book is to explore and try to make sense of these experiences using various theoretical concepts, vignettes and research findings in an attempt to understand racism, so that as therapists and counsellors we can offer informed interventions to victims of racism. For this reason I have decided to reflect on my personal experiences of institutional racism.

In my culture we have a saying: *Chinoziva ivhu kuti mwana wembeva anorwara.* The literal translation is, "Only the soil can tell that the baby of a fieldmouse is ill" because a fieldmouse nests in the bowels of Mother Earth. Hopefully, my contribution as an insider who has walked the tough walk will inform on what ails the baby of racial harmony, so that those offering therapy can contain and work more effectively with racism and cultural diversity. I also aim to improve the therapists' and counsellors' understanding of racial processes that might take place, or be recreated and re-enacted, in the consulting rooms.

Part One also explores issues around institutional racism, racial discrimination and victimization in a residential democratic therapeutic community. The community draws on Maxwell Jones' therapeutic community principles and the principles and theories of Tom Main, who worked with Foulkes in the Northfield Military Hospital in Birmingham. This therapeutic community uses methods similar to those used in the Northfield Experiment.

I explore the concept of projective identification, looking at what was projected into me and how I had to take legal action through the Employment Tribunal in order to give back these disowned projections. The psychological processes, conflicts and group dynamics evoked are discussed. Using the events of this first Employment Tribunal, the book highlights conflicting ideas between the legal system and group analysis in dealing with conflict. I also attempt to identify factors that perpetuate institutional racism.

I developed this paper further to illustrate how the Zimbabwean tradition of totems, in the use of animal metaphors, was embraced by this White therapeutic community. However, about four years later some of the senior clinicians banned the practice, claiming that I was working against the ethos of the therapeutic community because they perceived giving animal metaphors the same as giving concrete gifts to individuals. They also argued that it was potentially risky as they worried that I was placing myself in danger of attack by the residents. The book looks at how democracy was exercised by the residents to challenge this ban, and the fight to reinstate the animal metaphors demonstrates the power of democracy in a residential therapeutic community.

I then discuss a second Employment Tribunal focusing on issues of Black-on-Black betrayal and how that led to regression. The second Employment Tribunal highlights what happens when past and present collide. I also talk about what I believe to be the possible consequences of complaining about institutional racism: I suffered further victimization long after leaving the therapeutic community.

In the final chapters I discuss a third Employment Tribunal, looking at the impact of shame and guilt evoked in me by an incident I witnessed of a Black junior clinician whom I believe was racially discriminated against. None of her colleagues, either Black or White (including me), offered her much support. Feelings of shame and guilt are important to understand as they are often experienced when witnessing racial injustice. The significance of the third Employment Tribunal was in giving me an opportunity to recover from the damage I had suffered during the second Employment Tribunal.

Part One concludes by bringing all the different threads together.

CHAPTER ONE

What is racism?

1.1 Racism

The American Psychiatric Association (APA, July 2006) defines racism as a set of beliefs or practices that assume the existence of inherent and significant differences between the genetics of various groups of human beings, with these differences resulting in racial superiority, inferiority, or purity and in one group taking the social, political, and economical advantage over another by practicing racial discrimination, segregation, persecution, and domination.

1.1.1 Individual racism

Individual racism takes place when an individual degrades, ignores or ill-treats another person on the grounds of their race: for example, using racial jokes, unfair hiring, promoting, and firing of individuals.

1.1.2 Micro-aggressions

Chester Pierce was a psychiatrist who drew attention to micro-aggressions as a form of individual racism in the 1970s. The American

Psychiatric Glossary (8th edition cited in American Psychiatric Association, 2006) defines micro-aggressions as:

"Offensive mechanisms or actions by a person that are designed to keep other individuals in an inferior, dependent or helpless role. These actions are nonverbal and kinetic and they are well suited to control space, time, energy, and mobility of an individual (usually non-white or female), while producing feelings of degradation".

Some of these behaviours stem from unconscious attitudes of racial superiority and are not always intentional. However, they are unpleasant, shocking, depressing, and can grind down the individual's self-esteem.

1.1.3   Institutional/structural racism

This type of racism takes place at organizational or group level and can be built into policies in such a way that one group is favoured while excluding another on racial grounds. The Trade Union Congress report *"Root Out Racism" hotline: Exposing Racism At Work* (2000) defines institutional racism by quoting the definition in the Macpherson Inquiry Report into Stephen Lawrence's murder (Appendix 1):

"The collective failure of an organization to provide an appropriate and professional service to people because of their colour, culture or ethnic origin which can be seen or detected in processes, attitudes and behaviour which amounts to discrimination through unwitting prejudice, ignorance, thoughtlessness and racist stereotyping which disadvantages minority ethnic people".

The law holds employers responsible for any racism at work, therefore employers have to ensure that their employees behave appropriately. The law states that:

"Things done by a person in the course of his/her employment are treated as done by the employer whether or not done with the employer's approval or knowledge" (section 32 of the 1976 Act).

1.1.4   Racial discrimination

Racial discrimination occurs when power is used in acting out racial prejudice to control, deprive or exclude an individual on the basis of their race. It is unlawful to discriminate against any person, or group of people, on racial grounds. The law states that:

"By sections 1(1)(a) and 4(2) of the 1976 Act it is unlawful for an employer to treat an employee less favourably than he treats or would treat other employees on grounds of race. This is commonly referred to as direct race discrimination. An employer must not discriminate on racial grounds by subjecting the person to dismissal or any other detriment. Discrimination in the way that an employer affords an employee access to opportunities for promotion, transfer or training, or to any other benefits, facilities or services or by refusing or deliberately omitting to afford her access to them is also made unlawful under section 4(2)".

Complaints of racial discrimination can sometimes result in further victimization. The Law attempts to protect individuals from such victimization. It states that:

"Where a person alleges that there has been race discrimination or takes further action in pursuit of such an allegation, they have done what is referred to as 'a protected act'. If as a result within their employment they are treated less favourably because of having done the protected act, then they have been victimized within the meaning of the 1976 Act. It is unnecessary to establish that the original allegation of the breach of the Act was made out, as long as the allegation was made in good faith".

1.1.5   Stereotype

One of the oils that lubricate racism and racial discrimination is the way people are put into boxes, then stereotyped using this generalization as a standard measure of what we expect of an individual and what we associate with their particular group of people. Stereotyping stems from a process of categorization (for example, into social groups) which gives the individual a sense of belonging by identifying with that specific group. Historically, most groups have had an identified group they perceive as less superior, allowing for promotion of their own group as superior. There is a tendency of developing an in-group—belonging, and an out-group—not belonging (Dovidio & Gaertner, 1986).

Stereotypes are cognitive structures that people form about social categories in order to help them process information about people who are different from them. Therefore, stereotypes can only exist when differential beliefs and values become associated with the differentiated social categories created by the individual or group of people.

Hamilton and Trolier, cited in Dovidio and Gaertner (1986) discuss the development of stereotypes and how they are perpetuated as a result of the following processes (Ashmore & Del Boca, 1981):

Motivational processes: stereotypes serve the intrapsychic needs of the perceiver: for example, using degrading terms for Black people (calling an old man "boy") which promotes some White people's self-esteem and helps them cope with their own feelings of inadequacy. Sometimes the way the media reports events motivates the way a society processes that information, which then affects the perceptions and judgments formed about specific groups of people.

Socio-cultural orientation: these stereotypes are learnt through the process of socialization, such as learning from one's parents, family members, various social groups one belongs to, influential people in one's life (pop stars, footballers, notorious criminals) and the media. We learn about various groups and what to associate them with: Zimbabweans, Irish, English, Americans, Polish, Germans, Americans, Zambians, Nigerians, Jamaicans, Welsh, Scottish, French; Jews, Muslims, Roman Catholics and Jehovah's Witnesses. What associations come to your mind with each group? Where and what did you learn about them? What influenced your perception? What negative associations are attributed to your own group of people?

Stereotypes can be challenged and altered, for example through relearning from new or different experiences. Counselling and group psychotherapy offer the opportunity of having a new or different experience and a space for improving one's self-awareness by reflecting on what one has internalized from one's environment.

Cognitive structures and processes: Hamilton and Trolier define stereotype from a cognitive perspective as cognitive structures that hold the perceiver's knowledge, beliefs, and expectancies about other groups of people. This information may be distorted or inaccurate but will still have an impact on how we behave towards that group of people. For instance, if one believes that a certain group of people is inferior one is likely to be patronizing in the way one speaks or what one speaks about.

All stereotypes have a cognitive component and some have all three components. For example, racism is influenced by cognitive, motivational, and socio-cultural learning processes resulting in judgmental and behavioural manifestations.

Hamilton and Trolier discuss how stereotype influences what information we choose to hear and how we make sense of it based on what we have encoded in our brain and how we encode new information which will be used for future referencing.

They also demonstrate the effects of racial stereotyping on encoding information using Sagar and Schofield (1980), who studied the reaction of school children to drawings of cartoon stick figures of two boys sitting one in front of the other. These cartoons were accompanied by the following description:

"Mark was sitting at his desk, working on his social studies assignment, when David started poking him in the back with the eraser end of his pencil. Mark just kept on working. David kept poking him for a while, and then he finally stopped". Dovidio and Gaertner (1986, p. 143).

The participants were asked to rate David's behaviour on how playful, friendly, mean and threatening his behaviour was. Initially the David character was White, then changed to Black. What was interesting was that when David was Black his behaviour was perceived as more mean and threatening and less playful and friendly than when he was White, proving that stereotyping motivates how we perceive and interpret what we witness and what we become blind to.

Dalal (1997) states that stereotyping serves two functions, firstly of categorization and secondly as a means of instructions. There are two sorts:

1. stereotypes seen as a template that has coded into it what one may become. He gives an example of how Blacks become nurses but not psychiatrists.
2. stereotypes directing the mind as to what is to be seen. In my case, for instance, the institution I worked for ignored its scoring criteria, and the fact that I had scored highest in an interview, in favour of a White candidate who came third and scored the lowest. In a staff meeting where they discussed who to offer the job to they acknowledged that I had scored the highest. The Employment Tribunal later ruled this decision as racial victimization.

1.1.6   Internalized racism

It is important to acknowledge that we all have racial feelings, prejudices, beliefs, and stereotypic thoughts. The question is, are you aware of yours and are you aware of when you are likely to act them out? Although we have no control over how we feel, we are responsible for how we behave, even if the action is a direct result of how we feel. Stereotyping is not only about what others project onto you, but what you introject from around you—from the family and society at large.

Dalal (1997) suggests that stereotypes are strengthened because they are shared by a society as a whole. For example, I was brought up in a Black community in Zimbabwe (then known as Rhodesia) where it was socially accepted that Blacks and Whites lived in racially segregated areas and attended racially segregated schools. It was accepted that Whites were a privileged, superior race while Blacks were underprivileged and inferior. Although I was not conscious of this racial discrimination till my early teens, I was aware that the shade of one's skin was important and that it was socially accepted that the lighter the skin shade the more positive the attributes given to the person—superior, prettier, more intelligent—attributes similar to those given to White people. As a result of this socially accepted discrimination, some dark-skinned people used skin-lightening creams to achieve a lighter skin shade in the hope of gaining the privileged status, but they risked problematic skin conditions in old age. Some "burnt" their skin as it reacted to the chemicals in the skin-lightening creams, resulting in dark blotches. The other problem was that the cream was only applied on the face, so these women and men ended up with lighter faces and dark bodies, which often led to them being teased. They were called Fanta face and Coca-cola body.

Although I am a bold shade of black I did not feel the inferiority complex attached to my dark skin colour. Perhaps it was counteracted by the affluence of my family. However, I believe I unconsciously internalized some of the negative aspects attributed to dark-skinned people and had strong feelings about it. This is indicated by my self-chosen high school nickname "*Gangemukange svosve dema rinonhuwa*" shortened to *Gange*. It means a black ant which leaves a stink where it stings. Then there was my favourite teenage T-shirt on which I painted a slogan copied from my brother's MacDonald T-shirt: "*Black is beautiful, needs no crowning but justice*". I remember feeling very proud of my slogan.

At school I learnt that speaking my mother tongue, Shona, was an inferior thing to do. I remember at the age of eight being forced to speak English all the time at school except during Shona lessons. Our teacher used to give the first child he caught speaking Shona a placard with the word *"Traitor"* written on it in bold. Whoever was given the Traitor had to wear it around their neck until they caught someone else speaking Shona. They could then pass the placard on. The last child left with the Traitor at the end of the day was punished. Thus, from that tender age we quickly learnt to speak English, but the cost was internalizing the fact that our own language and culture was inferior, second-class to English, and that one is a traitor for speaking one's own language.

In my teens I realized that Blacks lived in cheaper houses in high density "locations" while Whites lived in bigger and better houses in low density suburbs; White children went to better schools and got better jobs; while White farmers occupied better land, Black families lived on smaller plots in less fertile areas. As a result of this injustice Black Zimbabweans arose to fight for our land and for equal rights. This is the society I was brought up in and the history I carry within me. My awareness of racial discrimination is strongly connected to fighting for one's rights and not accepting that the Other is better just because of their lighter skin colour.

Although I do not believe I am politically minded I still introjected the fighting spirit into me from the society I lived in, and it became part of who I am. Foulkes (1983) highlights the fact that one cannot separate the internal/external worlds, constitution/environment, individual/ society, phantasy/reality and body/mind. We are products of our environment.

My father had a great influence on me and my self-belief. For example, when I did something wrong he would give me an opportunity to put my case forward. If my argument was weak or showed that I had not thought through my actions I was punished, but if I could prove that I had thought things through I was let go, no matter how stupid the end result was. So, from a very young age I was taught to argue my cases and be my own lawyer. My father also taught me to fight for myself and that no-one need be better than me in everything: if they were I had chosen to allow it to happen. Growing up in a Black society in which my father was better off than most, and being unaware that Whites were more privileged than me, gave me confidence in who I am and what I am worth.

However, in multi-cultural societies today Black children learn early in life that White children are better than them. In her article, *Daring to Work with Internalized Racism* Rose (1997) described a Black child of nursery age refusing to play with a black doll yet crying for a white doll. When asked why he said, "I don't like it, it's black. I want a white dolly". When his mother told him, "but YOU'RE Black" he held his head down as if in shame and gave a heartfelt sob.

Rose further describes an experiment carried out by Clark and Clark (1939) cited in Rack (1982, pp. 68–69) in which children were given dolls to play with. Both children and dolls were of varied ethnic groups. Both Black and White children gave positive attributions to white dolls and negative attributions to black dolls. The White children identified with the white dolls in a more positive and comfortable position, *White doll is good and White doll is me.* On the other hand, the Black children's position appeared more confusing: *I am good—Black doll is bad. Black doll—White doll is me?*

In the above example, what is the Black child introjecting about who he is? What is the White child learning about the Other? Might the Black child end up with identity confusion? (If you are good you must be White and if you are bad you must be Black. I am Black therefore I must be …?).

Black children brought up in multi-racial communities tend to learn about racism, discrimination, and racial bullying at a younger age. I remember my daughter at four years of age coming home from nursery upset that she had lost her boyfriend to a four-year-old White girl because she was Brown; and my son at five years of age was upset at being called "poo-poo colour" at school. By the age of six he was already asking me questions such as, "Why did you marry a White boy when you're Brown? Did you like his freckles or was it because you wanted to live in England?" This presumably shows the impact of the media: the topic of bogus marriages was being covered on television at that time.

Years later my granddaughter, Tayler-Ray, was accused of being racist at the age of three by the staff at her nursery school. Her mother was told that if Tayler-Ray did not stop calling other three-year-olds "niggers" she would be expelled. Our dilemma was how to tell a three-year-old not to be racist. We tried to investigate where she had learnt about niggers but, because we were unable to have such a sophisticated conversation with her at her age, we could not find out. However, one day Tayler-Ray found her lost teddy bear in my car and started shouting with excitement, "Nigole! Nigole!" but to a politically correct ear it sounded like "Nigger-all! Nigger-all!"

My granddaughter got this teddy bear from her cousin Nicole as a christening present. It wore a T-shirt with Nicole's name on it but my granddaughter called it Nigole because she could not pronounce Nicole. My daughter took the teddy to the nursery and produced it in front of all the staff. Her daughter started jumping up and down shouting with excitement and they all agreed that she was saying "Nigole" and not "Nigger-all". The mystery was solved. However, it must have been difficult for my granddaughter to understand why grown-ups were getting angry with her when she was trying to tell them about her lost teddy bear.

I wonder what effect such racial experiences Black children carry have on them later in life when they become group analysts, therapists, or counsellors seeing White patients. What happens to White children brought up by racist parents, or children who are allowed to call other children "poo-poo colour", when they become group analysts, therapists, or counsellors seeing Black patients?

Foulkes (1983, p. 10) states that each individual "… is basically and centrally determined, inevitably, by the world in which he lives, by the community, the group, of which he forms as part".

What are we, as a society, creating for future generations? What does the future hold for our children?

CHAPTER TWO

The impact of internalized racism on delivering therapy

2.1 Clinical example one

When I facilitated a weekly women's group I lost three Black members at different times before realizing that they all followed a similar pattern of asking for a fee reduction for various personal reasons. When I agreed to reduce their fees without analysing the meaning of their requests they immediately dropped out.

When this was explored in supervision, I realized that with the Black patients I acted out my internalized racial stereotypic belief that Blacks are poorer than Whites. I automatically accepted their requests for fee reduction at face value. I believe the patients dropped out because they were checking out their own internalized racial stereotypic belief that Black therapists are not worth much, are not as good as White therapists. By agreeing to the fee reduction I was confirming the belief that I was not good enough and did not deserve to be paid as much as White therapists, thus devaluing their therapy and myself. When we started analysing this request for fee reduction in the group it opened up discussions about self-value and prejudices. The women stayed even when I denied the fee reduction because in their eyes I was saying, "*Yes, I am good and worth it*", thus valuing myself and their therapy.

2.2   Clinical example two

In another weekly group a White woman, A, informed me at assessment that she was not prepared to pay me the same amount as she paid her previous White therapist because it would be too much money for me, a Black therapist. One year later, A started missing payments. I took a longer time to raise this with her than I would have done with a Black person because of my stereotypic belief that Whites are rich. It did not occur to me that A could be having financial difficulties. When I eventually raised the issue of missed payments she admitted to having financial problems because she had given up her part-time job as a child-minder, but felt she could not ask for a fee reduction as that would stop her from feeling superior to me. This opened up group discussions about:

- Slave/master relationships: she felt like a slave and I was her master whom she perceived to be in control and with all the power. Her grandfather had warned her about Blacks coming to their country and taking all the better jobs. She was able to talk about her Black boss. Needless to say there was tension between them due to her internal conflict—she perceived her boss to be the enemy she had to fight following her grandfather's warning about Blacks taking over.
- The need to be shocking with her racist language was her way of hiding her vulnerability and hatred of feeling powerless and being controlled, because she experienced my dynamic administration and boundary-setting as controlling.
- Group members shared their guilty feelings around their parents' racist views, beliefs and attitudes. Eventually they worked towards owning their own individual racism they were projecting onto their parents.
- The group explored its struggle in challenging Black group members for fear of being seen as racist.

From these clinical examples I learnt about the importance of self-awareness of one's racial beliefs, feelings, prejudices, experiences and thoughts, and how lack of self-awareness can cause blind spots which interfere with therapy, as opportunities for exploration may not be picked up.

With this in mind it is my aim to promote racial self-awareness using my personal experiences. I also discuss theoretical concepts that are important to know about when working with clients of different race to us. By exploring these issues and making sense of them we are likely to enhance our skills as we achieve a better understanding of ourselves, which in turn frees us to receive projections without needing to defend against them. When a therapist is not defended the dynamics that might take place in the consulting room can be worked with empathy, sensitivity, understanding, and appropriately timed challenging that contain the client and reduce destructive re-enactment of the clients' conflicts in the consulting room. Being well equipped allows for a different holding experience that promotes personal growth.

CHAPTER THREE

The struggle to complain about racism

3.1   What made it difficult to complain?

3.1.1   Stereotypical beliefs

I suffered institutional racism, racial discrimination, and victimization at work over a three-year period without doing anything about it. I accepted that these were stereotypical beliefs/projections that Blacks need to learn to put up with. The last straw was when my eldest brother, Sam, died. I was refused compassionate leave because he was not considered a close relative, yet a White colleague was given compassionate leave for a father-in-law. I believe my complaints were about the stereotypical phantasies projected onto Blacks, who then become containers of these unwanted negative projections.

My experience of institutional racism made me feel perceived as:

- **Ignorant:** study leave was denied to me but not to White junior colleagues in similar positions to mine.
- **Aggressive/murderous:** expressed as a joke that if I became angry and killed a named colleague I could plead that in a moment of insanity I had mistaken him for a White farmer. This was said at

a time when farmers were being attacked and sometimes killed in my country, Zimbabwe, over land distribution.

- **Strong:** As a Black I felt that I was perceived as being strong as an ox, and despite the fact that I had one of the lowest sickness records— one day off in three years—a doctor's certificate was demanded of me after only one day off. (The local policy requested a doctor's certificate after a week off sick, and White colleagues with higher sickness records than mine were not asked to produce this sick certificate.)

- **Lazy:** the chairwoman of an interviewing panel wrote "lazy" on my job application form. She thought my curriculum vitae was five years old because it noted that I still worked part-time for my previous employer, but this was correct and already stated in my application. Missing that, she assumed I had stopped working and had not bothered to update my curriculum vitae, so she deemed me to be lazy.

- **Less intelligent/inferior:** After applying for an H grade post of Deputy Clinical Manager and being short-listed, I was offered an interview at a time I was presenting a paper in Manchester. I was refused an alternative appointment, even on the same day, yet a White colleague was encouraged and supported when he applied for promotion. Three months later I applied for an H grade Clinical Nurse Specialist post, but was refused promotion even though they openly discussed that I was the best of the three appointable candidates. The post was offered to my manager, a White woman who came third in the interview. Other colleagues, including a White clinician who was off sick, knew that I had been unsuccessful several days before I was told: I found out through the grapevine.

- **Mad/emotionally labile:** comments like *"You stick out like a sore thumb because you are psychiatric"*, *"Would it help if I say that you are mad?"* and *"Some people work here for free therapy"*, were made to me. Since the colleague who said I stuck out like a sore thumb would not apologize I kept raising the issue, and he commented that I was like a "weeping wound". Weeping wounds only heal with attention and treatment, but as the following story illustrates, this was lacking.

- **An immigrant:** As a Zimbabwean citizen this was correct, but I was discriminated against in that my employer refused me a clearance letter that would have saved me harassment by Immigration on my return to the United Kingdom after my brother's funeral.

I had told managers and colleagues that my brother Sam was seriously ill in a local hospital, and after his death I explained to a senior colleague that the family had to fly him back to Zimbabwe. Having mislaid my Zimbabwean passport containing my residence permit, I also asked for a letter stating that I worked full-time for the organization: this would prevent problems with Immigration on my return. This request was ignored, but while preparing to leave one of the senior clinicians sent me a letter by courier asking me to contact him as soon as possible because I was considered absent from work and in danger of losing my job—even though I had phoned to let them know what was happening.

I had two days to sort everything out: paperwork to fly Sam home, obtaining an emergency travel document from the Zimbabwean embassy, liaising with the undertakers in London, body-viewing before leaving the country and making sure we all caught the same flight. Since all adults in our immediate family were going we also had to drive the children to Pembroke in Wales, from where my father in-law would take them by ferry to Ireland. We then had to collect Sam's son, Tipei Winterton, from Heathrow, where he was arriving from Canada. My husband and I had so little time to pack that eventually my sister did it for us, so with all this going on, I was only able to contact the senior clinician from Gatwick Airport.

My sister and sister-in-law had both received flowers and condolence cards from their work colleagues. I had been sent flowers and cards from my two part-time jobs but nothing from my full-time job, and on my return was angry because I had anticipated at least some support, but instead they expected me to be grateful that the senior clinician I contacted had saved my job. Why was my employment at risk in the first place? No-one seemed to understand my distress about that, and even a Black colleague said I had targeted the White clinician who saved my job.

3.1.2   Analysing the possible dynamics

I also struggled to make a formal complaint because I was training in group analysis and was analysing my situation at work. For example, five of the six people concerned were senior authority figures, and I wondered whether my difficulties with them arose from an unconscious conflict with parental figures in my family. Four of them were men—could that be a reflection of unresolved difficulties with father figures?

The other struggle was that all six were White and were also colleagues I admired for various reasons. Had my admiration turned into a destructive envious attack?

On the other hand, one of Freud's well known catch-phrases is that sometimes a cigar is a cigar: we cannot ignore the reality of a situation.

3.1.3   Denial of institutional racism—shame and guilt

White (1989) talks about how a Black person carries disowned aspects of the White psyche, then becomes an extremely powerful "phobogenic object" whose presence threatens the return of the repressed. For others to take back those projections would ultimately entail them becoming conscious of White responsibility in all historical and present forms of exploitation of Blacks—guilt and shame may be experienced.

At work, outside formal meetings, some White colleagues would express their concern about how I was being treated. For example, after the meeting where the team discussed employing the White manager with the lowest score, two White colleagues were in tears when telling me what had happened. They were distressed because they felt that what had happened was very unfair, since I was extremely proficient and had scored the highest. Although one of them agreed to write a detailed account of the situation, the person did not want to be identified as the informer for fear of being victimized. So, while the willingness of White junior colleagues to support me made it possible for me to complain (because I was always made aware of what was happening behind my back), their unwillingness to be identified made complaining difficult, as I could not call them as witnesses.

While I accept this conscious decision to self-protect, I think there is another explanation as to why my two White colleagues found it difficult to acknowledge publicly what we all saw as racism. I concluded that they could be identifying with the whiteness of their White colleagues who made the decision to discriminate against me: this identification made them question their own involvement by association, hence their distress soon after the meeting. This distress possibly indicated their shame and guilt as a result of this identification, and in dealing with those uncomfortable feelings by confessing to me they separated themselves from their White colleagues.

I believe one of the reasons why it is difficult to self-challenge one's internalized racism is because the word "racist" has become too stereotyped. Just as "alcoholic" conjures up stereotypical images of homeless drunks sleeping on park benches but excludes company directors needing a shot of gin before starting the day, so "racist" conjures up an imago of the slave trade, apartheid in South Africa, skinheads or the National Front, but excludes ordinary-looking people who might be just as bigoted.

These conjured stereotypical imagoes of who society perceives as "racist" can make it difficult for Blacks to talk to Whites about experiences of racism and trust being listened to, even in therapy. There is a tendency to explain away the reality of a Black person's experience of racism: by denying it, the uncomfortable feelings evoked by the stories are buried and the focus is quickly shifted to the client's internal world. Looking for links from childhood experiences to explain the current situation allows for the denial of the burning reality of the present injustice. This is a defence against the shame and guilt experienced through the association of being White.

However, if a White group, White counsellor or White therapist tolerates the shame and guilt and rolls with the Black person in whatever direction they take them, then mentalization takes place, because by staying and understanding the Black person's experience of racism without giving premature interpretations, enough moss can be collected for analysis. Empathy, toleration of uncomfortable feelings evoked in the therapist, and attentive listening will enable the Black individual to let go of the present racist experience and move on to analysing his/her internal world—right back to the point of the initial traumatic experience of being treated unfairly, for example, within the family. In a group setting other group members of different races can then share similar family experiences around unfairness, discrimination, favouritism, and being an outsider.

On the other hand, if the Black member's reality of racism is denied it leads into a cul-de-sac, with the individual feeling alienated, misunderstood, unheard, gagged, stuck, and constipated with anger about the present situation. This makes it difficult for the individual to let go of the here-and-now experience in order to travel back in the past to see what has been evoked from there. When past and present collide and one is unable to see their link, interactions in the present become immature, regressed, and overloaded with extra baggage from the past.

The individual may be pushed into the paranoid–schizoid position and be unable to reflect on what else might be influencing the reaction. If the present reality is not acknowledged, the external sense of victimization and trauma experienced outside the consulting room can then be re-enacted in the consulting room.

3.1.4   Fear of abandonment

The final problem which made it difficult for me to complain about institutional racism was that I have a history of separation from my mother at a young age, the result of a 1960s migration to the United Kingdom. So, separation anxiety, fear of isolation, abandonment, and rejection held traumatic roots for me and had to be avoided at all cost. Complaining about powerful people seen as parental figures of the organization would result in the rest abandoning me. Fear of abandonment made me hesitate, but the situation at work could not carry on.

3.2   What made taking legal action easier?

3.2.1   The isolation of a minority

My workplace was predominately White. When I started there we were only two Black staff in a team of over thirty Whites. My relationship with the other Black colleague was like any other sibling relationship, ranging from pairing to rivalrous interaction. This was parallel to the residents' group we worked with, as we usually had a maximum of two Black residents in a community of up to twenty-nine residents. (This poses the question—why are so few Blacks involved in psychotherapy?)

Sometimes there was only one Black resident and it was difficult for them because it is better to have at least two people of the same skin colour per eight people. Although group members will have something in common in the matrix (culture, gender, class, education, hobbies, religion, sexuality, and employment), these similarities are not as obvious and immediate as skin colour. Having one different person can set up special treatment in reality or in phantasy, which can be experienced as both negative and positive and evoke feeling isolated or special. For both Blacks and Whites, feelings of envy, fear, paranoia, and persecutory anxiety may be evoked.

I believe being in the minority made it easier for me to take legal action because I felt no one was trying to see things from my point of view. The organization was failing to contain my distress, thus pushing me into wanting to prove the reality being ignored. To understand what failed for me I will discuss a vignette demonstrating how progress can be achieved when the distress of a minority person is contained:

Clinical example: A Black woman B, with a striking shoulder-length blonde wig, joined an out-patient group of seven Whites, three men and four women. The group had been meeting for two years prior to her joining. Patient Z, an Irish member married to a Black woman, welcomed B, saying how glad he was to have a Black woman in the group as it would allow for racial issues to be discussed. B took this remark as an attack and said at the top of her voice that she had no Black issues to discuss because she had no problems with her racial identity. She went on to talk about her high-powered job as a tutor at a nurse's training institute and how she could run our group single-handedly. Shocked by this highly charged response, the group fell silent. After some minutes B asked whether anyone minded her sitting on the floor: nobody objected so she did. Long silence.

Another woman, D, asked why B had chosen to sit on the floor. B explained that she had injured her back at work that morning while demonstrating how to handle and move patients. D offered her soft bag to lean on, which B accepted. She got up to sit on her chair, rolling up the bag to support her back. Something important had happened in that exchange. D and B began sharing similarities and the rest of the group joined in. The tense moment had passed.

Although Z had welcomed B because they had Black families in common, B was not aware of this due to Z's white skin colour. Without this knowledge B experienced Z's excitement at her arrival as an attack, an exclusion highlighting her difference as the only Black member in the group, so she responded with a counter-attack. Stereotyping influences how information is processed, and in this instance B's past experience of being perceived as the outsider in a team of White professionals became encoded because Blacks are seen as the problem, outsiders and inferior. Her anger about this was re-ignited by Z's welcoming statement, which she experienced as isolating her from the rest, and B was not going to allow history to repeat itself in this group. Fear and anxiety about joining an established group were defended against by appearing powerful and strong, possible feelings of inferiority were counteracted by talking about her high-powered job, and fear of being controlled by the White group was contained by suggesting that she could manage it single-handedly.

Listening to her rising voice one could imagine her attempt to raise herself up. Then she fell to the ground, sitting on the floor before reaching equilibrium and coming to the same level as everyone else.

3.2.2   Bollas' concept of extractive introjection

Bollas (1987) gives another interpretation to this vignette, that of extractive introjection as a defence mechanism, which is similar to projective identification in violating mutual relating, but in reverse. B's attack on the group paralysed it into silence, and having lost the capacity to think clearly, the group was left in a state of shock, shame and guilt. B extractively introjected Z by taking away Z's warm welcome and replacing it with feelings of guilt that he had done something wrong and was thus perceived as racist. His attempt to be helpful left him feeling helpless, while B made herself feel powerful and in control. The other members were able to stay with the shame and guilt induced through their associative identification with Z's White skin colour. If group members had attacked B for misunderstanding Z it is likely that B would have become more defensive, felt alienated and fallen into the paranoid–schizoid position, making it difficult for her to reflect and take responsibility for the consequences of her behaviour on others. Since no group member retaliated, B was able to reflect on her harshness, and the sense of guilt and shame made her feel humble, wanting to repair the damage.

D's expression of compassion and empathy restored the disturbed equilibrium and the group could heal by exchanging similar experiences with B, which made B feel embraced. I believe Z's established relationship with other group members enabled him not to react by trying to defend himself. He was able to recognize B's anxiety and talk about how anxious he had felt on his first day. The rest of the group reflected on their first experiences in the group, also identifying with B. This empathic response enabled reparation and healing to take place. The more complex dynamics of this session were further explored when B was more settled in the group.

In my case, however, my organization failed to provide a similar safe space to contain the distress of a minority member feeling alienated and attacked. When I complained of racial discrimination I was attacked further. To understand what made the space unsafe I will highlight some of the comments made by the organization's internal investigation team that was called in.

The report stated that some clinicians' behaviour was unacceptable: it crossed the expected professional line, was insensitive and lacked judgment, and internal structures for managing conflict were lacking, ambiguous or not followed. The report expressed concern over language used by some staff, which was described as "abrasive" and "confrontational", language that other staff found "cruel", "brutal" and "humiliating". All these conditions made the space unsafe to trust and to work collaboratively, as it pushed those involved into a paranoid–schizoid position where they were unable to show compassion for others or reflect objectively on their own behaviour.

In the clinical vignette the group did not rise to B's attack with a counter-attack: instead, D showed an interest in B's problem, allowing B to calm down. The group was able to reach a point of wanting to repair and work collaboratively. In my situation the organization failed to engage in any empathic understanding of my complaints. Instead, the digging of the "weeping wound" carried on without treating it, resting it or just allowing time and space for healing, so something else had to happen to resolve the difficult situation I was in. I could no longer carry on in that environment. I felt trapped.

Thorndycraft (2000) defines escaping in a way that summarized how I felt about the decision to take legal action. He says that such an action, desire, drive, or need is connected to a psychological state as a result of the individual feeling imprisoned, controlled, trapped, unfulfilled, paralysed and in fear of annihilation. The person feels pushed to do something about it: for example, escape or disengage. I felt pushed into a corner with no other choice but to fight back, so I took legal action.

CHAPTER FOUR

The black mother as a container

4.1   Taking care of projections

I felt I had become the container of unwanted feelings for my
organization, and this was destroying me. As a group conductor,
counsellor, or therapist one becomes a container of unwanted difficult
feelings through the process of projective identification. One has to be
aware of these projections, hold onto them, chew them over, and then
give them back to the patients in small digestible doses the patients can
manage.

In my culture a similar process takes place between a mother and
infant. When the infant suffers with colic the mother chews a *ruzoka*
root, which is extremely bitter and can only define a mother's love
because chewing it calls for a lot of dedication. The practice is that while
breast-feeding the mother chews the root, then removes her breast to
spit the *ruzoka* juice into the baby's mouth, like a mother bird feeding
her baby. She then quickly pushes back her breast and the baby does not
have a chance to taste the juice.

This mother-and-baby interaction is similar to the relationship
between a group conductor and his group. He receives projections
which he has to chew, no matter how bitter they are. He contains them

28

in his mouth, then gives them back to the patients surrounded by a containing atmosphere (the breast). The conductor, like the mother, monitors the consistency for each group member's colic and decides on the right time to give the *ruzoka* back. If underchewed (underprocessed interpretations or interpretations made too soon) it would be too weak to be effective. On the other hand, if overchewed (overprocessed interpretations or those given too late to be in the patient's or group's memory) it loses its punch. Patients, like the baby, do not understand how the *ruzoka* works but they experience the difference.

4.2   Failure to give back projections

However, if the mother chews without giving back the *ruzoka* the baby does not benefit and cries continuously, leaving the mother feeling bad. Similarly, if the group conductor, counsellor, or therapist accepts projections without processing and giving them back, therapy becomes ineffective. When projection takes place it leaves the patients undernourished and impoverished because they lose a part of themselves. By keeping the projections in me I was now an ineffective bad mother. The organization was refusing to open its mouth to receive back its projections.

What does the container do when filled up with disowned projections of being ignorant, mad/emotionally labile, a laughing stock, inferior, aggressive, and lazy? I had become a scapegoat, laden with all these unwanted burdens and abandoned in the wilderness. In group analysis the rest of the group is facilitated in taking back their projections and owning them by a process of identification and connection with the scapegoat. On the other hand, the scapegoat is facilitated in looking at her part in the process, thus identifying and understanding the hook that attracts the projections, and is encouraged to do something different about it.

However, what if the hook is the fact that one is Black? Projections made due to skin colour are difficult to deal with because one cannot modify one's skin colour. Like those 439 callers, I felt that my experiences of discrimination were because of my skin colour and it was killing me emotionally and professionally. I felt abandoned and forgotten in the wilderness. My cry was falling on deaf ears. What could I do?

I tried using a staff support group called Sensitivity Group but it felt insensitive, not allowing me to shed these projections by taking responsibility for what they were doing or saying, so we always ended up in heated arguments. I felt perceived as the problem and as having a chip on my shoulder. It was as if the destructive powers of the group had become murderous. Those who tried to support me were scapegoated, so most gave up and became silent.

This was happening in an organization of group analysts, doctors, psychologists, nurses, social workers, social therapists, and other therapists from various backgrounds (art and drama). I had chosen to work there because I understood it to be the cream of talking therapy that believed in the art of healing through talking. This reminded me of our village church bell, which makes a lot of noise getting the congregation in the pews but doesn't attend the service itself. Instead, it stays out resting in its tower—not practicing what it preaches. Some senior clinicians seemed to struggle to acknowledge their projections and focused in seeking for a potential patient in me.

The psychoanalytic approach to free myself of the unwanted, disowned negative projections having failed, the push to resign was so strong that I did so. However, impregnated with negativity and being a surrogate mother of this unwanted baby, I decided not to depart with a child not my own. I therefore withdrew my resignation. I felt strongly that I could not leave without cleansing my system of the poison injected in me through my painful experiences of institutional racism.

CHAPTER FIVE

The internal investigation

At first I complained internally about the institutional racism I was experiencing within the organization, but not being satisfied with the way my grievances were handled, I appealed. At that time a White member of the team put in her own grievance about an incident that had something in common with my complaints. I believe this helped to get the organization take my complaints more seriously, and a team of White senior officers was sent to carry out an internal investigation. They reported as follows:

Internal investigation findings
1 *Leadership*   a. There was an imbalance of power as the hierarchy was male dominated, there was a lack of sensitivity to gender role and an unfortunate air of "machismo" to it.   b. There had been a breakdown in leadership and a lack of clarity about management, sometimes areas of accountability and responsibility were not clear and that contributed to the resistance to altering familiar ways of doing things and implementing the organization's policies and procedures.

c.   Professional boundaries are blurred to such an extent that length in service accounts for more than skill, training, or professional based responsibilities; opinions of qualified staff including the most senior clinicians were not given priority over those of unqualified staff who had been in the post for longer time.

d.   Individuals in leadership roles were unable to exert effective leadership partly due to the roles being ambiguous and also the leadership being undermined by senior members who had been there for a long time and they challenged their authority and at times went above their heads to a more senior member.

e.   Leadership was unclear and confused about their role despite having a job description which clearly outlined their responsibility and accountability.

f.   Whilst groups are valued they do not provide an opportunity for individuals to explore on one-to-one their performances and receive personal direction and support.

2   Professional conduct

a.   The organization had lost sight of staff as people with their own rights and expectations about how they should be treated as employees.

b.   The behaviour of some clinicians was unacceptable and crossed the expected professional line; it was insensitive and lacked judgment; lacked common sense; lacked awareness of appropriate professional behaviour; the behaviour of some clinicians fell below standards expected of professionals and the internal structures for managing staff conflict were lacking, ambiguous, or not followed.

c.   Two of the investigators feedback that Ms Mubika's appeal was justified and one investigator went further to say that he had found the behaviour of one of the senior managers to be disruptive and arrogant that at one point he had to ask him to behave himself.

d.   It was extraordinary that the senior clinician who made the racial joke had not given a full immediate apology.

e.   The staff team had ceased to respond, possibly even at times did not recognize the inappropriateness of some behaviours. This helps to explain but not excuse the conduct of some of the staff.

3   Background of the events

The investigating panel considered the context when the complaints took place:

a.   There was concern about the staff turnover; accounts of staff members breaking down or taking sick leave occasioned by high levels of anxiety.

b. There was rapid change, high level of stress and demand occasioned by sickness and staff turnover and by the prolonged period of inquiry into the grievances.

The clinicians were caught up in an institutional process which affected all members including Ms Mubika whose grievances date from a long time ago and had not been raised at the time and others had not observed signs of distress at the time when the events occurred therefore it appears that there was considerable element of retrospective interpretation born out of frustration as her grievance seemed to be going nowhere and was a result of some institutional process.

4 Language used

a. The comment about a sore thumb had been unfortunate but not intended to be offensive and that Ms Mubika had not been distressed about it at the time it was said.
b. The panel expressed concern at the abrasive and confrontational style used in the staff group reflected in the terms staff used to describe it—cruel, brutal and humiliating and that the staff has lost all compassion or sensitivity for individuals.

5 Policies and procedure

a. There is concern at breaches of confidentiality around the process of recruitment.
b. Serious errors were found in the recruitment process and there was lack of familiarity with accepted practice and legislation; lack of awareness of Equal Opportunity legislation; failure to keep applications confidential; and there was inappropriate involvement of the whole team in decision-making, and leaking information about the outcome before the candidates were informed.

6 Difficulties in resolving the issues in-house

a. The general view was that everything can and should be sorted out "in-house". There was resentment directed towards the perpetrator (Ms Mubika) and officers of the wide organization who had been requested to resolve matters through the Grievance Procedure.
b. The panel recognizes that Ms Mubika is a sensitive person, and that even in relation to handling her compassionate leave, there were others who considered that she was overreacting and making unfair complaints; Ms Mubika did not always let people know what her plans were but at times expected preferential treatment.

> The panel concluded that Ms Mubika played some part in the difficulties that led to the grievance. It also commented on the reports that she stayed to "sort out" a senior clinician. The panel believes that it lost the opportunity to deal effectively with Ms Mubika's grievances and any further attempts merely made the situations and the relationships worse.

Initially I was given an abbreviated version of the above report, but then found out from a White colleague I previously complained about that there was a more comprehensive one. I insisted on having it. When I read it I felt blamed: for example, they claimed that I was overreacting and making unfair complaints about how my compassionate leave had been handled, yet they had refused me any compassionate leave, resulting in my using my annual leave to go to Zimbabwe for the funerals. As I had several bereavements within a short space of time I used most of my annual leave and ended up without any to use to accompany my daughter, Kimberly, to Zimbabwe when her father died. At fifteen years of age Kimberly had to make a ten-hour flight on her own to her father's funeral. (Her sister, Karen, had gone on holiday to Zimbabwe the day before, not knowing that their father was dying.)

Three months previously I had made a similar journey to my brother Sam's funeral. Although I had my husband, my nephew, two sisters, my sister-in-law, Sam's wife and my mother with me, the ten-hour flight was very traumatizing and distressing for us all, yet fifteen-year-old Kimberly had to do it on her own. Can you understand how maddening that thought is for a mother? To make matters worse, I was told that no other member of staff could be found to cover my night shift, not even for a few hours while I took Kimberly to the airport. Someone else had to take my daughter to the airport because I had to work so as to avoid another heated argument. Sam's death had left me feeling very vulnerable and without much emotional stamina to engage in further fights.

The first internal grievance hearing recommended that my compassionate leave be reinstated, but it was only after the appeal that I got back twenty-eight days of compassionate leave for the multiple bereavements—too late for my children. Therefore, to describe me as a "sensitive person" who was "overreacting" and "making unfair complaints" about how my compassionate leave was handled just summarizes the kind of organization I worked for.

I was not satisfied with the report because it left me feeling unfairly blamed, so I decided to seek outside help. I believed that the organization needed a reality check. In my eyes the internal system itself had become contaminated and diseased.

Therefore, I took legal action through the Employment Tribunal.

CHAPTER SIX

A push into the wilderness: the exile experience

6.1 The uprising

Following my writing to the Employment Tribunal I was suddenly transferred to another hospital. I was told it was easier for the organization to move me than move the several people I had complained about, and I was forbidden from making any contact with work colleagues or going anywhere near the unit. Senior officers requested a list of my personal belongings I kept at work, which they would collect for me.

Since I was not given a chance to say goodbye to colleagues and residents I wrote a farewell letter to all, giving an animal metaphor to describe three residents who were leaving in the following few weeks. It was interesting that that letter was left hanging on the notice board for over a year, long after all the residents I knew had left.

When I moved to the other hospital I was informed that the staff on my new ward would be told that I had been seconded for a few weeks to gain experience in working with psychiatric patients on an acute admission ward. As a result of my introjected racism I agreed to be introduced as someone lacking experience, agreed to take the inferior position of a novice, and not question why, even though I had worked for three years on a psychiatric acute admission unit as a senior clinician.

At the new hospital I met six staff I had worked with during my three years on the previous psychiatric acute admission unit. I had mentored two of them when they were student nurses and now they were to teach me. Role reversal? It took one of them pointing out how ridiculous the situation was for me to realize that I had agreed to take an inferior position. Pierre Turquet talks about the importance of defining boundaries between self (me) and the other (not me); the internal (within me) and the external (outside me) so as to know who is me and who is not me. Posing as an ignorant learner threatened to change me into the Other— the "not me" I could not recognize within me.

The time boundary of my past background (me known as an experienced mentor) and the present (me as an inexperienced learner) was incongruent. People who knew me as an experienced senior clinician were stuck in the previous time space and felt awkward teaching me because they knew I was the more qualified. This raised persecutory anxiety as to why I was really there. Some thought I was a spy and became suspicious of me. They started being careful about what they said and did around me, and the situation became so uncomfortable I started questioning what I was doing there. After such insight I refused to stay on the ward, hoping to be sent back to my former workplace, but instead I was sent home on special leave.

6.2   The exile experience

Special leave felt like being abandoned in the wilderness and was difficult to bear. My trade union and an organization dealing with racial equality abandoned me too: stating that racism is difficult to prove, they refused to get involved. I felt lonely, insecure and lost, and started idealizing the past, pretending that the situation at work was not as bad as I was making out. I wanted to return to how things were, with familiar faces and a routine ... but it was a phantasy.

I had been told that the special leave would last a few weeks but it lasted a year. This ran a traumatic parallel with my childhood experience of abandonment by my mother, who came to the United Kingdom for three years but stayed for ten. The waiting and not knowing when she would return was difficult to bear. Similarly, the waiting and not knowing when special leave would end was hard to bear. I was still not allowed any contact with work colleagues, and each week I sat at home, hoping this was my last week in isolation.

This ran another traumatic parallel of abandonment for me—by my youngest brother, Obediah, who ran away from home at age fifteen to fight in the Liberation War for the independence of our country, Zimbabwe. Blacks who went to war were known as comrades or freedom fighters by the local Zimbabweans and as guerrillas or *magandanga* (murderers) by the White oppressors. Black traitors were *vatengesi* (sellouts). Freedom fighters operated in areas where they were not known and were not allowed any contact with their families, but they were adequately supported by local youth. The local girls were known as *zvimbwido* and the boys as *mijibha*. If a freedom fighter was identified they all had to leave immediately or risk the Rhodesian army finding out—via Black traitors—resulting in their families being killed. I spent over four years not knowing whether my brother was alive or dead.

The pain of that separation was kick-started back to life during my exile. Not knowing when the special leave would end and not being allowed contact with colleagues was killing me. However, some junior White colleagues (like the youthful *zvimbwido* and *mijibha*) tried to support me, albeit clandestinely, but after some initial involvement I cut contact as it would have cost them their jobs. I did not want that on my conscience. I also decided against requesting colleagues to give evidence against their managers. I asked myself a similar question to that posed by Foulkes (1983, p. 113): "I had to ask myself one basic question: does what I am doing intensify and promote the hospital activities in toto or does it counteract this integration and have a disruptive effect?"

My intention was not to cause disruption or destroy the organization, and involving colleagues as witnesses would cause too much damage. I was not sure how I intended to win the case without a lawyer or witnesses and with some of the documents missing. The organization had seven witnesses, a solicitor, a lawyer and a barrister. Pierre Turquet describes the state I went into as disarray: detached and complete bewilderment. My world was falling apart.

I had to believe in our saying, *Rine manyanga hariputirwi* (that which has horns cannot be wrapped up)—the truth shall prevail.

CHAPTER SEVEN

First Employment Tribunal: white domination

7.1 Tug-of-war: group analysis versus legal system

With the Employment Tribunal hearing imminent, I became preoccupied with the conflicting objectives between group analysis and the legal system, such as:

- in group analysis the link between this external event and my internal world needed analysing and the splits brought together, but doing that at this point would jeopardize my chances of winning my case;
- in the legal system I aimed to win the case, but in order to accomplish this I had to maintain the good/bad split, focusing on the organization as all bad and thus blocking out any of its goodness;
- I had to focus on facts rather than feelings, because feelings would jeopardize my case. (In group analysis feelings are more important: facts are perceived as just stories, content that meanders round defensively);
- I had to prove I was a victim, whereas in group analysis there are no victims—just people who disown parts of themselves;
- taking legal action was a sign of maturity, but in group analysis it could be perceived as acting out, a sign of immaturity.

7.1.1   Contamination of my training

My eldest brother, Sam, died towards the end of my first year of training as a group analyst. I was about to assess patients for my training group, but because of the bereavement my training institution asked me to delay for six months.

At the end of this period work colleagues made it impossible for me to attend another telephone supervision, but my training institution, thinking me too distracted and thus unable to meet my training requirements, decided I had to wait a further six months. This meant staying on the course for another year. The act of refusing me time to attend the telephone supervision became one of my racial discrimination complaints the Employment Tribunal ruled in my favour. My employer accepted responsibility for that extra training year and paid all my costs—fees, accommodation, and travel.

I was the only person in my year group who had to stay on an extra year. This fed into my racial stereotypic belief system that Blacks are perceived as inferior and thick—as the only Black trainee I was expected to need extra time in training. I felt angry about that because I concluded that it had to be racism: the monster I perceived at my work place had followed me to my training, and I felt unfairly treated. I hated the course convenor and my supervisor, whom I blamed for this decision, and my therapy group became persecutory. Thorndycraft (2000) suggests that a group can be a safe, secure, holding and containing place, but Simpson (1995, p. 225) says it can be frightening, potentially self-destructive, overwhelming, and trapping, a "Persecutory Arena" (Nitsun, 1996, p. 43). I was now experiencing my training and my therapy group as a "persecutory arena".

Foulkes (1983, pp. 72–73) acknowledges that material brought forth in therapy is alive and multidimensional. Its incompleteness allows a variety of interpretations, stimulating each participant's own personal complexities to become fully engaged in the process. This can only be achieved if communication takes place in a permissive atmosphere where it is possible to formulate meaning for oneself and others, while at the same time receiving and understanding the formulations of one's problems as seen through others' eyes.

I felt too alienated to make such connections. Since racism, racial discrimination, and victimization are not within most White people's experience there was no sharing of similar experiences, and the isolation triggered feelings of being an outsider, as if I was the patient with eight

White therapists. I felt trapped and decided to drop out or risk losing my sanity.

This took me back to my father's death when I was eighteen. My family could not contain my grief for me and it felt as if I suddenly had many advisors telling me what was good for me. Previously, I would tell my father what I thought and we would discuss it, but these many advisors who did not understand me were driving me mad, so I ran away from home to live with a distant cousin I trusted.

When the extra year was added to my training, feelings of mistrust, of going mad, not being understood, not feeling held and contained by the group, the family and the training institution were triggered, and past and present intertwined. Although there was another colleague of mixed heritage completing in four years I did not identify with him at that time because, in my stereotypic world, light-skinned Blacks get the same privileges as Whites. I also blocked out thoughts about White trainees who, like me, had to stay behind for a year or more, reasoning that because they were not in my year group that did not count. Isolating myself from all who might feel the same as me, and determined to stew in self-pity, I sunk into it as the only black sheep in my year group doing four years' training in five. I felt suffocated and wanted to run away. Better to drop out than accept being treated like a second-class citizen.

Thorndycraft talks about an unconscious need to gain narcissistic gratification from the attention one gets from the group and the therapist when wishing to escape group therapy. This is what happened when I threatened to leave: they responded by encouraging me to stay and gave me the space to talk freely about how dreadful my experiences were. They did not try to justify or to pretend that the situation was not as bad as I experienced it to be. I felt listened to and understood. The "family" had contained me and my distress, so a different experience to running away was achieved. The persecutory group became safe and containing again.

The conflict between group analysis and the legal system was resolved by finding common ground. The group agreed not to analyse my conflict or to try and bring the splits together until after the hearing. As I was representing myself I had to stay focused, and my therapy group supported me by taking care of my emotional state, making me aware of emotions that would make me regress and containing me, particularly when feelings of abandonment worsened as my mother became terminally ill. I was supported in working through the trauma of our early separation and thus able to enjoy our last months together prior to letting her go. My mother died three weeks before the hearing.

7.1.2   Protecting my training: paranoid–schizoid position

The pressure to drop out of training had terrified me because I could not control it or think of any motivation to continue. I tried to stay for my family but that did not work because I knew they would understand and forgive me for dropping out, so those who loved me could not keep me in training. I thought of many other reasons to persuade myself to stay but nothing, it seemed, could provide the necessary rationale. Eventually I thought of my enemies, and how happy those who tried to sabotage my career—by making it difficult for me to meet the training commitments—would be if I dropped out. That produced the required reaction: holding on to my enemies' grinning faces propelled me to safety. I can honestly say "thank you" to them because only they could operate the brakes that arrested my self-destruction. Determined to wipe the grin off their faces, I stayed.

On further reflection, the decision to stay was also strengthened by an unconscious process of splitting: using denigration and idealization to protect my training, my sanity, and myself. White (1989) comments on Melanie Klein's theory (Klein, 1975, p. 49) that splitting is a stage of development which takes place around the age of four months when an infant has to split love/hate, good/bad. We all regress to this position of paranoid–schizoid when under stress, because we separate good from bad in order to protect what we treasure.

Klein (1959, p. 241) states that: "The splitting of persecutory figures which go to form part of the unconscious is bound up with the splitting off of idealized figures as well. Idealized figures are developed to protect the ego against the terrifying ones".

Kernberg (1975) looks at how splitting is used, particularly by people with a Personality Disorder diagnosis, to protect the good self and good object images from the dangerous presence of "all bad" images that can overwhelm the ego with anxiety.

While I split and projected the bad into my full-time work place I projected the good into my part-time job and idealized it. My part-time job mirrored back the positive by appreciating and supporting me, and that nourished my confidence and self-belief.

I also projected my self-destructiveness, which was choking my training through my desire to drop out, onto the course convenor and my supervisor whom I then blamed for pushing me towards dropping out rather than see their actions as supportive and constructive. Disowning my vulnerability, I projected it into my work place, becoming blind to any support offered not only by those in junior ranks, but also by a few senior clinicians without the authority to influence change.

While I felt confident as a result of the splitting I had done, it is important to remember that splitting causes an inability to reflect or think clearly, a lack of guilt feelings which normally enables us to take responsibility for the consequences of our actions, and a lack of concern for others. I needed to maintain the split because being concerned for the people I was taking to a hearing would sabotage my aim to win the case, so I got rid of my admiration, compassion, love and ability to forgive, and focused instead on the badness and abusiveness of the institutional racism I was experiencing. I used my hatred of what they had done to me to turn them all into bad objects. I was ready to represent myself.

7.2   The first Employment Tribunal hearing

Before the hearing I attended two interlocutory hearings to determine which complaints were "in time": that is, had occurred in the three months prior to contacting the Employment Tribunal. Incidents out of the three-month limit could only be accepted if linked to any within the time limit.

When I attended the hearing I was scared. I did not have any witnesses or legal support, while the organization had seven witnesses, all White—a Nurse Specialist, an acting Nurse Manager, a Clinical Nurse manager, a Consultant Psychotherapist, a Human Resources Manager, a Director and a Deputy Director. The hearing lasted eight days.

On the first day I was sworn in, for which I chose the Bible. I read my eighty-four-page statement, stopping now and then to allow perusal of evidence for each point I raised. We had two volumes containing 433 pages: the written evidence I had decided to rely on rather than call any witnesses. When I started reading the incidents around my brother's death my voice quavered. The Chair said I was tired because of the long read, and asked me to request someone else to carry on.

Since no-one objected my husband offered to continue, which was helpful in allowing me to stay focused.

After reading my statement the organization's barrister cross-examined me and the Chair and her panel came in with their own questions. The organization's seven witnesses followed the same routine of being sworn in, reading their statements and signing them; then I cross-examined them, with the Chair and her panel coming in to seek clarification from each witness.

I had originally intended styling my cross-examination after television courtroom dramas, but the barrister's method made me realize that I had framed my questions like a teacher setting a comprehension test to check her pupils' textual understanding. Fortunately I spent two days in the witness seat, and while answering the barrister's questions studied how he structured them. I then threw away my original list and started again, spending the nights perfecting my cross-examination technique.

Here are the Employment Tribunal findings:

The Employment Tribunal findings

1. The unanimous decision of the Employment Tribunal was that the organization victimized the Applicant contrary to Race Relations Act 1976 section 2 in that the interview panel failed to appoint her to the position of Clinical Nurse Specialist because she had earlier brought a grievance. Ms Mubika and her manager both applied for the post of Clinical Nurse Specialist. There were three appointable candidates at interview, of whom Ms Mubika performed the best and her manager the worst. As part of the Hospital selection procedure, subsequently critized by an internal panel and the tribunal, residents and staff were asked for feedback, and references were taken up. Her manager was subsequently offered the post. The tribunal considered that the panel's decision-making process was seriously flawed. The feedback did not undermine Ms Mubika's position as the best candidate after being interviewed. Ms Mubika's references were more positive than her manager's in respect of skills that were required for the post. The tribunal was driven to conclude that the panel did not like the outcome of the selection process and, by a procedure that was contrary to Equal Opportunities and fair selection, they recruited her manager. The tribunal inferred that Ms Mubika was not appointed to the post because she had submitted a grievance that constituted a protected act.

    Equal Opportunity was not observed, the panel was more negative to Ms Mubika devaluing her experience while they picked out the positive in the other candidate. The panel had difficulty in acknowledging obvious positives in Ms Mubika's case. The grievance mattered to some members of the panel.

2. The tribunal found direct race discrimination in the manager's refusal to accommodate Ms Mubika in relation to the interview for the Deputy Nurse Manager's post, contrasting her attitude of encouragement she later gave to another employee, her approach to Ms Mubika was unfavourable in comparison to a White staff whom she openly offered her support in the presence of people who would be short listing.

   The tribunal noted that Ms Mubika placed considerable emphasis on her profession and progress in her career and, although she was a "very robust person", the denial of two job opportunities within the space of three months, in what was a specialist field with limited opportunities for progression, was a major blow to her self-esteem. It was also significant that these setbacks occurred in the context of continuing employment, and were known to the colleagues alongside whom she worked. Over three years, there was a succession of incidents and discrimination by a range of people. Ms Mubika was particularly emotionally vulnerable at the time, as she was experiencing a number of bereavements. The tribunal considered that this was a case in the higher category of awards ...".

3. The organization discriminated against Ms Mubika on racial grounds in that:
   a. Ms Mubika was refused study leave when two White junior clinicians in a similar position were offered study leave.
   b. Ms Mubika was required to produce a doctor's certificate on her first day of sickness.
   c Ms Mubika was discriminated against when her manager took no action to assist her by providing her a letter for production to the Immigration authorities on her return to the United Kingdom.
   d. The organization discriminated against Ms Mubika by refusing to allow her to attend a telephone supervision.
   e The staff group discriminated against her when she was refused half a day's leave, and
   f. When a senior clinician made a racially discriminatory "joke".

Some complaints were dismissed as out of time, but of those that were allowed, eight out of thirteen were ruled in my favour. It was a great achievement—eight out of thirteen! No lawyer, no solicitor, no barrister and no witnesses! That was impressive.

I believe I could not prove the other five issues for the following reasons: lack of comparators; one incident was put down to the unsympathetic personality of the senior clinician rather than racism; it was stated that I got caught in a crossfire; the necessary documents could not be found and, since I was banned from the premises for a year, I could not get the evidence I needed. When I did eventually get it, it was ruled that re-opening the case to introduce new evidence was too costly and, in any event, unnecessary. I had won the majority of my complaints, so one more would not make much difference.

With an eight/thirteen win I felt I had established the reality of the institutional racism flourishing at that time in this organization. They had to review some of their policies and procedures, such as sick leave, compassionate leave, study leave, and the recruitment policy. I felt the chip on my shoulder lift because the organization could not ignore the Employment Tribunal's findings. They were written in black and white.

My initial reaction to winning was one of pleasure, but that was quietly replaced by distress. I cried because the Employment Tribunal had acknowledged what I had been saying all along, while the organization had refused to listen. However, thinking of myself as a victim of racism was of no comfort to me, because I was brought up *not* to be a victim and I felt shame that it was now official: I had allowed myself to be a victim for over three years and done nothing about it. My father, who taught me that I could only be a victim if I permitted it, would have turned in his grave.

However, after crying over what I had allowed others to do to me I regained my pride, because in spite of big organizations discouraging me by saying that racism and racial discrimination is hard to prove, I *had* eventually done something about it, and succeeded without any legal help.

Mazvimbakupa, my father, *would* have been proud of me.

CHAPTER EIGHT

The return of the prodigal daughter: depressive position

8.1 Mourning the loss

After the hearing I was asked to attend an interview to determine whether or not my return to work was a risk to the organization, although I did not understand what risk was envisaged. I was offered the option of not returning, of being transferred to another department of my choice within the organization, but declined because I needed to give back projections I might take with me if I left then. I was not ready to be run out of town.

When I came back from exile a Black clinician I expected to be proud of me (she had often complained of institutional racism at work) became angry and publicly accused me of having got rid of three White clinicians involved, in varying degrees, in my racial discrimination case. I did not feel responsible for these clinicians, but did feel guilty when recalling the stress two of them went through as witnesses during the hearing. True, they had struggled, but what had happened to me had to be stopped, and legal action had remained my only option. I comforted myself by rationalizing that since they had not been there at my request, I was not responsible for them attending the hearing.

I still felt sad, however, because I got on well with all three and liked them as individuals, although hating what they had done to me collectively. It was as if a destructive force had possessed my colleagues and turned them into a massive mob colluding into making abusive acts appear normal and acceptable, with those supporting me outside meetings remaining silent during meetings. This is why I was now not prepared to be made responsible for anyone's leaving—wthey had not cared about what was happening to me and, while not wanting them to leave, I did want the abuse to stop. Since I also cared about those who left, accepting responsibility for their leaving would stop me from mourning their loss, as it was my loss too. I had hoped we would all try to make sense of what had happened and learn from it, hence my return even though I knew it would be hard and painful.

One of the staff who left had enjoyed making Kleinian interpretations in quite a skilful manner. I recalled our lunch breaks together, during which I had tried to corrupt him into watching lunchtime junk soaps he had not seen before. We had in-depth discussions about those programmes, and I missed that. Another was interested in Lacan: we had talked and argued for hours on end about his work, but now our intellectual sparring was a thing of the past. When I hear about Lacan I think of that staff member and the times we worked together. The third was quite a caring and maternal person, sensitive to all of us but easily influenced, hence her inability to question the advice she was being given concerning actions which clearly discriminated against me. All three were good people whom I still respect. I felt sad that two of them had apparently been left to carry the burden of consequences of institutional racism, yet their actions had been supported by the now-invisible majority. What a betrayal!

Although the attack by a Black colleague was upsetting, at least she was up front about it, something I preferred to back-stabbing. When I returned, the change in Black colleagues who previously complained of institutional racism but were now distancing themselves from me marked a significant shift within the organization. For instance, after the initial cold shoulder by White colleagues they became friendly, including those I complained about and who had been found racially discriminating against me. On the other hand, the Black staff, and White staff from a Black culture, were those now being discriminating. What was deadly was that some appeared friendly to my face but stabbed me in the back, discussing me in my absence and agreeing to carry out an action plan I felt was unfair to me. I did not realize some of their involvement until after I left and saw written evidence of what they had said about me.

It was difficult for me to appreciate how powerful I was perceived to be because I had taken the organization to an employment tribunal and won my case, and how scared some of the staff were of my return, until one Halloween. We were told that the residents had declared it a no-swearing day. Any resident caught swearing paid ten pence and any staff who "swore" by using therapeutic terms like *feel/feeling, relate/relating* and *group* or *take it to the group* paid twenty pence.

A parallel process ran in the staff group. For example, when someone spoke of "feelings" I could "relate" to I chose to ignore him because I was annoyed with him for previously shutting me up. I later told him this, and he explained that talking to me filled him with anxiety and that *he* felt shut up. As he spoke I realized how much we mirrored each other's feelings. I had failed to hear some of my colleagues' view of me as a powerful and abusive person who, by taking legal action, had allowed intruders to examine the family's private affairs. Then I made them even more fearful by coming back when they expected me not to want to return, and by not showing that I felt scared, vulnerable or anxious. I was still angry about the way I had been treated and was being passively aggressive by pretending that I had not been affected at all, but now I had to cease attacking the breast and start feeding. It was time to bring the splits back together again.

First on the agenda was the need to stop attacking, which I connected to envy. Obholzer and Roberts (1994, p. 15) talk about envy as "spoiling envy" that works like a hidden spanner in the works through withholding or sabotage, causing and maintaining splits within the system.

When Klein links envy to the way an infant attacks its mother's breast she explains that the attack can also be a result of having had a good feed. Klein also talks about penis envy coming about as a defence against breast envy—the envy of women's possessions and attributions being more valued and envied than men's. The envious attack on the good breast can cause severe damage because it destroys the ability to enjoy, since enjoyment itself is attacked (Segal, 1992). However, the search of a father to protect the mother from the baby's attack protects the baby from staying stuck and supports it in making sense of good breast and bad breast dwelling together in the mother.

Hopper (2003) states that envy is a defence against the fear of annihilation, therefore the survival instinct can be experienced during the process of envious attack. Segal (1992) says anxieties in the paranoid–schizoid position are about survival from fears of persecution, annihilation, and suffocation.

I had projected the goodness from my organization into my part-time work for safe-keeping from the institutional racism I had been experiencing, and it was now time to reclaim it and put it back. I had to reopen my eyes to the goodness I had blocked out. This was a painful process because I still felt angry with those involved who were now giving me the cold shoulder. I should have been blanking *them* out for the abuse they put me through. I had to keep reminding myself that we were experiencing similar feelings. They were as angry with me as I was with them, and I had to accept that other people were also hurting, including those who had been unintentionally racist towards me. I had to give them time to recover, had to tolerate being put out in the cold. I now coped better with being ignored because I knew I must move on: bitterness would only destroy something good in me.

Engaging in the healing process felt like moving from a year of darkness into bright sunlight. I did not want to see the goodness blinding me but I knew the splitting had to come to an end. I needed to turn my envious attacks into admiration, so instead of down-playing a clever interpretation by someone I had hated, I made myself listen, albeit enviously, then swallowed the bitter pill of admiration by acknowledging the good contribution aloud. It felt like force-feeding and I hated doing it, but I knew I had to and with time it became easier.

8.2   The animal metaphors

On the other hand, some of my colleagues found it difficult to engage in a similar process of admiring my work and keeping their envy at bay. For example, during the 9:15 community meeting two days after my return, a resident who was leaving the following week asked me to give her an animal. She had been told by previous residents that if I came back before she left she should make sure I did this. I was initially surprised that the tradition of animal metaphors had been passed on and survived my long absence, but I then understood that my farewell letter, which still hung on the notice board, had served as a transitional object during my exile. Residents had used the animal metaphors to keep me alive in their minds.

In my practice I used my cultural tradition of totems. In Zimbabwe every Black Zimbabwean family has a totem they belong to: either an animal (ex. zebra called *Mbizi—Mazvimbakupa*), part of a body (ex. heart called *Moyo*) or nature (ex. water called *Mamvura*). The taboo is that one cannot marry someone of the same totem because that would be incestuous, and one cannot eat one's totem. The belief is that those who break the taboo will lose all their teeth or be struck by bad luck.

Freud (1950) wrote about a similar culture in *Totem and Taboo*, but referred to our culture as "primitive". In my metaphors I combined this "primitive" concept of animal totems and Klein's theory on projective identification. The resident's behaviour is projected onto an animal displaying similar characteristics, and the group looks at it and tries to understand the behaviour from a distance before translating it to their own behaviour. I found this encouraged residents to think creatively about their destructive behaviours. The metaphor demonstrates acceptance of a behaviour, then works with it in an understanding way. This helps them think about the purpose and the impact of their behaviour in the hope that the acquired insights will motivate change in those behaviours.

This is what the resident who asked for an animal was talking about. Since it was my first week back from exile I did not know her well enough, so relied on other staff to give me the information necessary to match her to an animal, and she was excited when she got it. Then other residents who were about to leave started asking for animals too. Using animal metaphors became popular again. Here are three examples:

Example 1

A kangaroo for S

Yours is the Kangaroo family—friendly, funny, and yet clear with boundaries once you establish where they are. Being friendly does not mean you cannot express your feelings, particularly of joy and anger. Kangas cannot feel the same at any given time or situation, but that does not mean you are belittling others' experiences if you feel happy when others are sad. You need to understand that it is OK to feel different and that your feelings are as important as the other person's. It also does not mean that your joy will be contaminated. The good and the bad need to co-exist. A Kanga worries that it can get abusive, murderous and out of control. Every Kanga has the potential to be abusive, every Kanga has murderous thoughts: some have come close to realizing how thin this dividing line is and it can be a frightening and shaming experience, but a Kanga has to remember that all experiences are important and need to be understood. To be able to show genuine concern for others you need to be aware of your own ability to be destructive and you have grown such an awareness, which is why others experience you as genuine, so do not judge yourself too harshly—just continue being a better Kanga.

As a Kanga you need to make sure that you use your pouch for the right purpose. A pouch is there to carry your baby and keep it free from trouble, abuse, and other misfortunes. As a Kanga there is a temptation to use it for hoarding all the thorns that prick you. Deal with the thorns as and when they happen, do not nurse them because they give birth to resentment, a parasite that will eat at you and will destroy you. A Kanga pouch used for thorn collection is dangerous because one day you will throw your baby in a bed of thorns. You have worked hard at identifying the thorny paths and how to slowly manoeuvre your way around them. Keep dealing with difficulties while they are still mole hills.

Sometimes a Kanga can feel the urge to punch out, but because Kangas are nice guys, instead of striking out it will bounce off to help the object of its anger. So, next time you are eager to help your enemy ask yourself if you need to stop and think how to say what you need to say. Also, look into your cooking and baking then make sure that your recipes are free of loaded feelings. Sometimes a cake is not just a cake but a sugary substance meant to give diarrhoea—passive aggression. If there are difficult feelings, express them first, then bake to congratulate the friendship you have made by telling them how they made you feel—that is genuine friendship, being honest and forgiving, including of yourself.

A Kanga has a reservoir of strength in its tail which keeps you going in times of struggle, but that makes it difficult for others to know when you need help. Stop soldiering and hopping on and give yourself permission to accept that you cannot be on top of the world at all times and that it is not just up to you to keep clocks ticking. Let others bake you a cake.

Well done for all the hard work you put into understanding yourself. You will do well if you keep doing what you have learnt. Bounce off with a pouchful of belief in yourself.

MJ

Example 2

A zebra for E

Yours is the zebra family, well known for its striking appearance that captures the attention of all. For you, how you look is important, but all zebra descendants need to be careful that their appearance does not take the focus away from the other qualities they have, such as intelligence, kindness, and warmth. Give such qualities a chance to shine through by not mesmerizing people into a trance with the dazzling outside appearance of the adorning black and white stripes. As a zebra you have to wise up to the effect of your stripes on yourself and on others.

The other function of the zebra's appearance is to hide its vulnerability from hunting lions. Sometimes being vulnerable is a virtue as it enables you to acknowledge when you are hurting. It helps you in setting boundaries around what is, or is not, acceptable to you, but then zebras have issues with boundary-setting because they are boundary pushers. Some say it is because of that clever scheming brain of yours and others say it is in the zebra's blood. Whatever it is, the issue of boundaries has to be taken seriously, and monitored at all times. They say the best police are those in touch with their criminal mind, so as the best boundary pusher it should be easy to police what you are doing with the rules of life. Just look at your coat and let it remind you to keep issues as clear as you possibly can.

Remember, boundaries are there not to imprison you or to be used to test how much others love and care about you. Boundaries are to protect you from being taken advantage of and from putting yourself in danger. They keep you safe and make life more predictable, but for a zebra that could be read as boring. You and boredom need to get married: you will be together for a long time. Boredom is part of life. If you are bored you are OK. Remember that puffing away smoky elements of the forest may bring excitement but it also breeds confusion, paranoia, misery and foolish thoughts, such as the lion is your best friend.

As a zebra you are warm and kind. You tend to take care of those who seem more vulnerable than you but you need to make sure that that is balanced by you getting your own share of care, otherwise you will become resentful. However, let us not forget the kick in the hind legs. The zebra's hind legs carry an aggression that is necessary to knock off old lion's teeth. A zebra knows when it is about to kick because it tends to apologize first. So, when you start the apology song it is time to pause and ask yourself how you can say what needs to be said without dressing it up with an apology. Any speech introduced with an apology when you have not done anything wrong loses its punch.

Be proud of your hard work because you deserve to be proud. Well done and good luck.

MJ

Example 3

A cheetah for S

You are the fastest in the cat family. Speed tends to be the pass-word for all your activities. Your way of thinking is faster than lightening because you are intelligent and logical in your approach. Sometimes emotions slow you down. It is good to stop and feel but avoid making decisions while you are in a pool of emotions. Keep respecting your feelings and bow to them. When calm you are ahead of others which can set you up for envious attacks. However, as a cheetah you have to learn to accept your gifts and appreciate them. Do not join envious personal attacks by attacking yourself. As one who attracts envy you need to be aware of your own envious feelings. Do not let them frighten you, just listen to them and follow their scent to their point of origin because if you figure out their form you can then work towards knowing, and getting, what your heart desires.

Unfortunately with speed you tend to miss out on little details and avoidance is a family trend. When things get tough cheetahs tend to avoid working them through and just speed past by cutting. You have to always keep your eye on your ability to cut either with words, hurting yourself or cutting off relationships which feel like hard work or are too painful. Many a delicious fruit is born out of sweat.

Remember that although a cheetah can never change its spots it can learn to live with them. Cheetahs, like all cat families, have claws though they try to minimize the damage they can cause because they are scared of their own vulnerability, power and aggression, but in those scary feelings is a seed of ambition waiting to burst open. Be aware of your own vulnerability, power, and aggression: you will need them as springboards to dive into a pool of creativity and self actualization.

At times, when a cheetah traps an enemy in its claws it will not let go. All cheetahs need to learn how to forgive. Sometimes one who is seen as the enemy is just a friend you have not bothered to understand, mostly because you are too alike. It is not a competition where the weakest has to give up the fight—instead, the strongest and cleverest gives up the fight in order to win greater things, for empty victory leaves a proud cheetah feeling deprived. Always leave room for dialogue but do not let those with voices full of milk and honey take advantage of you.

Remember that you are a cheetah, a fighter. Sometimes you pretend to be a millipede (or is it a centipede?) which, when it hits an obstacle, curls up, and hopes to die? A clever cheetah like you gives feedback that others are not ready to hear and they bite your head off. It just means that the feedback is too close to the bone, so think of a softer way of saying it and they will appreciate you. That is what friendship is about. When you get winded just stop to catch your breath or go and lick your wounds quietly, but then get up and have another go. You are not a "pede" so do not curl up and hope to die—that is avoidance, and every cheetah needs to be on the lookout for avoidance.

You have started the hard work and need to keep the momentum going. You have made good friends but the best friend you met during your year here is you. Be gentle and kind to yourself because there is only one you. Well done for all that hard work and good luck.

MJ

Our small therapy group had eight residents and three clinicians. Initially I gave animal metaphors to the residents in my group towards the end of their therapy to remind them of issues we had worked on, and the residents called it "being given an animal". It had started about four years previously when I worked with a White doctor from a Black culture who was brilliant with metaphors too, and our group enjoyed digging out and playing with the hidden meanings.

After about a year later, residents who were not in our small group began asking me for an animal. These requests were made during the community business meeting 9.15 (so-called because the meeting always started every morning except Sundays at 9.15 a.m.). The meeting was attended by all residents and all staff on duty—more than forty people. I would extemporise with shorter versions in this meeting.

As related, when I returned from my year in exile the animal metaphors became popular again, but after about three months I was ordered to stop giving them.

Four years later! Why? The Black senior clinician who told me to stop explained that a White colleague who previously made a racist joke to me and would not apologize until the internal investigation team forced him to, had expressed concern about my practice. The senior Black clinician said the rest of the team, including himself, shared those concerns, and that it had been agreed, in a business meeting I was not in, that I should stop. When I pushed for an explanation I was told that the White colleague felt "uncomfortable" about it, but as the story gained momentum on the grapevine some said they had heard I was buying little furry animals as gifts, while others said I was making little animals during art sessions to give to the residents.

I was asked to let the residents know that the animal metaphors had to stop, so I announced it in the 9.15 community meeting the following day. The residents were outraged. They said they found the animal metaphors interesting, funny and useful, because they all related to the given animal. They did not understand why it was being banned, but the idea of breast envy crossed my mind—an attack of a good feed. Despite the fury and questions flying about none of the staff offered an explanation, and I was left to defend a decision I did not agree with. After that I went away for a few days.

Melanie Klein recognizes the envious and greedy attacks made on the good object by the infant, resulting in damage and fragmentation.

When there is enough relationship between the fragments to allow some thinking about it the problem can be addressed.

Bion also focuses on the interaction between the container and the contained when envy is a factor, but instead of the two coming together in a way that results in mutual development, Bion suggests there is a reversal of the process, with thoughts becoming progressively depleted of meaning. There is a greedy or destructive interaction, a coming together in a mutually destructive way. In this, pain is not suffered but becomes progressively meaningless. Freud's answer was that the man who believed himself innocent was guilty in reality.

On my return I was told that the residents had challenged the staff team, and several community meetings were spent discussing the ban and working out how animal metaphors could continue. One of the senior clinicians insisted that the whole community be involved in making animal metaphors, but the residents objected because they wanted me to choose the animal. It was then suggested that the community comes up with the description, but the residents again objected, arguing that they preferred my version as it was good. Another suggestion was that other staff members get involved in the write-up but the staff refused because it seemed too difficult.

In the end the whole community came to a democratic agreement in the 9.15 community business meeting: I would announce the animal and the community would have a week to explore the connection between the given animal and the resident who was leaving. A week before discharge I would give the residents the written script, which their groups would discuss and analyse.

It was a pity that this practice of marrying cultural tradition (totems) and psychoanalytic theory (projective identification), resulting in a successful and effective union, was attacked. This was a White community that had embraced Black Zimbabwean diversity. From the start a junior clinician summarized the attack as envy, pointing out that within two days of my return residents were already interested in what I did, and admitting that he envied my relationship with residents. I always invest in building a strong therapeutic relationship: it invariably pays off, especially when working with high levels of distress and distrust while nevertheless needing to challenge people who, having suffered abuse, tend to experience most interactions as abusive.

It is true that unacknowledged envy is likely to be acted out. The team should have listened to the junior clinician and saved themselves the embarrassment of having to retract their decision. The residents' fight to hold on to the animal metaphors proved that one cannot keep a good thing down. The attack worked positively: it improved the practice and raised its profile as an effective therapeutic tool.

This event also showed how powerful the residents' voice is in a democratic therapeutic community. Taking the most senior clinician's suggestion of community involvement seriously, some started buying fluffy animals to match whatever was given to them, while others framed the scripts as presents for those leaving, thus making the practice even more powerful.

When I resigned all the residents wanted me to write them scripts for when they left, and more meetings were spent discussing this. In the end the community made another democratic decision—I would give animals to residents at the end of their therapy if they were leaving in the next three months. After writing scripts for the leavers I decided to be fair and wrote one long one for the whole community as my leaving present to them, which individuals could photocopy. Here is the farewell animal metaphor:

Animal Kingdom—the elephant community

You are a member of the Animal Kingdom—a community of elephants. As an elephant, the community stands feet astride on solid ground. The elephant's feet are made of structure, heavy solid structure which keeps the community safe and contained. Some have tried to bend structure and others thought they conquered it but we all know about mirages—illusions built by those who are in desperate need. So, if you find yourself thinking of ways of bending structure then identify yourself as one in desperate need of help.

However, the elephant does occasionally bend its feet, but that is only to cross over via the bridge of summit where an agenda is drawn for discussion and proposals. Therefore, when the urge to be creative hits you take it to summit but let me warn you that this is a different ball game. Crossing the summit bridge discourages impulsive decision-making ambushers but it also breeds frustration and anger while maintaining safety. Those used to sucking the teat of instant gratification scream like starving calves demanding instant change while the boring thoughtful worker-elephants guard the goal post. Trying to change structure can turn the 9.15 into an elephantiasis battlefield. It sounds like elephants gone crazy with ants stuck up their trunks—the bellowing sends the scared elephants scattering out. With time the structure kicks in, rules are reestablished. The elephants with the ants in their trunk sneeze and that opens their ears improving their hearing, and the scared discover that their feet are not made of clay and stand up to voice their opinion. A decision is reached—one elephant one vote that is democracy.

The struggle for the elephant family is in tolerating difference. Mother elephant has such a gigantic body that no elephant can feel her whole body with one touch. When elephants want to feel her they hug her and each calls out what they can feel—it's hard with a pointed tip; it's big and flat like a banana leaf and flaps about; it's round and wet and shuts when I poke into it; it's like a hose-pipe but fatter; it's big and flat like a bed with wrinkles, it's wet and crushes leaves. Who is right? Who can feel the Mama?

This could easily develop into elephantiasis, with each elephant wanting to convince the other that what they feel is the right feeling. Remember, one experience can produce different feelings, reactions and thoughts. What you feel is what is close to your heart, so listen to what is close to the other elephants' hearts. Be courageous when the elephantiasis heat stems from difference. Stop talking and do more listening: you might learn something new.

Your ears are the most important commodity in this community. Not only is the ear drum important to listen to the rapper-tap-tap of your neighbour but those banana ears are good for cooling the hot feedback you might get. There will be many a time you will have to listen to what you do not want to hear. Those are times better spent with your mouth shut—just wave those giant ears to cool the hot words of wisdom.

However, if the feedback is too hot avoid saying *"Bull-shit"*, *"It's your shit, deal with it"* or just *"shit"*. That is disrespectful because the first traumatic experience for a baby elephant is passing its first poo as it weighs more than a baby elephant can cope with. So, next time you hear yourself say , *"Bull-shit"*, *"That's bull-shit"*, *"It's your shit, deal with it"* or just a simple *"Shit!"*, take time out to remember the trauma that elephant went through to offer you its fresh manure. Of course fresh manure stinks and elephant's poo is no joke but still it is a gift given to you. You might not be able to appreciate it at that moment, but instead of ranting and raving like a victim let the sun (the community focus) gaze on you and the wind (the community voice) blow the fresh breath of wisdom exploring the meaning of that experience. If you allow this process to happen the stink will disappear and the fresh manure will dry—ready for your garden. You will see yourself grow and mature.

Elephants are well known for their memory, it goes too far back. Sometimes the elephant prefers to remember things that are harmful. This happens when elephants struggle with feelings of guilt, helplessness, pain, fear of being abandoned, or when burdened with emotional hang-over. Panic descends upon the community and the elephants refer to their memory bank that stores previous destructive behaviours. The urge to do something destructive kicks in just to stop the elephants from feeling these uncomfortable feelings. However, the educated elephants stop running away and stay with the feelings because that heals the weeping wound and frees their ability to think creatively and constructively.

Too much thinking and feeling can make an elephant sick. The ailing elephant is looked after by two doctors—Dr Surgery and Dr Community.

Between them two miracles are performed. Dr Surgery gives little smarties or sweet-tasting syrup (isn't that a lovely substitute for breast feeding?). Sometimes an elephant with a headache tracks its way to Dr Surgery who carries out an intensive examination with just one look and refers the ailing elephant to Dr Community, nodding wisely—*"Take it to groups"*.

Dr Community calls other learned elephants to sit in a circle and examine the ailing elephant from top to bottom, referring to their memory banks and reflecting on their own experiences. Dr Community is clever, with an empathetic tut-tut utters *"I know how you feel"* which might be heard as *I am understood* or *you mean I am not special?* Sometimes Dr Community offers a cold shower by saying *"What is your responsibility in all this?"* You mean I am not a victim?

Playing a victim can earn an instant sympathy vote but the ailing elephant stays locked in the shackles of helplessness and apathy. Do not be frightened to face the strength of your own aggression. If you embrace it and express your aggression safely then you will be able to separate abusiveness from the creative strength which feeds dreams and ambitions.

Let us not forget that some elephants visit Dr Surgery for company and attention. They turn up in surgery at odd times, and some even forget why they have come. Understandably, all elephants need a bit of attention but be upfront about it and be a teller!

Best regards,

MJ

(Two tellers were voted in every month to take the role of standing up in the middle of the 9.15 meeting and count votes,—an attention-seeking job, but someone had to do it.)

When I was leaving the residents requested that another member of staff takes over giving animal metaphors, but as no-one volunteered they were encouraged to talk about losing me and to recognize that the animal metaphors were part of the loss.

CHAPTER NINE

The white couple as a container

The other step I had to take towards recovery was with my training institution. The opportunity to understand how the racial discrimination had impacted my existence on the training came when we were playing around with phantasies about a locked room in the building during a large group session. Later that night I reflected on the theme of the locked room, and suddenly understood that for me it represented a room which held all my negative projections and fears which had threatened to choke my training. I had given the key to this dreaded room to the course convenor and my supervisor for safe keeping, which is why I hated them both as a couple. I hated them because they represented, or reminded me of, what they were containing for me—my negativity and the fearful projections I had disowned—and they were robust enough to contain the uncontainable on my behalf. This realization left me quite excited because I knew I was now ready to swallow the *ruzoka* and receive back the key to this feared room. I felt strong enough to reclaim my projections and take charge of my fears myself.

In the following large group meeting I requested the key by sharing my experience with the convenor and the group. Unfortunately, supervisors did not attend the large group, so I was unable to talk to my supervisor about this: I felt sad about that but happy that I had survived and grown through experiencing their survival of my rage. I had not killed them off.

I also felt sad about being left behind by my training year group, and complained in the large group about my fear of being overcooked in therapy due to having five years instead of four. I was allowed to vomit all the poison in my system about having to stay for another year and I so much enjoyed the wretching and throwing up of racial beliefs, stereotypical thoughts and feelings I had about being the black sheep of my year group that by the time my year group left me behind I was able to enjoy the extra year and used the time to blossom. I appreciated my training institution's ability to withstand my attacks. I believe that was what I internalized most in my final year in training, and that has enabled me to work more effectively with difficult and attacking people. I know I can survive their attacks in the same way my course convener, my supervisor, my therapy, and large groups had survived me. It was a year well-utilized.

In giving me the extra year, my training institution had presented me with the gift of a prickly pear—a gift with an itch. Initially it looks and feels like a curse, but when one accepts and works with it, the prickly pear turns into a blessing. The secret charm is in working through the itch. I believe I am a better group analyst for it and can honestly say it was worth the scratch.

CHAPTER TEN

The straw that broke my back

Foulkes (1983, p. 46), describing the changes at Northfield Military Hospital, says the hospital, which had been on "a very even keel under steady and experienced administration now became subject to more violent fluctuations. The changes had their upsetting effects, but at the same time they forced the hospital into greater contact with realities and produced a better integration of its functions".

After my year in exile I initially thought that a similar process was taking place in this therapeutic community. There was upset and anger about the recommendations made by both the organization's internal investigators and the Employment Tribunal, but in time some staff began appreciating the changes implemented.

However, when the dust settled I realized that not much had changed except that White colleagues appeared friendlier while Black colleagues became more hostile and attacking. For example, I still had problems getting time to attend my telephone supervision, but now the clinician involved was Black.

A few months after my return a White senior clinician I had complained about, and whose actions the Employment Tribunal found to be racially discriminatory, was promoted to a more powerful position.

On the other hand, I went for an interview for a Clinical Nurse Specialist post similar to the one I had been declared the best of three candidates for, beating my own White manager in the interview. The Employment Tribunal had highlighted that my reference feedback was much better than hers, yet she got the job. This time I was told that I had scored 12 out of 55. The only difference between the two posts was that the first was at a local community centre and the second at the residential therapeutic community I worked in. I had often acted in the post, so expected to score even higher than previously.

All the documents about the interview—candidates' application forms, interview questions, candidates' curriculum vitae, the panel's individual comments and individual scores—had disappeared. All they could find was a single piece of paper that stated I had scored 12 out of 55. How was this possible? I had been a member of their development team and involved in setting up similar units in other regions. This included recruiting and training staff, then supervising them when the new units opened. I therefore had the policies at the tips of my fingers in a field I specialized in: how could I score 12 out of 55? Did my experience and qualifications count for nothing? How did they short-list me? I really did not understand how that result came about, but it shocked me because I thought I had done better in this interview than the previous one.

There were ten questions and a presentation, each carrying a maximum score of 5 points. I am very good with presentations, yet was asked to believe that my highest score was 2 out of 5. For the interview as a whole, I was told that I scored two 2 s out of 5: the rest were ones and a zero. I know I answered nine questions very well, but struggled with one question asked by a Black senior clinician. He asked me to think about Clinical Governance and discuss a project I had been involved in during the past year, but they all knew I had only been back for three months following my year in exile (after the organization sent me home with strict instructions not to work and not to contact anyone from work).

So, the only project I had been involved in during the past year was taking the organization to an Employment Tribunal. I did not think talking about suing the organization as a way of improving its service would have been the best answer to give in order to get promoted, so I talked with enthusiasm about animal metaphors and how I use the concept of projective identification and totems. I outlined how it improved my practice and linked it to a research project I was working on. I had made a pretty good job of it because it was something the whole therapeutic community enjoyed, motivating them to talk in a playful manner about issues that are painful and difficult to talk about.

Not only did I not get the job, but I was also banned from giving the animal metaphors soon after this interview, following which the organization asked me to act in the very post for which I was made to believe I had scored 12 out 55.

I refused. Who would ask someone who scored 12 out of 55 to act in that same post? I would not unless I did not believe in the score. To me 12 out 55 means the person is useless and should not have been shortlisted. The fact that they wanted me to act in the H post proved, to me, that they did not believe in their decision either, but since I was not going to beg or be used, I refused to act in the post. I was threatened with disciplinary action but still refused. I was then asked to take up some of the duties with other G Grades but refused that too.

The Black senior clinician was advised to refer me to Human Resources because it was decided that I could not refuse. I was well aware that my job description stated I could act in the H Grade post in an emergency, but as far as I was concerned this was not an emergency: some of the senior posts had been vacant for nearly two years. Human Resources could not do anything to me so they seconded a new manager from another hospital into the post. However, I was left in no doubt that I would never be promoted in this organization and it had nothing to do with poor interviewing, lack of knowledge, skills or experience. I decided to leave.

The other reason motivating this decision was that I felt unsafe working in an environment where rules continually changed to fit in with the organization's needs at any given time. I found this maddening. For instance, when I came back from exile I was told that I could be transferred to any department within the organization. All I had to do was decide where I wanted to go. At that time I declined the offer because I was not ready to leave as I still held some hope that things could be worked through, but now I had lost that hope. I accepted that there was no future for me in this organization, but the problem was that I liked and enjoyed my job and found it difficult to give it up, so initially I tried to stay. I knew that the arrival of the H and I grades would be a challenging test and was not sure whether I would survive it, but I was willing to try. I explained all this to the senior clinicians and requested that should I find the situation unbearable I would be supported to transfer to another department. After being assured that I would be moved elsewhere within the organization, I did not bother to apply for alternative jobs.

However, when the White H and I grades were recruited I found it too difficult to stay and watch the "chosen ones" arrive. I spoke to the most senior clinician about being moved elsewhere and he said he understood why it was difficult for me and agreed that I needed to be supported to move on. He said he would find other options within the psychotherapy department but asked me, in the mean time, to keep an eye on what was being advertised internally that might interest me. When I saw an advert from the Deaf Child and Family Unit I thought it would be a good opportunity for me because I have always wanted to learn sign language and work with deaf people. I wrote to the senior clinicians requesting to be moved to the Deaf Child and Family Unit.

I also spoke to the business manager and he said he understood and supported my moving out of the therapeutic community. I conferred again with the most senior clinician and he arranged for me to meet with the Acting Chief Nurse, but later I found out that he and the Chair of the first interview panel that discriminated against me, who wrote "lazy" on my application, had written to each other stating that the meeting was to help them "to be seen" to be doing something about it should I take it further. To me this proved that they really did not intend to support my leaving.

Two days later the Acting Chief Nurse, who had previously said I could be transferred, now told me that I was too senior for transfer, yet I was still on the same grade as when they wanted to transfer me on my return from exile. They insisted that there was no policy which allowed them to transfer senior clinicians because their transfer scheme was only for grades A to F, not grade G and above. I questioned this because recently two White senior clinicians—one G grade (same grade as me) and another two grades above me (I grade) were transferred from this therapeutic community to other departments. I was told they were special cases. I then asked them to utilize the same transfer scheme they would have used when wanting to transfer me on my return from exile. They refused.

I was devastated because I just wanted to go. I felt suffocated. I had the impression that nobody really intended for me to leave.

They were facing a serious staffing crisis which they created through bad management because three senior posts had been left vacant for too long and the new seconded manager went off sick. I believe that they now needed me but only to use me, and I was not going to allow that to happen. I really did not want to be there anymore and I felt trapped because, on the promise that I would be transferred, I had not looked for an alternative job.

My phantasy was that they needed me because of the serious staff shortage. They would use me while they recruited White clinicians and I would be expected to support them into settling down into their posts. I have seen that happen to many Blacks: they groom White colleagues while they are left behind in lower grades. That would not happen to me. So, when they recruited the two senior White clinicians for the H and I posts I decided to leave before their arrival, but the first one arrived before I left. He was good and openly complimented my skills so I could not take my anger out on him for being the "chosen one". I did not want my envy to change me into something bitter and twisted, which would have happened had I stayed on to help groom the "chosen ones". I had to go.

I became angry. I felt they had been playing mind games of continuous contradictions with me, leaving me not knowing whether I was coming or going. People are known to be driven insane because of constantly changing goal posts. I thought of the time I asked for half a day's leave because I was upset about my daughters, who had gone to bury their father on their own. I became too upset to continue working, so asked to take annual leave for the rest of the day. The procedure at that time was that I ask for permission to take annual leave in a group meeting. My request was denied and we ended up in a heated argument, leaving me even more distressed.

Following this argument the vocal staff decided I should take time off sick. The discussion had been so heated that by the time I left the meeting I was very confused and scared—these people seemed convinced that I was sick, while I believed that, being in mourning, I was appropriately distressed. I was also appropriately angry, because I was just asking for half a day off with good reason and it was denied (a decision the Employment Tribunal later ruled as racially discriminatory). I was going mad with worry not knowing how my two distressed daughters were coping with the loss of their father in another country. It was their first time back in Zimbabwe after five years—to bury their father, and without their mother's support. If my colleagues were that concerned they could have offered me compassionate leave. In the last three months I had lost both my brother and the father of my children, a good friend I had last spoken to at my brother's funeral.

I was not going mad. In my culture, if someone is bereaved we offer support because we recognize that the person is likely to be vulnerable, but in this culture my mourning was interpreted as a sign of being on the verge of a mental breakdown. Similar arguments had occurred after I returned from my brother Sam's funeral, when I was told to be grateful that my manager saved my job. Now, three months later, we were having this row. For goodness's sake! I was just asking for half a day from my annual leave!

I left that meeting feeling close to the edge because I did not think I was being unreasonable, yet was made to feel as if I was going crazy. I went to see my doctor, who gave me two weeks off sick, but after a weekend's rest and talking to a psychologist friend I became clear again. There was nothing wrong with me that a good cry could not fix. I cancelled the two weeks' sick certificate because I knew that if I went off sick because some people told me I was sick, I would be handing over the control of my mind to a group with a history of some members suffering mental breakdowns while on duty. We always had a member of staff on long-term sick leave, and when they left another scapegoat was pushed into that position. From this experience I could well understand how a member of staff could leave this therapeutic community to be admitted onto a psychiatric unit, because that afternoon it could have been me. The push was cruel, almost convincing me that I was losing my sanity. Unforgivable.

It was clear that I was perceived as a troublemaker and I knew that I had to leave. Obholzer and Roberts (1994) talk about anxieties projected into vulnerable group members with the valence for expressing institutional dilemmas, but these members are seen as troublemakers. The troublemaker becomes an "institutional mouthpiece" into whom all the staff project their disquiet but distance themselves from, thus disowning that part of themselves by a process of projective identification. The troublemaker's behaviour is seen as a response to the unconscious needs of the organization.

It is important to see the organization as a whole and understand what the individual is expressing for them all. The solution is not to get rid of the troublemaker or vulnerable member, but to work out what is being played out for the organization as a whole. My organization failed to reflect on this and try to understand what I was expressing for it as a whole.

I felt that my sanity was at risk, and since this was more important than forcing back projections I had carried, I knew it was time to leave before being destroyed. Feeling trapped and suffocated, I resigned without a job to go to.

CHAPTER ELEVEN

Second Employment Tribunal: Black-on-Black betrayal

11.1 Regression

The second Employment Tribunal was triggered because of the injustice I experienced with Black and ethnic minority clinicians on returning from exile. However, when I tried to take legal action I was overwhelmed with emotions around betrayal by people I perceived to be my own, and I regressed. This painful experience demonstrates what happens when one regresses in the racial arena and how this quickly gets hooked into similar past non-racial experiences within the family. Hopefully this account will help therapists and counsellors understand the process of regression and how one needs to work with the parallel processes of past and present colliding. Understanding the impact of this collision is important in containing clients' distress and facilitating them in working safely through their regression.

Regression is a defence mechanism introduced by Freud, who connected it to the longing of a protective father. When individuals regress they revert to an earlier stage of development, reacting to a new situation as if back at that stage. Such behaviour is perceived as immature. Sometimes regression is entangled with avoidance behaviour, another

69

defence mechanism which, by avoiding the difficulty, does not deal with a situation in a mature way.

Boyer (1998), whose work is mainly with psychotic and very disturbed and regressed patients, says the therapist needs the capacity to tolerate regression and maintain therapeutic contact with the patient throughout the experience, ensuring that the therapeutic space remains consistent, optimistic and empathic, thus supporting the ego and the superego.

Jacobs (1998) talks about regression needing to be handled with care and skill. The therapist has to gauge how far the patient can go and stay in the chaos of the inner world facing terrifying feelings from the past. Besides knowing what the patient can manage, therapists need to know their own ability and capacity to hold patients without losing them, because regression is seen as descent into chaos. Counsellors and therapists have to remember that deliberate encouragement of regression is only for the most skilled. Even Winnicott—highly experienced and skilled—is known to only allow one patient at a time to enter a deep regressive phase (Jacobs, 1998, p. 203).

11.2   The betrayal

At the second Employment Tribunal I claimed constructive dismissal, racial discrimination and victimization. Some complaints were similar to those of the first tribunal, such as failing to get promotion and being stopped from attending telephone supervision. The difference between the cases was that the first involved White staff only, while the second involved Black and ethnic minority staff and White staff from a Black culture. This meant that I identified with all involved in the second Employment Tribunal, either racially or culturally. These clinicians were from various professional backgrounds—social therapists, managers, psychotherapists, nurses and doctors—but identifying with them was painful because I experienced their unfair treatment as betrayal by my own people.

The second Employment Tribunal panel consisted of three White men, and the organization's witnesses were all men, so I was in a roomful of men. That was intimidating but I convinced myself it would be all right because, having been raised in a male-dominated household, I expected a fair fight. When I was growing up I always found it safer to fight boys: they threw punches and did not bite or scratch like the girls.

On the first day the Chair decided there wasn't enough time to address all my complaints, and suggested that we focus only on the important ones. I agreed: being right at the beginning of the hearing the anxiety level was high and I felt intimidated by my surroundings, but I realized later that that decision weakened my case. Also, I did not understand some of the terms, unlike the previous Chair, this one did not often explain. Instead of asking for clarification, however, I just hoped that since the Chair was a man I would be all right—all I had to do was trust him. I did not question my blind trust in a stranger because the Chair did not feel like a stranger: I had turned him into my father, who listened, understood and knew what was best for me. I believed the Chair would give me a fair chance to present my case just as my father had been fair each time I presented my case. (Being a challenging child I presented a lot of cases before my father because I was in trouble most of the time.)

Although my complaints were similar to those of the first Employment Tribunal and the organization had the same number of witnesses (seven), this tribunal allocated the case just three days, whereas the first had allocated eight. I had believed the tribunal duty-bound to find enough time to ensure a fair hearing, and wondered why they had not allocated more days. They had our statements and knew there were seven witnesses and me, and were aware of the length of our statements, yet they allocated only three days. The first tribunal had found time for me to read my eighty-four-page statement, but this tribunal could not accommodate a seventy-seven-page statement; the first tribunal looked at every page of the 433 pages of written evidence and discussed them, yet this tribunal did not even open the 280-page bundle of evidence, and no one made any reference to its presence.

On the first day of the hearing I was asked to read my statement, but the Chair stopped me after a few pages, saying it was too long and there was not enough time to go through the whole document. He adjourned the hearing and instructed everyone to use the rest of the day to read my statement. At the start of the hearing I had pointed out that I had received one of the witness statements only the previous night, so the Chair said I could use the time to look at this late statement.

The following day I was cross-examined only briefly, so my hope of re-stating what I had written for everyone to hear was blown out the water. After the cross-examination the Chair said there were too many witnesses and not enough time to hear them all, so he reduced the seven witnesses to three. (Why ask me to spend the day looking at the statement of a witness who was not going to be called?) I had structured how I was going to cross-examine and had allocated questions of specific complaints to specific witnesses, but now I had to change both strategy and sequence.

Although the three witness statements were only between four and eight pages long, the Chair decided there was not enough time to hear them in full and instructed the witnesses to read only the paragraphs their barrister indicated, and with all this changing of goal posts I lost my footing with the whole proceeding. One witness left the witness seat before I had finished cross-examining him and when I pointed this out Chair told me that he was done. With another witness I realized that I had been given a different statement from the rest. In the statement I had, he had written that although he had never seen me (before the interview) he had heard about me, but in the statement the others had, that had been deleted. When I asked him about this his barrister intervened, saying that the point was not in the statement the panel had, therefore it did not exist. I thought the panel would make an inference to this because it could not have been a typing error, but the Chair accepted that the witness had never heard about me.

I also asked about the missing interview documents, drawing their attention to the organization's recruitment policy, which emphasized the importance of safeguarding interview information for a two-year period so that any case of discrimination brought against the organization could be defended. It was only ten months after the interview, and I felt that the Employment Tribunal could have made inference to the missing documents, but the Chair concluded that the Respondent was prejudiced by my delay in complaining.

There was no point in making submissions. From where I was sitting it all seemed an unfair fight. My stereotypic thinking that a combat with men would be a fair fist fight was shattered, and I was left feeling the pain from where the teeth had sunk in and the nails had drawn blood.

The Chair's summary stated that: "The Applicant made no submissions as such but agreed with the Chair's summary of her case namely that the interview panel conspired to prevent her promotion; that Black and Asian members were pursuing racially discriminatory policies on behalf of senior management and were merely on the panel for cosmetic purposes; that she should have been referred to Occupational Health after she refused to undertake H grade duties and the Respondent treated G grade and I grade differently by allowing them to transfer without interview".

In fact, I did not complain that I should have been referred to Occupational Health: I had refused to undertake any H grade duties so there was no point in the referral. However, I had said that if they insisted that I take the duties on, then they first had to refer me to Occupational Health. Since they did not insist, there was no need to complain.

My other complaint was not about "transfer without interview", but concerned policy surrounding the transfer of the White G and I grade colleagues. The organization had refused my transfer on grounds of there being no transfer policy for G grades and above, but if this was correct, what policy had been used to transfer the two White colleagues? Such unfairness was difficult to understand, and I was left wondering who really cared.

I will now look at the issue of the animal metaphors as an example of the level of lack of honesty the second Employment Tribunal had to work with.

Witnesses Two and Three were active in banning the animal metaphors, and when the ban was challenged they were also actively involved in negotiating how the animal metaphors could carry on, yet at the Employment Tribunal hearing they both denied that the ban was ever challenged and lifted. When the Chair asked one of them directly what he would have done had he found out that the animal tradition was still carrying on, he said he definitely would have stopped it because what I was doing was very worrying and I was putting myself in danger.

Danger? I had done this for over four years and not once did anyone express any negativity about the animal metaphors. Indeed, all were enthusiastic. Here are the views expressed at the second Employment Tribunal. If they are read with the memory of how the whole community (residents and staff) worked together and came to a democratic decision to re-instate the practice, this reading would sound ridiculous, if not pathetic:

Comments about the animal metaphors

Witness one

This Black clinician has never worked at the therapeutic community but had been invited to join the interview panel that scored me 12 out of 55. In his initial statement he wrote that although he had never seen me, before the interview, he had heard about me then he withdrew that statement. His views are based on what he seemed to have picked up from the interview and a discussion they had had after the interview. He stated that:

• He was concerned about me because I did not show an appreciation of how important it is to share information about my practice with my colleagues.
• I was using my animal tradition in isolation to other clinical practices and did not seem to form or work as part of a therapeutic community team.
• He believed that it is important that members of staff do not introduce new and different practices without full consultation with others.
• Although he said the animal tradition I was practicing was also my area of research at that time he later suggested that I did not appear to understand the importance of evidence-based clinical practice.

Witness two

Witness Two was one of the senior clinicians involved in banning the animal metaphors, and when the ban was challenged he was very involved in negotiating how the animal metaphors could be reinstated, offering suggestions on how the whole community could be involved. He told the Tribunal that:

• While it is acceptable that metaphors can be useful in therapy the process of giving personal individual gifts departs markedly from the therapeutic model of care.
• Giving a specific gift to a resident can potentially foster an intense individual attachment to a member of staff which then puts the member of staff at risk because this client group has impaired capacity to differentiate between present relationships with carers and past relationships with carers who have often been abusive. This intense feeling of closeness can easily slip into intense feelings of hatred, which have little to do with the current relationship. He had earlier given the following statistics about the client group we worked with:

Fifty percent have adult criminal convictions
Seventy-five percent have attempted suicide

Forty-five percent suffered sexual abuse

Seventy-five percent have had drug and alcohol abuse problem

Sixty percent severely self harm

- The animal metaphors may also incite intense rivalries between residents. The organization has had incidents in the past where residents have become very threatening towards staff to whom they previously had close attachment particularly around the time of leaving.
- He had genuine concern about my practice and also about the potential risk that I may be creating for myself. The decision to ask me to stop the practice was not a way of controlling me or underplaying my skills. This was because the residents can potentially be aggressive and for a clinician to give personal gifts to the residents has the potential of causing further stress and conflict which the resident may physically act upon. This could be detrimental to the health and safety of staff and residents.
- He explained that he met me with my line manager to discuss this and I agreed to stop giving the animal metaphors and that I raised this issue in supervision and other staff gave their professional input and it was decided that personal material was not to be used in the treatment model.

Witness three

Witness Three was the senior Black clinician who instructed me to stop using the animal metaphors and when this ban was challenged he was involved in the discussions on how the practice could be reinstated. He told the Employment Tribunal that:

- The practice of giving "concrete" material, that is a description of an animal is similar to giving a "gift" to a resident. This can cause residents to foster individual attachments to a particular member of staff and is not the usual practice.
- The model of care is that treatment is run via dialogue with residents and issues are resolved by talking rather than by giving "gifts" or "concrete" material.
- Staff is not encouraged to become drawn into individual practices as this can leave them in a vulnerable position and at risk.

He said my use of animal metaphors was discussed with the Director; and with the next most senior clinician and my line manager; then it was explored in supervision with other members of the team and it was decided that the descriptions of animals would not be given to residents on discharge.

Was this collective amnesia? What exactly is a gift? When someone talks about their dream in group psychotherapy we say they have given the group a gift because others relate to it and make sense of it. It becomes a group dream because it benefits all.

The animal metaphors were the same. The animal was given to one person but it was taken to groups and it became a group's property. The main reason I started writing the metaphors down was because some of the residents who requested the animal metaphors were not in any therapeutic groups with me for us to analyse the metaphor further, so a written script meant they could take it to their own therapy groups and do so without me. I never viewed this as something private between me and an individual because the exchange took place during the largest community business meeting which was attended by all residents and all staff on duty. There were over forty people in the room witnessing this.

The residents did not see it as a personal "gift" to an individual either because they all got involved in analysing the metaphor and learning from it, and since they all benefited there was no need to envy the individual who got the animal. I was left feeling that I had been practicing some sort of black magic which held residents in a spell and which nobody understood, and had to be stopped because it was potentially dangerous. The senior clinicians seemed to imply that I was using this alien practice in secret against the ethos of the community and that I was having individual relationships with residents.

Neither did I understand their wish to protect me from the residents. I never felt at risk at all. I was quite challenging of residents and used to address issues with them that other staff might fear to confront. I was able to do this because I invested in my therapeutic relationship with patients, relying on and trusting my ability to be not only professional and tactful, but also direct. There is a Yoruba (Nigerian) saying that describes my relationship with this group of people who evoke fear of aggression: *Oni surur ni o nfun wara kinihun mu* meaning *It takes great patience and tact to milk a female lion*. I could happily milk these female lions because of the time and effort I invested in our relationship and the genuine interest I showed in them. I felt quite safe with the residents, and even my leaving tea with them was memorable. They had baked a variety of cakes for this occasion, the masterpiece being one baked by a resident who was himself leaving soon, and I had given him the Kangaroo metaphor in this book. He baked a big dark chocolate cake with a white inscription "diarrhoea" on it. It was a joke inspired by the content of his animal metaphor, so we had a good laugh about the meaning of this and ate the cake, which was just amazing.

The residents also gave me a window flower box they made which had colourful drawings of animals and the inscription "MJ's ark" on it, and they presented me with a photo album of me with residents and staff engaged in various activities. From the staff team I believe my co-facilitator of the Garden and Maintenance Group chose the presents, a spade and an apple tree. The tree was similar to the one in our community garden, which both of us had a private standing joke about. She made sure I took those fond memories with me.

By contrast, the majority of staff leaving this therapeutic community were simply offered tea and Trust biscuits by the residents, so to say I was being protected from the residents was ridiculous. I was never in any danger. I believe the senior clinicians projected their own aggressive feelings/phantasies onto the residents. I needed protection from the envy of my senior colleagues, not the residents.

Listening to the two senior clinicians telling the tribunal that they banned the animal metaphors for good was an unbelievable and quite maddening experience. It was as if I had imagined the residents' rage and their challenging of the senior clinicians, as if I had imagined the whole therapeutic community, both residents and staff, working together in making democratic decisions to re-establish the "Animal Tradition". The very people who were involved in those discussions were now sitting in front of me denying that it ever happened. I felt as if I was going mad. I think it was this betrayal, rather than losing the case, that crashed me.

This account highlights the fact that having the same skin colour does not mean we have the same culture or that we understand, or are prepared to learn about, each other's cultures. It also highlights the tragically destructive forces found within ethnic minority groups. The sad thing is that most of the Blacks who treated me unfairly were themselves victims of racism. Why else would these men deny under oath that they were challenged and forced to reinstate the animal metaphors?

When I originally highlighted the issue of similar ethnicity to the Employment Tribunal I wondered whether one could put in a claim for racial discrimination if the other party is of the same race or culture as the claimant. Black-on-Black victimization is a big problem and needs to be understood and addressed: we Blacks can not only be ruthless with each other, but also be used by other race groups to attack our own kind, just as slave masters used Blacks to capture other Blacks during the slave trade.

It is no different today. One just needs to look at the history of African countries and how some of their leaders have betrayed their own people. In a documentary on Zimbabwe it was painful to watch Zimbabweans crawling through barbed wire and having chunks of flesh torn off their buttocks as they tried to escape into South Africa by crossing the crocodile-infested Limpopo River. It brought tears to my eyes.

Why do we, Black people, do this to each other?

CHAPTER TWELVE

Betrayal and regression

12.1   The Employment Tribunal's findings

Below is a summary of the Employment Tribunal's findings on the main complaints about promotion, refusal to transfer and constructive dismissal:

The Employment Tribunal's findings

The unanimous decision of the second Employment Tribunal was that the Applicant was not constructively dismissed and the complaints of victimization and race discrimination were dismissed.

a. Failure to promotion

- Ms Mubika did not ask for feedback from the panel and she had not complained about the unfairness of the interview at the time.
- Ms Mubika did not complain either because she did not believe that the panel had decided not to promote her because of her race or because she feared the consequences, and she agreed during the hearing that one of the witnesses was telling the truth when he had said she had failed the interview. Therefore the conclusion is that Ms Mubika did not complain because she did not believe that she had grounds to do so.

- The complaint had no merit. The conclusion is that the interview panel's decision was not influenced by Ms Mubika's race or previous case or earlier complaints. One panel member (*who had written in his original statement that he had heard about me*) had no knowledge of the complaints. There was no evidence that the members of the panel had colluded against promoting Ms Mubika or that clinicians on the panel from ethnic minorities were not free to make their own assessment of Ms Mubika's suitability for the position.
- The delay prejudiced the Organization. Interview notes kept by the panel members had been destroyed.
- The Organization had learnt the lessons from the previous case and had taken steps to ensure that Ms Mubika and all other employees were treated equally and fairly. There may have been bad feelings in some quarters arising out of her previous case, but there was no evidence that the conduct of the Organization amounted to a breach of contract or a repudiation of the employment contract. Indeed Ms Mubika's own evidence was that the Organization wanted her to stay at the hospital. Further that the Organization understood her wish to transfer within the hospital and supported it. The failure to transfer was itself not a breach of contract.
- There was an assertion by Ms Mubika that there was racism within the hospital as an institution. She produced no evidence whatsoever to support it. The Organization had taken steps to ensure equal and fair opportunities for all its employees and had taken note of the findings of the Employment Tribunal in connection with Ms Mubika's previous case. (*What evidence was given to support this?*) The very measures introduced by the Organization were suggested by Ms Mubika to perpetuate the discriminatory practices of which she had earlier complained about. Rather than there being a policy to discriminate against Ms Mubika in relation to promotion, she was encouraged to reapply for the job. She did not do so for what may have been understandable reasons.
- Rejection is hard to take. The possibility of further rejection may have deterred her. The Tribunal finds no support for Ms Mubika's assertion that the Organization operated a policy that discriminated against her in relation to promotion and that the policy was implemented by persons from minority racial backgrounds. When the opportunity arose to undertake H Grade duties Ms Mubika refused to do so until she received medical clearance.

In the findings the Chairman included the following memo I wrote to the Black senior clinician whom I felt was putting me under pressure to take on H grade duties for a job I had failed the interview by scoring 12 out of 55:

To: Team Leader
From: MJ Maher

I am responding to your memo of the 5th. I just want to reiterate what I have already said previously in the two meetings you were in attendance, which is that I am not able to take up any of the H Grade duties.

I believe the Organisation had over two years to fill in those posts but failed. As someone who applied for both H Grade posts and failed to get any one of them because of racial discrimination—confirmed by the Employment Tribunal in both cases—I feel I should not expose myself to a potential roller coaster I will not know how to get off.

I also want to make it clear before anyone decides to force me to take up a single task all of the following requirements are met first:

• A letter from my GP stating that I am capable of getting involved in this task without any possibility of harming my mental good health
• A referral to Occupational Health, followed by a report confirming that I will be alright to carry out an H-Grade task without impact on my mental good health
• A meeting with my union representative

Until the above requirements are met I would rather not discuss this issue even informally because I have respect for you and do not want this to get in the way of our good professional relationship, so let us stay professional.

While I empathize with the position the Organization finds itself in it was an accident waiting to happen—it just took too long.

(*I found it stressful to act in a post, or carry the duties of a post, I had applied for and did not get. If I am not good enough to appoint then why would I be good enough to do the job? I would have ended up feeling used and that would have depressed me and destroyed my self esteem. Is that difficult to understand?*)

Ms Mubika had decided for her own understandable reason that she wished to move on, and that she had to do so before September and that was the reason for her resignation.

In summary the Tribunal finds no constructive dismissal, no unfair dismissal and no race discrimination.

When the Chair read his findings I found it difficult to listen: it felt like blows falling all over my head, with me unable to protect myself because my hands were tied behind my back.

The points I had argued in my unread statement were not addressed at all. I expected those issues to be presented and the reasons for dismissing them given. For example, the decision I had to make concerning where I would run my second training group, which had to be set up by September, had no bearing on where I worked because I did not need to run the group within the Organization that employed me (my first training group was with a different organization). Thus, the September deadline for starting my second group had nothing to do with my feeling forced to leave without a job to go to.

If the senior clinicians had transferred me as promised I could have stayed within the Organization, but my distress obliged me to leave when the new H and I grades were recruited because I found myself in a conflict without resolution and did not want to take my frustrations out on those whose skin colour, I believed, proved to be the acceptable qualification for promotion. It was not their fault and I did not want to become bitter and twisted by staying on. This was clearly explained in my unread statement but the Chair preferred the explanation that I had to leave by September because of my training group. It seemed that my opinions did not matter, and I was left wondering whether the Chair and his panel had even read my statement, or just taken a day off. I guess I will never know.

During the hearing I had felt gagged by not reading my statement, and to now be told that I did not produce any evidence "whatsoever" was hard to take, especially as I had 280 pages of evidence that were never looked at during the entire hearing—not even once.

Another question I kept pondering over was how an Employment Tribunal could accept that important documents (interview questions, panel's individual notes and scores, candidates' applications) were destroyed while one piece of paper with the total scores survived. At the previous hearing these now-missing documents made it possible for us all to work out what actually happened in the interview. It felt as if the only lesson the Organization had learnt from that hearing was which documents to get rid of.

Again, how could an Employment Tribunal accept that all three witnesses vividly remembered one unfair question yet could not even vaguely remember the other nine? They remembered that the Black senior clinician had asked me to discuss a project I had been working on for the past year, yet they all knew that I had just returned from exile and had not been allowed to work for that year because the Organization had sent me home. That prejudiced my answering the question, and the Black clinician involved admitted at the hearing that it was unfair.

I also felt unjustly blamed. A case in point was the Chair saying my delay in complaining prejudiced the Organization, yet the Organization's own policy stated that interview papers had to be kept safe for two years, and the complaint was made at ten months. I felt my head explode with frustration: I wanted to walk out but knew I could not, and felt myself regressing to my early significant experiences. I fought against this by trying to play the smart Alec. How interesting, I thought, that some of the points I had raised, which were considered to be "out of time", had become "in time" during the hearing. For example:

a. I had complained about how the organization set up a "them and me" divide when I came back to work after a year in exile. I experienced a similar divide during the hearing as I watched the Chair and the barrister laugh on a couple of occasions about something I could not follow, while I fought against the paranoia creeping up my body like rigor mortis and threatening to arrest my train of thought.

b. The other complaint was that the organization had failed to discuss the Employment Tribunal proceedings and had minimized its findings. I felt that this was also re-enacted when one of my complaints was summarized by the Chair as "colleagues failed to offer condolences when her brother died". I did not care about not being offered condolences: what was cruel was that two weeks after coming back from burying my youngest brother, Obediah, on two occasions I was handed envelopes to put money in as my contribution to buy flowers and cards to express my deepest sympathy to two White colleagues who had each lost an elderly relative.

I had lost my eldest brother Sam (45), and less than two years later my mother, then six months later my youngest brother Obediah (42), without getting any such tender considerations. I had just buried Obediah, who left behind three minor children, yet I was treated as if my losses were insignificant. When I raised this in a meeting one of the colleagues who got flowers and a collective card of deepest sympathy spoke about how he had felt comforted by this kind gesture. I accept that it is not unlawful for an organization to be cruel, but since this was discriminatory practice I expected the Employment Tribunal's summary to include both White comparators I gave showing how White colleagues were treated differently following bereavement, and how I was expected to contribute to their privileged treatment. I felt that by leaving out this difference in treatment and minimizing my complaint by simply stating that "colleagues failed to offer condolences when her brother died", the Chair had depicted me as complaining about nothing.

12.2   Regression: the past and present collide

Listening to the Chair was winding me up and I wanted to walk out again, but had to take it on the chin. It was pushing me back in time, back to the most traumatic period of my life, when my father's death left me exposed and vulnerable and the changing rules rendered me confused. The rules my father brought me up to respect became redundant when he died, just as the policies this organization had made me respect became redundant at the hearing, with the resulting chaos and confusion making me once again vulnerable. My extended family seemed unable to understand the significance of these rules, just as this hearing did not seem to understand the significance of the organization's policies.

When my father died I felt blamed for being the daughter he brought me up to be: different from that expected in Shona culture. My father believed in the importance of independence, being clear to myself about what I do and say, and fighting for what is right. In traditional Shona culture, however, a daughter was expected to be submissive and dependent on a man, beginning with her father, who then passes her on to a husband. A child is dependent on its father, but if he dies the child is passed on to the *babamukuru*, big father (father's elder brother) or to the *babamunini*, small father (father's younger brother). The boys become men and after a year, at a ceremony to bring back the father's spirit into the family (*kurova guva*), the eldest boy, irrespective of age, is given his father's walking stick and his *gano* (hunting axe) as a sign of taking over as family head.

When my father died my family elders decided to take me up as a project and turn me into a proper Shona daughter. They interpreted my actions differently from what I meant, expecting me to accept that oppressive rules they insisted on were in my best interests. To me, however, such rules appeared neither good nor fair.

The hearing pushed me back to that era, back to dependence on men and being obligated to accept and follow their rules: telling me why I left the organization (even though it did not make sense) and rejecting the reasons I gave by ignoring them as if I never spoke (Of course, I did not speak because my written statement was never heard).

My family elders had done the same. When I spoke they turned a deaf ear, then put words in my mouth. My family predicted that I would be doomed because of my "hot-headedness". They called me a *nhinhi*, a tough seed that never softens or cooks no matter how long you boil it, but to me it basically proved that I was my father's child. The elders wanted to control my every move and I was not used to that: I just felt suffocated and betrayed, as if I had arrived from a different planet with a different set of rules. The world had gone crazy but was telling me that I was the crazy one. It felt the same at the second tribunal: I felt that I was declared the crazy one.

By the time I left the hearing I was experiencing a greater sense of fear than ever before, yet it felt familiar and in my mind it was located to the time my father died. I could not work out what the fear was about, but it was paralysing me. I fell silent while my husband expressed the outrage I felt. I kept thinking that when in quicksand, do not move. Just keep still and get your bearings right.

I tried to figure out where the fear was coming from. Maybe it was because I did not have a permanent job to go to ... no, the fear felt deeper than that. I tried looking for its source but I just could not work it out. However, I kept tracing the fear back to the time of my father's death, yet it did not feel directly connected. I was puzzled. His loss was a painful tragedy but not a frightening one, so where was the fear coming from?

After the confusion my family created for me, I ran away from home to live with a cousin who, although considered poor, understood me and helped me sort myself out. After the hearing I did a similar thing. I knew I was not emotionally strong as the fear stayed within me, and I was unable to process my anger because the fear threatened to drown me. I felt too vulnerable. I had to stand still or else drown in the quicksand of confusing emotions. I was afraid that the fear would consume me during the process of expressing my anger. It had to wait until I was stronger. When in quicksand, keep still. Moving means drowning. I stood still.

Gersie (1997, p. 35) states: "When talking does not get people anywhere, when tears are exhausted and rage is paralyzed, they cease to exercise authority over the events of their life. Devoid of authorship, deprived of agency and filled with a pervasive sense of helplessness, the person refrains from speaking their mind ... Thoughts about their reality, and the consideration of possible actions to change that reality, are not understood as problems to be explored. On the contrary, both the situation and the way of life are accepted as inevitability, necessary givens in a world out of which there is no escape, and beyond which no possibilities can be perceived". (Coles, 1989)

I felt helpless. I knew I had regressed badly and needed to be around people I trusted, people who believed in me and who would let me know I was all right. I had to depend on other people's judgment because I was too regressed to trust my own. Freud compared regression to an army needing to retreat to its secure base before facing the enemy again. I decided to retreat to the people I trusted until I was emotionally stable enough to deal with the struggles of living in a racist society. Therefore,

I retreated to my trusted part-time employer—the organization I had trained with when I first came to UK. I could only work at the lower grade of a newly qualified D grade nurse (back to being with the poor cousin) but that felt fine because of my association of poverty with sincerity, honesty, containing, comforting and genuine concern for my welfare. I felt nurtured by my part-time employer just as with my cousin, and the confusion began to settle.

When I received my written Employment Tribunal report I did not bother to read it immediately: I knew I was still too fragile and could not cope with severe negative emotional arousal. Any panel willing to believe I could score 12 out of 55 was not worth my time and was likely to drive me insane.

Since I was earning the equivalent of a newly qualified nurse we started feeling the financial pinch and re-mortgaged the house, but even though things began to balance out the fear was still there. Gersie (1997, p. 36) says we often put our memories of loss, shame, betrayal, and disappointment far from our desire to talk about them, believing that keeps us safer. Perhaps I had pushed my memories too far to recall but I kept trying to remember because the fear was crippling me and in order to get rid of it I had to find its origin and make sense of it. All I knew was that it was reignited at the second Employment Tribunal when the Chair read the findings. I knew it was connected to the time my father died, then ... blank. Maybe I felt his dying betrayed me? Possibly, but that thought did not make any emotional connection with the fear in me.

It took over a year to remember the source of my fear, and when I did it came back to me in a flash. When my father died, three months before my eighteenth birthday, I was confused because rules changed so abruptly. Everyone claimed to know what was best for me yet nobody was willing to listen to me. My opinions, which my father had respected and encouraged, were suddenly null and void. In my mind the experience at the Employment Tribunal triggered the feeling that my opinions did not matter, and that rules can be changed. They made me reduce the number of complaints because there was no time. No time to read my statement. No time to look at the evidence. No time for seven witnesses. No time for this, no time for that. No time, no time.

The loss of footing in life after my father's death became intertwined with the loss of footing at the tribunal hearing and I could not separate the two events. The past and the present had collided. Sources of comfort had now become sources of stress and distress.

The betrayal I experienced by my own people, my family, my Black colleagues and the Employment Tribunal left me feeling as if I was being hunted by a pride of lions. One minute I was happily galloping about within my family—a herd of zebras—then suddenly a pride of lions separated me from the rest of the herd, but I was not scared because I could see a few zebras around me. Then suddenly the few zebras that had given me comfort, confidence and protection from isolation started stripping off their skins, revealing lions hidden beneath. I was surrounded by a pride of hungry lions! The people I trusted had turned into hungry lions ready to pounce on me.

When my family turned into lions after my father's death because I challenged their advice, they labelled me a troublemaker. Nobody was listening to me or wanted to stand by me. I missed my father. His best friend, whom we knew as our *babamunini*, meaning our small father, came to see me. He had heard about my troubled soul and expressed concern, offering to have a chat with me away from everyone else to see how he could help. I felt relieved that at last someone would make time to hear me out and understand my views: someone who had known my father most of his life was going to listen to how awful it was to lose my father—who had been everything to me and made my world feel safe. I trusted my small father to take away the madness now being pumped into me. I was convinced that he would know exactly how I felt because he too would be missing his friend, therefore he would understand how I was hurting. He would realize that I made sense and was not going mad.

I then recalled an incident when I argued with my grandfather, who told my father that when he had tried to teach me manners I was rude to him. My father replied: "I wouldn't worry about that one. She knows what she is doing". I had felt comforted, trusted and understood, and now I strongly believed that since small father was my father's best friend he would be like my father, listening to me and respecting me. He would shrug off what others were saying and trust my opinion. He would say to them, "I wouldn't worry about that one, she knows what she is doing". Maybe he could even be the father I had lost. My heart filled with hope for the first time since my father's death.

I felt calm and hopeful as my small father drove me to his farm a few miles from Chivhu, a small town just outside Harare. The confusion was settling down. When we got to his farm and sat in the lounge he offered me alcohol, but everyone knew that I do not drink. Also, for a father to offer his daughter alcohol was a big taboo to break, at least to me, and alarm bells started ringing. I did not like that change of rules. At that time a girl who drank alcohol was perceived to be a loose woman, so why would my own small father want me to drink? My father never let me drink. I refused the alcohol.

My small father was friendly at first, saying that I looked tense and the alcohol would help me relax. Anyone would look tense if they had lost their father and the world was driving them mad. I did not like the look in his eyes either. I kept refusing the alcohol and he became irritable and insistent. I realized then that my small father was turning into a lion. I had to get out of there fast. I told him that I would only drink alcohol from a glass and not straight from the bottle. He got up to get the glass from his kitchen and I shot out through the window and legged it.

That sense of abuse of trust was the common feeling that made my past and present collide. I had expected to tell my story and be listened to, but was left feeling gagged and disregarded. I did not need to win the case, but I did need to be listened to in the same way I had expected my small father to listen to my distress. In both cases I ended up feeling that my trust had been betrayed. The fear clicked into place and it all started to make sense. This was the origin of the fear that had troubled me.

I then remembered more about this paralysing fear. After escaping from my father's best friend I ran into the forest, but now had to find my way back to Chivhu. Although I was scared I knew that if I walked along the main road my small father would find me so I stayed out of sight in the forest. After a while I could have gone to the main road and flagged down a car but I kept thinking "from the frying pan into the fire". No, the main road would be unsafe. Flagging down cars is common practice in Zimbabwe, but that day I just could not do it. I had lost my ability to trust.

Generally I am scared of trees and grass because of snakes and wild animals, but that day anger and fear clashed and kept me distracted. I could not think about my small father because it made me feel like a victim and feel sorry for myself, and that dragged me further into a deep black hole of helplessness and self-pity, making it impossible to fight. Who can I trust if not my father's best friend? I blamed my father for leaving me in this cruel world, for giving me stupid rules that crumbled under the weight of his death.

I used this anger to divert my attention from the fact that I was scared in the forest on my own. I had an intense conversation with my father. I cried my heart out in anger but at times could not stay focused and fear consumed my body. When that happened my imagination ran wild, turning the forest into a deadly jungle, then making the jungle spring to life. I visualized snakes just about to strike and the chattering of the monkeys—*I wonder if they would still chatter if they lost their father? Would they even notice?* I shook my head to clear the thought but it was replaced by another. *They say baboons can slap a human's skin off his face. I wish I could do that. There are many faces that need their skins slapped off.*

That thought opened the gates holding back similar stupid childhood horror stories about the jungle, and the fear came back. What was that noise? My heart missed a beat. Tension filled up my lungs and threatened to suffocate me. I let out a squeak as hot air forced itself out. Sweat poured down my brow.

As I approached a thicket of thorny bushes, the *mubayamhondoro*, my whole body tensed up and I became paralysed. My breathing sounded louder, summoning all the wild animals that had not yet seen me. I was now in the spotlight of danger. *Focus, focus* I whispered to myself. *Think about dad. What would he say? Yeah, what would he say about my situation? Well, he is not here now. He is busy resting with his grandfathers while I am being fed to the lions in this cruel, cruel world. How dare he!* The anger welled up and dispelled the fear. I took advantage of this and worked the anger into an inferno, becoming so angry that I did not notice I had just walked past the fear-inducing thicket of *mubayamhondoro* and up an anthill. I actually walked through the anthill without spotting the many holes often harbouring snakes. My anger prevented the smell of fear oozing out of me.

I thought about my father. I missed him so much and thinking about never seeing him again broke my heart and brought back the fear. I felt paralysed again and unable to walk any further, but forced myself to even though each step felt as if I was walking into the lion's den.

Either way I am going to die because soon it will be dark. The thought of darkness introduced the fear of ghosts. Ghosts! Snakes are nothing compared to ghosts! Ghosts are in a different category. My exhaustion disappeared and my feet grew wings, propelling me through the tall grass past balancing rocks that would normally scare me because baboons and monkeys like playing on them.

I tried to think of all the reasons why I was so angry with my father but the pain of losing him was too much and it brought back the fear. I could not get rid of the fear this time so I surrendered to it. *Come on wild beasts, come and do your worst because your worst is my passport to being with my father. So, come on. See if I care!* I worked the bravado till it turned into anger again, travelling through this vicious fear/anger cycle until I got to Chivhu.

On reflection I realized that after the hearing I did the same. Instead of being angry with the zebras that had turned into lions I directed the anger onto myself. Instead of allowing myself to feel like a victim I worked an image of me as the perpetrator, because being a victim would just pull me down further—down into a black hole of helplessness and self-pity. Being a victim made me feel weak, as if I was drowning, and the only way I could keep myself afloat was by being angry with myself. I built myself into this vindictive person who is not as good as she thinks she is. I recalled the Chair's comments about rejection: "Rejection is hard to take. The possibility of further rejection may have deterred her". Rejection is hard to take, rejection is hard to take. My head chanted the torturous words like a broken record, building up my self-hatred, which was good because it put some fire in my belly. I needed that. *Rejection is hard to take! Rejection is hard to take!*

I recalled the Employment Tribunal Chair's warm laughter with the barrister as they shared a joke and his warm farewell to the elderly Black man who had been recalled from retirement to be a witness, wishing him an enjoyable retirement. I worked on that to turn myself into a vindictive cow. *How could I bring an old man to a hearing? What is the matter with me? No respect for old people? Do I not know that in my culture old people never do anything wrong? They are an endangered species, are exempted from taking any responsibility for their actions.* I pumped up the volume on self-hatred. *This is madness. I did not ask him to be a witness. I am a victim ...* I quickly gagged that utterance of the voice of reason. This was not the time to play the victim ... *if in quicksand, keep still. Focus. You are not a victim. Victims have no energy to fight, therefore you are a perpetrator.* I carried on using my aggression to get out of this black hole of helplessness, of feeling like a nothing ... a toy God created for other races, and now my own race, to play with. A nothing ... *please, no self pity.*

I had to stay with the idea of being the perpetrator because it gave me power at a time I felt helpless and weak, so I wrote to the old man, apologizing for any distress I might have caused him. As an African I should respect my elders no matter what.

After running away from my small father I went home and cried myself to sleep. That night I had a vivid dream with a real presence of my father. We sat as we used to and talked through my difficulties. It was the first time since his death that I had a logical discussion with someone who understood me. The following morning everything seemed very clear. The confusion was gone and I felt calm and resolved. I knew what I had to do, so I packed my bags and ran away from home to live with a distant cousin who once worked for my father. The incident with my small father was wiped out of my memory. I must have felt that since nothing had happened it was an insignificant event, but now I realized that something did happen and it was a big deal—my ability to trust was damaged significantly at a time I was most vulnerable.

A few months later my brother Sam visited me at my cousin's. He said it would be best if we all stayed together at the ranch, and he wanted to take me home. My problem, however, was not with my siblings but with my father's extended family, and I was not strong enough to deal with them. Going back meant I would be looking after siblings and cousins, but I could not mother someone else when I felt like a lost child unable to exist without her father. I needed time to mourn him, to learn how to be without him, to find myself again. I needed to be in a place I felt safe and wanted, a place that did not make demands on me, a place that was stable, consistent and predictable, because my emotional reservoir was empty. I was not ready to leave my cousin.

Sam understood and did not insist on taking me back. The state I was in was well captured in Jacobs' vignette about Zara, "So the counselor, who at first had thought in terms of encouraging her to go out and begin mixing with people, soon realized that Zara needed to be able to retreat and find some safety; and that she needed to come out in her own good time, not under pressure". (Jacobs, 1998, p. 83)

I stayed with my cousin for a year, and continued dreaming about my father right through that period. Each time I was troubled, lonely, isolated or missing my father I would cry myself to sleep. He always came in my dreams and we would sit and discuss the problem the way we used to.

In my culture we believe that during the first year after death the deceased remains on earth sorting out unfinished business. After a year a ceremony called *kurova guva* is carried out to bring the deceased's spirit to join his ancestors, and exactly a year after my father's death I had my last dream, in which he told me I was ready to let him go. After that farewell dream I could not reach my father at all, no matter how much I cried. However, I listened to what he had said—that I was ready, so the next time Sam visited me I decided it was time to go back home. I was resolved and calm, and no family chaos could threaten me again. I had found myself.

CHAPTER THIRTEEN

Consequences of complaining about racism

13.1 The brown envelope

After leaving my full-time employment without a job to go to, looking for work became a priority. Having solid qualifications and an impressive work history, I was not worried, but my confidence started to evaporate when I could not secure a job. This was a new experience for me because previously I always got the first position I applied for.

For example, after training I carried on working for my training hospital as a D grade. An E grade post came up at a time when one usually got promoted after a minimum experience of six months post training. I was only four months post training but got the E grade job, despite competing against nurses with ten years experience.

The next jobs I applied for were both G grades: a charge nurse post at a therapeutic community and a Drug and Alcohol community nurse post. Although I was an E grade I was offered both jobs (jumping two grades, E to G), so chose the therapeutic community because I was veering towards group psychotherapy. Now, however, after six years as a G grade charge nurse I was unable to get a job, not even the Drug and Alcohol community nurse post I was previously offered. This post was subsequently re-advertised but I decided not to re-apply because

I knew I had fared well in the interview and there was nothing more I could do to improve my chances.

I kept applying for positions but the more I got rejected the more scared I became. I was losing my confidence. I started applying for lower grades but could not secure even an E grade post. I kept hearing that there was a shortage of nurses yet I could not get a job, not even as a newly qualified D grade. I began thinking that perhaps I was not as good as I thought. Maybe I deserved 12 out of 55.

It was while speaking to a Black psychologist about my situation that he told me about a "brown envelope" policy earmarking troublemakers, a stigma unidentified by the bearer but not the interviewing panel. He said that perhaps I had been given this so-called brown envelope which, by taking with me to interviews, alerted the interviewing panels not to offer me a job. His advice was that I needed to get rid of the brown envelope. I did not believe him at first, but after my sixth application was sent back with a note saying I had put insufficient stamps on the envelope and it arrived too late for me to be short listed, I knew that I had to stop and reflect.

There had to be a hidden meaning to this: the postage *was* sufficient because my application had not changed in size and I had sent other applications using the same first-class stamp without problems. Maybe my "brown envelope" was too heavy for a first-class stamp. I decided to stop applying for jobs: the Black doctor was right, I was carrying extra baggage, and needed to get rid of it first or drive myself insane. I believed that the shadow of my last job was casting its darkness everywhere I went.

I decided to lie low for a year while working as an agency nurse and a D grade bank nurse, because after that year I could apply for jobs without needing a reference from the therapeutic community. My colleagues knew what had happened and took care of me, making me feel wanted and respected. Although I was being paid a D grade rate and had to work long hours to make up the financial loss that did not matter because what was important was to feel safe. I had retreated again, back to being with the poor cousin I trusted to care for me.

I spent a year working solely for my part-time employer as a bank nurse and as an agency nurse, with people I could rely on to look after me, people I knew cared. My colleagues nurtured me back to good health, and twelve months later I was ready to seek full-time employment.

CHAPTER FOURTEEN

What's in a name?

14.1 MJ, not Em Jay

I used to think that a name is just for identification, but mine carried invisible baggage. A year after leaving the therapeutic community I had regained some of my confidence and was more settled. I had worked my way from a D grade agency nurse to a G grade within six months. After a year I was sure I had lost the brown envelope so started applying for full-time jobs again. Since I believed that my inability to secure employment was connected to my history with the therapeutic community, I decided to apply for a position outside the radius of that community, with the plan of moving closer to home later. My first application was at a senior level for a deputy manager's post and I got it. This confirmed that I had got rid of the brown envelope!

When my new boss phoned to offer me the job she was excited and spoke about how outstanding I had been at the interview and how she was looking forward to working with me. However, a couple of weeks later I phoned to enquire about something but she was not available, so I left my name—MJ—and my number for her to ring me back. When I originally applied for the job I had written my first name in full, which I rarely do, and during the interview I did not introduce myself, otherwise I would have said MJ, which is what I am usually called.

When my new boss returned my call she wanted to know whether I was the MJ who had worked at the therapeutic community. I did not understand her question because my curriculum vitae had a detailed account of my work history, which included the therapeutic community. When I confirmed that I had worked there she asked me about my name, and I explained that I use my initials. She fell silent for a while, then said she had not realized that people calling me MJ were using my initials. She assumed they meant Em Jay. She said she had heard a lot about me and, sounding different—less cheerful, less enthusiastic and almost cold—said she needed to consult with Human Resources.

Later, Human Resources contacted me requesting two more references. I questioned this because they already had the required two references and had offered me the job. I had never heard of a job that required four references, but they insisted so I sent them two more names. A few days later they contacted me again requesting another referee because one of those I had given was on a two-week holiday, and they suggested that to quicken the process I could ask someone from the therapeutic community. I said I did not grasp the logic of asking someone I had not seen in the last year to give me a reference when they could just wait two weeks. They accepted that and I got the position.

14.2   The burden of my name weighs me down

When I started work I knew I had to be patient with my new boss. My experience on returning to my previous work place after my year in exile had taught me how to be with people who had been poisoned by what they had heard about me and were being passively aggressive towards me. For example, a junior clinician newly employed while I was in exile reacted angrily to my return, so I chose to work with him by joining a group he facilitated. We co-facilitated our group well and our relationship improved. By the time I left he seemed to respect me and said how different I was from what he had heard. I was confident that my new boss would see that difference too. I felt grateful to her for offering me a chance to work even though I knew she would not have done so had she originally known that I was "the MJ".

Unfortunately, when I started work after a year of rather mundane employment I was hungry for challenges. I was very enthusiastic and the fact that I was more experienced than my boss did not help because I felt she saw me as a threat. I must have been irritating too, because the work I was expected to do covered various areas within my expertise and she dealt with this by continually reminding me that she was the boss. For example, when she gave me an Operational Policy to read I thought she wanted me to work on it so I engaged all my knowledge, experience and skills as a nurse, teacher, editor and therapist. On finishing the work, I brought back a very corrected document expecting some praise, but my boss was not impressed at all. She told me that I was supposed to just read it and not make any corrections. She then binned the copy I had worked on—all my hard work. From this experience I understood that I had to water down my enthusiasm and be more sensitive.

Our relationship did not improve. On one occasion she told me that as deputy manager I could attend meetings with senior external managers to discuss our projects. The two of us arranged to get together before the meeting, but when we met she told me she had changed her mind and it was no longer appropriate for me to attend. Since we were at a different site she took me to the staff canteen and bought me a cup of tea to sip while she attended the meeting. She gave me an information booklet to work on that I had already completed, because she felt I needed something to entertain myself with while waiting for her. I felt like a dog left in the car while its master gets on with the daily business.

Just before lunch the canteen staff threw me out because they needed to prepare the dining room for the lunch-hour rush. I watered down the anger at waiting that was starting to warm me up. I thought about my father. The thing my father and I argued about most was his annoying habit of leaving me in the car while he went to have a "quick chat" with someone, usually for thirty minutes or more. I always left his car unlocked and made my own way home. I know it has to do with having waited ten years for my mother's return. I can no longer bear waiting for someone not knowing how long the wait is going to be—not even my father would have got away with this. However, for this boss I waited. I did not complain. I just smiled and swallowed.

I smiled and swallowed other humiliating incidents too, because I felt she needed time to get to know me. I tried hard to make allowances for someone I believed was anxious because of hearsay about me. I knew that once she got to know me she would understand that what she had heard were just projections, but unfortunately we never got to that point because it became too much for me. Within the first month I decided to leave but was not sure whether I could get other employment after such a short period. I worried that this brief stay would reflect negatively on my chances but felt there was no harm in trying. I applied for a group psychotherapist's post that came up nearer home and at a higher grade (I grade, equivalent to Band 8a), but while waiting for the outcome of the interview my boss and I hit another iceberg.

She asked me to produce an information flyer using material our consultant had typed for me, but the document had extra handwritten information along the margin. I spent a whole day designing and preparing the flyer, and with hard labour produced something I was proud of. When I sent it through to my boss, expecting praise for a job well done ... there was silence. After thirty minutes she told me she was not going to use my flyer because it was full of inaccurate information, and instead of correcting it she had designed another flyer herself. Designed another flyer in just thirty minutes? I found it hard to believe she could design a flyer, one that took me all day, in thirty minutes. It was impossible. Later she told me she had deliberately added the inaccurate handwritten information to see if I would use my initiative by asking her if the given information was correct.

That was it! I decided there would be no more mind games. Enough was enough: no more smiling and no more swallowing. I wrote to the senior managers concerning all that had been happening and requested them to sort it out.

We were called to a meeting where she was asked to explain her actions but she walked out after a few minutes, saying I was shouting at her and she was not going to stay and be abused. I am not a shouter, especially when given the space to be listened to, but I was aware that one of my social stereotypic observations is that Blacks are perceived as loud and aggressive. I became concerned that she would be believed and the focus would shift from the issues I was raising to me personally. I needed to keep the focus on the situation at hand, so informed my managers that I wanted a written response from her before we met again because that way she had to explain her actions. She left the organization without giving a response.

Her leaving upset me because I did not want her to go. I understood she was anxious, but it was shocking to see someone so influenced by what she had heard about me. What could she possibly have been told to justify her behaviour? Whatever it was must have been really bad to change our initially warm exchange to this.

After she left I agreed to act in her post while waiting for the outcome of my interview for a group psychotherapist's post. I really did not want to stay, and even though I was encouraged to apply for the post when it was advertised, felt too responsible for her leaving to occupy her still-warm shoes. That would have been insensitive. Fortunately I got the group psychotherapist's job. Although I was sad about her leaving I was grateful for the poor way she had treated me because that motivated me to look for another position. Sometimes good comes out of bad experiences.

Getting the group psychotherapist's job boosted my confidence tremendously, because it proved I was not the idiot I was made out to be. I was excited as well: in less than two months of full-time employment I landed a job two grades above my acting post, something I had not thought possible within that short space of time. I had moved from being unable to get a permanent job, not even as a newly qualified D-grade nurse, to getting a G-grade and then an I-grade promotion in just two months! At the therapeutic community, a specialist unit, I had stayed on G-grade for six years. I was one of their best clinicians yet I failed three times to get promoted to the next H-grade. Now I had achieved an even higher grade!

To the second Employment Tribunal I say: rejection may be hard to take but one can survive it, and sometimes it's not a bad thing, especially for those of us who tend to hold on to what is toxic. Unfairness, however, can destroy. It nearly destroyed me.

14.3   The burden of my name in psychotherapy

Since going through the Employment Tribunal with one of the prominent organizations in psychotherapy I have found it difficult to rebuild my career within the professional community, and I believe this is because I am seen as a troublemaker. The difficulty I have is that some of those involved in the Employment Tribunal cases belong to the same professional body as me. I find that people I do not know have heard a lot about me and react with hostility or suspicion, and the fact that some doors still slam in my face makes me realize that I have not completely buried the brown envelope with certain psychotherapy organizations.

For example, I once applied for a post of a group conductor facilitating a group of trainee therapists. After applying I received a letter telling me that the criteria had changed and I did not meet the new requirements. How could the criteria change after applications have been submitted?

I shrugged my shoulders: when one door slams shut in my face another swings open behind me. I simply needed to turn around and find out which door it is. Better still, my friend John Allen says a door shuts because another *has* opened, making it a certainty. It's just a matter of looking for that open door. I have also learnt the art of not forcing open doors that are closing. I have a lot to offer. I do not need to beg.

A month after being told that I did not meet the new criteria a similar post was advertised by another organization that did not know anything about the burden of my name. I applied and got the job. It has proved to be a good opportunity for me because I have been able to develop within this organization by focusing my energy onto positive projects rather than having to fight for survival.

In some organizations, when I discuss my experiences the group splits. Some White British people attack me because they hear what I say as an envious attack on people they respect, but the majority of non-British White and a few White British support me. Some of the ethnic minority just ignore me and try to disassociate themselves. Sometimes I feel the north/south divide forming, with those who trained in London attacking me and closing ranks the most. The exceptions are the few who knew me from before or who have since worked with me, but the Londoners seem to feel more superior, hence the statement that I was envious. Fortunately, that does not bother me: it is a familiar pond to swim in because we had a similar division in Zimbabwe—those who went to schools in the capital, Harare, saw themselves as superior to those who went to schools outside the capital. I fitted in both camps because I went to Chishawasha Mission and St Dominic's, schools within Harare radius. I was seen as a town girl (I lived in Harare) but also as a country girl (I also lived in Chivhu). Similarly, in this country I place myself in both camps: I am a Londoner *and* a Northerner because I was trained in both regions—London and Manchester.

When I attend study days or conferences I worry about how I will be received on account of the projections my name carries. At these professional meetings some of my siblings from the therapeutic community talk to me and others do not, making it very obvious by chatting to someone close by while ignoring me. Most of those involved in the first tribunal, and those who worked directly with me, are happy to see me, while most of those involved in the second tribunal and those who have never worked directly with me but have heard about me tend to be hostile.

Being frozen out restricts my participation because I am made to feel like an outsider when I should have equal rights with everyone else. In the past, belonging used to be so important that I was prepared to pay the price, but since making sense of the fear triggered in me at the second Employment Tribunal I know that men can fail me and I will survive the disillusionment. I do not need to force my way in where I am not wanted. Sometimes one's own family can be toxic and moving away—as in my case, to a poorer distant cousin with better morals, a genuine regard for me and the ability to make me feel wanted, loved and cherished—is a better choice. I might meander around as I negotiate obstacles but I still get to my target destination. I am much happier than if I had stayed with a richer but abusive family whose terms and conditions stifled my personal growth with discriminatory rules.

It has been quite a rough ride, rough enough to leave me wondering what makes it possible for racism to flourish in any institution. We are good at looking far and wide for stereotypical racist imagoes, yet the people involved in my institutional racism case, and found guilty of direct race discrimination and victimization contrary to the Race Relations Act 1976, Section 2, are trained professionals. I am well aware that no-one is immune to racism—whether doctors, nurses, social therapists, psychotherapists, counsellors, or managers—but I had expected better understanding from my organization because it was an environment considered to be the cream of talking therapy, where the art is in listening, acceptance, and empathy. Nevertheless, the institutional racism there caused severe compassion fatigue.

CHAPTER FIFTEEN

Analysis of the second Employment Tribunal

15.1 Extractive introjection

In order to make sense of what happened at the second Employment Tribunal I turned to Bollas (1987). His concept of extractive introjection gives another explanation to Black-on-Black betrayal. Victims of consistent racist extractive introjection (being drained of one's positive mental function due to racial reasons) may end up identifying with the aggressor, taking on his personality and operating with a false self.

Some of my Black colleagues had talked to me about having suffered institutional racism themselves, so I expected some empathy, yet what they did to me felt no different from what the White clinicians did which led to the first Employment Tribunal. What felt worse was my reaction to the Black clinicians. I felt the treatment by Black and ethnic minority colleagues at a deeper level—a betrayal. Bang to core.

Bollas identifies four types of extractive introjection:

15.1.1 Theft of mental content

This occurs when one suggests an idea and someone else develops it further as if they thought of it first. It happened when I became a deputy manager for the third organization, where I was more experienced than my boss. Each time I suggested something she rejected it, but later incorporated it as if it was her idea. I did not get any acknowledgement, so was building her up while I got drained. In the end I stopped suggesting anything unless we were in a meeting with other people, or else I emailed her my ideas and copied in other managers. This, however, was not too bad: at least my ideas, which were part of who I am, were allowed to survive and grow even though someone else took credit for them.

On the other hand, the destruction of the animal metaphors went a step further because the aim was not to develop them—it was theft in order to destroy or kill them off. It felt as if they had taken something out of me that was as precious as gold dust, creative, effective and admired, and turned it into sawdust—rubbish, and perhaps even dangerous. At the second Employment Tribunal I was made to feel inferior, dishonest, stupid, unprofessional and infantile, while the witnesses made themselves look superior, smart, professional, knowledgeable and parental, needing to protect me from myself. It was the most painful experience of extractive introjection I have ever had—being robbed of an essential part of myself.

15.1.2 Theft of affective process

When someone makes a mistake he might feel surprised, shocked, and angry with himself, and that can lead to taking a depressive position where he reflects on his behaviour and accepts responsibility for the consequences. He might feel sad, guilty, and responsible and want to repair the damage, but if this process is stopped or interfered with, for example, harsh reaction towards the individual about how dreadful his behaviour was, or he is taken to court, he may become overwhelmed with shame and guilt. This could result in feeling forced to defend his behaviour in order to self-preserve against possible humiliation. He might become stubborn and deny or rationalize any wrongdoing, thus losing the reflective process that allows for reparation.

Sometimes I wonder whether some of the individuals from this organization had felt this overwhelming sense of shame, guilt and humiliation, because by taking them through yet another Employment Tribunal they had to fight for self-preservation no matter what it took. Wanting to believe in this possible explanation helped me survive the betrayal I felt at how hard they had denied what happened. They had pulled out all the stops—under oath.

15.1.3   Theft of mental structure

I could have proved that the use of animal metaphors continued after the ban by calling in witnesses involved in the 9.15 community meetings where reinstatement of the animal metaphors took place, but due to my upbringing I did not want to call on junior staff. As the eldest daughter I was trained to protect my siblings because they could not cope with the stresses of life like I could, so for me to call junior staff as witnesses was out of question: my conscience would not allow it. I believed that, like my siblings, my colleagues might not cope with the stress of an Employment Tribunal, especially as I would have expected them to speak against their seniors. I had relied on written evidence of the 9.15 diary to prove that the animal metaphors carried on, but to me it looked as if no one had looked at the written evidence.

At one point the scene at the Employment Tribunal hearing became a powerful observation for me. As I sat with three White male Employment Tribunal members, a White solicitor and a White barrister—all occupying positions of superiority in the proceedings of making a judgment on conflicts between Black and ethnic minority people—I felt the power of the White panel. It became our superego, waiting to give judgment on what they thought was justice.

In the slave/master situation, or where Whites are seen as superior and Blacks as inferior, the White person becomes the superego de-structuring the Black person's mind. When that happens the ego stops functioning from within because the Black person expects to be humiliated by the White person and loses the capacity to question—he aims to please or deceive the White person who is now his external superego. If the Black person's capacity to reason is denigrated, his mental structure (that which generates rational thought and problem-solving abilities) is dismantled, and as a result his self-esteem and self-confidence are eroded.

This is what happened when I could not read my seventy-seven-page statement or present my 280 pages of evidence. I was cross-examined for less than an hour and that was the only time I spoke about my case. I lost my confidence and self-esteem to the extent that I could not question what was being suggested, which was not helpful to me.

I just followed what the Chair was suggesting because I wanted to please him, and that destroyed me and my case. My ego was so crashed that I could not even be bothered to present my submissions, a task I had enjoyed at the first hearing. How could I summarize my arguments when I felt gagged? There was no point. When a Black person's ego stops functioning from within he is likely to behave like an idiot or a fool—displaying Uncle Tom's syndrome of wanting to please the White master.

The other thing that affected my functioning during the hearing was the joking between the White men, the Chair and the barrister. Since I could not understand their humour I became paranoid, a regressive state in which I was overwhelmed with a sense of the isolation of an outsider. This was made worse by my other Achilles' heel: the regressive reaction to constant changes of rules which left me feeling helpless and unsure of myself, resulting in further loss of confidence and the inability to challenge or disagree. I lost my self-esteem and confidence for a long time after the hearing. The destruction of my ego made it difficult for me to stand up for what I thought was right: it became easier to be deaf, dump and blind, and just do as I was told. A nodding dog. Nod. Nod. Nod. I had resigned and given up on myself. I had felt beaten and humiliated and that destroyed my spirit. I felt crashed.

15.1.4   Theft of the self

Bollas talks about the loss of a part of self, including loss of content, function and process, and one's sense of identity. The loss of personal history is a catastrophe one might not recover from.

A person who consistently has important elements and functions of his psyche extracted will feel that a primary injustice and may seek revenge, which is "a bitter and agitated despair that constitutes a form of unconscious mourning, as if the loss can only be undone by the law of Talion: an eye for an eye, a leg for a leg. In this respect, the law of talion is an unconscious act intended to recover the lost part of the self by violent intrusion into the other—to recover what has been stolen from oneself" (Bollas, 1987, p. 166).

Before going through the second Employment Tribunal I felt I had lost a part of myself and hoped to reclaim it by seeking justice, but because of the betrayal I experienced during the hearing I lost even more of myself. At the first tribunal I had split the good/bad and projected the bad into the organization and the good into my part-time job, but at the second tribunal I failed to do this, so during the hearing I still saw some good in the "bad" witnesses. For example, as I was the first witness the Chair asked me if I trusted one of the clinicians, Witness Two, who had been on the interview panel. I said I did because I was still hanging on to Witness Two's good side, thinking of the time he supported me in the past. However, when he took the stand I felt destroyed: he denied that the ban of the animal metaphors was ever challenged and insisted that he stopped it because I was putting myself in danger, yet he was involved in the discussions of reinstating the animal metaphors. When the Chair asked what he would have done had he found out that the animal tradition was still carrying on he said he would have made sure that it stopped, portraying the image of me continuing without his knowledge. I also found out from an email from the Chair of a previous interview panel I attended (who wrote "lazy" on my forms) that the meeting set up for me with the Acting Chief Nurse was so that they could be seen to be doing something in case I took it further.

The Employment Tribunal Chair concluded that the interview panel had been fair because I had said I trusted this panellist. I paid for my blind trust in men whom I used to believe always had my best interest at heart. Misguided trust.

15.2   What I got out of the second Employment Tribunal

I struggled to survive the betrayal I felt. At that time I was not conscious of any experiences of having been betrayed by paternal figures so I did not have the internal measure to help me make sense of this external experience. All the men in my early life had been protective of me—my father, grandfather and all my brothers—Sam, MacDonald and Obediah. The second Employment Tribunal had been all men—the Chair, the panel, the barrister and the witnesses, and that had given me a false sense of security. I believe that had they been women I would have survived their betrayal better because I am used to women disappointing and betraying me and am always prepared for it.

The second Employment Tribunal highlighted a weakness I was never aware of before: my blind trust in men. Although I had believed I coped well with the situation with my father's best friend (my small father), I now realized that I undermined its unconscious impact on me. I had filed away the betrayal attached to the paralysing fear of not being able to survive without my father and the fear I experienced on the journey back to Chivhu, and it took my experience at the second Employment Tribunal to revive it. I relived the feelings of the paralysing fear without remembering the incident itself, and that drove me mad because I did not understand what I was feeling and did not know how to make it stop or make myself feel better. Therefore, the second Employment Tribunal was important because it gave me the opportunity to work through past pain I did not even know I carried within me. I was able to update my filing system by becoming conscious of the painful incident with my small father, and could then separate the betrayal from the paralysing fear by understanding its source and making sense of it.

This experience has improved my relationship with men. It is now healthier, more real and less idealized. Knowing that men can let me down, I no longer react to the disillusionment they might cause as if it is so catastrophic that I regress close to losing my sanity. For that I will always be grateful to the second Employment Tribunal.

CHAPTER SIXTEEN

Third Employment Tribunal: the return of the spirit

16.1   Shame and guilt

The Third Employment Tribunal resulted from feelings of shame and guilt I found difficult to tolerate after failing to do something when witnessing discrimination against a Black junior clinician. Understanding the concept of shame and guilt is important when working with racism because those feelings tend to be evoked in both Black and White counsellors and therapists, and if not processed are likely to interfere with, and contaminate, the therapeutic processes of transference and countertransference.

The incident I had witnessed sat heavily on my conscience for a long time. The thought of my passivity was depressing because I did not like the change in me. I felt a sense of self-hatred at not having helped someone I believed was being racially discriminated against. I was not brought up to sit and watch the vulnerable suffer at the hands of the powerful. I tried to rationalize my passive behaviour but my conscience would not give me any reprieve from self-torment. Freud (2002, p. 79) states that:

"Conscience is the internal perception of the rejection of a particular wish operating within us ... This is even clearer in the case of consciousness of guilt—the perception of the internal condemnation of an act by which we have carried out a particular wish. To put forward any reason for this would seem superfluous: anyone who has a conscience must feel within him the justification for the condemnation, must feel the self-reproach for the act that has been carried out. This same characteristic is to be seen in the savage's attitude towards taboo".

Sometimes I find it difficult to read and digest Freud, especially in *Totem and Taboo*, because his language denigrates my culture, describing us as "primitive" and "savages". However, he identifies correctly the connection between our taboos and conscience, and that violation of a taboo produces a fearful sense of guilt even if the act is perpetrated in ignorance. It is true that in my culture we use taboo to control the choices we make, and even though no one knows where they originated (they are passed on from generation to generation) we do not question taboos because the fear of the consequences and the shame of it are enough to effectively ensure respecting and following them. Here are some examples of what is taboo:

a. You cannot steal from a field protected by a rukwa (a magic portion). If you do you will keep going in circles round that field until the owner comes to set you free. The humiliation deters anyone from stealing because one could never tell whether or not a field is protected by a rukwa.
b. *Ukatuka amai vako unotanda botso*: that is, if you insult your mother you will have much bad luck and the only remedy is to wear a sack and cover yourself in ash, then run round the village while children beat you up and humiliate you.
c. My culture believes in spare the rod and spoil the child. However, if you are about to beat your child and he runs behind your mother you can never beat that child for that offence because of *apotera*, he has found refuge. Beating a child who has sought shelter from his grandmother is considered to be a serious insult, equivalent to beating your own mother, and is also taboo.
d. When collecting *mazhanje*, a wild sweet fruit, you are not allowed to shake the tree. If you do you will be lost in the forest forever. The rationale is that when you shake the tree raw *mazhanje* drop, causing wastage, because the *mazhanje* which ripen on the tree are sweeter than those falling raw and ripening off the tree.

e. If someone disappears you are not allowed to cry just in case he has been taken by a *njuzu* (mermaid). If the family cries then the *njuzu* will kill him. The *Madziva* (water) traditional healers use water and products from the river to heal and are believed to have been trained by mermaids. I believe this taboo is to prevent people panicking; then they can search without becoming emotionally overwhelmed. Crying is seen as acceptance of defeat so we avoid crying for as long as we hold hope.

f. You do not eat a pregnant woman's favourite food; if you do you will suffer her cravings long after she has given birth. I believe this ensured that pregnant women enjoyed their delights without salivating hyenas on stand-by.

While most taboos are shame-inducing, some are guilt-inducing. To define guilt I will quote from Wallis and Poulton (2001, pp. 113–114) because they reflect on various authors' perceptions: "... guilt arises from our 'forgetting' our being—that is, failing to be authentic and to actualize our potential" (May, 1983). This ontological guilt was considered by May to be the foundation of all forms of guilt. Fromm (1956) claimed that guilt and shame derive from the same ontology as anxiety—that is, through "awareness of human separation, without reunion by love" (p. 8)—while Maslow (1968, p. 121) maintained that guilt stems from "not being true to yourself, to your own fate in life, to your own intrinsic nature".

I had failed to stick to my principles of being honest to myself and fight for what is right and fair. I knew I could challenge the White managers over what had happened, but that would be suicidal because I would be victimized. Part of me challenged my fear of victimization, insisting that I did not want to do anything because I would lose my comfortable privileged status of a respected senior clinician. I wondered whether Whites experience a similar conflict of interest when witnessing discrimination against Blacks. Do they do nothing for fear of losing their privileged status?

Wallis and Poulton discuss further how May (1983, p. 116) opposes the psychodynamic theories that anxiety and guilt stem from internalized structures (e.g., superego), stating that ontological "guilt does not come from cultural prohibitions or introjection of cultural mores; it is rooted in the fact of self awareness. Ontological guilt does not consist of I am guilty because I violate parental prohibitions, but arises from the fact that I can see myself as the one who chooses or fails to choose".

I believe it is impossible to rule out internalization because how I make choices is highly influenced by my introjected objects—the people, the relationships and cultural prohibitions I have internalized. Most of my choices are because of who I am, such as being my father's daughter, being a Zimbabwean woman, being a mother—all of which make me different from the next person. Also, some choices are so difficult that sometimes it feels as if there is no choice: for example, choosing not to assist the Black junior clinician stopped being about being true to myself and my principles: if I chose to challenge the White managers my family would suffer, as I would be victimized and most likely lose my job. The choice changed from being about what is right to being about choosing between my family and the Black junior clinician, knowing that whatever choice I made would affect one of them more than me personally.

Symington and Symington (1996, p. 6) state that psychoanalysts make interpretations concerning inner pain, regret, shame, guilt, or depression, thus facilitating the patient to tolerate these uncomfortable feelings because they are real and need to be accepted rather than avoided. Acceptance of these inner realities enhances mental growth. However, if the sense of shame and guilt becomes too overwhelming it is experienced in the paranoid–schizoid position, where splitting becomes a solution to avoid feeling shame and guilt.

Freud talks about self-torment and self-sabotage as the unconscious need for punishment as a result of the unconscious sense of guilt that defends against experiencing and staying with the intolerable guilt and concern for others. Not being able to tolerate these feelings could result in regressing from the depressive position into the paranoid–schizoid position, where the absence of a good object can be experienced as the presence of a bad object. For example, I failed to support the Black junior clinician and could not tolerate the guilt, so perceived myself as bad and needing to be punished.

Klein also talks about unconscious guilt and connects it to splitting. She believes in building an inner strength by encouraging awareness and acceptance of these difficult but real feelings.

When Littlewood and Lipsedge (1989) discuss patterns of mental illness they talk about how, in industrialized societies, guilt is common in depressed people. They also state that some religions are well known for encouraging guilt and appear to have a large number of depressed people. In some cultures children are brought up with guilt-inducing techniques and these societies have a higher number of depressed people than those who use shame-inducing techniques. My guilt was making me feel depressed but I realized that it was because I was in the depressive position which made me feel sad when reflecting on my unhelpful behaviour towards the Black junior clinician.

I am a Roman Catholic, brought up by Dominican nuns, so I am programmed to think "I have sinned, I feel guilty, I repent, I take my penance and I get forgiven". The absence of religion in this book was deliberate because I found it difficult to think about religion while going through the Employment Tribunal. I had to block it out because I could not tolerate the guilt I felt. I was taught to forgive so it felt as if I was going against my religious teachings, and during all the Employment Tribunal cases I stopped reciting the Our Father prayer because it made me feel incredibly guilty. Saying "forgive us our trespasses as we forgive those who trespass against us" was difficult because at that time I did not want to forgive, so saying it felt like telling a lie and that pricked my conscience. When I tried to justify my going through an Employment Tribunal I just ended up having a fight with God in my head for favouring and allowing the "chosen ones" to treat my race like their toys. That debate used to scare me because it always left me feeling even more guilty for being blasphemous.

So, for my peace of mind I stopped reciting Our Father. However, I liked Hail Mary because it just says, "Holy Mary Mother of God pray for us sinners now and at the hour of our death. Amen". This prayer left me feeling that Mary Mother of God accepts sinners and would take care of them through her prayers, making it all right for me to be an unforgiving sinner, at least for that moment. I carried on with my Hail Marys throughout the various cases.

So while I agree with May about having the ability to choose I strongly believe that whatever objects we internalize—people, culture, religion— all influence the choices we make in life.

Klein talks about guilt being experienced in the depressive position. This happens around three months of age when a baby can tolerate waiting. The baby begins to integrate conflicting experiences as it realizes that the breast/mother it loves is also the same breast/mother it attacks and hates. These feelings of love/hate are no longer split off into separate objects but are recognized to dwell in one object.

This realization enables the baby to wish for reparation of the damage it caused. If one is able to tolerate the sense of guilt and can reflect on it, the capacity to show concern for others can be achieved, resulting in the desire for reparation (Segal, 1992).

16.2   Impact of a change in management

When I began to understand the fear I had experienced during the second Employment Tribunal I started feeling more like myself—confident and content. When I reflected on the way I had been because of the fear, I felt ashamed at how submissive I had become, as if my body was there but the spirit had gone. I had become passive and accepting of abusive treatment. That was not me. One of the things I could not forgive myself for was the incident I witnessed while working as a bank nurse, during the year I could not find full-time employment because of the brown envelope.

The incident occurred in the organization I idealized, the hospital where I trained to be a nurse and where I first lived after arriving in the United Kingdom. It was the organization that supported me in all my further studies and celebrated my achievements with me, the organization that took me to its bosom and nurtured me during my troubled times. It was my safe haven, and I valued my colleagues there because of their care for me when the chips were down.

I had worked for this organization as a bank nurse for seventeen years—three years as an auxiliary bank nurse while I was a student nurse; then for six years as a staff nurse and bank nurse after qualifying; and eight years as a bank nurse after leaving to take on a charge nurse post at the therapeutic community. The patients used to joke that I should give them back the leaving present they bought me because I never left. I was attached to this organization and the umbilical cord could not be cut. During my first sixteen years this organization was a very happy, friendly, supportive, and hard working community.

Then management changed. The atmosphere changed. The new management was led by a White woman whom I will call Mother Superior. Mother Superior ruled by inducing fear and she used threats to keep us in line. There was an increase in Black and ethnic minority staff being investigated for various reasons and fired over minor issues. Some of the people suspended pending investigation went off sick long-term due to the pressure. I was one of the lucky few who were not targeted, and most Black colleagues believed it was because I was married to an Irishman, so they called me the Black Irish. Sometimes the name Black Irish was spat out with such force that it left me feeling like a traitor.

Some Black staff was moved from their current posts into less popular areas, while White colleagues were promoted into their now vacant posts. I was disheartened to see ethnic minority ward sisters who trained me get reduced to tears because of this injustice. They felt helpless and unable to do anything about it. Generally speaking, more Whites were being promoted while other races struggled, and those who did not get the jobs they thought they deserved went on sick leave, causing a rise in staff shortage which put demand on covering shifts. The pressure to work long hours was on everyone. I carried on working there because I felt I had to support others, as it was easier to work with regular staff.

There was a high staff turnover as more staff took early retirement just to get out of the place. In the past people would delay their retirement, and when they did retire they came back to work as bank nurses, but now they were never seen again. The organization used to sponsor retirement parties but now most people were refusing any management sponsorship because they were too angry or upset with the new management and wanted nothing from them. Morale nose-dived to a new low.

With all these problems we were always understaffed, resulting in a prioritization of our work and long working hours. In the past we spent time seeing patients one-to-one and offering structured talking sessions and activities on the wards, but now we hardly had time for patients, and the resultant acting-out behaviour increased as bored patients found unhelpful ways of keeping themselves and staff busy or entertained. There was very little support for staff: for example, when staff was assaulted there was no follow up by managers. In the past the manager would check on the victim but now there was silence unless Mother Superior believed there was something for which staff could be blamed. She would then interview staff in a way that was experienced as fault-finding or witch-hunting.

The staff defended against the anxiety of dismissal by forming cliques protecting their own. In the past, those making an error reported it to the manager because they knew they would be supported and the error became a learning opportunity for the whole team. Now, anyone making a mistake was protected by others in covering up, and those not in any clique were left hanging out to dry. Staff support went down, while complaints went up.

With all this unrest within the staff team the patients reacted by becoming more disturbed, as they did not feel contained. With limited interactions with staff, patients demanded attention, for example by engaging in serious fistfights which staff was occasionally unable to break up, requiring the assistance of security staff and police.

Sometimes patients targeted staff; if one did not do what they wanted they would accuse them of something. The investigations lasted too long. For example, a Black and an ethnic minority staff were sent on paid leave for nearly a year because a patient accused them of sleeping on duty. Why would it take that long to establish whether someone was sleeping on duty or not? In the meantime the organiza-tion was paying two more people to cover their shifts, a waste of money and resources.

Sometimes administering medication felt like walking through a mine field because doctors would decide to stop medication during a ward round but not carry it through by changing the prescription chart. Nurses had to use word of mouth to let others know what not to give, and if a nurse forgot to hand over this information there was a chance of administering discontinued medication. This was a dangerous practice, especially on wards relying on agency nurses unfamiliar with wards and patients.

Some patients, particularly those diagnosed with Borderline Personality Disorder, began competing to see who got one-to-one nursing, and when they succeeded they raised the bar even higher to see who stayed on it the longest. This resulted in more patients daring risky behaviour in order to be placed on one-to-one nursing, but my previous research showed that it is contra-indicative to nurse someone with a Borderline Personality Disorder diagnosis on one-to-one because of the secondary gains they enjoyed and because it took the responsibil-ity away from them. This group of patients challenged the nurses most, since no-one wanted to take the calculated risk of not placing them on one-to-one and setting limits with them, because the nurses feared being blamed when patients acted out. For calculated risks to work nurses needed to talk to patients more regularly in structured times so that patients had an opportunity to verbalize and reflect on their thoughts and feelings instead of communicating through acting out, but with the increase in one-to-one nursing there was further demand for more nurses, resulting in chronic staff shortages.

The other competitive sport these patients engaged in was absconding from hospital. Since psychiatric ward windows are designed not to open wide, there were no absconds through the windows, but some patients climbed up a tree in the courtyard to the roof and slid down a drainage pipe on the other side, while others managed to get the security swipe cards. One incident I witnessed was of a patient who absconded using a stolen security swipe card, and staff could not follow her because she slammed the door shut and the staff did not have another swipe card to get out. Obviously the patients were struggling with conflicting emotions about being in hospital—the wish for independence and the need for limit-setting (Obholzer & Roberts, 1994). We were failing to provide a containing environment because we did not have any staff support groups to contain us, for example by analysing our own parallel processes in order to make sense of the patients' behaviour. We needed to tune into our own countertransference feelings of hate and fear and make sense of our experiences but we failed to do this, resulting in some staff acting out too.

I became concerned about the unsafe practices and the chaos on the wards. I wrote to Mother Superior highlighting my concerns and copied the letter to the Chief Executive but neither responded, not even to acknowledge having received my letter. I wrote again to the Chief Executive, who was of ethnic minority origin, asking her to at least acknowledge my letter of concern but again she did not respond. So, we continued working in these trying conditions.

Since there was a demand for more staff the organization began using more agency staff, creating a different problem because it was felt that since most of them were just there for a day or so they did not show the same dedication as the regular staff. The other problem was that agency staff was paid more than regular or bank staff, creating resentment and rivalry, with the agency staff (the "outsider" who was favoured by earning more) becoming sitting ducks for negative projections, scapegoats blamed for most of the incompetence on the wards. Behr and Hearst (2005) say the attack on a scapegoat may revolve around disowned guilt and shame and lack of mutual identification, and reflective empathy.

One day I came on duty to be told that a patient who held the record of one of the top three absconders had absconded yet again. She did this before when I was on duty and we were short staffed, just three nurses on duty when we needed five. The three of us struggled because one had to go to Accident and Emergency with a sick patient who needed immediate medical attention, the other was nursing a patient on one-to-one and the third was administering medication, leaving the ward without staff to monitor the goings-on. I was able to talk the absconding patient into coming back, after which I reported the incident and questioned why the shift had been left without adequate cover. Management did not even respond. I believe that was because it was due to their own incompetence that the ward had been left so appallingly understaffed.

That week the same patient had absconded twice while on one-to-one nursing and in the care of White clinicians. However, on this occasion, still on one-to-one nursing but being looked after by a Black junior clinician, she went out through a window which had been tampered with so that it could open wide enough to slip through. Because the Black junior clinician who was looking after her did not belong to any clique to support her nobody was even talking to her as she stood alone in tears. I took her aside and asked her what had happened. It was clear to me that there was nothing the Black clinician could have done to stop the absconder because nobody had noticed the broken lock on the window. I reassured her of the patient's safety because, knowing the patient very well, I realized that for her it was just a game of wits.

The junior clinician calmed down and went home. Later she phoned me to check on the situation. She was very scared of Mother Superior, so I offered to help her prepare for her meeting with Mother Superior, but the following day she phoned again to say that Mother Superior had fired her over the phone. We were all shocked. I could not believe that Mother Superior could do that without even interviewing her or investigating the incident, especially as this was not the first time this patient had absconded while on one-to-one nursing. She had even been known to abscond from a secure unit that had two locked doors.

There was outrage but nobody dared say anything to Mother Superior for fear of becoming her next victim. Had she investigated how the patient absconded she would have found out that the hourly safety checks of the building were not carried out regularly and that that particular window was not on the checklist, otherwise someone would have noticed the broken lock. The other thing Mother Superior would have discovered was that the same patient absconded a few days before and staff had to drive around looking for her. They found her in the local shopping centre. The incident was recorded as "she attempted to abscond" but going out of the hospital ground is absconding.

Therefore, investigating this incident would have opened a Pandora's Box and exposed all these incidents of incompetence, dishonesty and the problem of staff shortage. It was apparently easier to sacrifice the inexperienced young Black junior clinician, but most importantly, we lost the opportunity to discuss and reflect on all these incidents and try to make sense of what the patient was attempting to communicate to us. I believe she wanted us to know that she was in the wrong place to get the help she needed because she required psychotherapy but was stuck on a psychiatric acute admission ward focusing on medication and not talking therapy. We were holding her like a prisoner when she needed treatment.

Most Black staff was angry about the firing of the Black junior clinician but no one did anything because we were all scared. I did not do anything because I knew that my shamrock as the "Black Irish" would not weather challenging this new management. I had no doubt that if I did anything about this I would be victimized, so I looked the other way and watched the young Black clinician get unfairly fired. I used to hate people like the one I had become, watching discrimination and unfairness and doing nothing because they are busy saving their own skin, but now I was one of them. That knowledge filled me with shame and guilt, but this time I had to put my family first. I had already put them through serious financial challenges by quitting my job without alternative employment. We were still recovering from that, so for once I had to forget about my principles.

However, when the fear in my bosom settled and I was in full-time employment I began feeling angry about who I had become. I felt I had been beaten into submission, bowing to what I experienced as racism, discrimination, victimization, and general unfairness. I could not get the young Black clinician out of my mind. I felt guilty because I had let her down and she could easily have been my own daughter. I tried to think of the support I had given her but my conscience would not give me a reprieve. *You are now a nodding dog.* My mind tortured me. I hated the new weak me and feared that I had developed Uncle Tom's syndrome—the nodding dog I have always despised. Words like "not being Black enough", being a "coconut", "house negro", "Uncle Tom" and "sell out" flooded my tortured mind as I imagined her disillusionment and rage at my passive role. As a fellow Black woman she would have expected me to at least do or say something, but I had remained paralysed.

Sad, very sad indeed. Nod, nod, nodding dog. Traitor!

My mind kept on silently tormenting me, massaging the shame and guilt I had felt back to life, and since I was now permanently employed I had no excuse for not doing anything about the injustice I had witnessed. I reasoned that even if I was victimized it would not affect my full-time employment. I also felt that I owed my colleagues some support in challenging the new management because what was happening needed to be stopped. No-one else would challenge them, but I could.

The letter I had written and copied to the Chief Executive had been ignored, so clearly no-one within the organization would do anything about it. On the other hand, I knew that I could not go outside the organization without raising the issues internally first, so I wrote a letter challenging Mother Superior about how they had treated the Black junior clinician. I explained why it was easier to scapegoat her. I suggested that she carried out an internal investigation to find out what actually happened. I also raised other issues, such as incorrect documentation of a serious incident which could have helped them find a more effective way of managing a vulnerable adult, unsafe documentation of prescription charts, and poor management of a traumatized patient. I highlighted the working conditions: staff shortages, lack of staff support, lack of debriefing after serious incidents, the impact of firing the Black junior clinician on staff morale (most staff felt guilty about what had happened to her as it could have been any of them), the need for a staff support group and the need for training staff in working with people with Borderline Personality Disorder. I offered to facilitate a free-of-charge staff support group for night staff and to send her dates for training and conferences on Borderline Personality Disorder which staff would find useful.

Once again the letter was ignored but, exactly as I feared, the mighty fist descended to strike: I received a letter telling me that management, represented by Mother Superior and her line manager (whom I will call Mr Overseer) had found out that I worked full-time for another organization. They claimed that since I had not informed them of my full-time employment they had not been able to monitor my working hours. I was suspended with immediate effect pending their investigation.

I thought this was ridiculous because they all knew that I worked for another organization full-time. This was obviously the only way they could punish me for challenging them. My irritation about my suspension came out in my response:

27th May

Dear (Mr Overseer),
Thank you for your letter dated 23rd May. Since I am not clear about what you are investigating I cannot comment except to share with you the thoughts which spontaneously popped into my mind that is as interesting as the excitement David Livingstone must have felt when he "discovered" *Mosi oa Tunya* and called it Victoria Falls.

I am eager to assist you but I need to let you know that I am away on leave from last week of July to third week of August, therefore I will not be available.

Yours sincerely,
MJ

Victoria Falls is one of Zimbabwe's greatest tourist attractions. The local people have always known the falls as *Mosi oa Tunya*, meaning the river that thunders, but David Livingstone disregarded that. Believing he had "discovered" the falls he decided to name them after Queen Victoria. The managers, like David Livingstone, were claiming to have "discovered" that I worked for another organization when it was already common knowledge, and I knew they had known about my full-time employment because:

a. When I applied for the Deputy Manager's post Human Resources requested four references and I was offered all four references by this organization's senior managers and clinicians. After getting the job I met them all to tell them and thank them. Two of these managers were responsible for allocating me the shifts I worked.
b. Most of the time, ward managers would phone me at my full-time employment when they needed me to work unplanned shifts, for example if someone went off sick. So, they knew how to reach me at work.
c. A year previously, on 1 st April, I had written to Mother Superior responding to her threatening letter to me for cancelling a shift

because my son had gone into hospital. I had explained about my full-time job and my grade. I also explained that I worked as a bank nurse to keep my nursing registration going, but I think I lacked tact in one paragraph which must have antagonized them. It stated:

  i. "Now let me clarify my position. You have treated me badly but I have never said anything because I choose not to. I have seen how badly you treat some staff and they can't say anything to you because you are standing on their oxygen supply. They need the Trust to pay their mortgages. You are not standing on my oxygen supply. I will survive long after the Trust stops my bank. Bank money was for my training which cost an arm and a leg fortunately you will be pleased to know that I have passed and I am now a qualified group analyst.... And you can only abuse me for as long as I let you".

  ii. Mr Overseer was given this letter in order to assist Mother Superior in dealing with the concerns I had raised (which he never did), so both Mother Superior and Mr Overseer knew I was employed elsewhere.

  d. Most recently, about a month before my suspension, on 9th April I wrote to a doctor and copied Mother Superior. In that letter I explained about my full-time employment and stated exactly what that post entailed.

With all the information I had about when I had informed them that I worked for another organization full-time, I questioned why both had failed to inform me that I needed to complete a declaration form. I had never kept my full-time employment a secret. When I returned from leave I was called to a meeting where I was handed the investigation report. I found out from the report that I had been investigated for fraud.

  F-R-A-U-D!
  I was shocked. Why fraud?

CHAPTER SEVENTEEN

Forewarned is forearmed

17.1 The fraud investigation

I believe fraud and theft are some of the stereotypic projections Blacks are saddled with but I had never imagined they would land in my lap. They did. My part-time employer had contacted my full-time employer and requested my work schedule and my sickness record. The part-time employer built a case using evidence of my work pattern over a five-month period from 19th October to 20th March. They compiled a table showing my daily working hours for both employers and the total, even calculating length of breaks between shifts.

It was shocking to realize that I was investigated for fraud without even knowing about it, and that my full-time employer had been informed. When I challenged the new management I had not considered the possibility of my new employment being at risk. It never crossed my mind. I had believed that the worst that could happen to me was losing my part-time employment. The realization that I could lose both jobs made me feel sick, nauseated and intruded upon.

Why fraud? A friend explained that some people go off sick in one job and spend that time working in another, hence their request for my sickness record. Fortunately I did not have any days off sick.

Here is a summary of their report:

Local counter fraud specialist investigation team interim report

Objectives:

a. To substantiate the facts of this case.
b. To ascertain whether any fraudulent actions had taken place.
c. To assist the organization in taking appropriate remedial action.
d. To make recommendations to improve controls within the organization.
e. To liaise with the Regional Fraud Team as appropriate.

Conclusion:

a. Ms Mubika had failed to declare a second employment as required by the organization's Standard of Business Conduct which clearly stated that failure to comply with the Standards of Business Conduct is a disciplinary issue which could result in dismissal or prosecution.
b. Ms Mubika had exceeded the maximum of sixty hours a week and therefore in breach of the organization's Collective Agreement for the Implementation of the Working Time Regulations 1998 (PER/006).
c. By working excessive hours without adequate breaks, Ms Mubika had put her own safety and that of service users at risk.

After reading the report I challenged Mr Overseer, presenting him with facts about how he and other managers knew that I worked for another organization. He wanted written evidence and I told him what I had: two letters I had written stating that I worked for another organization full-time, and four references written by his managers and senior clinicians. I also challenged the claim that having been unable to monitor my working time, they were unable to pick up that I had been working over sixty hours a week. I presented him with the hours I worked solely for his organization, well over sixty hours a week. I was actually working less hours a week since my second employment than when working solely for them.

Mother Superior was responsible for checking the duty rotas so she was aware of the hours I was working. She was also responsible for signing the monthly returns showing how many hours I worked in a month. She must have noticed that I was working more than sixty hours a week yet she seemed not bothered until I challenged her.

Often I was asked to work over the agreed hours because they could not find staff. When that happened the ward senior clinicians had to ask for special permission from managers-on-call first. I was not allowed to cancel shifts allocated to me. For example, when my son's hernia operation was brought forward I cancelled my shift the day before so they had plenty of time to get someone else, yet Mother Superior still accused me of putting the unit at risk and threatened that if I ever cancelled an allocated shift again I would not get any further work within the whole organization. Yet they now planned to prosecute me for working long hours! It did not make any sense because they had more to answer for than I had. Either they had not thought this through properly or they simply underestimated me.

I too had done my homework, making my own tables of the hours their managers and other clinical staff worked, which were above sixty hours a week. We all worked long hours because of the chronic staff shortage. I questioned why they had singled me out. I asked what they were going to do with all the people I had presented them with, including a good number of their managers. To challenge their claim that they could not monitor my hours, I presented them with my work schedule of the time I worked solely for them, clocking well over sixty hours a week.

With all this evidence the organization decided to drop the case against me, but I did not believe that just dropping the case was good enough because it was a serious accusation that could have cost me my career. Having a fraud conviction as a credential is bad for business. I believed that it was an aggressive action and that it was time the new managers learnt about accountability and how to treat staff fairly, so I sought outside help. I went to the Employment Tribunal.

When I was originally told that I was being investigated I informed both Mother Superior and Mr Overseer that when they finished their investigation I was going to take them to task for victimizing me. Their investigation complete, Mother Superior informed me that I could only work one Saturday night a week, but after a few days Mr Overseer wrote to say that to comply with the Working Time Regulation 1998 I could only work one night a fortnight. This did not make sense because the average working time under the Working Time Regulation 1998 is forty-eight hours a week and the maximum sixty hours. I worked 37.5 hours in my full-time employment, which meant I could work one night a week for my part-time employer, taking my total hours to 47.5 hours. I was the only one being asked to work once a fortnight: the rest carried on working sixty hours or more a week.

While it was true that at one point I agreed to work long hours due to the financial strain I had put my family under by leaving the therapeutic community without securing an alternative job, I also worked long hours out of loyalty because there was a serious shortage of staff. The long hours did not bother me because I enjoyed my work and I am used to hard work, but now I just felt used and that left a bad taste in me. Feeling victimized and discriminated against, I resigned.

17.2   The third Employment Tribunal hearing

I believe the new managers were used to ill-treating staff and getting away with it because no-one fought back, and never being challenged made them take it for granted that I would just roll over and be grateful that they did not prosecute me. Well, it was time they learnt about accountability and respect—after seventeen years of giving my all to this organization, being treated in this way was not acceptable. I knew that the Trust would not do anything because if their Chief Executive could ignore my letter containing a catalogue of serious concerns I had for both patients and staff, it was unlikely they would take up one individual case. I went to the Employment Tribunal.

The organization's legal team argued that I was not an employee so could not bring the organization to an Employment Tribunal, so a pre-hearing was called for the Employment Tribunal to ascertain whether or not I was an employee.

By the time we went to the pre-hearing Mother Superior had left the organization, so Mr Overseer and another clinician attended. It took two days. I liked the Chair, a White woman. She allowed time for reading our statements and signing them. I was able to read all twenty-eight pages of my statement and we looked at every single page of the 146 pages of evidence. The Chair took time to study the evidence and did not put words in my mouth. When not clear she asked questions. Her panel of two White men also asked relevant questions and were quite engaged in the process.

Their barrister challenged me about the suspension, saying I was not suspended, but I referred to Mr Overseer's letter which clearly stated I was. When I cross-examined Mr Overseer I was quite tough on him because I hated what he and Mother Superior had done, not just to me but to other staff who could not fight for what is right. I made sure that I addressed the difficult questions with him now because I knew

I could lose the case and not have another opportunity to expose what had been happening.

My written evidence included all my letters highlighting the incompetence and ill-treatment of staff. In my cross-examination I asked Mr Overseer about the suspension and challenged his interpretation of the Working Time Regulation of 1998, which he had misused to discriminate against me. He wanted to shift the focus to the David Livingstone letter but I used it to highlight the serious issue the letter raised and asked him to reflect on what he understood by the metaphor.

After presenting our submissions to the tribunal I felt proud of the way I had conducted myself. I felt confident the case would go in my favour. Unfortunately, after the hearing the Chair wrote to say she had not realized that her firm was connected to this Trust so she declared a conflict of interest and the hearing was aborted.

At a subsequent hearing Mr Overseer was reported to have gone on holiday abroad, but I had seen him just before the hearing and I pointed this out at the start. However, I agreed to proceed without Mr Overseer because I felt that, after his performance at the last hearing, if I was a legal representative for the organization I would have paid for his holiday myself just to get him out of the way, and for that reason I decided not to summon him. I felt that he had struggled during the hearing and felt sorry for him because Mother Superior had gone and he was left to carry the can. It felt unfair on him. I was sure he had learnt something from the last hearing and did not want to push him any more because I did not want him sitting on my conscience. I also believed I could still argue my points without him and that the notes from the aborted hearing would be available to refer to.

I found out during the hearing that it did not work like that. I think I had lost some of my rage since the implementation of significant changes, and Mother Superior and the Chief Executive who ignored my letter of concern had left. Unfortunately, without Mr Overseer I could not question the discriminatory actions around my suspension and the Working Time Regulations 1998, because the only other witness kept saying that she did not have the answers to the managerial questions I put to her, and because I liked her I could not push her.

This was another case of failure in engaging splitting as a helpful defence. My anger was not with my colleagues so there was no point in attacking this lone witness. Maybe it was also a sign that I was now better integrated and not capable of splitting good/bad because I could still hold on to the good in the presence of the bad. I had spent seventeen years with these people. I had known the only witness for seventeen years, working with her from the time I was a student and she a staff nurse, and we got on quite well. In my initial cross-examining I had tried to be tough with her but it just made me feel bad and rude because I just could not switch off the good between us and perceive her as a bad object representing bad management. I did not want our relationship to change, not even temporarily, because my relationship with her was more important than the case.

Here are the findings:

Employment Tribunal report finding of facts

a. Ms Mubika worked for this NHS organization for some seventeen years commencing from 18 August to 24th August.

b. The manager was clear in her evidence that once a bank nurse is on a rota cancellation was not possible unless it was an emergency. The bank nurse was therefore under an obligation to turn up for a shift once the rota was agreed. No payment was made for breaks and the payment was based on actual number of hours worked.

c. Allocation of wards and responsibility on the rota were assigned in accordance with the grade and experience of the nurse. In Ms Mubika's case she was often left to manage wards on shifts and prepare care plans.

d. Ms Mubika's absence on annual leave was recorded on the duty rota.

e. Ms Mubika argued before us that there was a verbal contract with one of the managers in which she had been promised that regular shifts would be provided to her on the nurse bank. We do not find that such a contract was ever reached. However, Ms Mubika worked regular shifts from the time she left full time employment till 24 August when she resigned. Indeed Mother Superior, the overall manager for all the wards acknowledges in a letter to Ms Mubika on 6 May that Ms Mubika worked regular bank nights as did Mr Overseer. This is further supported by Ms Mubika's most recent P60 showing an annual pay of £28.506 at a time when Ms Mubika's basic pay was anything between £18,230 and £22,015. The only absences from this regular pattern of working shifts on the nurse bank was four weeks three years ago when Ms Mubika went to Zimbabwe for four weeks as a result of her brother dying. (*I was paid annual leave for this.*)

f. On 23 May this year a legitimate investigation was launched into Ms Mubika's working hours and a copy of the organization's Disciplinary procedure was enclosed for Ms Mubika's benefit. Ms Mubika was told that pending the investigation the organization would not be able to offer any further bank work to Ms Mubika until an outcome was known.

g. As a result Ms Mubika was available for work as a bank nurse but prevented from offering her services as a nurse from 23 May until 23 June and thereafter she was only permitted to work one shift every fortnight (that is in any fortnight there was one week in which no work was permitted.) Ms Mubika worked as a bank nurse on this basis for the last time on 20 August.

I had worked for this organization for seventeen years without a break—expect when I challenged the new management and was suspended for a month—and after that I was only allowed to work one shift a fortnight.

For seventeen years I was treated as an employee. I was on the same rota as the full-time staff. My annual leave had to be booked in advance and was paid for when I took it. I was the only bank staff who also covered as a unit representative in charge of attending to any emergencies on all wards, and I manned the advice line on which the public phone in. At the beginning of the year the organization merged with two other organizations and I was sent a letter stating that:

"Your salary, current terms and conditions of service including your continuous service date will remain as present and will be protected by a Transfer Order from the Secretary of State. The only change will be that the New Trust will become your employer and will pay your salary .... Please accept this letter as formal notice from the Trust of your transfer to the New Trust on 1st April".

The letter was signed by all three chief executives of the merging organizations. To me it showed that the organization treated me as an employee.

On the question of whether I was an employee or not, the Employment Tribunal studied all this evidence and found as follows:

Employment Tribunal report

1. Law
There have been a number of authorities in this vexed area but the three essential ingredients for a relationship of an employer/employee to exist are;

a. The contract must impose an obligation to provide work personally,
b. There must be mutuality of obligation between employee and employer,
c. The employee must be subject to sufficient degree of control by the employer.

2. Conclusion

a. We address the first question as to whether or not there was a contract between the parties, and if so, whether it was a contract of employment. It seems to us that in this case Ms Mubika having agreed to work a particular shift or rota she was committed to work that shift/rota for as long as she was assigned to that shift or until the shift or rota came to an end for any particular reason. The organization had a similar view as evidenced by Mother Superior's letter to Ms Mubika where a purported cancellation of a shift was met with the threat of the removal of offers of future work thus making it clear that Ms Mubika was obliged to work once she had agreed a shift/rota. Similarly the witness in evidence confirmed that a bank nurse staff was expected to carry out her shift once agreed unless there were exceptional reasons preventing this e.g., sickness, illness in family.

b. The shifts/rotas were offered continuously to Ms Mubika on regular rolling basis for as long as necessary.

c. Ms Mubika was not subject to any close level of control when carrying out her duties as a nurse. However, as a highly qualified and experienced nurse we would not have expected any close control or supervision.

d. Ms Mubika carried out some training and attended training courses paid for by the organization.

e. When on the rare occasion or so Ms Mubika failed to attend for duty as agreed there was an enquiry at least as to her reasons for not attending and Ms Mubika could not substitute anyone else in her place.

f. She was subject to the disciplinary code and investigated in accordance with the organization's policy on WTR.

g. Ms Mubika worked as a nurse bank on regular basis working variable hours. Every time she worked a shift there was in our opinion mutuality of obligation in the individual contracts between Ms Mubika and the organization and these were contracts of service. There was a mutuality of obligation in each engagement on the shift in that the organization paid Ms Mubika for the work which Ms Mubika in turn agreed to do by way of providing nursing care as required by the Respondent.

3. Continuity of employment

a. The issue of continuity in this case focuses on the period of 23 May to 23 June this year and thereafter as Ms Mubika was only asked to work on the basis of one shift every fortnight with the last undertaken on 20th August. This was done for legitimate reasons relating to the Working Time Regulations 1998.

b. It was accepted by both parties that Ms Mubika did not work as a bank nurse during this period (for one month). On the findings we have made in this case and there been no contract of employment in this period, this period cannot count for continuity purposes and as section 212(3) of the ERA 1996 is inapplicable, Ms Mubika's continuity of employment was broken. Similarly, thereafter, in the period when Ms Mubika was only working one Saturday shift every fortnight, it follows that there was no contract of employment in each intervening week in which she did not work and hence continuity of employment after May was broken.

c. Not withstanding that Ms Mubika was engaged on a series of individual engagements, each amounting to a contract of employment during the period of provision of work, Ms Mubika does not have one year's unbroken continuous service for the purpose of S.108(1) of the ERA 1996. In any event the last shift that Ms Mubika worked was 20 August and this individual engagement came to an end on that day and on the day Ms Mubika resigned (24th August) there was no contract subsisting between Ms Mubika and the organization. Ms Mubika could therefore not have been constructively dismissed on that date.

I will discuss 3a.

- I was suspended pending investigation from 23 May to 23 June but I later found out that the investigation had already been completed, because the National Fraud Initiative Report was complied on 18th May and I was suspended on 23 May. The fraud investigation team was based at the organization's Headquarters so the report must have been available soon after completion. What was the point of suspending me when they had already completed their investigation?

- I was suspended for a month, yet the organization's policy states that "It may be necessary for an individual to be suspended from duty while an investigation is undertaken. This will be done when the continued presence of the employee might hinder an investigation, as a precaution against misconduct, or if it is in the employee's, their colleagues' or clients' best interest. It may also be necessary if the employee is pending a trial on criminal charges. A member of staff should not be suspended until the manager is certain that a suspension during disciplinary investigation is necessary. It may be appropriate for a short period of special leave (normally over 4 working days) to be used whilst an initial investigation takes place".

I believe I should not have been suspended because the organization had already completed its investigation and none of the reasons given in their policy justified suspension unless the organization was bringing criminal charges against me. I also believe that suspension (Mr Overseer called it suspension) cannot be counted as a break in service, especially if one was not disciplined following the conclusion of the investigation. I was paid annual leave during the time I was suspended.

The request that I work one shift a fortnight was not for legitimate reasons relating to the Working Time Regulations 1998 because those regulations state that I can work forty-eight hours a week. I worked 37.5 hours in my full-time employment so could work one night a week (ten hours), bringing the total time to 47.5 hours. This is what Mother Superior had suggested in her letter of 6 May, indicating to me that they knew the correct hours I could work. After my suspension was lifted Mr Overseer made me sign an opting-out form to enable me to work more than forty-eight hours a week. It stated that:

"Under the Working Time Regulations of 1998, no employee can be required to work more than an average of 48 hours per week in any 17 week period. However, if an individual employee wishes to work more than the 48 hour average, they may do so by formally opting out.

Working over 48 hours can come about in a number of ways, either multiple jobs or bank working with the Trust or a combination of employment with the Trust and other employers.

If you wish to opt out of the 48 hour average, please sign and return a copy of this letter. You may at any time decide that you no longer wish to be available for more than 48 hours average, on giving one month's notice in writing of your intention to terminate this agreement".

Given all this, how could an Employment Tribunal accept that asking me to work 47.5 hours a fortnight and not a week is a legitimate reason relating to the Working Time Regulation 1998? Also, I was the only person to whom this was being applied. Why an Employment Tribunal failed to rule that as discrimination aimed at breaking my continuity of service is beyond me.

When Mr Overseer suspended me I wrote to him stating that:

"I suggest that you do what you have to do but when you have finished with me I will be putting in a victimization claim because this is unfair. The organisation used me. You booked me more hours than I am supposed to work and when I cancelled shifts you threaten to stop giving me any work and now you discipline me for working long hours that you knew about".

I had forewarned them, and by creating this rule that discriminated against me and singled me out, they had forearmed themselves. I realized I had been stupid to forewarn them and they were clever enough to take me seriously and react accordingly. If I had worked every week as Mother Superior had suggested in her letter of 6 May (in accordance with the Working Time Regulation, 1998), I would not have broken my continuity of service and would have been considered an employee and they would have had to answer difficult questions, but by making me work once a fortnight I missed a week, and that week was seen by law as a break in continuity of service. Give them their due, that was clever. I was impressed.

The Employment Tribunal disappointed me. Having worked for this organization for seventeen years without a break, I was then given an enforced break by being singled out for a fraud investigation after challenging the new management. To me that was discrimination and victimization. Further discrimination and victimization took place in asking only me to work once a fortnight. If Mr Overseer had said he had decided to offer me just one shift a fortnight rather than claim he was following the Working Time Regulations 1998 that would have been different. Was it that difficult to understand?

I strongly believed that the Employment Tribunal had not understood the terms of the Working Time Regulations 1998 because no Chair in their right mind, I thought, would agree that the decision to ask me to work once a fortnight was legitimate, so I wrote asking for review. It was refused. Here is a summary of what the tribunal Chair said:

Employment Tribunal report

Refusal for an application for review under rule 34(3) of the 2004 rules
 	
The Chair refuses Ms Mubika's application for review of the reserved judgment.
    Ms Mubika wrote to the tribunal requesting a review of the tribunal's judgment on the grounds that the interests of justice require such a review (Rule 34(3) of the Employment Tribunal Constitution and Rules of Procedure Regulations, 2004).
    The interest of justice relied upon the following:
 	
a. That the policies of the Respondent prove that there was no break in Ms Mubika's employment.

b. That Mr Overseer failed to follow the correct disciplinary procedures.

c. That Mr Overseer advised Ms Mubika that she could only work one night a fortnight in accordance with the Working Time Regulations, 1998 and that this was not a decision made in accordance with the Working Time Regulations 1998.

The grounds on which a decision may be reviewed are that:

a. The decision was wrongly made as a result of an administrative error.
b. A party did not receive notice of the proceedings leading to the decision
c. The decision was made in the absence of a party.
d. New evidence has become available since the conclusion of the hearing to which the decision relates, provided that its existence could not have been reasonably known or foreseen at the time; or
e. The interest of justice requires such a review.

What the Employment Tribunal considered

a. Ms Mubika refers to notes of a previous pre-hearing in her application for review. There was an aborted hearing before a different tribunal where the Chairman kept notes. That hearing was aborted due to conflict issue arising after the evidence had been heard but before any judgment was delivered. This tribunal in reaching its judgment did not pay any regard to the notes of the aborted hearing and both parties were informed of this at the commencement of the hearing.
b. The grounds upon which Ms Mubika seeks review are matters which she raised at length in evidence before the tribunal and as such are matters which the Tribunal considered carefully in coming to its judgment. Ms Mubika herself accepts that she raised these points (namely the grounds) at the pre-hearing but that it was difficult to explain clearly without Mr Overseer who was unable to attend and was on holiday.
c. Ms Mubika made no application before the tribunal to either have the hearing adjourned so that Mr Overseer could attend or seek a witness summons. Ms Mubika was content to proceed in the absence of Mr Overseer.

Conclusion

In conclusion the Application for a Review is refused. It is well established that the Tribunal's discretion under paragraph 34(e) of the 2004 Rules is wide, but not boundless. There are simply no grounds on the information put before the Chairman to justify the review application succeeding. The matters raised in support of the application for review were placed before the tribunal at the prehearing review and given due consideration during the tribunal's deliberations and before reaching judgment.

In summary: the managers of this organization can discipline me, can demand that I work long hours and threaten me when I cancel. They can make me accountable for the hours I work even though they allocated them to me. They can investigate me. They can get me prosecuted for fraud ... but I have no right to question them or ask them to be accountable for discriminating against me, no right to do anything because I am just a bank nurse.

I still had fire in my belly about this so I appealed. Unfortunately I sent my appeal papers while in the hills of Cornwall and was told that they arrived six days late and were therefore out of time. Either Santa, Rudolph and the Christmas tribe had intervened by clogging the post rooms, or my subconscious was telling me to let it rest because I was now just being stubborn and I knew it.

So, I bowed to British justice!

CHAPTER EIGHTEEN

The cutting of the umbilical cord

Although I was disappointed with the third Employment Tribunal I was not upset. I wondered why.

The first question that came to mind was why I had done it. It all started because I could not sit with the guilt and shame of not having done anything to help the Black junior clinician. Therefore, losing the case felt like a well-deserved punishment for that sin of thinking more about my survival than my neighbour. I had confessed and was punished, so the slate could be wiped clean. That was the Roman Catholic in me. I could now forgive myself for not having done more to support the Black junior clinician. I could forgive myself for being a coward and not standing up for those being victimized.

When I feared victimization I had also wondered whether it was just a lame excuse for not wanting to get my hands dirty, but having experienced what I had feared I now understand how serious the consequences can be and how real my fear was. Never again will I pass harsh judgement on those who do not get involved, because I now understand the reality of being victimized. Personally, however, I will not stand by and watch any more, even when I know that the consequences will be harsh, because that destroys something good in me. However, had I not had solid evidence that the managers knew about my full-time

135

employment and that other staff, including their own managers, were being made to work over sixty hours a week, I would definitely have been destroyed. I would have lost both jobs.

However, the silver lining around this cloud was that I could now cut the umbilical cord attaching me to my training hospital. It was time for me to fly the nest and take a different path. I had delayed because of not wanting to give up the comfort of my first home in the UK, but now I felt ready to leave. I had paid back what I had got out of this place. I had supported my colleagues in making their plight known. I had done my best, but as my final act of support of Black nurses I wrote a fifty-nine-page document entitled *Racism, Discrimination, and Victimisation in the NHS: Can we dare break the chain?*

It contained all my personal experiences and was accompanied by a 375-page appendices of evidence. I sent the documents to various people and organizations:

> The three NHS Chief Executives
> Employment Tribunals Service
> My MP—Mr Richard Ottaway
> Commission for Racial Equality
> National Institute for Health & Clinical Excellence
> Mental Health Act Commission (because of patients on Section 3)
> The Parliamentary and Health Service Ombudsman
> Health and Safety Executive
> General Medical Council
> A trade union
> The Commission for Patients and Public Health
> Postgraduate Medical Education & Training Board
> The Information Centre
> NHS Institute for Innovation

Some returned the documents, stating they could not help me or did not want to be involved. Others wrote to give me advice on how to take legal action. One said that they had found the information interesting and were going to use it in training and asked me if I would be interested in taking part in their research.

The difference in the reaction of the three Chief Executives fascinated me most. The three were chosen because one belonged to the organization involved in the first and second Employment Tribunals, the other is my current boss and the third was involved in the third Employment Tribunal. Here are their reactions:

Chief One: A White man. He did not respond. My significant previous contact with him was when I found out that my White male colleague was being paid nearly six thousand pounds more than me. I wrote to make Chief One aware of this unfairness, and he responded immediately by asking Human Resources to sort it out. My pay was reviewed to match my colleague's and was backdated to the time I started working for this organization. This surprised me because I did not even have to fight. To tell the truth I was not bothered about it because I was just grateful to get the job and wanted a quiet life without starting battles again, but my colleague was more bothered about it and supported me to do something. This just marked the difference in treatment of staff by this organization. Therefore, when I wrote to ask Chief One to acknowledge the documents I had sent him I did not hesitate to accept his request to keep them, because of the fair way he had dealt with my complaint. However, he did not comment on the content.

Chief Two: A White man. Did not respond. His organization was involved with the first and second Employment Tribunals. When I asked him for an acknowledgement of the documents I had sent him, his Complaints Manager wrote back saying that the "department" was having problems in identifying the document and requested the name and address of the person I had sent it to. I sent them another set and explained that the information was confidential and too bulky to lose. In less than a fortnight I received both sets back with a letter saying he had no comment. That felt defensive to me and I was disappointed that he chose to return my documents rather than let his organization learn from them.

Chief Three: A White woman. Her organization was involved with the third Employment Tribunal, which happened before her time, during the silent ethnic minority Chief. Chief Three wrote to say she was touched by my effort and the way I had written the document, which was reflective; the account of issues was comprehensive with personal perspective and observations. She thanked me for giving her the opportunity to share my insight and reflect on things, and asked if I could work with her organization to further increase their understanding and knowledge as she recognized that my knowledge and experience were of immense value in taking their work forward.

The variations in the three responses made me wonder whether the organizations reflect their Chiefs' attitudes? The previous Chiefs of the third organization had been approachable and the staff was happy: then the takeover by the silent Chief matched the new management's negative attitude. Anyway, Chief Three arranged for me to meet with her Director of Workforce and Communication and the Director for Diversity and Inclusion. Both directors, one White and one Black, said my account shocked them and apologized for my negative experience with their organization. They asked if there was anything they could do to redress what had happened. One said she cried when she read about my experiences.

Both directors asked me to join their project on Human Rights Knowledge and Skills Framework Training. I was happy to do that as my leaving contribution—to participate in bringing change and fairness for my colleagues. I had worked for this organization for seventeen years. It had contributed to building the person I am today, so my leaving had to reflect the valued relationship I had had with this organization. In my culture we have a saying *"Kanda huyo kwaunobva, kwaunoenda husiku"*, meaning "throw a grinding stone where you are coming from, for where you are going is night/dark". Simply put, leave well for you might have to come back, and how you leave affects how you are welcomed back. On completing the Human Rights task I closed the door to my seventeen years with this organization. I threw my grinding stone and walked away with my head held high.

The umbilical cord was successfully cut.

CHAPTER NINETEEN

Making use of the black container

19.1 The art of listening

Taking legal action was seen by others as acting out. I believe acting out is important because it is part of a process that enables moving on, and allows for personal growth and development. I see it as a form of research, collecting data for analysis and reality-testing, then progressing to verbalizing the communication rather than acting it out. It is therefore important to explore the communication in the acting-out behaviour which, in the permissive therapeutic community, is tolerated and yet taken seriously.

When residents acted out, for example by self harming, they were considered discharged from the community, thus taking the acting-out behaviour seriously. They were given at least one day of assessment to attend all groups and if they missed any group a meeting was called and they had to explain to the whole community why they had missed the group and ask again for permission to stay. The aim was to ensure that the residents used this opportunity to talk about what they had done, explore the meaning of their behaviour and try to make sense of it. The important therapeutic intervention is that the residents were listened to, thus giving their acting-out behaviour a voice. A behaviour that might seem insane was analysed and made sense of because running through the emotional madness is a thread of logic, and if given a chance could be understood.

The following day the residents were given about five minutes each in the 9.15 community business meeting to explain what they had understood about their behaviour. Others gave feedback on their observations and experiences of being with them and the impact of their behaviour on them (reality testing/confronting). After the five minutes the community voted to decide whether they thought that the resident was capable of making use of the therapy being offered or not. Acting-out behaviour was eradicated by gaining insight and not by imposing an injunction not to do it again.

If acting-out behaviour is not tolerated and given the space for exploration so as to understand the communication it is trying to convey, the behaviour goes underground, that is, the residents would stop owning up to any acting-out behaviour that might still be taking place, or they may replace it with another inappropriate coping mechanism.

Being listened to is what highlighted the difference between the first and second Employment Tribunal for me. If I had lost the first case I would have been satisfied because I felt listened to. I read my whole statement—all eighty-four pages—and we studied the 433 pages of evidence, looking at every single page. The Chair, a Black Caribbean woman and her panel of two White men, were alert and engaged. The men asked a significant number of questions of all the witnesses as they sought clarification. The Chair played with the bundle of evidence as if with a concertina, going back and forth as she re-examined the evidence in an attempt to get to the bottom of things and get a grip of the facts in her search for justice. I could see that the panel had been listening.

At the third Employment Tribunal I presented my case and had felt listened to, especially at the first seating. I believe I got what I wanted at that hearing, and when it was aborted I only carried on with it because I had to see it through. Therefore losing the case did not matter. I was well-fed and satisfied by the first hearing.

On the other hand, at the second Employment Tribunal the White Chair and his panel of two White men chose not to hear my statement or open the bundle of 280 pages of evidence, which just sat there like a white elephant that nobody would dare, or bother to, talk about. At no time during the hearing was any of my evidence looked at, and the two members of the Employment Tribunal panel remained mute throughout. Not a single word from either. I had felt gagged and as a result suffered an emotional attack of regression.

When I left the first Employment Tribunal, winning most of my claims did not arrest my attention because something more important had happened: for the first time I had been in direct contact with a powerful Black woman. For the first time I could identify with a Black woman and could see myself in a position of power as a Black woman. Most of my emotional attachments and identifications have been with powerful Black men. Never before had I made an emotional identification with a powerful Black woman. This reminded me of a time at the therapeutic community when a Black student nurse showed great admiration for me and, feeling embarrassed, I ignored her. Now I understood what might have been going on for her, and I recognized the possibility of being seen by others as a role model.

With that recognition I realized that what was important for me was making demands on myself rather than others: for example, respecting myself first before expecting the same from anyone else. I carried the Black Chair with me because she made me understand that power is not just about fighting: it is about being professional, genuine, strong, sharp, fair, firm yet humble, respectful and compassionate. It is about giving real time, not "being seen" to be doing something. She was a female equivalent of my father, whereas I had only seen myself as a female version of my father, and now, for the first time, I had an idea of how to be myself rather than a female version of a man. I began to realize that I do not have to use a sledge hammer to smash my way through life, and to view letting go as a solution rather than a sign of defeat. I wanted that air of authority, power, wisdom, gentleness and respect that this Caribbean woman commanded, but this meant looking at how I contributed to some of the situations I found myself in.

From the second Employment Tribunal I left feeling very regressed. I now understood what it felt like when my patients talked about being abused and then feeling like double victims when they reported their abuse and nobody listened, or believed them. I went through the traumatic experience of fear in general and the fear of going mad because meanings had been changed when I was feeling vulnerable.

However, I still learnt important lessons through experiential learning, which can be painful. For instance, I became aware of my blind trust in men, and was forced to work on myself after the second Employment Tribunal in order to survive and maintain my sanity.

The regression I had experienced was so bad that I am convinced I could have drowned had I not had a supportive family—and friends who are psychologists and group analysts—to help me make sense of what was happening. I was also fortunate that my group therapy had done a good job on me. Those are the factors that kept me sane—and of course, being my father's daughter.

I have no doubt at all that I would have lost my sanity because the betrayal was very damaging. One has only to read the organization's own internal investigation report to understand the seriousness of the mental damage some staff suffered in this organization. My treatment was abusive and unfair. For example, they would not have given me back the twenty-eight days of compassionate leave had they believed I was treated fairly. Also, the fact that I got a two-grade promotion within the first two months of getting back into full-time employment proves to me that 12 out 55 could never be my style, yet they managed to convince an Employment Tribunal that it was a possibility. To me that was one of the greatest insults I have ever endured. I am not that stupid.

19.2 Acceptance of difference

It is interesting that the second Employment Tribunal was about similarity—same race or cultural background—yet we ended up highlighting our differences. On the other hand, the first Employment Tribunal was about difference, as all involved were White, yet we ended up finding mutual respect for each other's difference. I also learnt how with White colleagues we mirrored the same emotions for each other, giving us common ground to relate to each other. I realized that sometimes too much importance is placed on skin colour differences, because within the same skin colour there exist other significant differences and conflicts. For example, the use of totems was embraced by the majority of White people, both residents and clinicians, but some Black clinicians rejected it as foreign just because a White colleague said he felt "uncomfortable" about it. One Black senior clinician said he had never heard of it, as if that meant it did not exist. There was no sense of curiosity, or a desire to know more. The focus was on destroying it. This surprised me because I thought all Blacks have totems. It is sad that our difference focused on who is right or wrong instead of embracing each other's diversity and being curious about each other.

The ability to accept difference, successfully integrate and trade skills is important in achieving personal and collective goals in a multi-cultural society. Different races are better at different things, and accepting other people's differences will encourage them to accept, appreciate and adjust to a new culture, as acceptance of others eradicates the fear of the unknown. For example, when transplanting a seedling from a pot of dark compost into a garden of a different soil colour, the gardener (group conductor/therapist/counsellor) would not rinse off the dark compost before planting it because in order for the seedling to survive its roots should not be disturbed. In like manner, a Black individual should not be rinsed of his soil (culture) in order to survive in a White culture. The roots will grow beyond the dark compost, and the seedling will adapt and blossom in the new and different soil.

It is important that the individual, if possible, is allowed to work at their own pace of integration. Therefore, the decision to talk about racial issues should be guided by the readiness of the individual and the group, but sometimes that decision is taken away by unconscious processes such as transference and countertransference evoked in the here and now. The aim needs to be about understanding why what is happening at that particular moment. For example, if I walk into a room full of White women I might immediately be aware that we are all women (inclusive, defence against being alone) or I might become aware of being the only Black person (excluding, defence against being enmeshed, fear of losing one's identity, wanting to feel special). The work is in trying to understand why one reacts in one way and not the other at that particular moment, because that would give an understanding of the fears or feelings which influence one's reaction.

My reaction to losing the third Employment Tribunal case was of rejuvenation because I felt I had won back my self-respect. I had found my *umojo*. The spirit was back in the body, and I could now look in the mirror and like what I saw—me. Not the shivering, scared wreck. No, not that. The shame that caked my face had peeled off. The deep furrows that guilt had burrowed in my brow as I fought to squint out bad memories straightened out. The hair that had turned white from the stress of submission to what I felt was racism, discrimination and victimization remained white, but now reflected the wisdom of age suckled at the breast of experience. The smell of fear pumped into me at the second Employment Tribunal was squeezed out at the third Employment Tribunal like an overripe teenage pimple—painless. I walked tall as I emerged from the third hearing. I knew exactly how much I was worth. I knew I had recovered. No more the nodding dog. I had gone through the process of becoming Black in British society. What an experience!

PART II

ABANDONMENT: HIDE AND SEEK UNTIL
YOU FIND YOURSELF

INTRODUCTION

Cock-a-doodle-doo!
Cock-a-doodle-doo!

That is a victorious crow from the winner of the *Hide and Seek* game. In the Shona culture (Zimbabwean), during *Hide and Seek* if seekers fail to find the hiders they ask the hiders to crow—signifying victory. In group analysis similar *Hide and Seek* games are played but the patients crow to signify maturity. A therapist saying, "Paul has found his voice" is acknowledging reaching that stage of maturity.

Part Two was written as a clinical paper while I was training to be a group analyst. In this I explore the theme of abandonment within the *Hide and Seek* games played in the analytic groups I facilitated during my training as a group analyst. I show how fear from the past controlled my training group and how their experiences of abandonment, separation and loss influenced their reactions to breaks, to the loss of a group member, Ruby, and to my absence. These group and external events catapulted us all into our internal worlds, exposing the pain from the past hidden within. It gave us a chance to experience our destructiveness as we got into the paranoid–schizoid position followed by the relief of the survival of the objects of our love and hate. This allowed

147

integration of our different splits as we experienced the anger and sadness while grieving our losses—moving us into a depressive position as we achieved a sense of maturity.

A parallel process between my training group's experience and my personal experience in my own therapy group runs throughout Part Two, demonstrating that whether the therapist is Black or White we all have similar experiences which help us to understand how those of a different skin colour to us feel. I also explore the struggles of being a Black trainee experiencing institutional racism at work and the impact of that experience on my relationships within my predominately White training institution and on the training group of White patients I facilitated.

I chose abandonment to anchor myself because it plays an important part in my life: from early childhood, when my parents left us with our grandparents (I was six years of age when my mother came to United Kingdom), at eighteen when my father died, and during my group analytic training when my mother and two brothers died.

In order to understand abandonment we need to explore John Bowlby's work on the Attachment Theory, which emphasizes the importance of secure attachment between care-giver and child. Attachment behaviour is the key to human relationships and is pervasive throughout the animal world. When attachments are successfully negotiated during the developmental stages emotional growth and maturity follows.

As we know, one is as strong as one's weakest link. Part Two demonstrates how I worked on my weakness to a point of strength through exploration of abandonment and through experiencing, and making sense of, group processes such as mirroring, which enabled connection with painful emotions I had so far defended against. I use my experience with my second training group to bring to life my destructiveness which this group mirrored for me, thus making it possible for me to understand the intensity of my destructiveness. I show how my supervision group equipped me to deal with these difficulties, enabling me to contain my groups as they played *Hide and Seek* games till they found themselves.

I conclude by looking at how I bring Zimbabwean culture and group analytic culture together, enabling me to emerge as a solid Black Zimbabwean group analyst.

CHAPTER TWENTY

Personal history of abandonment

20.1 Family history

I am the eldest daughter of a family of six children—three boys and three girls. Our father did not want all of us to go to the same school so we were sent to different boarding schools in pairs—my elder brothers, Sam and MacDonald, went to St Philips, Chipuriro, and later to a boys' missionary school, St Ignatius, in Chishawasha, just outside Harare; my youngest brother, Obediah and I went to Chishawasha Mission, and later I went to a girls' missionary school, St. Dominic's in Chishawasha and Obbie went to Makumbe Mission and later to Daramombe Mission; my sisters Louisa and Tee went to Waddilove, Kwenda Mission, Makumbe Mission and St Francis of Assisi in Chivhu. Although we were separated during school terms we all kept each other in mind by sharing the same transitional object—Otis Redding's music. Listening to Otis Redding comforted us and kept us together when we were apart.

I have a powerful memory of my father's presence because he brought us up on his own but he must have been absent because he owned supermarkets and a hotel in Harare and Chivhu (a small town about 220 miles from Harare) and a ranch in Lancashire, about fifty miles from Chihvu.

I do not remember my mother till the age of four. This used to puzzle me but she later explained that she and my father lived in Zambia while we lived with our grandparents in Zimbabwe and we joined them when I was four. At the age of six my mother left us to come to United Kingdom for three years, which somehow got extended to ten years. This had a serious impact on me as I developed an irrational reaction to waiting. I will not wait past an agreed time.

Winnicott (1984) states that an infant is dependent on its mother's ability to make "good-enough" adaptation to its needs, but in my case my mother's needs came first, so separation took place and I developed defences against maternal deprivation.

Winnicott (1984, pp. 190–191) states: "… the infant must take over the environment function if the environment is not reliable, so that there is a hidden true self, and all that we can see is a false self engaged in the double task of hiding the true self and of complying with the demands that the world makes from moment to moment".

I was not aware of the impact of maternal deprivation because I did not know what to expect from a mother—I had defended against such loss in order to survive. I took on the role of mothering my younger siblings, protecting my true feelings of fear, vulnerability, sadness and distress by appearing strong, happy and unafraid as a way of protecting my siblings and myself. I was determined that my true self would not be found and yet yearned to be discovered, comforted and taken care of.

When my mother returned I was sixteen years of age. She tried to set boundaries for us but as teenagers we all felt too mature and independent to be mothered. We resented her attempts to look after us as if we were still ten years younger and experienced her as suffocating, so we rejected her. She could not contain our rage at her abandonment and, since she could not weather our protest, she left us again.

When my father died I could not cope with his loss because I felt that he was the only person who understood me. He encouraged independence and we enjoyed arguing with him but after his death, when I argued I was told I was being rude and disrespectful. I could not cope with the gap I was now experiencing between my father's rules and those of a Shona culture now being reinforced by my extended family, who had had little contact with me when my father was alive and so did not know me well enough to understand me. I feared that the change in rules would drive me insane so I ran away from home to live with my poorer distant cousin who, like my father, understood me and showed me the same respect and trust in my opinions and judgments as had my father. I tend to regress back to this traumatic event of losing my father and rules changing.

My brother Obediah was fifteen years of age when our father died. Obediah was my pair and he too ran away from Daramombe Mission school soon after our father's death to join the Liberation War fighting Ian Smith's regime to achieve independence. I always wonder why it was our pair, Obediah and I, who ran away. Was it a coincidence or was it something about the way we coped with loss as a pair? The middle pair?

CHAPTER TWENTY ONE

Sam's death: my past and present collide

21.1   The delay in my training

When I trained to be a group analyst with the Institute of Group Analysis (IGA) I did my introductory course in London but chose to do my diploma training in Manchester. Manchester Group Analysis North (GAN) training is a block training from Friday to Sunday once a month for ten months a year for a minimum of four years. I chose block training because I knew I needed to be away from home so that I could concentrate on myself without having to pull myself together after each session to return to being a wife, mother, aunt, sister and friend. In Manchester I could spend the whole weekend regressed and upset without worrying that my family would witness me in those states. The therapy was tough because we had five one-and-a-half hour therapy sessions in three days. You can imagine how intense seven-and-a-half hours of therapy in three days could be.

A year into my training, as I was preparing to assess patients for my first training group, my eldest brother, Sam, died. Raphael (1984, p. 402) states: "Each person must make his way through life encompassing two important facts. If he loves, there will be the great rewards of human intimacy, in its broadest sense; and yet when he does so, he becomes vulnerable to the exquisite agony of loss".

The loss of Sam was agonizing and unbearable. His death left me feeling very vulnerable. The reaction to Sam's death was that three of us sued our employers for unfair practice and institutional racism. We all associated Sam with fighting for justice and fairness. Sam would never have allowed the abuse I went through without a fight. I believe one of the reasons we fought for our rights at that time was that it was our way of sustaining our identification with Sam, because his loss was too painful to bear.

I did not know how to be vulnerable but I knew how to hide my feelings in my work and in taking care of others. I was ready to play *Hide and Seek*. However, my supervisor and the course convenor asked me to delay assessing for my group for six months. Later, after missing another telephone supervision, my training institution decided that I had too many things going on to be able to fulfil the course requirements satisfactorily so I was asked to postpone assessing for my training group for another six months. I was furious because, having a lot of responsibilities, there will always be things going on in my life. If I have to wait till the demands on me are those of an average person it would take me a lifetime to complete my training. I felt I should have been supported in focusing and carrying on with my training schedule despite what was going on.

The second delay was devastating because I went into the paranoid-schizoid position, where: "... the focus is very much on aggression or self and other directed destructiveness, much of it in the form of envy and fear of envy, and on grandiosity, ... The paranoid–schizoid position is also characterized by typical defences such as splitting and projective identification ..." (Waska, 2002, p. 4).

I had to use defence mechanisms such as extractive introjection and projective identification by hating the course convenor and my supervisor. I projected my anxieties, vulnerability, and helplessness into my supervisor and convinced myself that she was the one who could not cope when things were tough. I became the confident and experienced one because (I rationalized) I had been running groups for six years. Four weeks after my brother's death I was back at work running groups and doing quite well, so what was the problem here? I turned my supervisor into my mother, who set boundaries to contain me but I felt too mature, too independent and capable. I asked to be moved from her group to a male supervisor—my ideal father who understood me.

Sam was our father figure and when he died it felt as if I had lost my father and brother all in one. The pain was agonizing. The fear of going insane returned. I was thrown back to being eighteen, after my father's death and too many people telling me what was good for me as if I was an idiot and the pull to run away became strong. I considered transferring to the London course—a distant cousin who understood me. I had to remind myself of the reason why I chose Manchester. I felt trapped, sizing up one option, then abandoning it for another till I settled in my cage to the fact that if I really wanted to be a solid group analyst Manchester was the best place to be and that staying with my female supervisor would allow me to work through my relationship with my mother. I made running away not an option. I spent time in my small therapy group talking about this internal conflict and they were honest with me. It felt like having to eat cabbages, which I hated, but I knew it was good for me as it unblocked my internal digestive system. That saved me. Also, thinking about how pleased my enemies would be to learn that I had dropped out gave me the strength to hold onto my training.

One year after Sam's death I was more settled, and ready to assess for my training group.

CHAPTER TWENTY TWO

Hide and seek game

22.1   What is in the game?

Although *Hide and Seek* is a children's game it has valuable ingredients for ego training, such as:

22.1.1   Tolerating feelings of abandonment

Hide and Seek plays with the concept of separation and abandonment. In my group, feelings around separation and abandonment were evoked when breaks were announced, when I had to go away, when I fell asleep and missed the session, and when Sylvia, Ivy and Ruby left the group.

During my training I once introduced *Hide and Seek* game as a topic for discussion in the large group, but the discussion quickly moved on to talk about other games—*Murder in the Dark, Kiss Chase* and *Sardines*. The quick move to talk about other games evoked feelings of abandonment in me. It reminded me of similar feelings that were evoked when playing *Hide and Seek* and the game is abandoned while one is still in hiding and nobody bothers to call out that the game is over. However, I was able to recover and join in the discussion about the other games.

In my group, similar concepts surfaced, for example, when the group stops paying attention to a regular late comer or absentee like Martina. If the lateness or absenteeism is allowed to carry on without interpreting or trying to understand the communication behind it then the group has abandoned the game while still in play.

22.1.2 Tolerating ambivalence

Sometimes a child playing *Hide and Seek* hides in silly places, like behind the curtains with feet showing, behind a glass door or sitting in a washing basket with half the body out and the lid on a grinning face. There was a similar sense of ambivalence in my group—the wish not to be found and the desire to be found. For example, Robert stormed out of the group but waited in the corridor to be found. The group learns to tolerate mixed feelings of love and hate by surviving the attacks by its members and exploring the pain—looking beyond the surface. The surface might show one thing while the member feels something else. For instance, Howard became angry when he felt vulnerable so his anger hid his vulnerability; Martina's absence hid her fear of intimacy; Carol's anxiety hid feelings of aggression; Robert's silence hid his anger; and Sylvia's flight into good health (dropping out) hid her fear of dependence on the group and anger at being abandoned when the group went on break. The group seeks out its member by saying: "Martina, can we try to make sense of your lateness? Robert, you are too quiet today, what's wrong? You sound like a victim but I believe you are controlling the show here".

22.1.3 Risk-taking

When children learn to play *Hide and Seek*, the adults keep contact while searching by talking to themselves loudly, for example: "*Where can he/she be? I wonder if she/he is under the bed?*" This contact builds confidence and contains anxieties generated by fear of abandonment. Such contact is like an umbilical cord that enables venturing into uncharted waters. In my group, members maintained similar contact by saying, "You are not alone/on your own; I know what you mean; I can relate to that; I thought about you during the break; I am wondering how your week went considering what you spoke about last week; I will think of you on Saturday when you visit your father for the first time".

As the anxiety or fear is contained trust develops and the children begin to take bigger risks, such as hiding in dark scary places. The group members do similar things by moving on to explore deeper issues. For example, Carol disclosed her sexual abuse towards the end of her group therapy stating, "I was pretending that it never happened".

22.1.4   Tolerating disillusionment

Hide and Seek is an exciting and frightening game in which individuals engage in decoding clues to discover others or to lead to self-disclosure. Similar discoveries took place in my group as members supported each other in picking up signals and decoding them. During *Hide and Seek,* if the hider is not found he is asked to crow *"Cock-a-doodle doo!"*—signifying winning—as he finds his voice to say where he is. A similar thing happens when the group fails to pick up the signals of someone in hiding waiting to be found. Failing to find the hider creates space for achievement, a chance to crow *"Cock-a-doodle doo!"*—thus finding one's voice. For example, when Howard and Martina decided not to attend the group on Ruby's first day it gave others a chance to be more active and find the strength they never thought they had; and when I fell asleep and failed to attend the group, feelings of disillusionment were evoked and hidden rage unleashed. We had to work on the impact of these failings on individuals and on the group as a whole. What proved to be important was how the failure was managed and worked with, thus turning a disastrous event into an opportunity for growth.

22.1.5   Finding yourself

This is the final stage in playing *Hide and Seek*—when speaking and not acting out becomes the norm of communication. However, just because one has called out a few *Cock-a-doodle-doos* does not mean that this "mature" member will not play *Hide and Seek* again. The urge to play this game can return, especially when stressed and regressed. Therefore, it is important to find one's Achilles' heel so that one is aware of "what is me" and can become conscious of the "usual" unconscious defence reactions to certain situations. This enables doing things differently instead of repeating a fixed pattern from the past controlled by the unconscious mind like a puppet on a string.

CHAPTER TWENTY THREE

Reaction to abandonment: the loss of Ruby

23.1 My first training group

When I was ready to start assessing for my training group I arranged to run the group in a psychotherapy department under Dr Shaw, a consultant psychotherapist. In that department there were no Black patients on the waiting list or in therapy and I was the only Black therapist.

My training group started with eight members: three males—Robert, Howard, and Alex; and five females—Sylvia, Violet, Martina, Carol, and Ivy. The group lost Sylvia after forty-two sessions and Ivy after seventy-one sessions. When Sylvia left I assessed Ruby, who joined the group in session forty-nine but dropped out after one session.

I worked hard in getting a group culture going. The main problems were about attachment and committing to the group's boundaries. The group members met in the car park, offered each other lifts, mobile phones rang during sessions, and lateness and absenteeism were common. The group struggled with the lack of structure and wished to be given an agenda. They struggled with the lack of prescriptive answers from their leader. Robert threatened to drop out, Carol requested individual therapy and Sylvia wrote two farewell letters within the first three weeks. Eventually they settled down.

Initially there were varied *Hide and Seek* reactions to breaks. Howard, Sylvia and Martina extended their holiday in retaliation. Ivy got distressed and withdrawn because she found the unstructured time without the group to come to difficult. Robert stormed out of sessions. During each break Carol went on holiday to America, France, or Germany. When I interpreted her behaviour as her denial of dependence on the group she reacted by angrily denying this, but as she spoke she came to realize how important the group had become to her. She stopped going on holiday during each break to allow herself to miss the group. Initially she became suicidal just before each break, which was interpreted as her desire to be kept in mind as we all worried about her safety during the break. The group helped her to voice her anxieties rather than generate anxiety in other members so that they could experience how she felt.

I believe the group's reaction to breaks was influenced by their early childhood experiences of abandonment, separation and loss. Bateman and Holmes (1995, p. 236) state that: "Bowlby saw separation anxiety as a response to real parental inconsistency or absence in childhood, leading to clinging and fearful behaviour in the victim whose fears of being abandoned are realistic".

To help understand the link between early life experience of abandonment and one's reaction to separation, abandonment, and loss, I will reflect on the group members' reactions to the loss of a new member, Ruby.

23.2   Ruby's first and last session

Ruby: Is a sixty-five-year-old legal secretary and about to retire. She is widowed with no children. Her father was sent to prison for political reasons just before her birth and he was released when Ruby was eight years of age. On his release Ruby was not able to bond with him, but she envied the bond he had with her two brothers and a sister who were born after his release. Ruby was angry with her father for spoiling her special relationship with her mother. She feels she lost her mother to her father and her brothers and sister.

Ruby suffers from diabetes and is on insulin. She has no history of mental illness. She joined the group to deal with the impact of her upcoming retirement. Since she was given her retirement date Ruby has become depressed and anxious. She stated that her job meant everything to her and worried how she would cope when she becomes unemployed.

On Ruby's first day, session forty-nine, Howard and Martina were absent and Violet was late. The group started off with awkward silences. Robert was mute and Alex quiet. Ivy smiled nervously. Carol introduced herself and others followed her example. She then wished Howard was there as he was "good with words"—a wish to recreate a familiar family situation where her sisters and brother took the responsibility away from her.

Carol: Is a thirty-four-year-old high school teacher. Although she was not separated from her parents, she experienced her mother as emotionally absent. Her mother is a mortician at a local funeral parlour. Her father is a workaholic charge nurse at a local general hospital. She has two elder sisters and a brother. There is an age difference of twelve years between Carol and the third sibling, her brother. Carol's sisters treat her as if she is their baby rather than a sister and are overprotective of her. Therefore, Carol never learnt to take on any responsibilities as her siblings did most things for their "baby sister".

Carol suffers from anxiety and depression. She is on antidepressants. She joined the group to deal with her anxiety, sleep problems, and loneliness.

Carol explained about the group. She empathized with Ruby's position of being new, then spoke about how she had struggled with the group's lack of structure. Others related to what Carol was saying. They shared the difficult emotions they experienced on their first day and reassured Ruby that it gets easier.

Ruby introduced herself as Sophie, and I wondered whether I had mixed up her name. During her assessment she had been tearful and gentle, but now she was using a different name and appeared aggressive and angry. She experienced the group as attacking because they all started together and had been together for such a long time, making her feel excluded. The more she spoke the more resentful she became of the group's cohesion. She said she would not return. Violet became distressed, pleading with her to stay. I attempted to help her hear the group's support but failed.

Ruby did not return, and it took weeks to process the impact of her leaving. The group was upset and angry, first with me for exposing them to this agony, then with themselves, wondering if they could have done something differently. Robert spoke about how "nasty" he had been towards Ruby by being silent. He admitted to feeling angry with her as he feared having to talk about his sexual abuse again to someone new.

Robert: Is a fifty-seven-year-old gay hospital porter. He is a middle child with an elder brother and a younger sister. Robert had several separations from his mother in early childhood as she was often admitted onto a psychiatric unit. From the age of five to eleven Robert's elder brother sexually abused him. The abuse always took place when their mother was in hospital. His father worked night shifts at a local supermarket, therefore the children were left at home overnight on their own. Robert believes that his brother is responsible for him being gay because of the sexual abuse.

Robert has a diagnosis of Borderline Personality Disorder. He self-harms, has an eating disorder and misuses drugs and alcohol. He joined the group because he was concerned that his addictive behaviour was getting out of control. He also wanted help with his difficulties in forming and maintaining relationships.

Following Robert's talk about his fear of speaking about his abuse to a stranger, Carol became angry with Howard and Martina for being absent on Ruby's first day.

Howard: Is a thirty-six-year-old department store supervisor. He was separated from his father in early childhood due to work commitment. His father worked in Dubai. At twelve years of age his parents divorced. His father died when he was fifteen years of age. Howard, being the eldest child, had to leave school to earn a living and help his mother look after his two younger sisters.

Howard is married to a second wife. The first marriage failed following the death of his only son, Howard Junior, who committed suicide aged thirteen. They found out that he was being bullied at school. Howard became depressed and was put on medication. He is now scared of having another child because he feels responsible for Junior's death and believes he is not fit to be a father. He often flirts with the idea of committing suicide.

Howard joined the group to work on his aggression. He hides his anger by being "helpful" but occasionally he explodes. When he is being "helpful" other employees experience him as controlling.

Martina: Is a forty-seven-year-old hairdresser. Martina looked after her siblings from the age of five, when her mother died during child-birth.

Their father could not cope with the three young children so started drinking heavily. Martina looked after her two younger brothers until a concerned neighbour contacted social services and the children were taken into care. Since they were all sent to the same children's home Martina carried on looking after her brothers.

Martina suffers from depression but is not on medication. She joined the group because she could not cope with the guilt she felt following her brother's arrest for an armed robbery. Martina felt responsible because she believed that had she brought him up well he would not be doing such bad things.

We looked at Howard and Martina's passive aggression in failing to attend the group on Ruby's first day and encouraged them to express how they felt. Howard spoke of feeling fed up with looking after other people and wanted others to do it. Howard and Martina shared their experiences of looking after siblings when their parents abandoned them. The group reflected on how Carol had used this opportunity to come out of her shell and show her strength. They praised her and gave feedback on how confident and supportive she had been. They also acknowledged their dependence on Howard to lead them and reflected on the pressure they impose on him. They discussed how others needed to take on this responsibility as Carol had done.

We also explored Violet's distress as she desperately pleaded with Ruby to stay.

Violet: Is fifty-nine years old and unemployed. Her only sister died when Violet was a baby. Her mother was a seamstress and her father a missionary. Violet's parents were disowned by her paternal family because they objected to her father marrying a divorcee. Her mother was an only child who grew up in an orphanage, so Violet does not have any maternal relatives.

Violet's mother died six years ago and her father died some months before she joined the group. Following her father's death, Violet discovered that her mother had had two children by her first marriage. She hired a private detective who located them in Birmingham, but they rejected her because they did not want to have anything to do with "that woman"—their mother—who abandoned them.

Violet has no history of mental illness. She joined the group to work on her anger towards her mother for not telling her the truth. Violet is not in any relationship and has no children.

Violet reflected on the time she spent a lot of money to hire a private detective to find her half-siblings and how they rejected her just as Ruby had rejected the group. She became more distressed as she recalled her experience. Others related to feelings of rejection. It took some weeks to process what losing Ruby had triggered off for Violet about her relationship with her mother, who died at a time Violet felt she needed her most.

Ivy was angry with me and later with the group for not being able to hold onto Ruby, stating that Ruby would have been good for her because they were of a similar age with similar experiences.

Ivy: Is a sixty-four-year-old retired head of social services. Ivy is an only child. Her father was an alcoholic who was often so comatose that Ivy sometimes thought him dead. She recalls dreading coming from school in fear of finding her father dead on the kitchen floor. Ivy's father died twenty years ago of an alcohol-related illness. Ivy blamed her mother for not loving her father enough to save him. She often described her mother as a very cold woman. Ivy's mother was an invalid for a year and died during the course of the group, two weeks before my mother's death.

Ivy suffers from depression and severe anxiety but refuses to take any medication for fear of becoming an addict like her father. She joined the group to deal with the impact of her retirement.

Ivy talked about feeling like an outsider because the rest of the group was too young to understand the impact of retirement. The group encouraged her to talk about her experiences: even though others might not have had similar experiences they would find a common thread. The theme of being an outsider was shared and explored; Robert spoke of being the only person who was sexually abused, Howard was the only married man and Martina was the only one brought up in care. The discussion moved on to talk about the group matrix they shared (Foulkes, 1990, p. 291).

I invited Ruby to meet with me so that we could reflect on what had happened. She spoke of feeling anxious because the group worked well together. She related this to her early life—her siblings were closer to each other in age and had a better relationship with their father. He had been there for their births, whereas in Ruby's case he only met her after his release when she was eight years old and they failed to bond. She grew up feeling like an outsider within her own family and that painful feeling had been evoked in the group. My attempt to help her hear the group's support reminded her of her parents taking her siblings' side.

On reflection I had failed to attend to her persecuting internal world, so she could not accept or trust the embracing external world which had become her excluding family. I could have paid more attention to how she was feeling at that moment and given her internal world space to be explored, for example by asking: "*What is difficult about being here today? What are you feeling now, when did you experience these feelings before?*" The group would have identified with her feelings of being the outsider.

Ruby was able to make sense of what had happened, but she nevertheless asked to join a new group rather than an established one. Although I knew that my group would have offered Ruby a chance for a different experience, now was not the right time because my mother was dying and the group was in crisis due to my pending departure. It was too early for Ruby to be able to survive my absence so soon after joining the group. Therefore, I arranged for Dr Shaw to see her about joining a different group.

Foulkes and Anthony (1973, p. 137) state that: "The timing for the admission of the new member is an important factor, since a great deal depends on the development of the group at that point. If the group is at a crisis, then the new member may well precipitate a catastrophic disruption ...".

My experience with Ruby made me think more about how I assess someone joining an established group and to pay more attention to their history, so that when something is being reenacted I would be quicker at picking it up and in containing the regressed member by assisting the group in understanding, and working through, the dynamics evoked.

CHAPTER TWENTY FOUR

Mother's death: the impact of planned absence

24.1   Preparing for separation

When my mother became terminally ill, my supervision group and Dr Shaw helped me prepare the group for my absence. I told my group that I anticipated going away for four weeks without further notice and that Dr Shaw would look after them in my absence. This information was met with silence, then distress and anger, especially as I could not give them a date or the reason for my absence. I had decided not to give any personal information because it would influence their behaviour towards me and would also affect their freedom of spontaneity. Here is an extract from the last group session before my mother's death:

The group last met two days before my mother's death. Howard started off the group by asking me which frost I preferred, wet or dry? The atmosphere was playful and the following conversation took place:

Sylvia: They have predicted blizzards, all students will turn up including truants just to test out the teachers. *An active discussion takes place. Martina and Violet walk in late.*

Martina: (*The group truant*) I was not expecting you, MJ. I have been looking forward to enjoying today's session without having to work hard.

> *The group becomes manic. I address the avoidance and refer to last week's distress and anxiety around my pending absence.*
>
> **Ivy:** *(Lost her mother two weeks ago and is in denial of the impact of the loss.)* What makes you think we are anxious or that we are going to miss you? We will be off to the pub for a good time. *Laughter.*
>
> **Sylvia:** Carol, I thought about you. You were very upset last week.
>
> **Carol:** I can't remember why I was upset. *She then talks about her fear of the dark. She remembers being given a key to let herself into the house after school but felt too young to have a key. She talks of feeling struck by the incongruence between the childish dolls and toys she used to play with and the responsibility of the key hanging round her neck. The discussion about people's fears continues. My attempt to connect the discussion to the fear of the unknown surrounding my pending absence or to think about the key of responsibility I was giving them was ignored. Instead they carried on locating their fear outside the group.*
>
> **Alex:** *Relates to the fear of the dark and loneliness. He talks about how he used to enjoy being on his own talking to his dog which is now dead. He expressed his fear of his mother dying as she is getting older and less active.*
>
> **Robert:** *Relates to the fear of the dark, and to the fear of his mother dying. I ask him about walking out of the session last week. He appears surprised that I remembered. He then spoke of having felt suffocated and that he hates sitting next to me. He concludes by saying: "I will explain to the rest when MJ is away".*

The group was struggling with its ambivalent feelings of love and hate for me. They treated my absence like Ivy treated her mother's death: by denying its impact on them. However, Sylvia dropped out of the group soon afterwards.

Sylvia is a thirty-two-year-old career adviser attached to local high schools. She was adopted at the age of two but only found out about her adoption when she turned sixteen. Her adoptive parents explained that she is special because they chose her and her mother always made her feel special by being available all the time. Sylvia's family history of an ever-present (perfect) mother did not prepare her to cope with failure, being failed or disillusioned with the added conflicting emotions of rejection and abandonment by her biological parents. Sylvia could not cope when her marriage failed and she blamed herself even though her husband eloped with another woman.

Sylvia suffers from manic depression and is on medication. She has four children under the age of ten. She made several suicide attempts (overdosing and self-harming) following the breakup of her marriage.

She joined the group to deal with the impact of her divorce and to learn how to express her anger safely.

When Sylvia left she explained that she did not need therapy any more because she had resolved her problems. I believe she perceived my absence as a failure she could not recover from. She could not cope with a therapist who let her down, who, like her birth mother, abandoned her.

Robert and Alex located their anger and anxiety about my abandoning them onto the fear of losing their mothers and the loss of Alex's faithful dog that was always there to listen to him—unlike me, the abandoning parent.

Alex is forty-three years old and unemployed. He has an older sister who is married. Alex still lives at home with his mother and an elderly aunt. His mother does everything for him and gives him pocket money to buy computer games. Alex sleeps all day and plays on the computer all night. He used to get out walking his dog, but since the dog's death three years ago he has avoided going out. Alex believes that he cannot survive without his mother and is convinced that he will commit suicide when she dies.

Alex was separated from his mother at two years of age when he was hospitalized with meningitis. His father died in a traffic accident when he was seven years of age. Following his father's death, Alex's aunt came to live with them to support his mother, who was not coping well on her own. Alex suffers from depression and is on medication. He joined the group to learn how to make friends.

I was also struck by the power of the unconscious mind at work as Alex and Robert's fear of losing their mothers was turning out to be my reality. The group did not feel safe enough to deal with its mixed feelings about my absence.

24.2   Coming together after separation

During my absence the group met three times with Dr Shaw. Here is an extract from the first session on my return:

> Robert spoke of having missed me, he had worried that I would not come back. He spoke about how hard it had been at home because his brother who sexually abused him was involved in a road traffic accident which left him disabled in a wheelchair and needing total care, so he has come back to live at home. Robert spoke about how he now hates being home.

Carol: *I know what you mean. I hated going home when I had an abusive partner. I could feel the anxiety level going up as I got closer to the house. I could feel my stomach churn and dreaded getting home.*
Howard: *I'm opposite to you. It's not about going home, I dread going to work. I wake up at six and immediately start thinking about work.* He then spoke of being frightened of losing his job even though his team is doing well and he knows that it is an irrational fear. A long reflective silence followed.
Carol: *I'm just realising how hard it must be for Robert at home.*
Robert: *It's not so much about what happened in the past but that my brother is now back living at home.* I ask him: Would it help to talk more about your relationship with your brother? *What relationship? I can't talk about it.* What is the fear? *Losing control. The group might cope with listening to me but I'm afraid that I will go home and kill my brother.* Long silence. *I wish I had a different relationship with my brother, like when our grandfather died and I had to support him.* Silence. *Maybe it will be the same when mother dies.* Silence. Reflective and depressed atmosphere settled in the group.

The silence was suddenly followed by a manic atmosphere as they compared Dr Shaw to me. In the following weeks they talked about the impact of my absence and Dr Shaw taking over. It had evoked different issues for all. For example, for Robert the sexual abuse had become more alive because it happened during his mother's absence and his father was too preoccupied with work to notice. Robert became angry with Dr. Shaw who had become the available father. However, he spoke about the abuse in a detached manner. For Carol, Dr Shaw became the caring but not so present father and I was the dominating distant mother. Violet became angry and distressed linking it to feeling abandoned by her mother who died and left her on her own with a lot to sort out. Howard remained the strong one who looked after his siblings. Martina said she was not affected by the absence, defending against maternal deprivation and the rage about her mother dying when she was only five years old, leaving her to look after her siblings?

CHAPTER TWENTY FIVE

Obediah's death: the impact of unplanned absence

25.1   Coping with unplanned break

Six months after my mother's death and two weeks before Christmas the group was preparing for the Christmas break and Carol was working on her suicidal feelings triggered by the pending holiday. My youngest brother, Obediah, became seriously ill and I had to go abroad immediately. I felt I was abandoning the group at a crucial time. Dr Shaw could only join them for half an hour but I knew the group was now mature enough to meet on its own. After some consultation with my supervisor and Dr Shaw, I wrote a letter to the group. Dr Shaw took it to them. I explained that due to unforeseen circumstances I had to go away. I asked them to decide on whether to meet on their own or not, explaining that should they agree to meet they needed to understand how important it was that they all turn up. I asked them to decide in the presence of Dr Shaw, as he would need to arrange for someone to prepare the room for them. I used the group's language in my letter as a familiar transitional object to hold them together and contain them with familiarity during my absence, just as my siblings and I had used Otis Redding music to keep each other in mind when we were apart. Winnicott (1998, p. 197) states that:

"All these transitional objects and transitional phenomena enable the child to stand frustrations and deprivations and the presentations of the new situations".

I was away for four weeks because my brother passed away two weeks after my arrival. I understand that when Dr Shaw walked into the group room Robert walked out but Carol brought him back. The group decided to meet twice and they all turned up. After that they had a planned two-week Christmas break.

On my return I sent letters to all members confirming the return date. My absence was raised in the first session back as follows:

Howard: I was not bothered because I knew that whatever you had to do was important and you would be back. (*Where were his feelings about being left, abandoned or let down?*)

Carol: I thought it was something to do with your family because you gave us holiday dates then left earlier, it must be something you had anticipated but it happened sooner than you thought. (*What about the fact that I left when she was feeling suicidal? Is she protecting me from her anger or it is a sign of maturity?*)

Howard: I was more worried about Robert. Robert you seemed most affected and you walked out when Dr Shaw came in. (*Was he protecting me from his own anger? Looking for others to express his anger for him as he has done with his siblings? Or was he asking Robert to express what the group was finding difficult to talk about?*)

Robert: I could not be with him. *Some manic attack on Dr Shaw by Robert, Howard, and Martina.* Malcolm Pines (1979) states that:

"... what the conductor must note, eternally be alert to, is what of all this that is verbalised is accepted within the psychological life space of the group. For much will be disclaimed and cast out beyond the group boundary, and given an apparently independent existence out there in some other area of psychological space ...".

I commented: Dr Shaw seems to be a good reliable Teddy Bear who gets the bashing when you are angry with the mother who abandoned you. *Laughter* followed by reflective silence.

Robert: You are right. I was not angry with Dr Shaw, I was angry with you, actually I am still angry with you, not angry more of disappointed, for selfish reasons.

Ivy : Yes. I was disappointed too but I thought you had a good reason.
Robert : I thought of two things:

1. That you were not coming back and Dr Shaw had come to tell us that someone else is taking over in which case I did not want to know and I was going to drop out.
2. That Dr Shaw had come to say the group was ending. It was confusing. I spoke to my doctor and told him that even if *she* comes back how would I know that *she* would stay or would be off again? *Laughter.* Yes, I called you *she.*

I believe the laughter was to cover up the nervousness Robert had expressed on behalf of the group, a nervousness they could not express because they were protecting me from their rage. I had to take the fear of my disappearance again seriously and encouraged them to talk more about it.

In the following sessions they were able to talk about their anger with me and link it to their life experiences of being left for more important things/people than them. For example, Martina's siblings were more important to her mother than she was, Robert's father considered his work more important than his family and Violet remembered a time her mother left her at home sick while she went to work. They concluded that I had abandoned them to attend to other more important things and they were able to be angry about it. If I had told them of my bereavement I would have gagged them and defeated the purpose of therapy, as they might have felt obliged to take care of me. I believe they would have felt guilty about the feelings they had experienced at being abandoned.

CHAPTER TWENTY SIX

Reaction to the group ending: unspeakable rage

26.1   Group's past and present collide

My group was scheduled to run for two years. A few months towards the end of the group I announced the date of the last day of therapy. Following this announcement the members engaged in *Hide and Seek* games through passive aggressive behaviour, such as coming in late, being absent without leaving messages, being negative and demanding individual attention. Ivy dropped out in session seventy-one, killing the group before it killed her.

26.1.1   Session seventy-nine

Howard was on holiday abroad, Violet had missed the previous session and on return said she was in no mood for fighting and did not want to explain herself or have her behaviour analysed. She also told us she had resigned from her job. The group had worked hard with her on commitment resulting in accepting a full-time job, and her resignation was experienced as an attack on the group.

Robert arrived late. When others enquired he stated, "MJ told us to be direct so I will be direct. I met Ivy. She really looks better, the best

I have ever seen her and that is because she has stopped coming here". Robert then complained about the group making him worse.

I recalled my supervision group saying the group's phantasy was to kill me off because they were choosing to reject the group before it rejected them when it ended. When I told the group this they all laughed and immediately focused their attention to their sitting positions. They were in the same chairs as on their first day. I observed that they were sitting in gender pairs and I compared it to Noah's ark, then wondered what storm was threatening them as a group. Robert got angry, saying I always made interpretations of where he sat. Then he stormed out. Other group members refused to go after him because they felt he needed to learn to do things differently to running away and expecting to be persuaded back.

When I left the room at the end of the session I saw Robert waiting in the corridor I walk through.

CHAPTER TWENTY SEVEN

Disillusionment: the attack of the absent breast

27.1   Sleeping through the session

The following week I met with my employer to talk about the continuing racism I was experiencing at work. The meeting was unproductive and left me feeling furious. That evening I was supposed to facilitate my group. I decided to rest for a few minutes but fell asleep, waking up at 4.30 p.m. just as the group was ending. I panicked because it was too late to contact the group. I wondered what this was about. I became aware of how angry I had been about being in a predominately White workplace and feeling unappreciated and racially discriminated against. My group members were all White, so did I resent them for being White? Was I failing to keep my anger with one White group separate from the other White group? Was that my unconscious retaliation?

What had happened clearly showed that I needed to talk in my own group therapy about how I felt about being a Black therapist working with White patients in a racist society.

I phoned my supervisor, fearful that he would see my falling asleep as being unprofessional and uncommitted. I expected to be punished. I considered lying about why I had missed the group but decided to be honest and face the consequence. When I spoke to my supervisor he

175

surprised me by seeing my sleeping as part of the group dynamics to be discussed with my supervision group. On that day we focused on the immediate action I needed to take. I wrote to the group members apologizing for my absence and confirming that the group would meet the following week as usual. I was relieved that I did not need to explain why I had failed to attend.

My supervision group explored how I was acting out the group's phantasy of killing me off and suggested that I help them voice their anger with me for ending the group. I said I had tried that but it was not working. My supervisor suggested that I change my approach—to think about how I felt about the group ending.

I had enjoyed my group and we had worked hard together. They had become an important part of me and I had learnt a lot from them in our common journey. I would miss them. I realized that my group was like my first baby and its ending felt like abandoning them, and that made me the same as my abandoning mother. In my small therapy group I worked on my ability to abandon. Like my mother I left my children to come to the United Kingdom. The guilt of making my children experience the pain I went through when my mother left me made me rationalize that I was not as bad as my mother because I only left them for four years and not ten, like my mother. I had to work on the guilt I felt and acknowledge the impact of abandoning my children for four years.

It was hard to see myself in the same light as my mother. However, by identifying with her I became emotionally closer to her and understood her better, even though she had passed away. I felt sad at the missed opportunities but became calmer within myself and content with the mother I had had and the mother I had become.

I also worked on the trauma of my father's death and realized I had made an unconscious promise not to let my children become too dependent on me for fear of them going to pieces when I die, as I did when my father died. I saw that I was doing the same with the group. When they spoke about missing me and the group it made me feel as if I had made them too dependent on the group and me. It made me feel guilty, like a bad parent who creates dependence on herself before abandoning her children.

Raphael (1984, p. 402), states that: "Some dare not involve themselves intimately with others, because they cannot bear the thought of the pain of separating from them or of eventually losing them.

They may be especially vulnerable, perhaps, because they suffered and did not resolve such pain in early childhood".

I realized that I had stopped listening to the group talking about missing me because of the guilt it evoked in me. I had to learn that it is all right to be valued and missed because we had dared to be involved. I began to value my relationship with my father and accept that it was normal to miss him. He did not fail me by being there for me as I did not fail my group by being there for them. Our relationship lives on long after the physical contact stops because we internalize the relationship.

CHAPTER TWENTY EIGHT

Finding themselves: pain is gain

28.1   Working toward ending therapy

Remembering what my supervisor and the supervision group said, I spoke in the group about how I would miss them, and suddenly the group became angry with me. Carol spoke of the injustice in the group: I expected them to explain themselves yet did not explain my own absences. She felt disillusioned and let down by me. I had failed to be the ever-present breast.

The group responded to Carol with pleasure because she had found her voice. She had never been able to express her anger with me. Carol responded to the group's reaction by becoming tearful, saying how important I had become to her. She then disclosed having been sexually abused at twelve years of age by her friend's father when she went to a sleepover. She had never told anyone about it. She apologized to Robert for not being able to talk about it earlier when he spoke about his sexual abuse and explained that she had been trying to pretend it never happened. She was able to work through the shame and guilt she felt. The group held her warmly.

Robert also found his voice in expressing his anger instead of his usual behaviour of storming out. He spoke of feeling angry with me.

He had felt responsible for my absence when I fell asleep because he had walked out of the previous session in anger. He had phoned the unit to see if I was all right. He spoke about how furious he felt when he received my letter because he knew I was all right. Robert became so angry that his shouting was frightening and nearly getting out of control, but then Carol reminded him of a time he once said that he would never ring me and she quoted his declaration "even if she was the Queen of Sheba", and that calmed him down immediately. He said he was a different man now and talked about how he valued me and the group.

Robert explained that the nightmares about his sexual abuse had started again and he blamed me for making him worse. This time he spoke about the sexual abuse with emotion. It was scary for the whole group because he became so regressed, curling up in the chair into a foetal position. Sometimes his lips moved but without a sound coming out. We talked about how scared he must have felt. He became angry with his mother, of whom he had been so protective; maybe he was able to do that because I had survived his anger. The group was able to stay with him and contain his distress.

Howard thought I had staged my absence because they had stopped working. Violet became angry with him because she felt he did not give them a chance to decide whether to stay or go home. Suddenly the group became heated—most were angry with Howard for trying to replace me.

I commented: "It seemed Howard's effort to protect the group by keeping you all together is not appreciated".

The heat died. Howard spoke of his fear of the group falling apart, linking it to the trauma of his parents' divorce. The group shared his fear but also talked about how he becomes controlling when he is frightened, worried or scared instead of talking about how he feels. This helped him understand the rebellion he sometimes faces with the employees he supervises. The group's reaction to being controlled helped him understand how his work colleagues might feel when he is worried about sales going down and he becomes controlling as a way of keeping them together and focused.

This led to talking about his son's suicide and how his anger and pride had made him rigidly controlling when he felt vulnerable and at a loss. Howard became angry with himself for failing to notice that his son was being bullied at school. He talked about his guilt which made it difficult for him to mourn the loss of his son because he felt he did not deserve to be a father. Howard became distressed. He regretted not having sought therapy earlier because he now knew how to listen and hear. He believed that had he had therapy earlier he would have found out about the bullying and his son would still be alive. He sobbed in the silence of the group's presence.

Howard's relationship with the group changed as he allowed them to support and take care of him when he was vulnerable in the group. Initially his level of distress worried the group because they had never seen him upset before. He usually got depressed and on two occasions he was so depressed and suicidal that I had to arrange for hospital admission for him, but he continued attending the group from the hospital. On this occasion I worried about him getting depressed again, so asked him to contact me if necessary, but he did not. The following session he appeared settled and resolved. He had survived being vulnerable, sad and distressed without going into depression. He was surprised that he felt all right about being vulnerable in front of other people. Howard was also surprised at how emotional he felt about the group ending. The following sessions he began to talk about life after the group and the possibilities of starting a family with his wife. He felt ready to be a father again.

Violet said she was not bothered by my absence because she understood that I could not be there. I said how unlike her to be so accepting and that she sounded resigned. She spoke about having resigned from her work. The group had worked hard with her to get her to commit herself to a full-time job, as she struggled with commitment. On exploration she was able to express her anger with me and it freed the space for further exploration, which led us to understand that giving up the job was her way of punishing the group for ending—by rejecting its help. She became distressed about missing her mother. Later, Violet was able to withdraw her resignation.

Alex said he was not affected at all by my absence but later he spoke about his fear of the group ending. The group projected their own fear of not surviving onto Alex and wanted something done to make sure he was not lost. We worked hard to get each member to own and share the fear of not being able to manage without the group. However, I referred Alex to Dr Shaw to consider him for an open-ended group because he needed longer-term work on himself, as suicide when his mother dies remained a strong option.

Martina responded to the group ending by missing more sessions. It was like playing *Hide and Seek* in the mountains where one could hear the giggles to mark her presence but was unable to locate her because the echo vibrated everywhere—in her siblings. In one session she spoke about her regret at missed opportunities as she could have made better use of the group than she had done. I agreed with her but also added that maybe she had gone as far as she was ready to go for the moment.

The group worked on what she was doing for them, which was mainly about acting out the rejection they all felt.

CHAPTER TWENTY NINE

Where is the hope in therapy?

Towards the end of therapy a group member brought *This be the Verse*, a poem by Philip Larkin, for the group. It starts with:

> They fuck you up, your mum and dad.
> They may not mean to, but they do.
> They fill you with the faults they had
> And add some extra just for you.

I have had a number of patients talk about this poem with mixed feelings. Some have used it to explain why they do not want to have children—they do not want to pass on their gene of misery and inflict their pain onto another human being. This sentiment is powerfully evoked in the final lines:

> Man hands on misery to man.
> It deepens like a coastal shelf.
> Get out as early as you can,
> And don't have any kids yourself.

In this group they started off by joking about how the therapist "fucks you up" but they did not want to explore it in a serious manner.

Some quickly moved on to getting angry that the poem gives parents an excuse for their bad parenting. A discussion on family traits took place—with history repeating itself, what hope is there for them? Are they victims of family curses or can they break the spell of misfortune? One voiced a thought that parents should take responsibility for their mistakes and not make excuses, but others (mostly parents themselves) defended them, saying that their parents' generation never got the opportunity of breaking the spell through therapy. They talked about how important their therapy had been in turning their lives around—in breaking the spell. They expressed their appreciation of the time in the group.

Carol agreed that therapy does change relationships, recalling a time she spoke of feeling suicidal, and Violet suggested she talked to her mother about how she felt. Carol had explained that she was unable to talk to her mother about her feelings and the group had looked at how much she had changed and that she was now ready to have a different relationship with her mother. Carol had trusted the group's feedback and was able to be honest with her mother about finding it difficult to talk to her about how she feels. Her mother responded by identifying with her and spoke of her difficult rela- tionship with her own mother. She expressed a desire not to repeat her mother's mistakes and recalled how they used to be closer when Carol played with Jenny the beanie doll. Carol became excited that her mother remembered her first doll, and that realization made her feel that her mother knew her more than she had thought, and the acknowledgement of her own mistakes enabled Carol to talk to her mother about her suicidal thoughts and her anger with her. They cried together. That experience was very significant to her healing process.

This reminded me of when I visited my mother in hospital and she was asleep. I played Otis Reddings' tape and she woke up. "That's the boys music," she whispered, half asleep. She had recognized our transitional object! I felt connected and understood that she held the same transitional object as the rest of us. Without therapy I would have focused on "It's *the boys*" because I would have felt excluded, but today what mattered most was that *she knew*. I had never thought that my mother knew about our shared transitional object. I realized that defences not only repress the pain, but also repress pleasure and highlight the negative.

While Larkin's poem powerfully portrays the pain and anger about the damage caused by our parents in bringing us up, it stays stuck in playing *Hide and Seek* games without the hope of finding oneself. Yes, our parents might "fuck us up" in childhood but we carry on "fucking ourselves up" in adulthood. It is not the living parent but the internalized parent we carry within us that "fucks us up". We have choices, and in Part Two I have demonstrated how my White group and I, a Black group therapist, worked together in analytic groups to find ourselves by reliving our fears and working them through instead of running away. The psychotherapeutic interventions give us the opportunity to have different experiences, enhancing the healing process of our emotional wounds. Whether one is Black or White and is of a different skin colour to the therapist, a deep understanding of issues being explored in therapy can be achieved as we all share similar family experiences. The psychotherapeutic space holds the hope for breaking these destructive cycles, therefore past faults, pain, and emotional damage do not need to be passed on.

CHAPTER THIRTY

Celebrating the final separation

The group wanted to celebrate its ending. Howard invited us to his house for a barbecue. I questioned the attack on the group boundaries but that just created a group joke that they would barbecue me. My supervision group thought that was positive as it signified the wish to internalize me. Others wanted to go to the pub, and I wondered whether that was an attack on the group room. They laughed, but played with the idea, ending by paying tribute to it. They acknowledged how much good and painful work had been contained in that room and how important it was for the room to be part of the ending. The idea of going to the pub was dumped.

We explored the avoidance in wanting to celebrate the ending but still they wanted to mark it positively and show their appreciation. Someone suggested bringing food, which generated excitement leading to sibling rivalry anxieties such as competition—whose food would be the best and whose would be left uneaten. Some thought food would spoil the ending and others felt it was important because it symbolized the psychological feed they shared. The room vibrated with *Cock-a-doodle-dos!* as everyone contributed to the discussion, unlike the first session where depression held them together and what I said was accepted without questioning. They felt free to express their individual views. Foukles (1990, p. 279) states that: "The true therapist has, I believe, a creative function—in a way like an artist, in a way like a scientist, in a way like an educator. If he can avoid wanting to educate people in his own image, he will be able to help them creatively to become themselves ...".

In the end the group agreed to leave it to the individuals to choose to bring some food or not. We agreed to maintain the group time boundary by finishing on time.

On the last day Robert spoke of his struggle with endings. He talked about the pull to reject the group before it rejected him and how on his last day at school he had wanted to thank his science teacher, but it was too painful so he missed the last day at school. He became upset, but pleased that he was able to come and say goodbye and thanked everyone for the support, thus valuing himself and his experience in the group.

Violet also spoke of finding endings difficult. She reminded us how she had planned to leave the group prematurely, tearfully saying she needed a holiday. Violet thanked the group for holding on to her to the end.

The group reflected on what had changed in each of them, what memories stood out about each member. They reflected on their first impressions and first experiences of each other and how their opinions changed with time and working together. They wondered what they would be doing at this time in the weeks to come.

They wanted to know what I would be doing, whether I was starting a new group. Would the "new babies" meet in their group room? This led to wanting to know if I had any children of my own, how big my wardrobe must be, which outfit each one of them would remember me by and why, and what each of my looks meant. They played a guessing game about my looks, commented that I had a memory like an elephant and imitated my voice, accent and facial expression (or lack of expression) while recalling my catch phrases—*Take the group with you, Not group amnesia again! Why don't you play/roll with the idea?* Then there were tears of mixed feelings and appreciation. In the last thirty minutes they shared the food; not everyone brought something but everybody ate. It was like letting go of home-leavers rather than abandoning them. I felt like a proud mother witnessing her children come of age. There is still a lot of work ahead but they have the necessary tools with them that are wrapped in hope.

They had played *Hide and Seek,* worked on the fears from the past, struggled with the ambivalent feelings of love and hate evoked by the fear of loss, separation, and abandonment, and survived the conflict of not wanting to be found but hoping to be found. Their destructive impulses were experienced, tolerated, explored and understood. The group had provided containment so risks were taken and the members reached varied levels of maturity.

Martina missed the last session. I invited her for an individual session to come and close her experience with the group, which she accepted. Two weeks after the group ended Violet sent a bouquet of flowers to the department with a thank-you card. Her final act of having the last word.

CHAPTER THIRTY ONE

Finding myself: the halls of mirrors

31.1   My second training group

My training required that I facilitate another group, and this second training group was instrumental in my personal growth as it made me understand my difficulties with connecting with feelings of fear and vulnerability. The group mirrored that part of me I had abandoned—the distressed abandoned child left by her mother, coping with difficult feelings of vulnerability and fear of abandonment by projecting them onto her siblings and taking care of those feelings by mothering her siblings.

For my second training group I decided to have an experience in co-facilitating a group, so I chose a drug and alcohol rehabilitation therapeutic community. I arranged to co-facilitate a group with Rodney, a senior clinician. The drug and alcohol rehabilitation unit I chose was one I had worked in for six years but which was now going through a process of change. It had previously offered residential and day programmes but management had decided to let go of the residential part.

The clients were angry about this decision because it meant losing the guesting facility. Guesting is when an ex-client who believes that he or she is in danger of relapse contacts the unit to request an opportunity to stay for three days and work on whatever is causing the craving. This three-days' stay was called guesting, as the client was not admitted but was a guest to the unit. This model of relapse prevention was based on an observation that suggests that the craving, if tolerated and not acted upon by drinking, would come to pass. However, the individual needed to identify and then work on what was evoking the urge to drink and deal with it, otherwise it would only be a matter of time before he or she succumbed to the urge. Fighting the urge to drink without trying to understand what is causing it is called "white knuckling" and is not safe, as the next drink is just round the corner. Both staff and clients agreed that the loss of the guesting facility was a big disaster because nothing could replace it and it had saved many lives.

The other form of relapse prevention treatment offered was psychotherapy in a group called Relapse Prevention Group. Clients who had gone through the rehabilitation programme and been discharged, and those who were about to be discharged, attended this group. Its aim was to help members identify when they were setting themselves up for a drink and to deal with the problem before they relapsed. They also talked about the social challenges they might be facing and found ways of dealing with problems without looking for a solution at the bottom of a bottle. They reminded each other about how they had dealt with similar problems in the past and linked it to their upbringing. They encouraged each other to take risks in new situations after talking it through in the group. This was the group I had decided to run as my second training group.

With all the changes that were taking place, Rodney was pulled in all directions—dealing with rewriting policies to suit the new structure, attending various meetings about the changes with external managers, meeting with staff and clients to update them on the changes and sorting out other unit responsibilities. It became difficult for him to commit to cofacilitating the group with me so we decided that I would conduct the group on my own.

Although the changes affected all, the vulnerability became located in the new clients. The ex-clients formed a committee to present their views to management. Annamore, who was in my Relapse Prevention Group, was one of the founder members of this committee. Annamore's parents were killed in a road traffic accident when she was two weeks old. She was adopted by an abusive family and coped by drinking.

When I started the group I introduced the following dynamic administration:

- I prepare the group room in advance instead of individuals getting their own chairs.
- I put a table with a box of tissues in the centre—previously tissues were banned because it was believed that tissues symbolized getting rid of tears or discouraging expression of distressing emotions.
- I took responsibility for time-keeping instead of one of them banging on the wall to signify the beginning and the end of the session.
- If a group member was not attending he or she would be expected to let the group know in advance. Previously they just did not turn up.

It was difficult to enforce these boundaries because I had worked on this unit before starting my training as a group analyst and had not known that the above dynamic administration was the therapist's responsibility. To them I was still the same person who was now introducing new rules after six years without any explanation, and most of the ex-clients met my decisions with anger. I was introducing new ideas at a time when management was introducing new changes which they were angry about, so the two became linked together. However, the clients found it easier to attack my changes. They took out their frustrations about the changes imposed by managers that were beyond their control, on this group because they felt able to challenge my changes.

The first six sessions were blocked with antigroup behaviour as the members became destructive, criticizing the changes in the unit and the staff for destroying their chances of recovery, and me for changing their group by setting new rules—the breast was poisoned so no feeding could take place.

When I entered the room for session six, the table and the tissues had disappeared and the note of apology I had left on the table was placed on my chair. I sat down and paid attention to my countertransference feelings so as to make sense of what was being communicated to me. I felt furious, aggressive, rejected and rejecting. *How dare they? Why do I bother? I wish I could just get up and go.* Instead I sat, listened and observed calmly. The conversation was a struggle, with Annamore trying hard to cover up the silences by drawing in individuals with direct questions. Then silence again. Foulkes and Anthony (1973, p. 156) state that: "Silences represent an important communication in the group, and the therapist must endeavour to understand the many different meanings".

This silence was pregnant, heralding a group storm. I said: "I wonder whether it would be helpful to talk about what is going on in the group at the moment".

Annamore responded: "We don't like the way you run this group. You took our power away and we have decided to take it back. I wanted to shut you up and I have succeeded. We don't want you here".

I felt punched right in my stomach, needing to catch my breath. I just wanted to get up and leave, but instead I took myself out of the group and watched them with my third eye. I saw myself in Annamore—me after Sam's death, feeling abandoned and frightened, refusing to feed, attacking the breast—my supervisor who was trying to look after me.

Foulkes' mirror phenomena flooded back to me: "The group situation has been likened to a 'hall of mirrors' where an individual is confronted with various aspects of his social, psychological, or body image. By careful inner assessment of these aspects, he can achieve in time a personal image of himself not grossly out of keeping with the external and objective evaluation. He can discover his real identity and link it up with past identities" (Foulkes & Anthony, 1973, p. 150).

I was now in my supervisor's shoes. At that moment I experienced the strength of my attack on my supervisor who tried to take care of me, just as I was trying to care for this rejecting, rejected group. I was shocked by the realization of the power of my rejection. I went into the depressive position where the focus "... is on love, understanding, concern, reparation, desire, and various forms of regard for the object (*my supervisor*) as well as on destructiveness and guilt" (Waska, 2002, p. 4).

I felt closer to my supervisor. Identifying with her made me feel strong and confident because I knew I was better integrated: I had introjected enough of her to know that I would survive the present attack. She survived mine, therefore with a bit of her in me I was sure that I would definitely survive Annamore and this group in mourning.

I also identified with my mother when she returned from the United Kingdom and we attacked her rules, hiding our fear of being abandoned again as we pushed her to leave sooner rather than later. My father, like Rodney, had been preoccupied with running the businesses and had not been there to set boundaries for us. He had let us make our own rules. I realized now that that responsibility at that age put pressure on me to grow up too quickly so as to parent my younger siblings when I too needed to be looked after.

Hopper (2003, p. 116) states: "Envy might serve as a defence against the anxiety inherent in feelings of personal and social powerlessness or helplessness, aphanisis or annihilation anxiety, confusion and other forms of "nameless dread".

Although I understood the theory of what was happening I knew that the group was not ready for feeding with interpretations. It needed to be held firmly in order to calm down before it was ready to feed. An angry and distressed baby will not breast-feed—it will either bite the nipple or choke on the milk. What it needs is to be cuddled and comforted till it rides through its rage. So, I cuddled the group firmly by reinforcing the boundaries I had set and explained that they were not for discussion but we could talk about how they felt about it and that I was there to stay. With that the group settled. Someone went to get the table and the box of tissues and the group was ready to feed.

CHAPTER THIRTY TWO

Celebration of two cultures

I n the Shona culture we say: *Kandiro kanoenda kunobva kamwe* (a little plate goes where another came from). It means that when you receive a gift you thank the person by sending back another gift.

It is also our tradition for one to spend one's first salary on gifts for parents and grandparents, to mark the shift into adulthood. Therefore, it felt important for me to mark my departure from being a trainee group analyst to becoming a qualified group analyst and a colleague to my tutors. However, I found myself in conflict because, in group analysis, giving presents to your analyst could be seen as a sign of immaturity, as failure to say what needs to be said.

I took my dilemma to my small therapy group and talked through how I could marry the two cultures I now belonged to—the Shona culture and Group Analysis.

In my last large group I explained about my culture and invited others to join me in carrying out my tradition. I passed labelled presents to the person next to me who passed it on till it got to the tutor. All presents were hand-made in Zimbabwe. I gave this speech:

The lecturer: For me you represent the theory. I give you three clay pots. I have struggled with the fear of being envied (paranoid–schizoid position), and when I presented my clinical paper (*Racial Discrimination: A cry in the wilderness*) you re-framed my fear of being envied by others to my need to be aware of when I "self-envy", that is, self-sabotage. I had divided the group into two to avoid being with some members whom I feared would attack my work but you asked us to stay together. You taught me about putting my faith in the group because the group as a whole was lively, interested, impressed, encouraging, and supportive. I also learnt to be more concerned about my own destructiveness which I can project into other people, then dress up my self-sabotaging acts in the disguise of self-protection. By dividing the group I was not protecting myself; instead I was attacking my own good work because I would have missed the feedback from half of the group.

In Shona we say *Mapudzi anowira kusina hari* (Gourds—pumpkin family—fall to those without clay pots to cook in), meaning, talents fall to those incapable of utilizing them. I feel that my last year has been about making clay pots for myself to cook my gourds. I had the talents but lacked the clay pots—the capacity for optimum utilization. I thank you for that.

My supervisor: Thank you and the supervision group for teaching me about containment, playfulness and creativity. I got you two drums. I remember when I was ten going to village dances where we danced to the rhythm of the drums in the moonlight evenings. We took turns to dance in the circle, displaying individual styles, learning to be creative, trying out new styles copied from others and adapting them to suit our own individual rhythms. That is similar to what I am taking with me from my supervision group—the experience of taking my turn in the circle, feeling contained to take risks in trying out new styles, adapting what I learnt from others to my own rhythm. I thank my supervision group for giving me the confidence and belief in myself; not to be afraid to make mistakes and to be honest as I learn from my mistakes. I thank you all.

The course convenor: Because of the financial cost of losing three members of my family within a short period I could not afford to pay my fees for some time and I found it humiliating to ask for help, but you as the course convenor made it easy for me. You taught me to ask for help when vulnerable. I give you a motor bike—made from wire. I am scared of motorbikes so they represent my fears. If I have to get on a motorbike

I have to trust the other person and hang on to them. That is a strong image to take with me—if fearful or vulnerable to remember the motor-bike, that is—to ask for a lift and hold on to others. Thank you.

The group analyst: Taking on many responsibilities is part of my culture, but you as a group was not afraid of being politically incorrect and challenged me. I give you a doll of a Zimbabwean mother carrying her baby on her back, a hoe over her shoulder and firewood on her head. This doll represents the multiple responsibilities I carry as a Black Zimbabwean mother. You gave me the ability to question the unquestionable because sometimes what is first presented might take a different meaning on exploration. For example, insisting on exploring why I say "elopement" when speaking about my "allotment". As a foreigner I felt it is my privilege to use wrong words. Political correctness would have failed to make me reflect on this and it was useful because it made me aware of my ability to forcefully get what I desire (elopement) instead of waiting to be allocated (allotment). This has helped me understand that I have a choice, for example, not to fight all the time for what I want but is denied to me, and that sometimes not fighting leaves space for receiving better things given with pleasure. I am now in a job I enjoy because of this insight.

The mother-and-baby dichotomy holds defences for me, so be aware of what is under the mask because sometimes the mother is dependent upon her baby.

Thank you and the small group not only for making me eat my cabbages but for nurturing me so well that now I grow my own cabbages.

I also give the female members of the team *tsero*—woven flat containers made of reeds, bamboo or grass. For example, the container on the front cover containing corn and maize. *Tsero* are also used by women to separate nuts from shells. One throws the mixture of shelled nuts and their shells into the air using the *rusero* (singular form of *tsero*) and the wind blows away the shells. Sometimes a few nuts get blown away. For me it represented my difficulties with letting go—to abandon the few blown-away nuts and value those left in the *rusero*. (*This was the most challenging imagery I took with me. A year after training it preoccupied me, proving that therapy carries on long after the sessions stop.*)

After my speech the large group joined in playing with the concepts I had introduced and made their own free associations with the presents and the wrappings. Others spoke about what they were taking with them, gave feedback on my impact on the course and how they would miss me, and I heard and digested what was being offered without playing deaf. I even enjoyed the thought of being missed. It was an inclusive farewell.

I knew that I was ready to fly the nest.

PART III

CAN PSYCHOTHERAPY

PENETRATE
BEYOND SKIN
COLOUR?

TRAINEE COUNSELLORS' RESPONSES
TO QUESTIONS OF SKIN COLOUR

ACKNOWLEDGEMENTS

Part Three looks at a research I conducted for my MSc in Psychology with Manchester Metropolitan University. The research was carried out with Westminster Pastoral Foundation Therapy (WPF Therapy) trainee counsellors.

I would like to thank my supervisor, Professor Ian Parker, for the support and encouragement that helped me stay focused, and for assisting me in building my confidence in the work I had to do so that I could enjoy the frightening task I undertook.

Thanks to Lesley Murdin, Christine Driver, Lykke Leszczynski, Stephen Crawford, John Stewart, Claire Umar, Vera Richards-Fothergill, Martyn Head and other WPF Therapy staff for giving me the opportunity and support to carry out this research, and many thanks to their committed trainee counsellors who participated in the research and the group that allowed for challenging discussions on diversity. Both participated with enthusiasm, honesty, and courage. My sincere gratitude for the lessons I learnt.

I would also like to thank South London & Maudsley NHS Foundation Trust (SLAM) staff—Fran Bristow, my former manager, who continued to support me with practical help and advice, my manager Caron Gaw for being interested and for offering me time to carry out the research, my team mates Dr Anita Timans, Marcus Page, John Harding, Stuart Colquhoun, Nicki Makin, Lyn Ezzekiel, Elaine Ofomi, and Barbara Moore for being challenging guinea pigs in testing the research tools and giving constructive feedback; Chris Okoro, Luke Sullivan, Dr. Julie Steel, Ryan Little, and Yomna El-Guindy for technological advice and John Gale and Liz Wealand for the literal support. Many thanks to the SLAM service users who spoke about their experiences at the Black History event. Thanks to Pam Russell from SLAM Communications for supporting us in applying for funding to celebrate Black History. Some of the funds have lubricated most of the work in this research.

Thanks to my family and friends: my friend Amy Manchersaw, a clinical psychologist, for being there and keeping stress at bay and for agreeing to work more than she bargained for without complaining, and to her husband David Muggleston for keeping the ship afloat by calming the stormy weather with non-analytic support and by being just an ordinary down-to-earth guy.

Thanks to my husband, Gary, for being there for me and for fathering and mothering our children while I was on another planet, and for ferrying me to and from Manchester; to my father-in-law, Seamus Maher, whose enjoyment and admiration of my suffering motivates me to do my best, and mother-in-law Maureen Maher, who always takes my work seriously and whose belief in the power of prayer fills me with confidence that it will be all right. She always believes in me and in whatever I do.

Thanks to my girls Karen Mpo Zinaka, my make-up artist (sorry the video failed to pick up her efforts, I just became a "black blob") and for all the meals she brought to work when I became too engrossed to eat, Kim Nomathemba Zinaka for sharing with me the excitement of some of the findings and Kiara Thembile Maher for helping me learn my lines and recite my poem with the "right moves" for the video.

Thanks to my boys: my eldest son, Bryan Themba Maher—the reality-confronter who refused to help with the research (reminding me that it is my homework, not his) but laboured on the artwork and joined me in toiling at the allotment to create the background for the front cover. My baby son Brendan Thabiso Seamus Maher, who showed an interest and youthful enthusiasm in the project, asking many questions and constantly enquiring if I was planning to be like Mandela or Martin Lurther King, and insisting that I get a role model like those two. Boy, my son can dream! And he has a mouth to match his vivid imagination.

Special thanks to my grand-daughter, Tayler-Ray Thandiwe Zinaka, another reality-confronter like Uncle Bryan, who insisted that I drink her "pretend tea" when I was at my busiest and refused to go away because drinking her "tea" was more important than my "stupid work".

Special welcome to my three grandsons AJ (Anthony Joy Thulani) Zinaka and Ethan Alexandra Themba Zinaka, born during the incubation of this research, and OvAngelo-Kai Tamas—all bringing hope for the future and symbolizing unity of people of different races and cultures.

To my nephew, Blackson Tafadzwa Mubika, another allotment helper, and my niece Trish Cathrine Mubika, both Obediah's children, who are now ours and whose art at tea-making with others was well appreciated since they made sure I was well watered. Tea was flowing like *Musi oa Tunya* (the Victoria Falls)!

I felt well supported. Thank you all.

INTRODUCTION

The research I carried out explores the responses of trainee counsellors to some of the factors that influence change in a counsellor's ability to work with someone of a different skin colour.

The opening quotation by Nelson Mandela captures my philosophy about working together, Blacks and Whites, rather than blaming one race for another race's misfortunes. It is important that we explore the racial attitudes, beliefs, stereotypical thinking, and prejudices we have internalized and see how they interfere with our work with clients. How can we, as counsellors and therapists, work with those of different skin colour effectively?

The research was carried out with WPF Therapy trainee counsellors. WPF Therapy is a counselling and psychotherapy training institution that also offers individual and group therapy.

The research engaged the trainees in a questionnaire and a training video that encouraged self-reflection on internalized racism while explaining the link between child developmental stages and reactions to racist experiences. The trainees were then given a second questionnaire to investigate the effectiveness of the video as a training tool, followed by a semi-structured interview. In the interview the trainees reflected on their experiences around racism and identified factors that influenced the change in their answers between the first and second questionnaires.

The focus was mainly on the process, as the aim was to investigate the trainees' responses that revealed attitudes which interfere with their ability to work effectively with clients of different skin colour. The research identified and analysed common themes, patterns, differences, and similarities in responses. It analysed the identified changes between the first and second questionnaires. The significance of these findings is discussed and any factors significant to change are explored.

CHAPTER THIRTY THREE

Choice of the research topic

"Some may say that research or theory that is determined by highly personal factors should not be trusted. Others will say that no one in their right mind would bother with the arduous business of research without a history of personal reasons" (Stern, 1985, p. ix).

Personal and professional experiences influenced my choice of this topic. First, my personal experience of institutional racism, racial discrimination, and victimization discussed in Parts One and Two, which left me questioning my own internalized racism that allowed me to suffer over three years of racism without complaining.

When my attention was drawn to the fact that I treated Black clients differently to White clients I became more curious about how my internalized racism affected my work in general as a Black psychotherapist working with predominantly White clients. I also became interested in knowing how aware other counsellors and therapists are of their internalized racism and how it affects their work with clients of a different skin colour. I became interested in investigating the factors that affect the relationship between therapists and clients of different skin colour.

As I progressed in my thinking about this research I realized I could make better sense of it by using my personal experiences. I became excited but my mind kept somersaulting about in response to what I was reading about other researchers' work and as a result of discussions with my colleagues and my own observations as a group analyst.

Holloway's states that: "I try to explain how I came up with the questions I did and how they changed as I went along. It would be impossible to present these questions fully without talking about myself: the point I was at in my life and its history, the political and cultural conditions which produced it, how these shaped my interest in certain areas of contemporary social theory. These factors together produce the conditions which make possible my research questions and shaped how I addressed them". Holloway 1989: four cited in Banister, Burman, Parker, Taylor, and Tindall (1994, p. 144).

Therefore, my second reason for choosing this topic was to make sense of my experiences, and reading Holloway's work reassured me of the possibility of talking about myself as a vehicle for clarifying what I wanted to discuss.

The third reason was that my psychotherapy department was offered funds by South London and Maudsley NHS Foundation Trust (SLAM) to celebrate the Black History Month. At our first event I presented a paper on *Psychotherapy Penetrates Beyond Skin Colour* to a group of NHS professionals, service users and their carers and friends. The presentation focused on the similarities in child developmental stages of Black and White children from birth to adulthood, linking childhood experiences to racial experiences in adulthood (Appendix 2).

Below is the information on the ethnicity of the people who attended the Black History event:

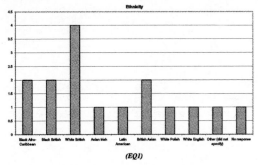

Figure 1.

Thirty people attended the event (Figure 1): sixteen staff, ten service users/patients/clients, and four carers and friends of the service users. Although it was a Black History event, White people were in the majority, making me realize that the issue of skin colour is not just for Blacks. It affects everybody. The presentation received so much positive feedback that I decided to develop the topic into a research question—from *Psychotherapy penetrates beyond skin colour* to *Can psychotherapy penetrate beyond skin colour?*

CHAPTER THIRTY FOUR

The grounding theories

In the following chapter I discuss concepts that are important when working with difference, such as Bowlby's Attachment Theory; Winnicott's concept of Hate in Countertransference; Klein's concepts of paranoid–schizoid position, projective identification and depressive position; various perceptions on the concept of internalization and Bollas' concept of extractive introjection. I also look at some essential definitions, such as culture, cultural competence, colour blind, racial ideology, racism, internalized racism, institutional racism, and cultural racism.

34.1   Attachment theory

Attachment Theory was first developed by Bowlby as he studied the mother-baby bond and how it is affected by separation, deprivation, and bereavement. Bretherton (1992) discusses how Mary Ainsworth developed the theory further by seeing the attachment figure as a *"secure base"* from which an infant can explore the world. Ainsworth transformed it into a methodology, making it possible to test Bowlby's ideas empirically.

Attachment Theory refers to the "state" and "quality" of the person's attachments. It is about contact, proximity, feeling contained, held, comforted and secure. Holmes, talking about Attachment Theory, shows how interpersonal experiences become internalized as personality or attachment style, which influences future relationships and connects the political with the personal. Marris (1991) cited in Holmes (1993, p. 204) states that: "This is the ... link between sociology and psychological understanding: the experience of attachment, which ... influences the growth of personality, is itself both the product of a culture, and determinant of how that culture of attachment itself, but all our ideas of order, authority, security and control".

Bowlby was motivated by the work of Lorenz (1952) on goslings, how they displayed survival-innate behaviour of "anxiety" by cheeping and searching when separated from their mother/surrogate mother as a way of keeping their parent close for protection. This was related to humans. Bowlby studied infants' behaviour and concluded that the bond between an infant and its caregiver is strengthened by a consistent, sensitive and responsive carer. From this experience the infant is able to form a secure attachment which is internalized and forms part of the person's personality for future interpersonal relationships.

Stern (1985) spoke about the "attunement" of the caregiver. It is during these early formative years that some children are looked after by nannies/au pair, and in multicultural societies an attachment can be formed with nannies/au pair of different skin colour to them who then become their internalized objects. The same happens with infants adopted by parents of different skin colour to themselves. Greenberg and Mitchell (1983) state that everyone carries within himself a world made up of all he has seen and loved and keeps coming back to that world. Future relationships are moulded around these early childhood imagos.

34.2   Hate in Countertransference

Historically, the relationship between Blacks and Whites has been clouded with hate and fear. Therefore, it is important for counsellors and therapists to work through their own feelings of hate and fear, as they can be evoked in transference and countertransference.

Winnicott (1947) invites us to pay attention to the "nature of the emotional burden" on practitioners when working with clients who evoke hate and fear in them. He says that as much as we love our clients we cannot "avoid hating them and fearing them" and being aware of this makes our motives less driven by hate or fear. Not acknowledging or paying attention to the emotions evoked in the therapist can lead the therapist into acting out those feelings. The hate needs to be interpreted at an appropriate time and expressed as "objective or justified hate" in order for the practitioner to be real and available to his/her patients.

Bowlby also talked about the projection of "internal dangers", for example feelings of rage and hatred, which are projected onto the neutral environment of the therapeutic space (Holmes, 1993). Sometimes in therapy the rage that is projected onto skin colour is this "internal danger" and a skilled therapist would explore what is at the bottom of such intense feelings.

34.3   Kleinian concepts

34.3.1   Paranoid–schizoid position

When working with difference it is important to understand Klein's defence mechanisms. Segal (1992) explains Klein's concepts of paranoid-schizoid and depressive positions as defence mechanisms that deal with anxiety. She believes that we move from one to the other as we cope with stressful situations or experiences.

Frosh (1991, p. 50) quotes Klein (1946, p. 4): "I hold that anxiety arises from operation of the death instinct within the child, is felt as a fear of annihilation (death) and takes the form of fear of persecution. The fear of the destructive impulse seems to attach itself at once to an object—or rather it is experienced as the fear of uncontrollable, overpowering object".

Frosh shows how Klein's theories can be categorized as object relations and explains that the difference with other theorists is that others put their significance of libidinal and destructive drives as the driving forces, while Klein connects the drives to a specific object, for example the breast.

Dealing with difference can induce anxiety which can result in a process of splitting, for example black/white, good/bad, colonizer/ colonized, master/slave, oppressor/oppressed, victim/perpetrator. Historically, Whites have contained the goodness and Blacks the badness. The good (White) is idealized and the bad (Black) is denigrated.

However, these days the opposite also takes place: in some Black communities Whites are denigrated and Blacks are idealized.

This Black/White split has dominated and troubled multicultural societies, making it easy to get into the paranoid–schizoid position as a way of coping with the anxieties evoked by the split. Experiencing feelings of hatred and envy can trigger off destructive and aggressive phantasies, making the world unsafe and resulting in breeding mistrust, suspicion and fear of persecution. In the paranoid–schizoid position there is a lack of concern for the other, so no sense of loss or guilt is experienced over one's destructive and aggressive behaviour. In therapy, when these feelings become too powerful to contain within oneself, they are split off and projected onto the "neutral environment"—the bad breast—the therapist, who has to contain them, chew them like the *ruzoka* and make them safe by analysing them, then give them back to the client in forms that the client can accept and digest, for example through interpretation.

34.3.2 Projective identification

Projective identification takes place during the paranoid–schizoid position. It is an active way of getting rid of one's uncomfortable or undesirable feelings/thoughts/behaviour by disowning them and pushing them into someone else who might display a similar behaviour/thought connected to these unwanted feelings. This is where others respond by saying a pot is calling the kettle black.

34.3.3 Depressive position

The depressive position can be achieved when the containing mother/therapist is able to give back the digested badness. The person is able to take back their projections and reflect on the consequences experienced as a result of their actions or lack of action. A sense of guilt and sadness about the loss is achieved and an acceptance that both good and bad can dwell together in one body. It is a position of maturity.

34.4 Internalization

The reaction to racism has an impact on our inner world in as much as our internal world influences how we experience and react to racism in the external world. Wallis and Poulton (2001, p. 6) define internalization by quoting Walrond-Skinner (1986, p. 186): Internalization is a "process whereby the individual transfers a relationship with an external object into his internal world' and it encompasses incorporation, introjection and identification as mechanisms that create internal mental representations out of objects and events. Wallis and Poulton discuss the different ways of internalizing, which I developed further by linking them to racist experiences as follows:

34.4.1   Identification with the aggressor—ego psychology

Anna Freud introduced the concept of identification with the aggressor in *The Ego and the Mechanisms of Defence*. It is a defence mechanism that develops during superego development in an attempt to cope with internal and external threats. For example, just as a child identifies with an aggressive father, so a victim of racism may introject and identify with a racist by taking up racist behaviour (such as oppressive and fear-inducing characteristics) as a means of coping with the fear or anxiety evoked in him/her by the racist. The critical function of the superego is externalized and projected into the Other. If the superego develops it allows for self-criticism, which enables one to reflect on one's behaviour so as to take responsibility for any wrong-doing. However, if the superego fails to develop, the individual will continue to see nothing wrong with their behaviour and internal racism is likely to be established.

When Wallis and Poulton (2001, pp. 30–31) discuss Sandler's concept of the internal representational world, they talk about how a child carries various images of significant people and of itself in order to help the ego function in its adaptive and defensive work. For example, when my patients relate how they dealt with a difficult situation they say: "I thought about what you/a group member would say in this situation and I knew what to do; I took you all with me to face my manager whom I was dreading to meet and you gave me the confidence to face him".

This is a sign of the beginning of the process of internalization of other group members and the therapist that influences how the client reacts in a given difficult situation. With time and practice the ego is strengthened and the group member or client will not need the external concrete representations to give them confidence because they internalize them. Therefore, a person brought up by a racist parent or in a racist society will introject racist representations and in their absence the person will still be influenced by this internalized racism, often without being conscious of it.

34.4.2   Internalizations in response to fear of loss

Mahler built a theory of internalization from a developmental model based on observations of the child-parent relationship. She believed the quality of that relationship is essential in achieving a stable sense of self and others. Healthy internalization is achieved through an available parent who is present to engage positively with the child. At sixteen to twenty-five months a child develops a sense of being a separate individual. Internalizations are driven by the fear of losing the parental love. If the parent is available, loving and responsive the child develops healthy internalizations, but if this child-parent bond fails, the child may develop negative attachments, for example splitting of objects into "good" and "bad" (Mahler et al., 1975) cited in Wallis and Poulton (2001).

Mahler's theory also applies to the experience of some Black people in an employer/employee relationship, where similar dynamics take place. In the employer/employee (parent/child) relationship the employer needs to be positively available and responsive. For example, when I had problems with a supervisor and my employer intervened. I got a new supervisor—the organization proved to be available and responsive and I was able to stay focused and blossomed from that experience; and when I found out that I was earning less than my male White colleague the organization was responsive and quickly sorted out the problem. They gained my respect and I felt contained. On the other hand, in a racist organization that availability is mostly present in White/White relationships but lacking in most White/Black relationships. When my organization became an unavailable and unresponsive parent due to the institutional racism that was not being acknowledged and dealt with, I ended up surviving through splitting so as to preserve any goodness that I treasured. My part-time job became the "good object" and my full-time job became the "bad object", and I became blind to any good in my full-time job.

Initially the fear of rejection controlled me—the fear of losing the parental/organizational love. For some time I could not complain about the racism because I wanted to fit in, even at the cost of losing myself. However, it came to a point where I felt that I had lost the parental/organizational love anyway. I felt exposed because I felt blamed for being oversensitive. I feared that more abuse would take place because, by locating the problem in me instead of addressing the institutional racism, colleagues would read that as permission to carry on with their discriminatory behaviour since they were not asked to be accountable for their actions.

I also believe that I struggled in this organization because my healthy internalized relationship with my father and brothers would not allow me to accept a long-term abusive relationship without a fight. Although I lacked an available, responsive, loving external parent in the organization I had an available, responsive, loving internalized parent within me. If I had internalized an equally abusive parent I would not have taken legal action. It is likely that I would have succumbed to the learnt helplessness.

34.5   Essential definitions

34.5.1   Culture

Culture is "the set of norms or behavioural patterns, meanings, life-styles, and values shared and utilized by members of a determined human group ... includes ... social relationships, language, religion, ethical principles, traditions, technology, legal norms and even financial philosophies" Alar on in Oldham, Skodol, and Bender (2005, p. 561).

Suman (1991, p. 9) states that culture: "... is now often seen as something 'inside' a person—a psychological state (D' Andrade, 1984) ...".

It is important to understand that since race or skin colour cannot determine one's culture, a Black person can internalize a White culture and vice versa if they are brought up in such an environment. For example, in some African countries it is common for White babies to be cared for by Black women and they often grow up in the company of their nannies' children/grandchildren, resulting in internalizing the Black culture. In the programme Big Brother, a British Channel Four television reality show, we witnessed the unforgiving reaction of a society to a young White woman who had internalized a language used by her Black friends. Young Emily, a White contestant, joked with Charlie, a Black contestant she was friendly with by calling her "nigger". Although we are aware of some Black people calling one another "nigger" it seemed unacceptable for a White person to call her Black friend "nigger" without causing offence. Although Emily explained that back in her hometown her Black friends and herself call each other "nigger" in friendly banter, the unforgiving society decided to take it out of her naïve context and put it into its own context. As a result young Emily was pulled out of the programme.

We ask White people to respect us, yet we say it is fine for us to carry on abusing each other because we are of the same skin colour. Abuse is abuse. What is taboo for Whites should be taboo for Blacks too. One thing I learnt from Big Brother is that language needs to be the same, either acceptable or unacceptable, regardless of colour or race. If we have an "in language" then we should be prepared to allow those we invite into our "in club" to use the same "in language".

My phantasy is that some of the people who get offended by the naïve Emilys of this world have never suffered real racism, because those who have can tell the difference between misuse of power and naïvety. However, of those who have suffered racism and find the Emilys offending, my assumption would be that they might find her an object for displacing an anger they failed to discharge at the people who deserved it, and the Emilys are just easy and convenient punch bags—society's scapegoats.

Black children adopted by White couples—for example, Black children adopted by actress Angelina Jolie or singer Madonna—are likely to internalize a White culture. Black people who internalize a White culture are often misunderstood and get called "coconuts" or "bounty" (dark outside but white inside): however, that just indicates their attackers' ignorance because culture is not determined by skin colour or race.

34.5.2   Cultural competence

Cultural competence is the ability to work effectively with people from various ethnic, cultural, political, economic, and religious backgrounds with the capacity to be aware of how one's culture influences how one views others. (North Carolina Division of Social Services, 1991: p. 1 cited in Sullivan, Harris, Collado & Chen, 2006, p. 988).

34.5.3   Colour-blind racial ideology

Neville, Spanierman, and Doan (2006) define colour-blindness as the denial, distortion, and/or minimization of race and racism.

Colour-blindness is based on a dominant race allowing individuals, groups, and systems consciously or unconsciously to justify racism and encourage the racial status quo.

Schofield, in Dovidio and Gaertner (1986, pp. 237–241) discusses the consequences of colour-blindness by reflecting on a research carried out at an American school, Wexler Middle School, with 1200 Black and White children. The school provided a "positive environment for interracial education" by offering equal status to Black and White staff and pupils. Schofield highlights how race became invisible because at this school, acknowledging one's awareness of the other's race was perceived as a sign of prejudice. She gives an example of an interviewer who asks a teacher to confirm whether he only had one White girl in his class. The teacher was unable to confirm without referring to his class register first, then said, "You know, you're right. I never noticed that ... I guess that is a good thing".

Not noticing that he only had one White pupil proved to him that he was not prejudiced. How is it possible not to notice the only White student in a class of Black students? This is similar to my experience when I asked thirty participants at a Black History event to describe me in one word. Not one person, either Black or White, described me as black: they explained that they had thought about it but decided not to say "black" because they did not want to offend me, yet describing me as "scatty" was considered to be fine.

This story reminds me of a time when my daughter was in a White school. Each time she got into any mischief a description of a tall Black student always narrowed the search down to one person—Kim, so she felt restricted in her struggle to cross the bridge from childhood to adulthood. Her White friends became reluctant to get into any mischief with her because they did not need sniffer dogs to be caught out. Is that racism? It may feel unfair for her but that is who she is.

To demonstrate further that not talking about race does not stop people's behaviour from being influenced by race I will discuss a research by Schofield. Schofield showed how in the above school they observed teachers and students during school activities for about 200 hours. In that time they noticed that both students and teachers made less than twenty-five race references, yet when the students were interviewed they seemed race conscious. When they observed the students during the lunch break, they noticed that they socialized within their race groups, for example only six out of 119 White and ninety Black children sat next to someone of a different race. Sagar and Schofiled (1977), cited in Dovidio and Gaertner (1986, p. 241).

34.5.4 Racism

Jones (1972, p. 172) cited in Dovidio and Gaertner (1986) states that racism: "Results from transformation of race prejudice and/or ethnocentrism through the exercise of power against a racial group defined as inferior, by individuals and institutions with the intentional or unintentional support of the entire culture".

Kovel (1984, p. xcvii) cited in Frosh (1991, p. 77) states: "The racist relation is one ... in which the white self is created out of the violation of the black self, through its inclusion and degradation. Racism degrades the Other to constitute the dominant self, and its social order".

Racism is no longer about Whites degrading Blacks because more Blacks are now in positions of power and some degrade Whites, particularly in countries that were colonized and where Blacks fought for their independence. In South Africa, Nelson Mandela—the first Black South African president—avoided this plight of role reversal by introducing reconciliation between Blacks and Whites. Similarly, in counselling and psychotherapy the issue of power has shifted as more Blacks train in the talking therapies impacting on the therapeutic relationship. For example, the White client discussed in Part One who struggled to pay for her therapy but would not negotiate for a lower fee. This was because she wanted to maintain her perceived position of power over me, a Black therapist whose perceived power threatened her, and which therefore had to be tamed by paying more than she could afford.

Lago and Thompson (1996, p. 16) quote Troyna (1993, p. 15): "What is evident is that racism is an ideology which is continually changing, being interrupted and reconstructed, and which often appears in contradictory forms. As such, its reproduction in schools and elsewhere can be expected to be complex, multi-faceted and historically specific ... specific forms of racism can be expected to change and inherited racist discourse are likely to be re-constituted. New circumstances are likely to lead to new formulations of racism".

According to Krause (1998, p. 161) "race" in Anglo-American terminology is a "colonial" and "postmodern" product. In the 1800s race referred to phenotypical features such as skin colour, hair colour and texture, eyes and stature, but with time it now refers to a hierarchy that places Blacks and ethnic minority people at the bottom. Therefore, racism has become a political relationship.

34.5.5 Internalized racism

Foulkes (1983, p. 10) states that each individual: "... is basically and centrally determined, inevitably, by the world in which he lives, by the community, the group, of which he forms as part". Therefore, a child growing up in a racist society will absorb and internalize the racist culture and his/her behaviour, attitude, and belief system will be consciously or unconsciously racist.

34.5.6 Institutional racism

Institutional racism "is represented by the double standards, and differential treatment inherent in our justice, education, medical, government, housing, and other social systems" Okun (1996, p. 220) cited in Paniagua (2001, pp. 9–10) "[Ethnic minorities] are hired to meet affirmative action quotas but are given less significant or powerful responsibilities in the job ...".

In Part One I highlighted how an organization's policies might enable institutional racism to take place, thus allowing White colleagues to receive better treatment. For example, being offered opportunities to study and develop themselves, and preferential treatment to secure their promotion. The institution had to review its policies such as study leave, recruitment policy and compassionate leave in order to ensure fair treatment of all staff.

34.5.7 Cultural racism

Cultural racism "is based on the assumption that White is the norm, that people of colour are inherently inferior, less intelligent ... [and considered] as uncivilized, emotional labile, and prone to violence" (Okun, 1996, p. 218 cited in Paniagua, 2001, pp. 9–10).

In Part One I discussed the findings by the first Employment Tribunal of my personal experiences of cultural and institutional racism, also showing my interpretation of the racial stereotypical thinking behind what happened to me, such as being perceived as inferior, stupid, emotionally labile, lazy, and murderous or prone to violence.

CHAPTER THIRTY FIVE

The history of skin colour

35.1 The history

Fernando (1991) talks about how powerful skin colour has been for many years and that judgements were made, and are still being made, based on one's skin colour.

Knox (1950) cited in Fernando (1991) maintained that external characteristics, mainly skin colour, reflected internal ones such as intelligence and propensity for cultural pursuits; that dark-skinned people were generally inferior.

There have been many movements set up to fight against such attitudes in the hope of achieving equality, as captured in Martin Luther King's speech cited in Allen (2005, p. xvii):

"I have a dream ... that my four children will one day live in a nation where they will not be judged by the colour of their skin, but by the content of their character".

Sue and Sue (1990, p. 75) cite several writers (Harrison, 1975; Kochman, 1981; Stanback & Pearce, 1985; Thomas, 1969; Willie, Kramer & Brown, 1973) who have shown how Blacks—in response to their slave heritage—adopted passive behaviour. I identify this as silent acceptance of situations one is forced into, such as acceptance of being treated as if one is invisible; a sense of resignation, giving up or withdrawing; wanting to please (also known as Uncle Tom's Syndrome) and avoidance of any form of self-expression. These behaviours are adopted as survival strategies when living in a racist society but are not exclusive to the "slave heritage" response because similar survival behaviours are adopted by survivors of neglect and physical, sexual and emotional abuse. Racism, however, tends to get special treatment which breeds fear of normalizing or challenging some of these experiences.

Fanon (1952, p. 42) quotes Mayotte Capecia: "I should have liked to be married, but to a white man. But a woman of color is never altogether respectable in a white man's eyes. Even when he loves her".

Mayotte wrote this in 1948, showing how the desire for a White skin has been a preoccupation of some Blacks.

I found Jackson (2000) fascinating because she comes from the same country as me so we share a similar interest in issues of skin colour. She discusses how Blacks in Africa and the Diaspora perpetuate a hierarchy of "shadeism" (skin colour) and how they ascribe social value and meaning. For example, light skin stood for good, handsome, intelligent, dark skin for bad and ugly. She captures well the mentality of the society we were brought up in.

However, I disagree with Jackson for placing the birth of "shadeism" in slavery only. She fails to address another factor more immediate to the Zimbabwean culture—colonialism. Zimbabwe is a landlocked country, so was too far from the sea for any profitable slave trade. Our folk stories do not mention slavery except in reference to tribal wars, where women were captured to be wives or slaves of the conquering tribe and the captured men were trained to be warriors strengthening the conqueror's army. I became aware of slavery when I studied African history and even then slavery was placed, in my mind, in Zanzibar.

Colonialism, on the other hand, impacted on Zimbabwe. We grew up with words like "you kaffir" (equivalent to "you nigger"). Therefore, I have a more emotional reaction to being called "kaffir" than "nigger" because that is what I grew up with in a country that was divided according to one's complexion. Segregation was established as early as 1892 when the Salisbury Sanitary Board established a Location for huts to be built by African workers. In 1900 there were only twenty-six huts. In 1907 a new Location of 25ha was established. It was 4 km from town and next to the cemetery, slaughter poles and night soil disposal works. No shops were allowed until 1939. In 1930 the Land Apportionment Act divided the country into Blacks, Coloureds (mixed heritage) and Whites (Sayce, 1987).

Black families were separated from their fathers because the men had to go to towns seeking for work. The accommodation they were provided with was only suitable for single men, so wives and children were left to live in the countryside. The only women who were found in towns were seen as prostitutes and terms like *"bhonirukisheni"* ("born in locations" meaning a city child) were used to describe people without morals. A hierarchy of colour was formed, with Blacks at the bottom and Whites at the top enjoying the privileged position of living with their families in towns or on large fertile farms. Because of these injustices Black Zimbabweans went to war, the *Chimurenga*—the Liberation War to claim back our country. Following Zimbabwe's independence an old problem arose: Blacks fighting each other during tribal and political conflicts, thus forcing the country to genuflect to starvation, homelessness, poverty, and other Black man-made miseries.

35.2   The conflict among black people

One cannot discuss skin colour without looking at the conflict among Blacks which existed even during slavery days. Allen (2005, p. 315) writes about the first slave traders in Africa being Black and how they betrayed "their fellow-citizen". Allen gives the following quotation:

> *"Concerning the trade on this [West African] Coast, we notified your Highness that nowadays the natives no longer occupy themselves with the search for gold, but rather make war on each other in order to furnish [us with] slaves ... The Gold Coast has changed into a complete Slave Coast".*
>
> William De la Palma, Director, Dutch West India Co.
> September 5, 1705.

Black-on-Black hatred is also highlighted by Jackson (2000, p. 547), who quotes from a 1712 speech by Willie Lynch, a British slave owner, about how he controlled slaves by using differences like age, colour and skin shade. Of skin shade he said: "You must use the dark skin slaves versus light skin slaves and the light skin slaves versus the dark skin slaves".

This Black-on-Black betrayal is painfully portrayed in the film Roots, set in 1767, in the scene when Black African, Kunta Kinte, is hunted down, trapped like an animal and captured by four Black men to be sold as a slave.

The hatred between some Black people in the United Kingdom is mainly played out between Nigerians/Ghanaians, Africans/Caribbeans and Black Afro-Caribbeans/Asians. I have been told that the Nigerian/Ghanaian conflict has a historical root often experienced when one nation seeks refuge in the neighbouring country. Then in the early 1980s the Ghanaian refugees were forced to flee Nigeria. Instead of using suitcases, most had to use big striped plastic bags which are now called "Ghana must go home" or just "Ghana Must Gos". My understanding of the African/Caribbean conflict is that most Africans were left to work on their own land while Caribbeans were taken into slavery. One argument is that Caribbeans strongly relate to slave history and are teased by being called "slave children" with "a slave mentality". On the other hand, some Caribbeans believe that Africans are too colonized and ignorant of their slave history.

The other argument is that Caribbeans do not have many role models in influential positions, while Africans (for example Nigerians) stayed in Africa, where they learnt to be driven by powerful Black role models—such as doctors and lawyers—in prominent positions.

Some Africans argue that the tension between Caribbeans and Africans is because they feel rejected by Caribbeans, who see Africans as "too dark", yet others say some Caribbeans will accept that their ancestors came from African countries like Ghana.

My observation is that most Caribbeans have English surnames, so one is unable to tell from the surname that the person is Caribbean, whereas most African surnames are in their own language and thus identifiable as African. Therefore, it is difficult to tell how many Caribbeans are in positions of power or are successful because their names could be mistaken for White English names. There also seem to be more successful and powerful women than men in the Caribbean society.

The other issue that seems to divide Blacks is that of skin shade. Light-skinned Caribbeans are called "slave babies" because one of their ancestors must have conceived with the White master. Light-skinned

Blacks are also referred to as "house slaves" and are hated because historically they were seen as "nearly White" and got better treatment working in the house, while darker-skinned Blacks were referred to as "field slaves". They were treated harshly and were destined to toil the land.

I believe some marriages and relationships between Africans and Caribbeans struggle to survive because of these historical conflicts. The other relationships that seem to struggle are between the Blacks and Asians. One explanation I got was that because of the Asian cast system, Africans and Caribbeans are too dark and therefore are at the bottom of their social ladder. The other explanation was that Asians classify people by their ethnicity: Europeans at the top of the ladder, followed by Asians and then Afro-Caribceans at the bottom. It does not matter whether the Afro-Caribbean is lighter skinned than the Asian or not: they are seen as inferior. However, because of some Asians' love of whiter skin shade the envy of the lighter-skinned Africans and Caribbeans often results in envious attacks. Therefore, some Asian families struggle to accept the Afro-Caribbean/Asian relationships. Conversely, White/Asian relationships seem to work better because Whites are at the top of the skin shade ladder and therefore they are readily accepted.

CHAPTER THIRTY SIX

The minority identity development model

36.1   The minority identity development model

Constantine, Warren, and Miville (2005) looked at the racial identity theory as the individual's psychological processes within a socio-political and cultural environment or society in which power is differentiated by race.

Lago and Thomas (1991) discuss the Minority Identity Development Model based on the work of Atkinson et al. (1989). Jackson (2000) uses a similar model by William Cross which I found more provocative because it is put in the context of a culture I grew up in. For example, when she discusses the Encounter stage, she states that as the Black person challenges the concept of Black being bad and White being good, there is a slow realization that there are intelligent, and successful, Blacks, and that not all Blacks are dishonest. That is so provocative that it pushes for an emotive reaction and the message is in danger of getting lost. I disagree with what Jackson says because I grew up in a Black community, and from very early childhood I knew, and still believe, that my father was one of the most intelligent, successful and powerful men in my society, closely followed by my grandfather. My father was respected by both Blacks and Whites, and from a very young age I grew up wanting to be as intelligent, powerful and successful as he was.

I found the explanation given by Vandiver, Fhagen-Smith, Cokley, Cross Jr, and Worrell (2001) on Cross's Nigrescence Model (1971) less provocative and enabling identification with some of what is discussed, even though I still disagree with several of their views. For example, they explain nigrescence by quoting Parham and Helms (1991, p. 320) as "to become Black". I was born Black and have always been clear about who I am. I only started doubting myself after coming to England, when I discovered that being Black had a different meaning and obliged me to go through the process of "becoming Black" in a British society. This process became clearer as I wrote Part One and reflected on my racial experiences.

I will discuss the Minority Identity Development Model using the three identity clusters of Cross's revised Nigrescene Model (1991) discussed by Vandiver, Fhagen-Smith, Cokley, Cross Jr, and Worrell (2001)—Pre-encounter identity clusters; Immersion-Emersion identity clusters; and Internalization identity clusters, while reflecting on my personal experiences in relation to the different stages.

36.2   Pre-encounter

A Black person is perceived as desiring to be White, therefore his/her assimilation of White behaviour, attitudes, and culture is understood as Black self-hatred and anti-Black. I believe our Black history of slavery and colonization inflicted a level of suffering, humiliation, poverty, and loss of identity that not only destroyed self-esteem and promoted self-hatred for allowing such degrading things to happen, but also created a desire to be part of the "dominating and privileged" White race. Jackson gives hair-straightening, and the use of skin-lightening cream, as ways of assimilating Whites, stating that these acts could be understood as "I hate my hair and I hate my skin colour, therefore I hate being Black".

For me the desire to be White is evoked by envy: for example, when my White colleagues get promoted and I do not, even though I am better qualified than them; when White colleagues get offered study leave while I am expected to dance for the same privilege; when White colleagues make hurtful racial jokes about me, and when I do not laugh am told that I lack a sense of humour. Who would not desire recognition for their achievements? Would you not like to have the same opportunities as your colleagues? Would you not want to be treated with respect rather than be a source of cheap entertainment?

It is hard to be Black in a multi-racial racist society. As a Black person I find my professional journey meandering about in a thorny, rocky and infertile wilderness, while my White colleagues were offered smooth shortcuts to the oasis. They have it easy and I would like to have it easier too. So yes, in those moments of despair brought about by racial injustice I have hated being Black because it is tough. I would dare anyone to go through some of my experiences, as discussed in Part One, and see if they would not, just for one moment, wish they were not Black.

A Black person who is seen as pro-White is understood to be anti-Black, as evidenced, for example, in the reaction to mixed race/mixed heritage relationships. When a Black person goes out with a White person it is read, particularly in the Black community, as meaning that the Black person is anti-Black. This, however, shows a lack of understanding: one might go out with someone because they are attracted to the person rather than their skin colour.

Cross (1991) reviewed his concepts in recognition that the Pre-encounter is actually more complex than originally thought. When Cross reviewed the Pre-encounter stage he put it into two categories—the Assimilation stage and the anti-Black stage.

36.2.1 The Assimilation stage

In the Assimilation stage Black individuals identify with the White group but not for racial reasons: for instance, being British and talking about being proud to be British. However, some Blacks find it difficult to accept Blacks in Assimilation stage who see themselves as British because they say British feels "white". They perceive being British as a betrayal of their country of origin (or their parents' countries of origin), so they tease the Black British or accuse them of becoming too westernized, being a coconut or a bounty (brown outside but white inside).

36.2.2 Anti-Black stage

A Black person with an anti-Black identity may feel that Black hatred is reinforced by social and historical experiences. Cross (1991) talks about the impact of an educational system with a distorted history which can cause a Black person, by internalizing, to begin questioning his/her self worth, causing feelings of self-hatred. In Zimbabwe the arrival of missionaries brought confusion because our culture was seen as pagan and primitive and we were referred to as savages, and when I was growing up the promotion of anti-Black was reinforced. For instance, we were not allowed to speak our mother-tongue at school except during Shona lessons; our tradition of naming children with meaningful Shona names after grandparents, parents and siblings was changed to naming children with Christian names of saints; the traditional healers who had treated people for centuries were now called witch doctors and seen as evil, making it sinful and shameful to visit a traditional healer, and eating with one's fingers instead of using a knife and fork was now seen as uncivilized. All these changes resulted in Blacks internalizing anti-Black attitudes.

In our multi-racial United Kingdom society one of my experiences of racial self-hatred was when witnessing the young Black junior clinician being fired by White managers. It evoked the same historical sense of helplessness under White domination, because I felt in no position to challenge the White managers: I was not a permanent employee and they could stop offering me work in a blink. Nevertheless, I hated myself for my consent by silence.

I believe that the anti-Black experience only occurs in the presence of Whites. For example, experiencing my father's best friend's betrayal did not make me think less of his race or make me anti-Black, because we were in a Black community. On the other hand, being betrayed by my Black colleagues made me extremely conscious of my anti-Black sentiments, because in a multi-racial community I was very aware of their race.

36.3   Immersion-emersion stage

There are two identities in this stage:

a. Intense Black Involvement—all that is Black is good.
b. Anti-White—all that is White is bad/evil.

36.3.1   Intense Black involvement

This stage is characterized by soaking oneself in blackness through seeking information that enhances embracing it, such as learning about the historical achievements of significant Blacks; seeking Black role models; a desire to know more about one's culture and also the motivation to spread this knowledge through writing, music, and participating in Black activities that promote Black social consciousness.

I was brought up with intense Black involvement, learning about my culture from a very young, pre-school age. During school holidays all the grandchildren would visit our grandmother at her countryside homestead in Chivhu. In the evenings after supper we would sit around my grandmother and listen to folk stories. She always started them with, *Paivapo!* (Once upon a time). Then, after each of the first three lines of her story she would pause, a cue for us to eagerly respond with *Dzepfunde!* or *Zviri munzeve. I cannot translate *Dzepfunde!* because it is a sound, but it means "we are listening" and *Zviri munzeve!* translates as "it is in the ear"—in other words, we are listening. After the third *Dzepfunde! / Zviri munzeve!* my grandmother would continue. I enjoyed her stories because they were always interactive, with us joining her in a song or in repetitive chanting with varying loudness, for example, when she described the hare creeping towards a target we would creep with the hare by chanting in rhythm to his footsteps. We started at a distance chanting loudly, *Ini nyange, ini nyange, ini terere!* (I creep, I creep and I listen!) and as we got closer to the target grandmother signalled us to lower our voices. We responded by lowering our bodies too ... lower and lower ... until she worked us—coordinating our rhythm like a conductor working his orchestra—into tiny, whispering, almost invisible balls. Afterwards we would discuss the moral of the story, for in every folk story there was always a lesson.

This is how we learnt about our culture, our ancestors, life in the past, our tradition and what happens to animals that do not respect their elders or follow their traditions. On other nights we competed in two groups—guessing the hidden meanings to our Shona sayings. We exercised our observational skills looking at *madimikira* (sayings with opposite meanings to what you say) and *zvirahwe* (proverbs). For example, *rakazvirova rikazhamba* (it beats itself up, then cries out loudly). Can you guess what bird does that?

Another example, *azvuva sanzu azvuva nemashizha aro* (he/she who drags a branch will drag it with its leaves). Can you guess what that means?

Sometimes we played musical games but the most exciting nights were when there was a full moon, because then we could go out to sing and dance to the rhythm of drums. Country dance is very different from the city ballroom dance. It is like dirty dancing and was important because it was at such occasions that relationships were formed. So some danced to attract future husbands and wives, but being a tomboy I danced to show off. I certainly have the moves.

It was also during these visits to my grandmother's that my cousins and I got our sex education. Culturally, sex education was the responsibility of paternal grandmothers and aunts for the girls and paternal grandfathers and uncles for the boys. The maternal side did not get involved in sex education because the child belonged to the father. Therefore, for me, school holidays were mainly about learning about being a Black Zimbabwean, a Shona, of the Zezuru tribe.

On the other hand, the process of "becoming Black" in the United Kingdom took a painfully different route for me. The institutional racism was just heart-breaking because I was not used to being abused just because I am Black. The experiences I went through expelled destructive gases as I became overwhelmed with feelings of rage, anxiety, fear, shame and guilt. I was furious with the White managers for the way they treated me and felt ashamed and guilty for the way I treated the Black junior clinician who was discriminated against. In those desperate situations it is difficult to promote Black involvement because there are consequences for fighting against institutional racism, and in my case I exposed my family to the pain of those consequences. However, the feelings of rage, shame and guilt drove me to do something about it despite my fear of the consequences. I felt the fighting spirit rekindled in me to war against this injustice. That was the same spirit that led to the uprising of Zimbabweans fighting for our independence, even though the consequences were war and death. In so doing, we revived our culture (and an interest in our history) after years of being told it was pagan and unacceptable, eventually valuing both our culture and history. In true Zimbabwean spirit, I was ready to face the consequences of valuing my colleagues, because that meant valuing myself too.

36.3.2   Anti-White attitudes

Initially Cross (1978) stated that during this period the Black person tends to denigrate Whites and White culture, but the 1991 review identified two types of anti-White: one a result of racism and White domination, the other a result of stereotyping. (In my clinical examples I discussed my late recognition of a White member struggling to pay her fees because of my stereotypical belief that Whites are rich—that could be seen as anti-White based on stereotyping.)

The anti-White as a result of racism comes about as a way of redressing injustice. Cross states that the overt expression of denigrating what is White is not as common as during and soon after the Civil Rights movement. This is also true of some African countries: in Zimbabwe during the Liberation War and soon after independence some Black Zimbabweans were angrier with the Whites than during Ian Smith's regime, before the Liberation War. I believe this was due mainly to a raised awareness of the impact of colonization on Blacks and of how privileged Whites were. We, Black Zimbabweans, had lost our fertile land to White settlers, and had also lost part of our cultural heritage because it was portrayed as pagan and primitive by White missionaries.

After independence some of the anger was directed at religion, and the interest in Zimbabwean culture increased. Organizations such as the Zimbabwe Institute of National Traditional Healers' Association (ZINTA) were formed to raise the profile of Zimbabwean traditional medicine, and that action was seen as rebelling against the Western ideology that had so negatively portrayed our culture and traditions. More people returned to naming their children with African names—a tradition eroded by the practice of baptizing believers and naming them after Christian (mainly English) saints. On streets, buildings, hospitals, and schools, names of White settlers were changed to those of Black freedom fighters, and places with negative connotations were changed to more positive ones. Salisbury became Harare, Enkeldorn became Chivhumudhara (now just known as Chivu); street names like Rhodes Ave, Selous Ave, David Livingstone, Queen Elizabeth, and others became Samora Machel (the late president of Mozambique who was a close friend of Zimbabweans), Robert Mugabe, Herbert Chitepo, Tongogara, Jason Moyo, and Zimbabwe Ruins became Great Zimbabwe. This reclamation of Zimbabwean culture could be perceived as anti-White because it was going against what was done by the White settlers and White missionaries who had oppressed Black Zimbabweans.

Hooks (1992) also talks about the difference between anti-White as a result of White oppression and anti-White because of the stereotype of White people. Cross suggested that anti-White attitudes can remain as part of a Black person's identity, for example, disowning a son or daughter for marrying someone of a different race or unprovoked racial attacks on strangers just because they are of a different race.

36.4   Internalization stage

Cross's (1971) earlier model consisted of two stages:

- Internalization stage

Black people let go of the anger and guilt of immersion-emersion stage and accept themselves as Black in a more real manner without the split of one race as all good and the other as all bad. It is a stage I compare with Klein's depressive position of reflective maturity.

- Internalization-commitment stage

This is a "self healing" stage where inferiority and insecurity are replaced with Black pride and self-love and getting involved in diverse activist organizations. After the third Employment Tribunal I felt more at peace, more secure in knowing that I did not need to prove myself. Going through an Employment Tribunal was to prove that I was not as inferior as I was being portrayed. It was the only way I knew how, maybe because I grew up with a father who encouraged me to fight for my rights from a very young age.

Having reached this point of self-healing, I began to think of more creative and less stressful ways of fighting racism. I also became more confident and secure within myself, so when an organization does not appreciate my work I just walk away. Instead of gate-crashing parties where I'm not wanted, I now only walk through doors that are open to me. It is their loss. I am that good and full of self-love.

Cross revised these two stages (Internalization and Internalization-Commitment) and combined them as just Internalization. The new version recognized differences of opinion in internalized Blacks. Cross (1991, 1995) introduced three ideologies in relation to the diversity of internalized identities—(a) Black Nationalism, (b) Biculturalism, and (c) Multiculturalism.

36.5   Black Nationalism

Black Nationalism advocates Black empowerment, economic inde-pendence, and awareness of Black history and Black culture. Cross (1971, 1991, 1995) talks of two forms of Black Nationalism—separatist and inclusive:

Separatist view: This came from Pan-African ideology advocating that Africans in America return to Africa, and it encouraged racial segregation in the United States. Frederickson (1995) cited in Vandiver, Fhagen-Smith, Cokley, Cross Jr, and Worrell (2001).

Inclusive view: DuBois' view of inclusion advocated Black consciousness within American society (educational, political, and cultural systems) and for Blacks to have equal opportunities. Fighting racism and oppression through political inclusion of non-Blacks was also advocated.

While it is not easy to fight against racism and oppression it is worth the effort. For example, a year after I complained about the treatment of the Black junior clinician I was invited by the same organization to assist them with their policies on Human Rights. I accepted the offer because I saw it as an opportunity to make a difference by participating in improving the treatment of Blacks and ethnic minority staff working for this multi-racial organization.

Black Nationalism's position was reviewed (Cross, 1991) and moved from the Immersion-Emersion stage to the Internalization stage because Cross recognized that it served an important positive position in those who reached the latter. Blacks in Internalization stage are more open and less defensive, and although they will still fight racism and oppression, they are more willing to accept other cultures.

36.6   Internalized bicultural identity

The Black person embraces two cultures, for example being Zimbabwean and British, without idealizing one and denigrating the other as in the previous stages.

36.7   Internalized multicultural identity

A strong grounding in one's Black identity enables the individual to welcome and identify with more than one other culture at an equal level. It also includes the capacity to accept others' differences and a willingness to join their causes. For example, I identify with being Zimbabwean, British, and Irish.

I speak Shona most of the time because gossiping in English does not bring out the flavour of the discussion. There are some words one can never translate because we use sound a lot, for example *akati kubu!* She/he went *kubu!*—is a comic fall. *Akati bhi!* She/he went *bhi*—is a heavy fall, and *Akati do!* She/he went *do!*—is a clean fall. The three sentences describe three different types of fall, differentiated by the sound of the fall. In English all three would be translated as "She/he fell" of which the literal translation is *Akadonha*, but does not describe how he fell. I cannot translate the sounds but the closest one is *Akati bhi!*—a heavy fall, which can be translated to "She/he fell with a thud". Without sound the language becomes too blunt for a Shona speaker. In Shona one can be precise with the words and can smell, taste, feel, and touch from the sounds given.

Another Zimbabwean characteristic is that my present home holds both Zimbabwean town *and* country features—it reminds me of Sam's Glenlone home in Harare with its uphill site, and we grow corn and pumpkins around the house just like a typical Zimbabwean country homestead. It's a shame I cannot have cows grazing in the back garden and chickens roaming about!

I cannot put my finger on what British things I do but that is not surprising because most British people do not know what defines being British. I came from a British colony and some of the British things we do are too familiar for me to see the difference, which perhaps is a sign that mine is a colonized mind. However, I often hear my family complain that I am becoming too British. When I was training, both in counselling and as a group analyst I was often accused of behaving as if I am the "Queen Mother" because I always managed to get people to treat me as if I were special. For example, I arranged for hotel room service for five years including Saturdays—a day the hotel did not serve meals to any of its residents, but they served me. I thought that was because I am a nice person or that I have a "lost puppy" look that provokes maternal instincts in most people: either that or it was a sign that I grew up in a hotel and can speak the language. Whatever it is, it irritated some and fascinated others.

The British me enjoys the utter junk on British television, so instead of socializing in pubs during my free time I settle for a night of total television rubbish—Coronation Street, Eastenders, Emerdale, Blind Date, Big Brother … just joyful pleasure! Then Heartbeat and The Royal with their golden oldies' music—the pure honey of British rubbish, but what television bliss!

I feel that Kilkenny, in Ireland, is my other home. The houses look very Zimbabwean, mostly bungalows with beautiful large gardens surrounded by durall or stone walls. However, I sometimes feel sad that I have destroyed my culture. For example, my family's totem is zebra and my older children's totem is lion, but my younger children have no totem because that is passed on through the father, and my husband's culture does not believe in totems. None of my younger children (and some of their cousins, my sisters Tee and Louisa's children) or my grandchildren have totems because their fathers are Nigerian, English, Jamaican, Jewish, and Romanian. So, all Zimbabwean women who marry outside their totem-carrying culture kill off this tradition, while the Zimbabwean men pass it onto their children. Some White Zimbabweans have adopted totems but it is not the same because one is born into it. We are very proud of this tradition because that is what makes us special and different from other cultures.

My husband, who is Irish, enjoys being Zimbabwean. He has perfected the art of kissing his teeth when he is irritated and he is better at it than most Africans I know. He gets involved in any traditional ceremony with enthusiasm. For example, before we were married in church in the United Kingdom we went to Zimbabwe for the traditional ceremony, where he paid the *lobola*, the bridal price. My brother sold me quite cheaply and I was not impressed at all, but being a daughter I had no say on how much I was worth. However, it was a pleasure to watch my husband's face when he was introduced, to his horror, to all the women who were now his "wives"—all my sisters, paternal cousins and my brothers' daughters. It was also a pleasure to watch him clap, *ngusvuro*—a clapping done by men when greeting their in-laws, and it's louder for mothers-in-law (my mother and my brothers' wives are all mothers-in-law). It is a technique that is achieved by the way one arches the palms and fingers so that some air is trapped, giving a *ngusvuro* sound, different from a clapping sound. Children clap with fingers pointing in one direction, men beat the *ngusvuro* and women clap with the fingers crossing. When my brother and mother died my husband performed his traditional duties as a son-in-law very well, including cooking *sadza* in big drums to feed the mourners.

We do not decide on what part of each other's culture we take on because that is a personal decision. For example, in my culture a son-in-law never touches his mother-in-law; to greet her he goes down on one knee and beats the *ngusvuro* while looking down. My husband used to kiss my mother, to her initial horror, but that was eventually accepted. The other thing my husband will not do is eat caterpillars, *madora*. He did the respectful tasting but immediately drew a line on that one. At the *lobola* ceremony he was expected to provide and slaughter a goat as a sign that he would be able to provide for me. He got the goat all right but he chickened out of slaughtering it by paying someone else to do it for him. He had it very easy because in the past a man would not be allowed to marry until he proved himself a man by killing a wild animal. The animal had to be big enough (a lion, buffalo, kudu) to provide a hide that could be used to make something—clothes, blankets, drums—so no fluffy little harmless hares. My husband was scared of killing a goat but he denies that and talks instead about animal rights. In the olden days men who were unable to kill were destined to become confirmed bachelors.

I also have things at which I draw the line. For example, I would never call my in-laws by their first names. That is unheard of. So when my in-laws asked me to call them by their first names I just smiled politely and then quietly drew my line. However, I think I have had it easier than my husband, because his culture does not make many demands on a daughter-in-law, whereas in my village a daughter-in-law would be expected to wake up early and have warm water ready for the in-laws to wash, have most of the daily chores done and breakfast ready. I was prepared to do that but in Ireland they all go to bed around three or four in the morning and still wake up early. I just could not do it, because by the time I got up my mother-in-law would have had her breakfast and my father-in-law would have gone to work. I eventually gave up trying to follow my culture because it just made me feel guilty. My parents would have been disappointed in me, but I reasoned that my in-laws would rather I sat around the table with them and talked all night. We never run out of conversation and we always go to bed after three in the morning. Therefore, I was happy to adjust to this part of Irish culture.

I enjoy being Irish, sometimes dressing up like a leprechaun in a bright orange wig and green attire, shivering bravely in the bitter streets of Dublin on a normal rainy, cold Irish day, cheering and waving my Irish flag at the St Patrick's Day floats passing by. In September 2007 I went to Ireland to watch our team, the Kilkenny Senior Hurling Team, play Limerick in the All-Ireland Hurling final. As a Kilkenny Cat I felt so proud wearing my black and amber glanbia Cill Chainnigh shirt with black trousers. It was an emotional event because James McGarry, our best goalkeeper for the past few years, had lost his wife Vanessa in a tragic road traffic accident a few weeks before the final so he could not play. PJ Ryan, who had taken over as the best incoming goalkeeper, had broken his arm in the All-Ireland semi-final match, but fortunately he made a miraculous recovery to play. We worried that his arm might not allow him to last the match.

The night before the hurling match my father-in-law gave us background information on each player, adding his personal knowledge of them. Being a retired postman who started doing his rounds at age fifteen, he knows nearly everyone personally. My father-in-law does not tell a story—he weaves a verbal tapestry, using many threads in all directions until a full picture is formed. He is an artist at story-telling. For example, when he talked about James McGarry he meandered to talk about his father Seamus, then ten minutes later he came back to talk about James, "You can never meet a nicer, modest guy like James McGarry". Then he told us of the time James helped him when he was delivering the newspapers.

My father-in-law is a serious sportsman. His first love is soccer but he also played hurling for Kilkenny, and in the 1950s that was a problem because of the Gaelic Athletic Association (GAA) Rule 42, now known as Rule 44. According to that rule, if one played any British sports which were referred to as the garrison games (such as soccer, tennis, cricket, and rugby) one was not allowed to play in any Irish games or even be a spectator. The GAA was formed to promote Irish sport such as hurling, handball, Gaelic football, rounders, and camogie. The British government tried to ban the GAA but it survived. The GAA is responsible for The All-Ireland Hurling Championship, in which all thirty-two counties compete. My father-in-law talked about how happy he was when Rule 42 was changed to allow for British games to be played because in 1955 his hurling team was playing in the finals. When he arrived for the match he was not permitted to enter the stadium because the gatekeeper knew he played soccer, and if he had played and been found out his team would have forfeited the game. My father-in-law had to go back home. He could neither play nor watch his team play. However, his team won and they all sent for him to join in the celebrations.

The other moment of glory my father-in-law related was the first time rugby was played in Croke Park in 2007. I understand that Croker (Croke Park) was the Mecca of Irish sport, so to have a British team play in Croker was a miracle, and to allow them to sing *God Save the Queen* was unbelievable. He talked about how the Irish nation was glued to the television to watch what would happen after years of anti-British atmosphere. The GAA had requested that the nation honour their guests but there were some demonstrators and the main objection was allowing God Save the Queen to be sung. On the day the British team was greeted with respect, and when they sang God Save the Queen the whole stadium was dead silent, applauding at the end. When the Irish team sang their anthem Amh n Na bhFiann, A Soldier Song which was written by Peadar Kearney in 1907, the atmosphere in the stadium was just electric. "You have to understand this (that is my father-in-law's catch phrase)—watching these 18-stone mountains of men sing with floods of tears streaming down their faces was something you had to see to believe. There was no dry eye in Ireland ...".

So, the following day when we watched the match the players were not just players on the pitch but men I knew personally. All I needed to do now was put faces to names. We all stood up for the anthem and my heart filled up as I recalled last night's story about the crying rugby players. I felt very emotional and connected to the Irish pride. We watched the players sing. There was Brian Cody, whom my father-in-law (he was his postman) described as one of the most successful managers in the hurling history, so far winning five out of eight finals and only losing the first two; Henry Shefflin, our captain, best scoring forward in Ireland, a free taker and penalty taker, the boy wonder and Pelé of hurling. He is our talisman—the key player. Tommy Walsh—left wing back, he has won all stars in four different positions, which I understand is an amazing achievement, and he can be put to play any position; Martin Comerford—full forward, he is our target man who wins the ball and distributes it; Noel Hickey—our fantastic full back, just returned after ill health; Michael Kavanagh—our right full back, I think he has won five or six All-Ireland medals, superb defender; Fast Eddie Brennan—our right corner forward, when playing well he can explode in a couple of minutes and P. J. Ryan—our invalid, playing less than four weeks after a major injury. ... oh, the match is starting.

The match was electric and I was a true Irish with the Irish history pumping around my system. I was buzzing. The match was tense because a lot was at stake. We won the game, and the jubilation was just unbelievable. The presentation of the trophy, the Liam McCarthy Cup, was even more tense and poignant. Our team captain Henry Shefflin gave a very emotional delivery that portrayed how close the team was.

He dedicated the trophy to the memory of Vanessa McGarry. When he lifted the trophy young Darragh McGarry came on the stage and his father James McGarry lifted him up so that he could lift the trophy with Shefflin. Tears flowed to the roar of the cheering. There was not a dry eye in Ireland and I now understood what my father-in-law meant by that. The McGarry's tragedy had become the teams' and Kilkenny's tragedy. We were all united in the bitter-sweet moment. My husband and I decided to stay for the homecoming even though it meant going back to England on the day we were working.

For the homecoming we lined the High Street to welcome the team back to Kilkenny. We stood opposite Dores butchers, all dressed in our stripes in a range of styles to mark the various years gone by—black-and-amber T-shirts, sweatshirts and tracksuits. We waved our flags while the little babies sat in their pushchairs sucking their sooth-ers wondering what was going on, older people rested on their walking sticks in great anticipation and the raucous bunch of youth squeezed their hooters for more noise. The team drove slowly down in a con-voy led by cars from the local Kilkenny Carlow Community Radio. The boys stood on top of the double-decker bus waving, all dressed in striped light blue shirts and beige trousers. Mine being the only black face in a sea of Irish people drew attention, and I felt very pleased when some of them pointed and waved at me—a personalized wave. When the bus drove past we followed it to the temporary stage set up in the car park behind Dunne Stores in the market car park. Mayor Fitzpatrick and all members of the cooperation were there. Bishop Forrestal was there. And I was there witnessing the start of Kilkenny making a history of unbeatable wins!

When I came back the following morning the plane was delayed, leaving me without any time to go home and change, so I was still wearing my black-and-amber shirt. As I walked through the streets of London to my therapy group I felt very Irish and emotionally patriotic. I was dying for someone to ask about my shirt but no-one did. Silence. In Ireland everyone outside Kilkenny, in the streets, at the airport (well, it felt like everyone) was cheering us and shouting "Well done!" for winning. In London there was silence until I got to my group, the only place I was hoping no one would recognize the significance of my shirt because therapists do not discuss their personal lives with clients, but one group member knew. The only person in the whole of London

I could not talk to about the excitement and pride I felt was the only one who wanted to know!

Internalization of another culture can be fun and inclusive. The internalization of multicultural identity is an unconscious process one might not be aware of until others point it out, or when one starts to reflect.

36.7   Further discussion

The other reason I preferred the way Vandiver, Fhagen-Smith, Cokley, Cross, Jr, and Worrell (2001) presented the Black Identity Model is that they address the Black/Black hatred and place it in Pre-encounter stage, which Jackson fails to address. For example, Jackson explains hair-straightening by Blacks as a desire to be White but fails to address other possible explanations, such as fear of abuse by Black teachers who hit Black school children with hard-to-manage hair across the knuckles with sharp-edged rulers. Straightening hair made it easier to manage and kept the knuckle-bashing at bay. The teachers' behaviour could be understood as anti-Black or self-hatred projected onto the Black students with typical Black Zimbabwean hair. We call it "the hard Mashona" hair because it never responds to combing.

In Palmer and Laungani (1999, p. 11), Rawson, Whitehead and Luthra raise some issues to think about in connection with this model. They state that it "is not intended to be linear and applicable to every minority. It should not be assumed that all black and ethnic people start at the pre-encounter stages. Many young people have a positive sense of themselves and their racial identity from childhood".

I agree with their observation: having lived in segregated Black areas with very little contact with Whites, and without television until the early 1970s, there was no reason for us to envy Whites because we did not see how privileged they were. Our extended families provided supportive role models who created a sense of belonging, thus allowing for secure attachments to be formed. Therefore, it is a phantasy to suggest that a Black person starts by being "out of touch with himself/herself" and that he/she only achieves a sense of security in the fifth stage of development. Here is a good illustration from personal experience.

The first Whites I met were nuns, but since they seemed poor and worked too hard I found no reason to envy them. However, in my late twenties I went to South Africa with my brother Sam. On our way back home we decided to get rid of our South African rands because

Zimbabwe's currency is dollars, so in the last town before crossing into Zimbabwe we went to a supermarket. As we were about to walk through the door everyone around us became excited, indicating that we go around the side. When we did we could not find a door so went back. The same thing happened. After the third attempt we worked out that being in South Africa during apartheid meant Blacks were not allowed in supermarkets. Where they were pointing for us to go to was a small window we could be served from. Sam and I decided we were not that desperate and gave the money away to some Black children standing by.

If I had grown up in such an environment, where racism was so in one's face, I too might perhaps have started out hating being Black and envying Whites, but with my upbringing this was certainly not the case.

CHAPTER THIRTY SEVEN

The White identity development model

The White Identity Development Model is similar to the Black Identity Model. It was introduced by Helms (1984) cited in Lago and Thompson (1996) and later Sue et al. (1998) further worked on it. The model consisted of six stages:

37.1   Contact stage

At this stage Whites have limited contact with Blacks and are unaware of racism. However, they are influenced by the historical stereotypic belief that Whites are superior and Blacks are inferior, and accept that belief without questioning it. They ignore the differences and maintain an unawareness of the privileges they experience from institutional and cultural racism. Colour-blindness is promoted as positive. I have had White and light-skinned ethnic minority people say to me "We don't notice that you are Black", when I am such a bold shade of black. Some say "Anyway it doesn't make any difference to me. At the end of the day we are all human beings", Eeh ... try living my life. You will certainly feel the pinch and realize that one's skin colour does matter in the present society.

37.2   Disintegration stage

Whites in this stage overidentify with Blacks, developing paternalistic attitudes towards them. They might believe that *"we are all the same and equal"* but they do not treat Blacks as equals. They feel conflicted because they see themselves as non-racist yet ignore the unfairness they witness Blacks being exposed to. They may be torn between being loyal to other Whites and "doing the right thing". However, there is an awareness of their own privileged position, with a sense of guilt or ambivalence about being treated better than other races. For example, when I was a senior staff nurse I had a friend, a junior White nurse, working on the same ward with me. We both decided to enroll on an Introduction to Counselling Skill course. We both applied for funding from our employer at the same time.

The organization offered to pay her fee in full, protected her study days and offered her paid study leave. I was denied the funding and study leave. We had two days off a week, so I used one of my days off to attend college. If I was allocated to work on my college day I was told that it was my responsibility to find a replacement. This happened quite often and I used to ask my husband, who worked on the next ward, to work my shift so I could attend college. Later, I would use my only day off to pay back the shift by working on his ward. The junior nurse felt guilty, uncomfortable, and embarrassed that although we worked on the same ward and attended the same class, she was well supported while I was not. She tried to make it better by looking for a possible explanation to justify the situation, but in the end we had to accept and acknowledge that it was unfair and was not her fault. By acknowledging this we managed to protect our friendship. I was angry about the situation and the following year applied to go on to the Diploma in Counselling, and channelled my anger into fighting for funding. I got it.

37.3   Reintegration stage

Reintegration is seen as regression because of Whites' idealization of their own racial group as superior and the denigration of Blacks as inferior. They selectively distort information and blame Blacks for their difficulties, hence maintaining the racism status quo. For example, when I complained about racism at work the internal investigation team concluded I was "oversensitive" and denied any racism within the organization. They gave a few "reasonable" explanations. I kept being told I was using the "race card" for sympathy; that I was provoking to be treated differently because I was being difficult or expected special treatment; that I must be doing something wrong or that it was my fault because I was unable to ignore things and tended to complain too much. Other Black colleagues seemed not to mind the same treatment, but since I was not accustomed to being abused, the problem was always located in me rather than considering the possibility of institutional racism.

37.4   Pseudo-independence stage

This stage is entered as a result of a painful/insightful incident which forces Whites to review their beliefs and way of thinking. For example, following the unprovoked fatal racial attack on Stephen Lawrence, more Whites began to acknowledge the existence of racism, and institutions became more involved in fighting racism and discrimination. There is an intellectual acceptance of other races as Whites begin to understand and acknowledge their contribution to the existence of racism. A different relationship is built based on how similar Blacks are to them, but these are limited relationships because they still hold on to their subtle sense of superiority over, and intolerance of, other races. For example, I often hear White colleagues prefix their stereotypic prejudices when talking about Black people with, "You are different". Another example is when some Blacks are promoted into higher posts to prove that the organization is not racist, but are not given the authority that comes with the post. Therefore, the discrimination and prejudice can become more subtle and sophisticated—it becomes an intellectual game.

37.5   Immersion-emersion stage

The White person seeks and internalizes a personal definition of Whiteness and racism. At this stage the individual takes a further step in self-exploration, at a deep emotional level, of what it means to be White. Challenging their prejudices, beliefs, and stereotypic thinking, they undertake diversity training that promotes racial self-awareness, or explore this in their own therapy.

37.6   Autonomy stage

Promoting self-awareness reduces feelings of guilt, allowing for acceptance of one's own contribution in perpetuating racism and letting go the belief that Whites are superior, a cut above others. In Autonomy the White person is internally comfortable around issues of difference and the reality of racism. There is an internalization of non-racist racial identity, an acceptance and respect of other races and an appreciation of racial similarities and differences.

Constantine, Juby, and Liang (2001) reflect on Helms' (1984, 1990) statement that healthy White Racial Identity Development occurs when Whites abandon racist attitudes and move towards a non-racist identity. Kernahan and Wolfgram (2003) state that Tatum (1997) identified two developmental tasks for Whites:

a. abandoning individual racism
b. recognizing and opposing cultural and institutional racism.

While these stages of development are helpful in challenging thinking, they might also encourage complacence, because White colleagues can use their training in diversity, or the fact that their friends or partners are Black, as a reason why they cannot be racist. Achieving Autonomy does not mean one doesn't need to think about these issues any more. I believe some people who have reached the Autonomy stage can regress to earlier stages (for example, back to Contact stage) as they witness racism but are too scared to get involved. They become blind to cultural and institutional racism.

While the Racial Identity Development Model stages are useful in reflecting on dynamics that might be taking place, I still prefer the psychoanalytic view that one's upbringing influences the present interactions and relationships. For example, some Whites treat Blacks with respect and appreciation because they were brought up to respect other people and not because they have gone through the stages of developing a White Racial Identity. I believe racism and racist attitudes are a result of what one internalized from within the family and the society one is brought up in. These behaviours are then replayed in adult life.

CHAPTER THIRTY EIGHT

Psychoanalytical interpretation of racism

Winnicott (1984, p. 132) states, "in psychotherapy nothing really new ever happens; the best that can happen is something that was not completed in an individual's development originally becomes to some extent completed at a late date, in the course of the treatment".

The basis of my research is that the experiences we go through in later life are simply a repetition of what began in our early formative years. Our preoccupation with certain issues is an attempt to understand or communicate early childhood experiences for which, being pre-verbal, we had no words.

For example, in the research questionnaire (Appendix 3) question 14 is a vignette about Mr. Smith, who walked into the consulting room and said "… there is no point of sitting down because I am racist and you are Black".

According to the White Identity Development Model Mr. Smith would be seen as in stage three (reintegration, hostility towards Blacks) and by agreeing to work with him the therapist could be perceived as suffering from "Uncle Tom's syndrome" for being a fool who tolerates abuse.

However, in psychoanalytic thinking Mr. Smith's behaviour is understood as a meaningful communication. His problem is not with the therapist's skin colour. He is talking to himself about himself. He wants the therapist to understand that there is something about him that is not acceptable, that cannot be sat with. His only way of making the therapist understand how he feels is by projecting his feelings of rejection, humiliation and vulnerability into the therapist (transference), thus making the therapist experience how he feels (countertransference).

When the therapist picked up these unconscious communications and interpreted them, Mr. Smith was able to talk about the pain of his rejection by his father because he was born with a strawberry birth mark across his face which was referred to as a "skin condition". Mr. Smith has carried this rejection within himself (internalized rejection). When he saw the therapist he feared rejection so he became his rejecting father and turned the therapist into himself—the rejected object. Himself rejected because of his "skin condition" or skin colour (strawberry mark), he was now rejecting the other because of her skin colour. By offering to work with him the therapist showed she could survive his rage and he could trust her to contain him.

For Mr. Smith the therapist's skin colour became a powerful point of connection with her. He could talk about rejection in a racist register because it provided him with some power that allowed verbal articulation which, with skilled help, he was able to connect back to the pre-verbal vulnerable child unable to articulate his experience of rejection.

Mr. Smith was in therapy for four years and continuously worked to understand his racist attitude. In one session a group member talked about the group being like a family. Mr. Smith objected, saying the therapist could never be his mother.

"For a start she is Black and my mother is White," he said.

"How does it feel to have a Black mother?" the therapist responded.

After a long silence he answered, "You would have made a better mother than my own mother".

That could be seen as progression to autonomy (acceptance of similarities), but when Mr. Smith was threatened with separation from the group he regressed, once again showing racial hostility. For example, the organization changed its treatment time to eighteen months, so Mr. Smith, who had been in therapy for four years, was given his leaving date. He experienced that as rejection and the racist language returned.

"This is not your country, who do you think you are to tell me what to do? Go back to your country!"

This clinical example illustrates how one can regress to an earlier stage in the racial identity development depending on one's experience at a given time.

Looking at Kohut's theory of self-psychology, Mr. Smith's traumatic rejection by his father resulted in his failure to alter his grandiose self and the idealized self. Mr. Smith idealized his father and his ideas and feelings needed to be "empathically mirrored" for the grandiose self to be modified into a mature capacity for self-approval, self-nurturing and healthy ambition. Unable to provide this, his father rejected him, resulting in failure in the development of self-object, hence Mr. Smith's continued display of grandiose behaviour.

At the age of four Mr. Smith's parents divorced and he blamed his mother (the bad denigrated object) for failing to be an ideal wife who could hold on to the father (the good idealized object).

Kohut (1971, p. 28) cited in Wallis and Poulton (2001, pp. 46–47) states that: "… if the child experiences traumatic disappointments in the admired adult, then the idealised parent imago, too, is retained in its unaltered form, is not transformed into tension-regulating psychic structure, does not attain the status of an accessible introject, but remains an archaic, transitional self-object that is required for the maintenance of narcissistic homeostasis".

Kohut states that in the treatment of narcissistic personalities this grandiose self and the idealized parent imago are encountered in transference, as in Mr. Smith perceiving the Black therapist as unworthy to sit down with him. During the course of therapy the self-object transferences were worked through in the group's and the therapist's relationship with Mr. Smith, who continuously set up the therapist to reject him by pushing boundaries, sometimes involving others. For example, after one group session Mr. Smith seduced some group members into going to his house for a birthday party—challenging the therapist's authority of no contact outside the group. The therapist was robust enough to reinforce the boundaries and kept interpreting his behaviour without rejecting or humiliating him. The group began to reflect and understand its own behaviour in connection to his dynamics, their own individual dynamics and those of the group as a whole. The consequences of boundary-pushing had a painful impact on the group as a whole as two members ended up fighting, and Mr. Smith began to understand and appreciate the need for boundaries. He started to care about how his behaviour was affecting the group and settled down to work, but it took some months to process the issues and feelings evoked by breaking both individual and group boundaries.

Mr. Smith had tested the therapist's resilience and felt he could trust her and the group to contain him without the fear of rejection. He began to get in touch with his anger with his father for leaving him and his fear that his father might have rejected the family because of his skin condition. That was the pain and the fear he carried within, and when he could not bear it he projected the burden of the rejection onto his unfailing available mother, whom he trusted to survive his rage. Later he projected these difficult feelings onto the group, which contained them for him before processing them. As he started taking back his projections his relationship with his mother began to change, and by the time he was ready to leave the group Mr. Smith had developed a different relationship with his mother. He had great respect for her and appreciated what she had done for him.

Winnicott introduced the concept of the good-enough mother who is able to hold and contain (Bion) her infant. He talked about the importance of a "holding environment" for the infant, whereby mother's attunement mirrors the child's inner experience. The child assimilates or internalizes these mirrored experiences, which in turn establish the foundation and structure of the self. As the child matures the mother becomes less preoccupied with mirroring, facilitating progress through the critical stages of separation and differentiation (Winnicott, 1949, 1958).

Kernberg believed that identity is built from identification with, and internalization of, a relationship with an object instead of the object itself. The relationship between the child and the object is partially determined by the affect tone (libidinal versus aggressive) the child brings into the interaction. Internalized objects will be experienced as good or bad depending on the tone in the interaction. Kernberg states that the ego, the superego and the unconscious are derived from internalization of good and bad objects. The ego comes into being through the use of introjection for defensive purposes; superego is comprised of early primitive introjected images and integrated images of ideal object and realistic parental demands and prohibitions. The unconscious is made up of "rejected introjection and identification systems" (Kernberg, 1975, p. 35).

Winnicott (1950, 1958) believed that a child who internalizes a "bad relationship" between his parents may behave as if "possessed" by the quarrelling parents. This child learns to engineer fights with those around him by engaging the real external "badness" as a projection of what was bad within himself.

Hinshelwood (1994, p. 97) states that: "If objects are internalized in a process that is angry and hostile—that is, with phantasies of aggressive biting and tearing to pieces, and so on—then the state of the internal world is persecutory and dominated by hostile internal objects".

Lacan's theory focuses on the "mirror stage" between six and eighteen months, a time a child recognizes its own image in the mirror. Since the infant sees its image every time it looks in the mirror it believes this ever-present mirror image to be a representation of who he is. A parallel is drawn with the introjected mother, who is also unfailingly ever-present. Construction of the mirror-image is also derived from infantile narcissism, most evident in the child's delight when viewing his or her reflected image. Lacan believes that the moment the infant is expressing excitement at seeing itself in the mirror is the moment of the "libidinal dynamism" of narcissism, and narcissism is the foundation of all identifications because the individual sees part of himself reflected in relations to others (Lacan, 1977, p. 12).

CHAPTER THIRTY NINE

Qualitative methodology

39.1   The research

While working on this research I found the following definition from Nelson et al., (1992, p. 4) cited in Denzin and Lincoln (2000, p. 7) quite grounding:

> "Qualitative research is an interdisciplinary, transdisciplinary, and sometimes counterdisciplinary field .... Qualitative research is many things at the same time. It is multiparadigmatic in focus. Its practitioners are sensitive to the value of the multimethod approach. They are committed to the naturalistic perspective and to the interpretive understanding of human experience ...".

This definition captures the process this research took me through, the excitement about what I was finding and the fear of being overwhelmed by "many things at the same time". It was orgasmic surrendering to the intense experience somehow out of one's control yet needing to be interpreted and understood from various standpoints.

I took the post-positivism stance of using multiple methods as a way "of capturing as much of reality as possible" using several methods:

questionnaires, vignettes, a training video and face-to-face interviews (Tindall, 1994). This enabled me to collect data from various sources so that I could use triangulation by looking from a range of standpoints, scrutinizing for consistency and contradictions, checking and double-checking the collected data. Tindall, citing Reason and Rowan (1981, p. 247), states that: "The validity of research is much enhanced by systematic use of feedback loops and by going around the research cycle several times".

I was aware that this research was born of personal experiences and interests. It is also an emotive topic and to get the best out of it I used personal reflexivity (Tindall, 1994) which enabled me to explain the context of my ideas and my position in the debate of the impact of skin colour. I felt confident that the psychological work I did on myself in my analysis, particularly around racial experiences, would enable me to be relatively objective, and containing of the participants. I also relied on my supervisor, my psychologist friend and a group analyst colleague to give me constructive feedback as I progressed.

Tindall (1994, p. 150) cites other researchers who have used personal reflexivity: Callaway (1981, p. 470), talking about the use of "ourselves as our own sources", Marshall (1984, p. 190) in *Women Managers: Travellers in a Male World*, Kitzinger's (1987, 1993) work on feminism and lesbianism, Holloway's (1989) work on the meanings of gender in adult heterosexual relations and Oakley's *Sociology of Housework* (1985).

Being a group analyst helped in framing my interview questions in such a way as to give trainees the freedom and security to speak about their own experiences (Parker, 2005).

39.2   Method

39.2.1   The three-phase creative cycle

I followed Kelly's (1955) three-phase creativity cycle cited in Tindall (1994, p. 144).

Phase one: circumspection—I involved my team in trying out the research tools. It was useful in highlighting blind spots and I used their feedback to improve the effectiveness of my tools.

Phase two: pre-emption—I worked with four people: my supervisor, an ex-manager, a colleague group analyst, and my psychologist friend. They helped me to be more focused but it was difficult at times because we did not always agree.

Phase three: control—I tested the questionnaires on other group therapists, counsellors, and psychologists within my department. However, since there was only one black therapist I invited the administrator to join in so that I had feedback from another Black person's perspective.

I used these three phases in designing the research tools—the questionnaire, interview schedule, consent form, information sheet, and training video. Some of this work is discussed under design and procedure. Here is the feedback I received at phase one of designing the research questionnaire (Appendix 3):

Therapeutic intervention service team feedback

1. Question 4. Ethnicity
Initially I had planned to use the tick-a-box system we use at work but it provoked a discussion around where one places oneself—where does one belong? The tick-a-box forces one to fit into a category and it was felt that it would be more interesting to let the participants decide on how they see themselves.

A Black colleague said she felt uncomfortable thinking of herself as Black British because she felt disloyal to her country of birth—Nigeria. This lead to another lengthy discussion on ethnicity. A man of mixed heritage (Irish/ Caribbean) felt disloyal to his West Indian side; a Scottish/ English man was not happy about being classified as White British and an English man felt comfortable with the White British classification but thought that it was boring. In the end I cancelled the tick-a-box option and decided to let participants make their own choice of how they describe their ethnicity.

It was suggested that I add a question to pick up the ethnicity of the parents because one therapist thought that would allow for more background information about their diversity. She saw herself as White British but her parents were Jewish.

2. Question 8a
My colleagues recommended that I change *Do you ever discuss issues of skin colour?* to *Have you ever discussed issues of skin colour?*

3. Questions 8b
provoked a passionate discussion. Some requested that I take out neighbours because they felt that nobody talks to their neighbours about issues of one's skin colour. However, a man of mixed heritage said that he engages in lengthy discussions with his White neighbours because his neighbour's wife was seriously assaulted by a Black man and they wanted to make sense of it. I talk to my neighbour of mixed-heritage, about the whiteness of our neighbourhood seen in the local culture and we exchange our experiences of racism. With my White neighbour at the back we share recipes and I offer her my Zimbabwean garden produce, and with my White neighbour on my right we engage in "polite"

252 RACISM AND CULTURAL DIVERSITY

conflicts due to cultural differences, for example different views about the value of the ornamental trees—to his horror, I chopped mine down and replaced them with fruit-bearing trees. In Zimbabwe a village home is surrounded by an orchard, barren trees are left to grow wild in the forests while the beautiful mauve Jakaranda trees adorn the avenues of Harare, the capital city.

At my allotment I talk to two old Irishmen—John and Tommy—about my husband's lack of green fingers, and they compensate for their kinsman's hatred of gardening and redeem their tribe by helping me and encouraging me. My Jamaican neighbour, who has lived in this country for fifty-five years, talks about how he is made to feel more Jamaican in the United Kingdom and more English in Jamaica, where he is referred to as the "queen's mad child" because he seems to be rushing about all the time while everyone else takes it slow and easy. We also exchange recipes, for example how to cook pumpkin leaves. My White English neighbours, a couple, talk about their admiration of my balancing act of carrying my grandson on my back, a pumpkin on my head and a *tsero*/basketful of pumpkin leaves/maize in my arms. They are fascinated by the various crops I grow—English sweet corn, Jamaican maize, Ghanaian maize, maroon pop corn and Zimbabwean maize (*chibange*). Their attempts to tell the difference between the different varieties of corn fascinate me.

After a lengthy discussion I decided to include neighbours in the question.

4. Question 10

Stated, "*In a therapeutic relationship, do you think the counsellor and client of different skin colour can achieve a deeper understanding of the issues they are working on?*"

It was suggested that I change deeper to deep. However, some felt uncomfortable with this question but could not put their finger on why.

5. Questions 11a and 12a

My colleagues reacted to this exercise by rebelling, either by putting the same number for all statements instead of rating them. Others wrote comments of irritation curtained by jokes that made it difficult to peep into their unconscious reactions. Nobody was clear about why they reacted to those two questions the way they did.

6. Question 13

It was suggested that I add this important question: *What anxieties do you have when you are about to meet a client of a different skin colour to yourself?*

7. Other issues that came up

Some of the interesting discussions were about how White colleagues said they could tell that the questionnaire was designed by a Black person because of the language.

One White member reported feeling defensive when answering the questionnaire. She stated that when seeing a client she wants to convey that she

QUALITATIVE METHODOLOGY 253

is not racist and that she is trustworthy. However, she acknowledged that this could be unhelpful as it felt defensive. Her feedback was useful to me because it emphasized the importance of debriefing after the research to mop up feelings evoked during the research.

Another White member said that skin colour is a Black preoccupation. On further exploration it was concluded that Whites avoid talking about skin colour because it makes them feel like racists.

A Black member felt strongly that skin colour runs deeper for a Black person than the superficial seen by Whites as it represents everything—oppression, racism, slavery, history, colonization, social, economical and political injustices.

We also looked at the paradox of skin colour which is just skin deep yet the consequences go deeper penetrating into the heart.

39.2.2 The research tools

I followed Kelly's (1955) three phases in designing the letter to participants, the information sheet, the research schedule and the consent form. When the first draft was ready I piloted it on my work colleagues—three White therapists, one mixed-heritage therapist and a Black administrator. On completion of further work in response to their feedback, I distributed the tool to the rest of the team for final comments before I was satisfied that it was ready for use.

Here are the final copies of the research tools:

i. Letter to the participants

Letter to the participant

Dear,

Thank you for offering to participate in the research entitled *"Can Psychotherapy Penetrate Beyond Skin Colour?"*
I am enclosing the following information for you:

- **Information sheet**—it tells you about the research. It states the aim, explains about the participants, confidentiality and the method to be used in carrying out this research.
- **The consent form**—draws your attention to what you are assigning yourself for and it explains about your right to withdraw from the research. It is important that I receive the signed consent form prior to your participation in the research.
- **Research questionnaire** (Appendix 3)—Can you please complete the questionnaire prior to attending the Video Day and bring it with you?

On the Video Day you will be given the second questionnaire. You will be asked to pick a number that you are expected to write on both questionnaires so as to match the two questionnaires by the same person. You then hand in the first questionnaire and take the second one with you. The second questionnaire will be collected on the day you attend your face-to-face interview. The interview dates and the group debriefing date will be arranged on the Video Day.

Thank you.
Yours sincerely,
MJ

ii.   Information sheet

Information sheet

Research title: Can psychotherapy penetrate beyond skin colour?

The Aim:
To explore some of the factors that influence change in a counsellor's ability to work with someone of a different skin colour.

The research will investigate trainee counsellors' attitudes, level of self-awareness, and qualities considered important in a counsellor. I hope to explore connections between talking about a subject and being more aware of factors that improve the therapeutic relationship between people of different skin colour.

The participants:
The participants are trainee counsellors from four different WPF Therapy training groups. They are of different skin colour and mixed gender.

Confidentiality:
The participants will be expected to write their age, gender, ethnicity, and their parents' countries of origin. Some people might consider this an invasion of their privacy, however, this information is important to this research but it will not be used to identify who they are. Should a participant be concerned about their identity being uncovered, for example if he/she is the only Black/White person or the only woman/man and if he/she thinks it would prejudice his/her response he/she has the choice to withdraw from the research.

At the beginning of the research the participants will pick a number from a container and that is the number they will write on both questionnaires so that we can match the two questionnaires.

There is an optional activity that involves a face-to-face interview. Participants are asked to make a decision about this before they join the research. However, they are allowed to change their minds should they so wish.

All information collected will be handled confidentially. The data collected will be kept on my USB Mass storage device and will not be disclosed to unauthorized persons.

WPH Therapy will not be involved in the actual research, but they will get the report of the findings.

Method:

1. Participants will complete a consent form before joining the research.
2. Participants will pick a number they will use right through the research.
3. Participants will complete the first questionnaire.
4. A thirty-minute video will be shown and the participants will complete the second questionnaire.
5. This will be followed by a thirty-minute individual face-to-face audio-recorded interview.
6. When all the participants have been interviewed they will be invited to join a group debriefing. During the debriefing the participants will be given time to share their experience of the research. It will not be a structured space but a facilitated space for them to explore issues raised during the research so that they leave the research feeling supported and grounded by the experience. They can also decide whether they would like to know about the findings and how they would like to be informed.

iii.   Research poster

If we can become more aware and accepting of our unconscious/internalized racism, will we be more effective in working with difference and in penetrating beyond skin colour?

- The Attachment Theory encourages exploration beyond the external presentation, so what animal do you think you see?
- **Aim:** To explore some of the factors that influence change in a counsellor's ability to work with someone of a different skin colour.
- **Design:** Initial briefing of participants, completion of a questionnaire, watching a video followed by another questionnaire and face-to-face interview, concluding with group debriefing.
- **Proposed analysis**: Identifying and analysing common themes, patterns, differences and similarities in responses.
- Identifying and analysing changes between the first and second questionnaire by the same person and in comparison to the group as a whole.
- Assessing whether any of the changes are significant.
- Evaluating whether the outcome of field research supports or disconfirms the hypothesis.
- Ascertaining which, if any, factors were most significant of any change.
- **Contact: MJ   Email: Phone: iv.   Consent form**

iv.   Consent form

Consent form
Can psychotherapy penetrate beyond skin colour?
Consent to participate in the research
I .... give my consent to participate in this research. I am aware that: a. I will be asked to complete a research questionnaire that requires personal details, such as age, ethnicity, and my parents' country of origin. I have been made aware that this information is important for this research and will not be used for identification of participants' contributions. b. I will watch a video followed by completing another research questionnaire. c. I will participate in the face-to-face interview that will be audio-recorded.

d. I have the right to see the transcript of my interview and to change or delete any sections of it should I so choose.
e. Should I decide to withdraw from the research I have the right to do so at any time.
f. At the end of the research I will be given the space to discuss my experience with other participants.

SIGNED: ....
DATE: ....

v. Questionnaire

When I designed the research questionnaire I used the feedback from the Black History event, my experience as a Black therapist and as a Black patient in a White analytic therapy group, and my findings from the literature research.

The research questionnaire vignette (Appendix 2, Question 14) was important for measuring whether the video was an effective training tool that can influence change in the trainee counsellors' attitudes and the way they work with clients of different skin colour. This was done by comparing their responses before and after watching the training video.

vi. Interview schedule

The participants were asked the following questions:

Interview schedule
Can psychotherapy penetrate beyond the skin?

1. What did you notice about your feelings when completing the questionnaires?
2. How important is the issue of skin colour to you?
3. Are you aware of any changes in your answers between the first and second questionnaire?
4. If there are, do you know what made you change your mind?
5. Since joining the research, do you think your way of viewing some things has changed? If yes, what has changed and why?
6. Do you think it is essential for clients to be seen by a counsellor of the same skin colour as themselves?
7. What personal qualities and counselling skills are required when working with someone of a different skin colour?

8. What specific factors would you bear in mind when you first meet a client of a different skin colour to yours?
9. What do you think about the vignette? Can you suggest any improvements?
10. Would you have worked with Mr. Smith? What factors would have influenced your decision?
11. What do you think about the video? Can you suggest any ways of improving it?
12. Are there any additional issues you would like to see included in this research?

Designing the interview questions followed a similar process of piloting the schedule with five colleagues before testing it with the rest of the team. Here are some of the rationales for asking the questions:

- **Question 1**—was in response to the feedback by one of my colleagues that she had had an emotional response to the questionnaire.
- **Question 2**—gives the participants an opportunity to say more about themselves and their personal experiences around skin colour.
- **Questions 3, 4, 5**—assess whether participants were aware of any changes in the way they answered the questions. If so, they identified what influenced them. This also helped me identify other external factors that influenced the change.
- **Questions 6, 7, 8**—these questions were asked before in the questionnaire but this gave participants an opportunity to elaborate.
- **Questions 10, 11**—require the participants to express an opinion on the vignette and the video. The purpose was to test the hypothesis as the influences to change were identified and discussed.
- **Question 12**—aims at involving participants in influencing the future of this research by identifying what could have been missed out or how the research could be further developed.

vii.   Video presentation
Initially I wanted to use the video of my presentation at the first Black History event because of its effectiveness in raising racial awareness by exploring similarities in the development of Black and White children from birth to adulthood and linking it to racial experiences. Unfortunately, the sound was poor because the oversensitive microphone had picked up noise from construction work outside the room,

so I decided to shoot another video. I rewrote the presentation and included the audience's responses. I also built in long pauses so that research participants could respond and reflect on their own personal responses. I reduced the number of slides so that the presentation lasted exactly thirty minutes, including a three-minute demonstration at the end. Here is the explanation of the video slides (Appendix 2):

Video presentation
• *Slide* 1—Introduces the Black History event.
• *Slide* 2—Explains a group activity in which I asked the participants to describe me in one word.
• *Slide* 3—Looks at the list of the words used to describe me.
• *Slide* 4—Highlights the words avoided—**black, fat, short.**
• *Slides* 5 *and* 6—*What do you see when you look at me?* A poem I wrote for the Black History event.
• *Slides* 7 *and* 8—Explains the rationale for choosing the lion logo.
• *Slide* 9—Shows a picture of a kitten looking in a mirror seeing a lion. This picture was bought at a South African market and the illustrator is unknown.
• *Slides* 10 *to* 20—Explain child development stages from infancy to adulthood and how these early experiences might link with racial experiences in adulthood.
• *Slide* 21—Explains the relationship between the internal and external worlds.
• *Slide* 22—Explains the derogatory racial words some people use.
• *Slide* 23—Was accompanied by a three-minute video demonstration. This is the only part from the original presentation that was put in because it was important to hear the audience's reaction. I walk in carrying a baby on my back. I compare my role as a psychotherapist to that of a mother and explain the intuitive, intimate bond I have with my group members to the one I have with my baby and how I am attuned to its different cries and understand the meaning of each cry. I then ask the audience to pay attention to their reaction to my next move and to pay attention to their first thought and feeling. I take the baby off my back and reveal a blonde white doll. The surprise that the doll is white is loud. I comment that if this is the reaction to me and a white doll then surely a similar reaction happens when a Black therapist sees a White client and vice versa. This is the mother/baby scene that is captured on the front cover of this book. What was your reaction?

CHAPTER FORTY

Procedure

40.1 Recruiting

I planned to recruit four volunteer participants from each of the four training year groups. I met with the WPF Therapy programme managers and a student representative to discuss the best ways of recruiting participants. Since I facilitated the experiential group of half of Mode A first year trainees we agreed to exclude all Mode A first years.

Initially I circulated the research poster and information sheet via the programme managers and the student representative. The response was poor. I met again with the programme managers and they arranged for me to talk directly to the trainees for ten minutes at the end of their last seminars. The response was more positive, and to those interested I gave an envelope containing a letter to the participants, the information sheet and the research questionnaire.

40.2 The participants

Fourteen trainees volunteered to participate in the research but one dropped out at the beginning of the research. The thirteen participants who completed consisted of ten women and three men. Here are their details:

Number	Gender	Age	Ethnicity	Parents	Religion
1	Female	38	White British	White British	None
2	Female	56	White British	White British	C/E
3	Female	38	White British	White British	Christian
4	Female	40	British Chinese	English/ Malaysian	Buddhist Viens
5	Female	55	White American	American/ German	Christian
6	Male	45	Black African	African	Christian
7	Female	49	White British	British/ New Zealander	Atheist
8	Female	40	British mixed race	Ghanaian/ English	C/E
9	Female	55	White British	Canadian/ Jewish German	None
10	Male	55	White British	English/ Mexican	C/E
11	Male	32	White British	White British	Christian
12	Female	33	White French	Moroccan/ German	N/A
13	Female	49	White American	Americans	N/A
14	Female	Dropped out			

Figure 1.

I divided the participants into two group:

- **Three Black participants:**   Black British—two women of mixed heritage
  Black African—one man
- **Eleven White participants:**   White British—five women and two men
  White American—two women
  White French—one woman,
  One drop-out

The ages of the participants ranged from thirty-two to fifty-six years with a mean average age of forty-five. All participants are in personal therapy as one of the training requirements.

On recruitment we agreed on dates for viewing the video and that participants would bring back the signed consent forms and the first completed questionnaires.

I set the video in one of the training rooms. On the viewing day I checked their signed consent forms and participants picked an identification number to match their questionnaires and the interview transcripts. They collected the second questionnaire and we arranged the interview dates. After completing these formalities participants watched the video. I stayed in the room making notes of our reactions while watching the video. After watching the video participants left the room without any discussion.

The face-to-face interview took place within a week of watching the video. However, some preferred to do it on the same day after watching the video as they were going on holiday. The interviews were carried out in two buildings. When the interviews were completed I wrote to all participants offering two dates for group debriefing.

Invitation to debriefing

Dear participant,

Thank you for participating in this research. I am arranging for a group discussion on Tuesday 12th September from 3 p.m. to 4.30 p.m. or Thursday 14th September from 6 p.m. to 7.25 p.m. It is important that we meet as a large group in order to gain more by sharing the experience of participating in this research.

Attendance is voluntary but considering that it was an emotive research I would appreciate if you could make an effort to attend and make sense of some of the puzzling emotions that might have been experienced, and it is also important to understand that others felt more or less the same.

Looking forward to meeting you again.

Yours sincerely,
MJ

Nobody attended on either day and I only received one apology on the day. Later other participants contacted me with various explanations, expressing a desire to meet again.

CHAPTER FORTY ONE

Research findings: important qualities of a counsellor

41.1   The important qualities of a counsellor

The research Question 11a required the participants to choose six out of fifteen qualities they thought were most important when working with clients of different skin colour to themselves. They ranked them from 1 to 6 starting with 1 as the most important scoring 6 points and the sixth choice scoring one point. Here are the findings of the total combined scores from all year groups of the qualities they consider most important:

a.   Before training

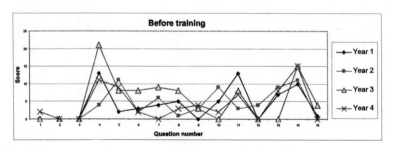

Figure 1.

1st Item 14: Having worked on one's own feelings around separation, abandonment, alienation, loss, rejection scored 51 points.

2nd Item 4: Ability to tolerate not knowing scored 49 points.

3rd Item 11: Ability to make use of the transference and counter-transference scored 31 points.

4th Item 5: Sensitivity to cultural variations scored 30 points.

5th Item 13: Ability to convey empathic understanding scored 24 points.

6th Item 7: Capacity to separate own issues from the client's scored 19 points.

b. After training

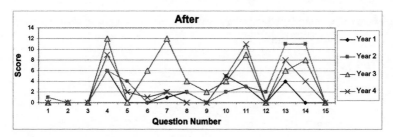

Figure 2.

After training Items 4, 13, 11, 14, 7 remained in top six.

Item 10: Being non-judgmental joined at 6th position.

c. Individual year groups

Here are the individual findings for each year group:

i. 1st years

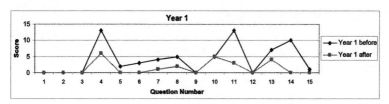

Figure 3.

The first years chose the following as the top six most important qualities in a counsellor working with someone of a different colour:

1st Item 4: Ability to tolerate not knowing.
2nd Item 11: Ability to make use of the transference and counter-transference.
3rd Item 14: Having worked on one's own feelings around separation, abandonment, alienation, loss, rejection.
4th Item 13: Ability to convey empathic understanding.
5th joint position:

- **Item 8:** Ability to be honest in supervision.
- **Item 10:** Being non-judgmental.

After training Items 4, 10, 13, 11, 8 remained in top six.

- **Item 7:** Capacity to separate own issues from the client's joined at 6th position.

ii. 2nd years

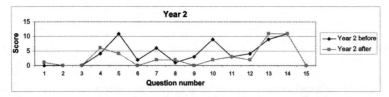

Figure 4.

The second years chose the following as the top six most important qualities in a counsellor working with someone of a different colour:

1st joint position:

- **Item 5:** Sensitivity to cultural variations.
- **Item 14:** Having worked on one's own feelings around separation, abandonment, alienation, loss, rejection.

3rd joint position:

- **Items 10:** Being non-judgmental.
- **Item 13:** Ability to convey empathic understanding.

5th joint position:

- **Item 4:** Ability to tolerate not knowing.
- **Item 12:** Capacity to be neutral.

After training Item 13, 14, 4, 5 remained top six.

> **Item 11:** Ability to make use of the transference and counter-transference joined at 5th position.

6th joint position:

- **Items 7:** Capacity to separate own issues from the client's.
- **Item 8:** Ability to be honest in supervision.

iii. 3rd years

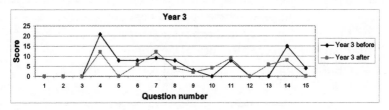

Figure 5.

The third years chose the following:

> **1st Item 4:** Ability to tolerate not knowing
> **2nd Item 14:** Having worked on one's own feelings around separa-tion, abandonment, alienation, loss, rejection.
> **3rd Item 7:** Capacity to separate own issues from the client's.

4th joint:

- **Item 6:** Ability to establish boundaries while aware of the power issues within the counsellor/client relationship.
- **Item 8:** Ability to be honest in supervision.
- **Item 5:** Sensitivity to cultural variations.

After training Items 4, 7, 14, 6 remained in the top six.

> **Item 11:** Ability to make use of the transference and counter-transference joined in 3rd position.
> **Item 13:** Ability to convey empathic understanding joined in 6th position.

iv. 4th years

The fourth years chose the following:

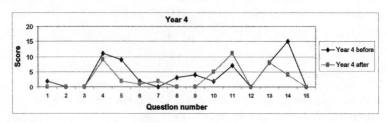

Figure 6.

1st Item 14: Having worked on one's own feelings around separation, abandonment, alienation, loss, rejection.
2nd Item 4: Ability to tolerate not knowing.
3rd Item 5: Sensitivity to cultural variations.
4th Item 13: Ability to convey empathic understanding.
5th Item 11: Ability to make use of the transference and counter-transference.
6th Item 9: Willingness to learn about the client's culture.

After training Items 11, 4, 13, 14, 5, remained in top six.

Item 10:   Being non-judgmental came in 4th position.
6th joint position:

- **Item 5:** Sensitivity to cultural variations.
- **Item 7:** Capacity to separate own issues from the client's.

CHAPTER FORTY TWO

Research findings: important awareness qualities of a counsellor

Question 12a was similar to Question 11a but it listed awareness qualities necessary for a counsellor working with someone of a different skin colour to themselves. Here are the findings:

a. Before training

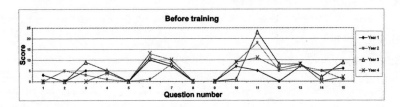

Figure 1.

    1st Item 11: An awareness of one's own prejudices about people of a different colour scored 57 points.

    2nd Item 6: An awareness that skin colour and culture are not the same scored 35 points.

    3rd Item 7: An awareness of the importance of family structures/ beliefs/values and their impact on the individual.

4th Item 13: An awareness of one's blind spots/weaknesses scored 30 points.

5th Item 10: An awareness of the impact of cultural practices, traditions, customs, beliefs and values on one's identity scored 26 points.

6th Item 12: An awareness of stereotypical beliefs around different cutures scored 19 points.

b. After training

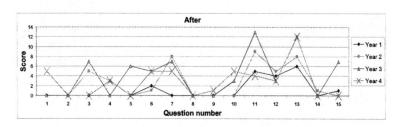

Figure 2.

After training Items 13, 11, 7, 12, 6 remained in top six.

Item 3: An awareness of the impact of loss on depression, formation of conscience and development of empathy join in 6th position.

a. The significant differences

Here are the significant differences observed among the four year groups:

i. 1st years

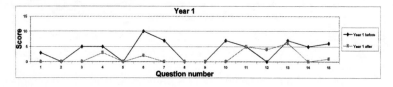

Figure 3.

The first years chose the following:

1st Item 6: An awareness that skin colour and culture are not the same.

2nd Item 13: An awareness of one's blind spots/weaknesses.

3rd Item 10: An awareness of the impact of cultural practices, traditions, customs, beliefs, values, on one's identity.

4th Item 7: An awareness of the importance of family structures/ beliefs/values and their impact on the individual.

5th Item 15: An awareness of the various transitions a client is having to make.

6th joint position

- **Item 11:** An awareness of one's own prejudices about people of a different colour.
- **Item 14:** An awareness of the importance of family history to one's identity.
- **Item 4:** An awareness of the impact of the processes of immigration, racism, discrimination, and harassment on mental health.
- **Item 3:** An awareness of the impact of loss on depression, formation of conscience, and development of empathy.

After training Items 13, 11, 4, 6, 15 remained in top six.

Item 12: An awareness of stereotypical beliefs around different cultures joined in 3rd position.

ii. 2nd years

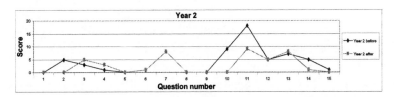

Figure 4.

The second years chose the following differences:

1st Item 11: An awareness of one's own prejudices about people of a different colour.

2nd Item 10: An awareness of the impact of cultural practices, traditions, customs, beliefs, values, on one's identity.

3rd Item 7: An awareness of the importance of family structures/ beliefs/values and their impact on the individual.

4th Item 13: An awareness of one's blind spots/weaknesses.

5th joint:

- **Items 2:** An awareness of the impact of "culture shock", "survivor's guilt"
- **Item 12:** An awareness of stereotypical beliefs around different cultures
- **Item 14:** An awareness of the importance of family history to one's identity

After training Items **11, 13, 7, 12,** remained in the top six.

Item 3:   An awareness of the impact of loss on depression, formation of conscience and development of empathy joined in 4th position and,

Item 4:   An awareness of the impact of the processes of immigration, racism, discrimination, and harassment on mental health joined in 6th position.

iii. 3rd years

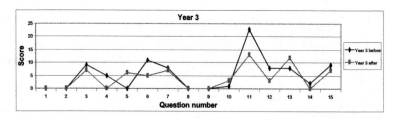

Figure 5.

The third years chose the following:

1st Item 11:   An awareness of one's own prejudices about people of a different colour.

2nd Item 6:   An awareness that skin colour and culture are not the same.

3rd Item 3:   An awareness of the impact of loss on depression, formation of conscience, and development of empathy.

4rd Item 15:   An awareness of the various transitions a client is having to make.

5th joint position:

- **Item 7:** An awareness of the importance of family structures/beliefs/values and their impact on the individual.
- **Item 12:** An awareness of stereotypical beliefs around different cultures.
- **Item 13:** An awareness of one's blind spots/weaknesses.

After training Items 11, 13, 3, 7, 15, remained in top six.

> **Item 5:** Awareness that one treats everyone the same joined in at 6th position.

iv. 4th years

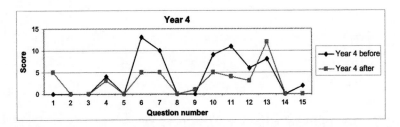

Figure 6.

The fourth years chose the following:

> **1st Item 6:** An awareness that skin colour and culture are not the same.
> **2nd Item 11:** An awareness of one's own prejudices about people of a different colour.
> **3rd Item 7:** An awareness of the importance of family structures/beliefs/values and their impact on the individual.
> **4th Item 10:** An awareness of the impact of cultural practices, traditions, customs, beliefs, values, on one's identity.
> **5th Item 13:** An awareness of one's blind spots/weaknesses.
> **6th Item 12:** An awareness of stereotypical beliefs around different cultures.

After training Items 13, 6, 7, 10, 11 remained in top six.

> **Item 1:** An awareness of Attachment Theory joined in 2nd position.

CHAPTER FORTY THREE

Analysis of predictable findings

43.1 The difference between the first and second questionnaires

There were some changes in answers between the first and second questionnaires. In the first questionnaire answers were more generalized, in the second they were more focused in the present, the first more "textbook", the second reflected more on personal experiences. For example, one answer was about the personal experience of being bullied at school and how it would help in understanding some Blacks' experiences.

There were more noticeable changes in the quality of the verbal responses to Question 14b: *How would you have responded*? In the first questionnaire the responses tended to be defensive, "you feel the need to speak to a qualified counsellor", and sometimes provocative/ rejecting "I'm not your best friend" and in the second questionnaire these phrases were taken out.

In the first questionnaire some responses were long-winded (anxiety?) and in a potentially aggressive situation it is more containing to say less: however, in the second questionnaire most of the longer responses had been shortened.

A few who had given vague responses in the first questionnaire said more in the second: for example: "Explore further" in the first questionnaire became "I should like to think that I could have worked with his opening remark but I am not sure".

On the other hand a few did not change their first responses; they just wrote "see previous questionnaire". Most of these participants had given a well-thought-out first response.

Only one participant's second response was more defensive in comparison to the initial response.

43.2   The connection between talking and effectiveness

In Question 8 participants were asked to identify the people they discuss issues of skin colour with and how often. Figure 1 shows the result.

Group	Often	Sometimes	Never	Total
1. Friends	Both – 3, 6, 7, 9, 16 Same – 0 Different **Total = 5**	Both – 1, 2, 4, 12, 20 Same – 10, 15 Different – 13 **Total = 8**	Both – 0 Same – 0 Different – 0 **Total = 0**	**13** **0 never**
2. Family	Both – 6 Same – 9 Different – 0 **Total = 2**	Both – 4, 7, 13 Same – 1, 2, 3, 12, 15, 16 Different – 10 **Total = 9**	Both – 3, 20 Same – 0 Different – 0 **Total = 2**	**11** **2 never**
3. Neighbours	Both – 9 Same – 0 Different – 0 **Total = 1**	Both – 6 Same – 0 Different – 1, 7, 9 **Total = 4**	Both – 15, 16 Same – 2, 10, 12 Different – 3, 13, 20 **Total = 8**	**5** **8 never**
4. Your Patient	Both – 0 Same – 0 Different – 6 **Total = 1**	Both – 3, 6 Same – 0 Different – 9, 7, 10, 13, 15 Unspecified – 2 **Total = 8**	Both – 0 Same – 1, 12, 16 Different – 7 **Total = 4**	**9** **4 never**

5. Work colleagues	Both – 10, 12, 16	Both – 2, 6, 7, 9, 15, 20	Both – 0	**11** **0 never**
	Same – 3	Same – 0	Same – 0	
	Different – 0	Different – 13	Different – 0	
	Total = 4	**Total = 7**	**Total = 0**	
6. Your therapist	Both – 0	Both – 0	Both – 0	**8** **4 never**
	Same – 6	Same – 3, 10, 15	Same – 2, 9, 12, 16	
	Different – 0	Different – 7, 13, 20 Unspecified– 2	Different – 0	
	Total = 1	**Total = 7**	**Total = 4**	
7. Your training body	Both – 16	Both – 3, 6, 9, 20	Both – 0	**9** **2 never**
	Same – 0	Same – 4, 15	Same – 12	
	Different – 0	Different – 7, 13	Different –0	
			Unspecified – 2	
	Total = 1	**Total = 8**	**Total = 2**	
8. Other Strangers on the bus		Both – 6 **Total = 1**		**1**

Key
Both—Black and White
Different—People of different skin colour from the participant
Same—People of same skin colour with the participant
The numbers next to both, same and different are the participants'
identification numbers.

Figure 1.

The information in Figure 1 was compared to the responses participants
gave to Question 14b about the vignette: *How would you have responded?*
The findings suggest a link between talking about skin colour and being
able to confidently contain a client expressing racial prejudice. Here are
the findings:

a. Four participants said they did not talk to their therapists, of whom two did not talk to their patients either, and two did not talk to their neighbours. These four participants seemed to struggle most with responding to Mr. Smith. Two were able to acknowledge their fear and not knowing what to do. One stated that because she is White the situation would not arise, therefore did not give a response. Some participants in this group used defensive language, for example "you feel the need to speak to a qualified counsellor". There also seemed to be a sense of guilt in this group, "I'd put a foot wrong" and "I had done something offensive". Three participants out of the whole group did not return their second questionnaires and all three were from this group of four.

b. One participant stated that he talked to his therapist but not to his patients of different skin colour. His response started by acknowledging his fear and not knowing how to respond, but he proceeded to give a response that showed some sensitivity.

c. Three participants stated that they did not talk to their neighbours only. Their responses were confident, direct and containing, using words like, "work together", "I appreciate what you have just said," "you have made such an effort", "you are right". They did not repeat the negativity. However, there was one provocative statement "I'm not your best friend" but it is in the middle of calming words and might not have sounded as provocative as it could standing on its own. Therefore not talking to one's neighbours about skin colour issues seemed not to affect the therapist's confidence in dealing with racial prejudice.

d. Two participants did not talk to their families only. However, one worked with refugees and asylum seekers in "an environment and landscape of being politically correct" and his response was direct, containing, and showed confidence. The other, a religious participant, was less confident but more calming. In the second response she/he said she/he would acknowledge the client's "right to be racist". However, not talking to one's family did not seem to affect the trainee's ability in working with a client expressing racial prejudice.

e. The last three spoke to everyone and one even added an additional category of "strangers". All three showed confidence with direct responses that demonstrated reflective practice of what they would consider, the hypothesis they would think about to "try to tease out" these issues. Their interventions were containing because they clarified boundaries and confidentiality, gave appropriate apology, and established a collaborative working alliance by using words like "work together", and they let Mr. Smith know that he would be involved in the decision-making on how to proceed.

43.3   The gap between theory and practice

Participants chose the *Ability to make use of transference and counter-transference* as one of the top six important qualities in a counsellor. They seemed to have a good grasp of the concept. However, most failed to put that understanding into practice when faced with the situation in the vignette. They experienced the countertransference feelings of fear, anger, aggression and rejection they were picking up from the client but they owned those feelings as their own rather than an unconscious communication they had received. As a consequence of doing this they became angry, frightened and attacking of the counsellor and rejected any identification with her, resulting in failing to hold the client in mind.

43.4   The isolation

There was a sense of isolation experienced by the Black trainees who strongly identified with being Black and by some of the non-British White participants. Here are their reactions to the isolation.

43.4.1   A "militant" Black participant

One Black trainee felt angry about her isolation. She felt she was left to raise "the difficult bits of things that people don't want to raise", such as why diversity was talked about in the last seminar instead of working with difference throughout training. This trainee usually found herself being the only Black person in training, at work and in social environment. She is aware of her difference and that other people feel "uncomfortable" when she raises difficult racial issues, and that makes her feel excluded, rejected, and sad. Being part of the research made her feel "strengthened" by the realization that she did not have to take total responsibility for raising the issue of difference and skin colour with colleagues and other people. The research has been *"quite useful"* in helping her understand that there are other people who are thinking about these issues and that there is work going on even though she does not have contact with them. She comments: "… a video/presentation like that in the training, in our training, would have been very useful, very helpful. It would have allowed or opened up discussion that never happens in the training and that is one thing I do regret, and actually by being part of this research just highlighted for me an isolation which I think I was ignoring … there is isolation in the training that I feel and that's highlighted by doing the research and it is probably the reason why I said I would do it. I was slightly disappointed with the number of people who said that they would take part. Not completely surprised, but disappointed".

43.4.2   A religious Black participant

This participant seemed to lack trust in others and responded to the isolation by denying any difficulties with it. In the questionnaire, when asked whether the issue of skin colour is important to the participant, the participant denied it stating "… I don't think clients are as concerned about colour as counsellors seem to exaggerate".

However, the participant later disclosed a racist incident experienced when having to lead in prayer at a funeral. A relative of the deceased shouted that he was not going to let their relative be buried by a Black person. This participant raised very important but difficult and painful issues of rejection: the need for a Black person to prove him/herself because of the projections placed upon one's skin colour. How can a Black person trust in a racially hostile society? How does one's culture (for example, the Christian faith) affect interactions with clients who evoke aggressive, negative feelings in the counsellor? How can the conflict between these evoked hateful feelings and the religious teachings of love and forgiveness be worked with?

43.4.3   White participants

The isolation was also experienced by some of the White non-British participants who stated that, "it feels institutionally White British … I often feel at odds here too, but you can't tell from looking at me … only when I open my mouth". She described her experience as "different" and "difficult". She also raised the fact that race is not prioritized and that it was "compartmentalized" instead of "being a continual framework throughout all work".

A few like her thought race is not prioritized because WPF Therapy is predominantly White and that "White people and White people very rarely talk about race" but some questioned why, in a situation that is "predominantly White do we need to talk about that? (race)" Therefore, race and a few other differences are left towards the end of every module when "nobody has any energy, and there is nowhere to carry it on to".

43.4.4   Issues of power

Issues of power came into play but mostly in a subtle way. For example:

- A male participant who had worked in production said he did not "hundred percent like the video", its format, the lack of "professional editing", "the content I don't think evoked much in me in comparison to the questionnaire", and that it was "too long" so he switched off halfway through the video because he had had enough.
- A few women balanced the Dictaphone on the edge of their crossed knees, swinging it to and fro. Watching this filled me with anxiety and fear of the Dictaphone falling off and breaking. I found myself asking the question, "Who controls this research?"

CHAPTER FORTY FOUR

Analysis of unpredictable findings

44.1   Kleinian concepts

It was not surprising to see Kleinian concepts of projective identification, splitting, paranoid–schizoid, and depressive positions develop during the process of this research, but what was surprising was how they developed.

44.1.1   Splitting: impact of political correctness

The process of ranking Question 11a and 12a was interesting because it raised the issue of who gets pressurized to be politically correct. There was a split in the reaction of Black and White participants. Most White participants had split the tables into two groups—psychodynamic stance and cultural stance. Having done that, they felt that they had to choose a side—psychodynamic or cultural? Some White participants felt they had to be politically correct instead of sticking to a decision they felt was right. It left them feeling angry, irritated, confused and indignant. In the feedback section of Question 12 most just wrote "no comment". One admitted that he gave short answers in retaliation.

It was only through the face-to-face interviews that I was able to understand their responses to this exercise. Here are some of the White participants' comments about it:

- *It felt like there was a split in the questionnaire. You could either be race conscious, colour conscious or you could be analytically conscious ... (internal world).*
- *I didn't feel comfortable making a hierarchy of numbers in the questionnaire.*
- *Sometimes it felt frustrating having to put things into an order ... .*
- *As the questionnaire progressed, my response was—I don't know what's being asked of me. Confusion about the grading.*
- *I found myself getting quite indignant and irritated by it because there seemed to be two different sorts of answers ... answers about psychodynamic theory ... the other set of answers was to do with political, ideological, cultural sociological kind of contextual things to do with cultural issues ... .*

The Black participants did not comment on the psychodynamic/ cultural split. They seemed unaware of it. They also did not have the same concern of being politically correct and they felt comfortable making their decisions based on what they believed in. However, one Black participant was left reflecting on her personal experience of racism due to her skin tone and how, when she was older, she realized that her skin tone was no different to others but she had "incorporated a feeling of myself as being very different including my race and skin tone".

The other was left with feelings of guilt because the exercise challenged the way she raises, or fails to address, issues of skin colour with her patients. She recalled some "specific incidents" when she missed it and on reflection felt she could have worked with the issue more than she did. The third said the questions were not difficult but did not say more about it.

Here are some of the comments from the Black participants on the same exercise:

- *A challenging exercise but one that made me think about how much social constructs can and do impinge on our internal world and our unconscious. Knowing oneself is, I believe, the key; our work is about two people finding a connection.*
- *Very difficult ... I realised that I was looking at a mixture of personal qualities and openness/honesty in the work rather than the same skin colour.*

I feel that it is of primary importance that the client is seen as a distinct individual rather than typecast by their skin colour.

All participants reported that after seeing the video they found it easier to complete this section of the second questionnaire and that they did not have the same emotional response as before. Here are some of their comments:

- *What I found interesting about your video is that it puts it very firmly within that psychotherapeutic context—skin colour within it you know, and I feel that that is the case.*
- *When ranking the attributes second time I felt more comfortable in writing the psychodynamic ones due to the video and reflecting ... I thought the point in the film we saw was a very good one, it is easy to stereotype Black society as the underprivileged and that is not necessarily the case.*

44.1.2 Paranoid–schizoid position

i. On the same Questions 11a and 12a of the first questionnaire some participants took a paranoid–schizoid position by feeling tricked. For example, "I felt I was being set up for a fall".

ii. The other activity that evoked suspicious/paranoid thoughts was the vignette. Some participants had assumed that the counsellor was White. However, some could play with the discovery of their assumed stereotypical thoughts/beliefs and understood them as introjections from their social environment: "The twist in the tale was very masterful really that it just played into all my culturally determined stereotypical assumptions that by definition ... Ping! my mind goes, right, the counsellor is White, straight away. Of course that is the world I have grown up in".

  On the other hand others could not hide their irritation with this "trick". One suggested that the vignette should have given the full description of the counsellor and spelt it out that she is Black instead of letting the client tell them.

iii. Some participants considered the poor quality of the video another "trick", "a deliberate act that you did not want to show yourself". Others thought my invisibility was a clever "trick" to emphasize the points being raised by the video and that it mirrored the invisibility of Blacks.

44.1.3   Depressive position

Two participants felt sad when they reflected on their answers to Question 8b because, after completing their charts on who and how often they spoke about issues of skin colour, they realized that they did not speak about it as much as they thought they did. They felt sad, "very uncomfortable" and "guilty". One said, "I hadn't thought about things in quite the way the questions forced me to think about things ... the guilt was more that I don't do much thinking about it as perhaps I thought I ought to".

44.2   Supervision

Overall, participants did not choose the *Ability to be honest in supervision* as one of the top six qualities. However, the first-years placed it in fifth position both times and the third years chose it second and not first time while fourth years chose it first time but not second time. In the interview supervision was mentioned once by one participant and in the questionnaire another participant expressed some anger towards supervisors for not enabling them to use supervision effectively.

44.3   White internalization of Black

Again, it was not surprising to find a White participant who internalized her Black nanny but it was surprising considering the small number of participants. It was also surprising to realize how much that internalization affects one's perception of things that might seem obvious to others. For example, the one White participant who was brought up by a Black nanny recalled being interviewed by a psychologist at the age of four because she had made a black doll. She was the only child at her kindergarten who made a black doll and that raised concern. Her father associated with Blacks as equals. She feels that she suffered racism and experienced a "kind of incomprehensible, irrational gap between me and other (White) people ... I can't explain it and I don't know if it's an identification (with Black people)".

On the day she completed her first questionnaire before coming to watch the video, she talked to her therapist about an experience she had talked about "a couple of times before" but for the first time her therapist realized that her nanny was Black.

When watching the video, she related to the discussion on internalization of Black culture by White children brought up by Black nannies and had found it fascinating. However, the demonstration with the white doll left her puzzled because she could not understand why the video audience was excited and had to investigate before realizing that it was because the doll was white and blonde. Other participants had reacted at the same time as the audience—shocked and surprised. One participant commented: "It was a shocking image, and it was really interesting to see a Black woman with a white baby doll child ... something about the physical closeness of having that baby on your back, which very much brought to mind mother images and mother thoughts ...".

On the other hand, to this one participant that close bond between a Black mother figure and a White baby was natural and could be noticed in the way she prefixes her nanny's name with "my" and gets animated when talking about her.

44.4   Groups within groups

When the research started I had two groups, one of White participants, the other of Black participants, but as we progressed more groups emerged within those groups.

44.4.1   White participants identifying with Black culture

This was a group of White participants who closely related to Blacks. One grew up surrounded by Blacks. The other worked and socialized with Blacks and has a child of mixed heritage. They talked about feeling included and identified with the Black culture in their choice of food, music, and the sports teams they support. This group was more comfortable with me, and was fascinated by the research and related to it more personally with stories. We felt comfortable and connected. The language was sometimes metaphoric.

Their response to the research was of enthusiasm. I felt so emotionally connected and seduced that I did not encourage keeping within the time boundary.

44.4.2   Black participant identifying more with White culture

This participant spoke about how, when she was younger, others defined her as different. Her friends were from other cultures but also classified as the "*Other*". Through therapy and self exploration she does not define herself by "*colour*" any more. Talking to her in the interview, she has internalized a White culture and was comfortable and confident about her identity.

I responded warmly to her. Although I felt distantly connected I felt respectful and admired the work she has done on herself.

44.4.3   White group with White identity

The majority of the participants in this group had lived abroad in Africa, St Lucia, Japan, and Mexico. They had personally been in incidents where they were attacked or treated unfairly because of their white skin colour. They experienced how "uncomfortable" and "painful" it was to be different and to be "viewed as less", "an immigrant and culturally inferior" while they viewed themselves as "superior". They either retaliated against the position they found themselves in by disparaging their attackers, "belittling them" or rationalizing, for example by telling themselves it was not as bad as the experiences Blacks go through, or reassuring themselves by thinking that they were the privileged ones. They were more theoretical and studious. They joined the research for personal reasons and were more challenging of me.

I felt attacked at times, but was also fascinated and wanted more of "their wisdom". I identified with their ability to despise and to feel superior. I felt comfortable to push and challenge them more because I knew they could take it. It was an intellectual connection.

44.4.4   Black participants with Black identity

These participants were conscious of being Black and different. In most situations they found themselves the only Black person. One fights for Black recognition and the other finds the complaints about his/her accent more difficult to deal with than those about his/her skin colour. They tended to feel excluded, rejected, and sad.

I identified with their ability to deny any vulnerability by being strong and wanting to fight for their rights or by denying and thinking that they cannot be bothered. I felt protective of them. We shared a love of folk stories. I challenged them but in a more supportive way. I had an emotional connection with them.

44.4.5   White group fearful of racism

This group did not have personal experience of racial attacks but had witnessed Blacks, including friends, being attacked, humiliated, or treated unfairly while they themselves were held in the privileged position. They were left feeling guilty and responsible for what had happened. This group talked about wanting to be liked, and held a fear of the stereotypical ideology, for example being scared of a "bunch of black boys" or "a lot of black people in one place". One talked about being affected by the race riots of the 1960s, the ghettos and the "reported statistics". They worried about what other people might think of them, and had a fear of offending and of being seen as "exploiting" Blacks. Some of them felt uncomfortable being in the minority. They felt isolated, with a sense of not belonging and a wish to identify with Black participants. One joined the research as a way of supporting one of the Black trainees, whom she felt carried the burden of racial difference.

I found myself mirroring them by being careful about how I said what I said and trying hard not to say the wrong thing. I could not push or challenge them.

CHAPTER FORTY FIVE

Reflexive analysis

arker (1994, p. 2) states that a qualitative research is "the interpretative study of a specified issue or problem in which the researcher is central to the sense that is made". Therefore, in order to make better sense of my findings it is necessary to think about my personal position in this research. Baxter, Hughes, and Tight (2001) stress the importance of making one's role and position in the research clear so as to assert ownership and to enable recognition of possible limitations, influences, and biases of one's own perspective.

45.1 As a student and researcher

When I started this research I was scared because I am not an academic: I am a clinician and a creative writer. I had a supervisor who is very academic, and after reading some of his work I was not only impressed but also intimidated. I felt that my research could never be good enough. We talked about it and he was very grounding. He encouraged me to present my research at the university's Research Open Day and that built my confidence, especially as others showed great interest in my research.

Being a creative writer interfered with my role as a researcher because I was continuously seduced into following stories and ended up with too much information. This overwhelmed me and it was difficult to stay focused.

45.2 As a group analyst

I believe that it is what happens during the formative years that also pulls us into the racism food chain and perpetuates it by being racist—including Blacks—or by being victims with secondary gains. My own experience of racism linked with my first experience of being treated unfairly during my formative years. I failed to complain for over three years because the adult experience of racism made me regress to the age of six, where I coped with unfairness by keeping quiet. Through tracing this acceptance of discrimination to its roots in therapy and understanding it, I started dealing with racism in a more mature way.

During my training I was the only Black African trainee in my year group and I was the only Black person in my analytic therapy group among seven White trainees and a White group analyst. Therefore, I understood the isolation and the fears experienced by some of the Black and non-British White participants. My own experience helped me become attuned to the psychological processes taking place for some of the participants. Burman (1994, p. 51) in her chapter on interviewing, suggested responding to and following up issues raised by a participant as an advantage of semi-structured interviewing, as it is more open and flexible. I was able to follow and raise an awareness of their unconscious fears. For example, all participants found the vignette emotionally provoking. The difficult feelings that were expressed were of shock, anger, fear, rejection, and relief that it had not happened to them.

Some participants identified with the counsellor in the vignette and that provoked some anxiety in them which was expressed as anger with the counsellor. For example:

Sample of interview transcript: Projective identification

"... there was something so disrespectful about it on her side. But when I was thinking about it I was thinking—I usually call my clients by their first names. I don't know, it was a difficult situation, I was glad that I wasn't there because I would have been scared ... just when I thought I had got through the hard strip of the questionnaire .... That was a very tough one.

There was a big difference in my opinion in what I wrote for my response between before and after the video. I was more angry with the counsellor the first time ... I felt that the counsellor made too many assumptions in her approach to start with, and that it had kind of gone from nothing, the zero before they had even met, to a potentially violent situation. I thought that the counsellor sort of sparked that a little bit ... I don't think that you should introduce yourself, say to a client by first name without thinking about how they might feel, what their views are about that sort of thing. Also the client is fifty-five and that is even the more reason to be thinking that a person of that generation will be of Mr. This and Miss That. That was the first thing. Of course she didn't know that he was going to have love and hate tattoos, you can't make any assumptions about what those tattoos may or may not mean. But then she was potentially in a very difficult position because he followed her into a private room and then said '*I am a racist*'. It was very odd actually. I just felt somehow this just doesn't feel quite right but I couldn't quite work out what was right, and so what I picked on was the fault I found in the counsellor, I think that was it".

"Was it easier for you to do that?"

"Yes, it was, because I didn't know. There were too many conflicts being presented. I think it was partly because I felt that was a situation that I could very easily be in myself and I would not know what I to do."

"Do you think by looking at what the counsellor did wrong, you were reassuring yourself that you wouldn't do that therefore would stop the situation?"

"Well, I hate to say it but I think you are probably right. I think there is something in that; it was much easier to do that. When I did it the second time, it was a lot easier to see the conflict and to think about the conflict that the client was presenting just in those few minutes. It helped me to find the right words that I might say, or what I might do, but there was a conflict that the client was presenting in everything that he did. I was less concerned about the fact that the counsellor called him 'Jimmy' or 'James' or whatever, which is important, but it is not as important as what else was happening at the time".

"When you imagined yourself in that position, what did you think?"

"I have an expectation that one day something like that will happen. I hope it doesn't, but the reality is that if I carry on doing this kind of work, that it might well happen especially if I work in the National Health Service (NHS), I think. I don't know, there was something about that immediate rejection without even finding out whether the counsellor is any good at what she is supposed to be doing for you, a decision made on the basis of the counsellor's skin colour".

From the above it is clear that the vignette was shocking and had aroused difficult feelings for all trainees. Supervision would have been the appropriate place to process all this, yet no-one thought of taking it to supervision. However, it is difficult to make use of supervision when one is angry or feels unable to trust the supervision space. My experience as a trainee group analyst enabled me to understand the anger and lack of trust in supervisors expressed overtly and covertly by the participants.

As discussed in Part One and Part Two, I lost trust in my supervisor but I was able to talk about it. We made sense of the dynamics taking place and my supervisor created a space for me to experience being vulnerable instead of using my old coping strategies of looking after other people. I hated it but my supervisor was robust enough not to be intimidated by being seen as my persecutor and the racist. I used my personal therapy group to process some of the dynamics evoked in me and my therapy group was not afraid to be politically incorrect, which allowed me to vomit my rage onto them. I gained more by staying with my supervisor and addressing our difficult relationship, and that enabled me to internalize my supervisor's stamina and ability to contain the rage of a frightened person defending against feeling vulnerable by denying his/her dependency on others. This experience enabled me to be sensitive to the participants' silence, frustration and fear concerning their supervision.

45.3   As a Black Zimbabwean woman

My culture and my experience as a Black Zimbabwean woman and a mother influenced the way I conducted this research—for example, in the way I spoke in the video and how I carried the "baby" on my back. In the interview I was quite maternal in the way I contained the participants.

45.4   As an editor

When the participant who had worked in production said he switched off from watching the video because of its poor production, I understood his communication better from my experience as an editor. When I came to the UK I had just left my position as an editor but still had an editor's eye, so when I tried to read the local newspaper I just felt frustrated and irritated because it was so badly edited that I found myself editing it as I read. I felt superior and irritated, so I stopped reading this paper. Therefore, I could relate to this participant's sense of superiority and irritation rather than see it from the historical stand of my superior White master. Achieving this understanding enabled me to admire him and try to look for another meaning to his reaction. If I had taken the historical stand of my White master I would have been irritated (countertransference—picking up his irritation) and dismissed the interaction, resulting in losing the opportunity he had created for seeking another explanation, and that proved to be important.

45.5   As an observer

While observing the participants watch the video I found that my reaction was split depending on the participants' skin colour.

With White participants I felt embarrassed about all the grammatical errors I made in the video, for example when I said "Describe me in one word, describe me *with* one word". Why did I have to repeat the instruction? The worst was when I said, "Here are some of the adjectives and verbs used to describe me". I could hear my teacher, Teacher Chari, when I was nine years old hammering into us, "a *verb* is a *doing* word, a *verb* is a *doing* word". I felt so stupid for including doing words when talking about descriptive words.

On the other hand, with Black participants a grammatical error felt forgivable, but I was horrified when I heard myself talk about Blacks being more skin-shade conscious because I kept saying "they" which meant I was excluding myself. *How so British!* I could hear my superego crash me. I felt ashamed—like a traitor.

45.6   As an African

I have always been aware of Black Caribbean clients being angry with me at the start of their therapy but I never understood what triggered off their rage until I engaged in this research and learnt about the conflict between Africans and Caribbeans.

One day I commented to a Caribbean member of the group, who was excited about having a Black group conductor, about the possibility of my letting him down and he perceived it as rejection. He was enraged by my rejection. He thought that either the hatred between Africans and Caribbeans was being played out between us or that I was pushing him harder because he was the only Black person in his year group and I was making sure that he succeeded. It was quite a powerful and honest interaction: it shocked me but also made me realize how real the African/Caribbean conflict is.

I had heard about the African/Caribbean conflict from my husband, who told me that on his ward they do not let an African nurse look after a disturbed/excitable Caribbean patient and vice versa because it made the patients' condition worse as they became more paranoid and verbally aggressive towards the nurse. When I talked to other Blacks about this I was told that it was just a White man trying to make us hate each other, so I dismissed it.

However, my interaction with this Caribbean group member happened in a robust group that allowed us to explore the issues of Black/Black relationships. This has improved my work with Caribbean patients because on reflection I realized that they got angry with me when I prepared them for my disappointing them, which they always experienced as rejection. I started questioning my need to prepare "clingy" clients for rejection and traced it to my own fear of anyone being dependent on me, because I was very clingy and dependent on my father and when he died I could not cope with the loss. I was out of my mind with grief, therefore I never wanted to inflict the same pain onto anyone else.

The power struggle among most Blacks is common: for example, Zimbabweans saw themselves as more superior than Zambians and Malawians. My early childhood was spent in Zambia and when I came back to Zimbabwe I had a tough time because of my Zambian accent. My extended family laughed at me for being Zambian, calling me a *"mubwidi"*, *"achimwene"* all derogatory words for a Zambian. I quickly lost the accent and the language, something I now regret. However, Zimbabweans fleeing into South Africa are now being perceived as the poor, inferior and unwanted cousins. Being an immigrant in any country seems to put one in the inferior position of a beggar who has come to take without anything worthwhile to offer in return.

CHAPTER FORTY SIX

Discussion of findings

46.1 Looking beyond the superficial

Whose research is it? was the question I asked myself when some of the women balanced the dictaphone on their knees. It looked vulnerable and fragile but I resisted the urge to ask them to make it safe. Instead, I wondered what that was about and it led me to that question—whose research is it? It was terrifying to think that I depended on the participants to complete my research, but their enthusiasm assured me that they relied on me to complete it. I thought of a group cliché—"trust the process"—and knew that I did not need to take responsibility of the dictaphone or worry about the research. I trusted the process, allowing the research to become "our" research.

When one participant said he switched off halfway through the video I was disappointed, because all the other participants had criticized the quality of the video but had still found it interesting. Was he being envious? Was he being the superior White master?

I was sure that those two explanations were not correct because of my experience with this participant. Recalling my reaction to reading a badly edited newspaper helped me understand the third explanation. The research presents skin colour as a barrier and it questions whether we can go past that barrier and penetrate beyond it. Focusing on similarities can seduce us into thinking that skin colour is insignificant, in the same way that the participants' enjoyment of the video might make us forget the reality of its poor quality. Therefore this participant reminded us of that reality and its importance.

Although this research confirms the hypothesis that psychotherapy can penetrate beyond skin colour, the above participant warns us not to underestimate the impact of one's skin colour because visual presentations impact on our motivation to engage or not. Skin colour carries a history—slavery, colonization, conflict among people of different skin colour and among people of the same skin colour. Foukles (1966, p. 152) reinforces the impact of such social functions when he states that "social permeating the deepest levels of the psyche" of the individual who is pre-conditioned to "the core by his community ... and his personality and his character are imprinted vitally by the group in which he is raised". Therefore, it is important to understand how we are affected by our environment.

46.2   Political correctness

The split between Black and White participants' reactions was fascinating. I am not sure why I am surprised because I was aware of Whites being more conscious about being politically correct while Blacks enjoy freedom of speech as demonstrated by the story of Emily from the Big Brother programme. This has made me think more about how difficult it is for White colleagues. I now appreciate my training group more because it did not worry much about being politically correct. It is important for counsellors and therapists to be able to withstand negative transference, even if they are perceived as racists.

In the vignette, some participants could not cope with the negative transference, so they blamed the counsellor for provoking it. Negative transference will take place and cannot be avoided, but it has its own therapeutic value. Some therapeutic communities have worked successfully with it, for example, at a local therapeutic community the treatment of people with a diagnosis of Personality Disorder was based on the following ethos which allowed for, and contained, conflict and negative transference:

Democratization: equal power in the community; for instance, they used democracy to fight against senior clinicians' decision to ban the animal metaphors. If the senior staff had carried on insisting on the ban the issue would have gone to a vote and since there were more residents than staff the residents would have won, especially as some clinicians were also against the ban.

Communalism: sharing amenities and free communication. The residents and clinicians lived together, and all carried out some of the domestic chores. For example, one day a week residents and staff met to allocate domestic chores (cleaning the kitchen, toilets, meeting room and so on). In the evening two clinicians joined the residents for supper and evening activities such as indoor games and watching television. The staff bedroom was along the same corridor as the residents' and no bedrooms had locks. At the Drug and Alcohol Rehabilitation Therapeutic Community there was a similar shared living, but at night all staff went home so the residents took care of themselves overnight.

Reality Confrontation: there was continuous analysing and interpreting of residents' behaviour as seen by themselves and by others. The treatment was twenty-four hours a day. If there was a crisis or if someone needed support the community came together no matter what time of the day or night it was. Any inappropriate behaviour was explored in smaller therapy groups then discussed in the 9.15 community meeting where the rest of the community gave feedback on its meaning and impact on others.

Permissiveness: community members tolerated behaviour that might be distressing or seen as "deviant", thus creating an opportunity to analyse and make sense of it (Rapoport, 1960, p. 60). However, life-threatening behaviour which put others at risk was not tolerated: fire setting, lighting a candle, playing with the fire equipment (extinguishers, hose, alarm) and playing along the railway line. Breaking a major rule ended in an immediate discharge.

In the Drug and Alcohol therapeutic community similar permissiveness operated, except for drinking and taking drugs. They had random alcohol and drug tests or, if one was suspected of drinking, one was breathalysed. If positive, then the person was discharged immediately. At Open meetings, which were attended by recovering addicts, their families and friends, no-one could attend the meeting if they had consumed alcohol or taken drugs less than twenty-four hours before the meeting. If found out they were asked to leave immediately but welcomed to the next meeting where this was discussed and others gave feedback on how their drinking impacted on them.

It was through permissiveness that Mr. Smith's use of a racist register was tolerated, analysed and understood.

CHAPTER FORTY SEVEN

Issues for training and clinical practice

47.1   Allocation of clients to counsellors

My experience is that Black patients tend to be allocated to Black counsellors/therapists and the assumption is that they share the same culture. However, society is changing and such assumptions will need checking for the following reasons:

47.1.1   Skin colour does not determine a person's culture

Some Blacks have internalized a White culture and vice versa. The participant who was brought up by a Black nanny demonstrated the impact of internalizing a different culture and how she became blind to Black/White difference.

More people are growing up in different cultures, and with the increase in people adopting children of different skin colour to themselves (as publicized by Madonna and Angelina Jolie) more children will be internalizing different cultures. Unlike the racial identity development models, the model I am proposing, of linking child development with racial experiences, will remain effective, because it is not dependent on the skin colour of the individual but on what they internalize from the society they grow up in.

47.1.2   Conflict among Black people

Are counsellors and therapists aware of the conflicts and dynamics among different Black people? It is important to be sensitive to it so that it is picked up and worked with as soon as it emerges. It is necessary not to assume that Black counsellors and therapists will evoke positive transferences for Black clients, because the reality is that they can also evoke negative transferences which can be quite powerful. For example, if a Black client is in anti-Black or self-hatred stage they are unlikely to react positively to having a Black therapist. This is not to say that Black therapists cannot work with Black clients. The point is that all therapists need to be aware of the possible challenges that might come into play so that they are prepared and can allow the processes to take their course rather than become defensive.

47.1.3   An increase in Black counsellors/therapists and clients

There is an increase in Blacks training to be counsellors or therapists and also in Black clients seeking talking therapy. With the increase in immigration, are the training institutions preparing their trainees enough to work with people from different cultures? We need to take seriously the participants' fear of working with aggression that tends to be projected on to a "bunch of Black boys" who historically have contained projections of violence. Are the trainees being prepared adequately by analysing their own projections so that they can work effectively with the Black boys and Black men they fear? One participant captured what others expressed as the institution's lack of concern for issues of skin colour by saying she is White and that situation does not apply to her, but things are changing and this defence mechanism will not support those who are scared of what gets projected onto Black people. Training is paramount.

47.1.4   Isolation

The isolation experienced by Black and non-British White participants could have been less overwhelming if trainees from different year groups were given opportunities to share their experiences with each other. As shown by the research, some participants, both Black and White, discussed similar observations and raised similar questions, but in isolation. My personal experience of the isolation was less intense because my training was in groups, so I had various groups to talk about it, for example during lectures, in therapy, supervision and the large group where I met with others from other year groups.

Some participants suggested using the WPF Therapy Saturday workshops. However, WPF Therapy trainees training in individual therapy seem to be scared of groups, as evidenced by the failure to attend the debriefing group. My experience with the WPF Therapy experiential groups I have facilitated is that in the first few weeks members are preoccupied with paranoid and persecutory fear of being attacked by the group and they dread coming until they have been in the group for a month or so. I believe that in order to effectively explore issues of difference in group, training institutions need to build a culture for group exploration first for those training in individual therapy.

The other way of containing the isolation is in supervision, as the isolation is likely to present itself in the work the trainees do. It is also important to explore it in personal therapy.

47.2   Skin colour and bonding

This research has shown that unconscious racism interferes with working effectively with people of different skin colour. All participants admitted to feeling anxious when they meet a client of different skin colour for the first time. Two participants said they would feel anxious about the same things whether the client was Black or White.

The trainees raised the following concerns:

Anxieties about the first meeting

a. Fear of not understanding & being understood
Six participants commented on the fear of not being able to understand or being understood, for example:

- "How will we understand each other?" X 2
- "Will they be worried that I won't be able to understand where they are coming from?"
- "Will I not be able to understand something well enough which is of great importance to them?"

- "Will I miss something important?"
- "Will I unintentionally upset someone?"

b. Prejudice
Five participants said they get anxious because they worry about prejudice, for example:

- "How will our prejudice manifest itself in the work?" X 2
- "Will my own prejudices become part of the work?"
- "Will they be prejudiced against me?"

c. Acceptance
Three participants identified fear of not being accepted:

- "Might I not be what they want?"
- "Will they accept me?" X 2

d. Rejection
Two participants wrote about fear of rejection:

- "Will I be rejected?" X 2

e. Other anxieties
Individual participants were anxious about acknowledging race issues; how their own internalized racism would manifest itself; whether they could be trusted; whether they would be judged; what assumptions they might make; whether they would be able to work with negative transference; fear of being abused/insulted/challenged or becoming "an object of discrimination"; how their blind spots/weaknesses make it difficult to see or pick up dynamics taking place; whether they would act out something harmful; whether defence mechanisms/preconceived ideas, stereotypical beliefs/thoughts would stop them from being open to explore, see or think.

These questions focus on difference, and as demonstrated by this research, difference can evoke anxieties which then seek the support of defence mechanisms such as paranoid–schizoid position, resulting in splitting into good/bad and Black/White. The counsellor/therapist might become emotionally unavailable as she/he becomes defensive by being politically correct, suspicious, provocative, anxious, detached, fearful, rejecting, or wanting to please.

Without the emotional availability the bond between counsellor/therapist and client cannot be achieved and the counsellor/therapist would not be able to provide the secure base needed to reflect and to explore.

The reaction by the White participants to Questions 11a and 12a, and the parallel process of my different reaction to Black and White participants watching the video, prove that skin colour has an impact on how we react to others and how others react to us. Therefore, external presentation, such as skin colour, has an impact on us and it is important to address this superficial barrier in order to work effectively. If we underplay the significance of skin colour at first contact we are unlikely to process our anxieties, making it difficult for us to get hold of the clients because we are more likely to act out our anxieties. Current studies show that American Indians, Asian Americans, Blacks, and Hispanics tend to under-utilize traditional mental health services (Sue, Allen & Conaway, 1975; Sue & McKinney, 1974; Sue, McKinney, Allen & Hall 1974). Other findings indicate that ethnic minority clients are likely to end therapy at a rate above fifty percent after first contact in comparison to less than thirty percent of White clients (cited in Sue & Sue, 1990).

On the other hand, putting trainees through racial self-awareness training reflecting on their racial experiences and using the child development model that links with racial experiences seemed to contain these anxieties. The strength of the video was focusing on similarities, so the participants could think about how they connect with their clients rather than worry about the impact of being different. The improvement is evident from the way they answered the second questionnaire. After watching the video the participants were more confident and containing of their client and less emotionally aroused and overwhelmed. They focused on being connected with the client, "working together"—a collaborative alliance.

However, not noticing the colour difference means we could miss something. This is well illustrated by the participant who was brought up by a Black nanny. She could not see the impact of a Black woman with a White "baby". However, being on the research she began to switch on something which enabled her to talk to her therapist in a different way, allowing her to be heard differently.

47.4 Supervision

It was surprising that the ability to be honest in supervision was not in the top six important qualities in a counsellor. I also expected supervision to be mentioned when participants found the vignette difficult, because supervision is where issues around transference and countertransference are explored and one's fears, doubts and emotions aroused by clients are reflected on and made sense of. It is also in supervision that blind spots and weaknesses are identified and if necessary the supervisor can facilitate the trainees in identifying what needs to be explored in personal therapy for further understanding. Therefore, it is important that the trainees are able to trust their supervisor in order to be able to expose their vulnerability for further exploration so as to strengthen their weaknesses.

The BAC Code of Ethics and Practice for the Supervision of Counsellors (British Association for Counselling, 1987) states that "The primary purpose of supervision is to ensure that the counsellor is addressing the needs of the client". Supervision aims to protect the client and support the counsellor, but if there is no trust in the supervisory space neither will be achieved.

The silence about supervision made me wonder whether there was a problem with it, because I noticed that when participants are not happy about something they fall silent rather than express negative thoughts. For example, they wrote full answers to all the questions except Questions 11b and 12b, which had many "no comments". However, it became clear that "no comment" was a pregnant silence loaded with feelings of anxiety, anger, indignation, and frustration. It was only by using a different method—semi-structured interview—that we were able to reveal these negative feelings and thoughts arrested in the silence.

One participant wrote about how trainees are unable to use supervision effectively because the attitude of some of the supervisors makes it difficult for them to be honest. This explained part of the loaded silence about supervision.

As mentioned before, being angry or even hating one's supervisor is a common occurrence: however, what is important is to be able to voice these difficulties and try to make sense of them, using the supervision space and talking in one's own therapy. It is possible to regress in supervision and project out the "internal danger" (Winnicott, 1984) onto the supervisor. Supervision can make one feel vulnerable and exposed as one reflects on one's practice, so it is important to be able to trust the supervisor whose duty is to hold, support and contain the supervisee. Sometimes the dynamics of the patient are played out between the trainee and the supervisor, particularly when working with Borderline Personality Disorder or Drug and Alcohol Addiction, where splitting is used as a defence against accessing help. This needs to be reflected on and the splits brought together as a way of containing the patient.

On the other hand, if the supervisor/supervisee relationship fails to work due to difficulties they are experiencing with each other— for example, when the client's transference is re-enacted between supervisor/supervisee without any attempt to make sense of it in relation to the work with the client; when the supervisee's personal dynamics are evoked but not taken to personal therapy for further work, or when the supervisor's unresolved issues result in abuse of power— then changing one's supervisor would be best. It is important that the supervisee feels safe and contained to be able to be honest. A contained supervisee means a contained client and contained group.

When working in a multi-cultural setting the other possibility to consider is whether the supervisor lacks experience in working multiculturally. Constantine, Warren, and Miville (2005) state that supervision can be compromised if the supervisor has not done enough work in multicultural training or does not have much experience in working with clients of different skin colour. Constantine (1997) found in a study that seventy percent of the supervisors had never trained in cross-cultural or multicultural counselling courses. Therefore, it is essential for trainees to make the training institution aware of their difficulties, and for the institution to take such complaints seriously and support their supervisors by offering/ensuring adequate training.

Most trainees questioned why diversity is not taught continuously throughout the year. I believe this can be incorporated in training: discussion groups, looking at vignettes. Gainor and Constantine (2002) cited in Constantine, Warren, and Miville (2005) report that trainees who receive more supervision focusing on multicultural issues tend to display a higher ability in multicultural case conceptualization than those who do not. In this research it has been evident that trainees working in multicultural environments who got supervision at work responded to the "racist" client with confidence by being direct and containing. Also, trainees who spoke about skin colour with various people, particularly their therapists, were confident and containing of the "racist" client.

The first-year group was the only one that ranked ability to be honest in supervision as one of the top six important qualities both times. Vespia, Heckman-Stone, and Delworth (2002) found that junior supervisees graded *"Asks for help when appropriate"* of greatest importance, unlike other trainees, and they referred to the developmental theory

(Stoltenberg et al., 1998) reflective of the need for help and structure at earlier stages of training. Supervision is always important whether one is in training or is qualified: however, the degree of need might lessen as one begins to internalize a supervisor in them. There will always be blind spots to be identified and understood, and supervision is the place to discuss and weed them out. It is similar to gardening, the more you weed the less the weeds, with blind spots the more one in honest in supervision the more insight is gained which eradicates blind spots.

47.5 Training

The results of this research provide data supporting the association between training in racial self-awareness and the ability to respond more appropriately to a "racist" client. The responses to the second questionnaire showed that most trainees were more confident, competent and containing after watching the video. They were less defensive, less emotionally aroused and did not act out the feelings evoked in them (countertransference), unlike when they first answered the questionnaire. Thus, the training was effective, and since the video was efficient as a training tool, I heeded the feedback about its poor quality and had the video redone professionally. On reflection, I now believe that a group discussion soon after watching the video would be more productive, as participants can share ideas such as making use of supervision.

Constantine, Juby, and Liang (2001) stress the importance of multicultural training. They state: "In recent decades, marital and family therapy (MFr) training programs have increasingly recognized the importance of preparing practitioners to become multiculturally competent (e.g., Falicov, 1983, 1988, 1995; Haley, 1998; McGoldrick, Giordano & Pearce, 1996)".

Wheeler (2000) highlighted how assessments of trainees' competence are made based on their personality, training, supervisors' input, successful therapy outcome, reflection of personal experience and how they relate to tutors and others rather than feedback from the client. Some participants felt that the power of the vignette was in the fact that it came direct from the client. They expressed a wish to have similar vignettes for discussion and suggested a similar research carried out with clients so that they are given a voice.

47.6   Personal therapy

From the findings, participants who did not talk to their therapists about issues around skin colour struggled most in responding to Mr. Smith. Sue and Sue (1990) highlight the emphasis by some "multicultural experts", such as Corvin and Wiggins (1989), Helms (1984) and Ponterotto (1988), for the need for White counsellors to deal with their concepts of whiteness and to examine their own racism. The same applies to Black counsellors because, by exploring issues around one's skin colour in therapy, one gains confidence in talking about it and dealing with negative transference or idealization.

During the interview some participants talked about personal racial experiences that seemed painful and needed to be processed and understood further in personal therapy.

47.7   Further observations

47.7.1   Participants' feedback

While this research has clarified some issues it also raised more questions for the participants, such as:

Participants' observations and questions
1. Everybody is different but I think there is something special about racism but I can't quite put my finger on what it is.
2. The area of London that I live in there is a very big Turkish population … they probably suffer terrible discrimination although they are the biggest ethnic minority group.
3. Am I downplaying something because I am uncomfortable or because I don't want it to be a big deal?
4. (*Talking about who should take on these researches.*) "… how many people are out there potentially doing this research? I bet it is not very many. It is not an area that by definition many choose to go into and I would imagine, like yourself, it's the Black psychotherapists or analysts or members of the analytical community who are concentrating on it and a hazard a guess that the analytical world is still very much dominated by White middle class, women or men, but mainly women and therefore people who do that research in the grand arena in the community are really a very small minority". Why should it be like that?

5. Do you think you could work with somebody of a different race, culture, religion?
6. There are some Black tutors but so far I have been taught by White people, why?
7. The racial mix across my group is pretty wide. I'm interested to know if there is any positive discrimination working in terms of the people that you (WPF Therapy) take on as trainees?
8. How is therapy perceived in African or Caribbean cultures? What is it like to go and see somebody who is part of your family or part of your community?
9. Is it appropriate that all Black service users are seen by Black counsellors/therapists?
10. What's going to be done to encourage Black people to become counsellors/therapists?
11. How do we make sure that the experiences of Black service users are taken into consideration in the training of counsellors and therapists?
12. I think that something like this really gets people to actually think about how they feel about skin colour/race but how can the barriers be challenged so that one can look at similarities as well as differences?
13. I have been led to believe that diversity training in most institutes is dealt with as an add on. It is not actually talked about as integral to the training because there is not a lot of writing about it.
14. I would like to know what is going to happen with this research in terms of what is going to be done with it?
15. I would like to think that there are people within the NHS who are doing this kind of work, thinking about the provision of services for all users of the services, and thinking about the most appropriate treatment.
16. We are hearing a lot about Cognitive Behavioural Therapy (CBT) as being the panacea for depression, for every kind of difficulty, but actually, what are we doing in psychotherapy/psycho-dynamic/group psychotherapy to show what is appropriate for some people?
17. What is the counsellor/therapist's purpose? To change a culture or is it to help the client/patient with whatever it is he/she is bringing into therapy?
18. Is our aim to help the client or is it to prove a point?
19. I tried to get a Black client to explore the issue of her race but she didn't want to, and I wondered whether that was because I am White, she said her other counsellor was White and it made no difference. How does one start a dialogue about race issues in therapy?
20. The most challenging counselling is done with the people who are most similar to me, because that is where I find it more difficult to keep in mind that we are different.
21. Do clients/patients/service users have a right to be racist?

Following the participants' suggestions of getting clients' views I organized the next Black History event on the topic *What makes an effective therapist/counsellor/practitioner?* The service users debated on that topic.

47.7.2   The training video

For the following Black History event we were given more money than the previous year, so used some of it to get the training video re-produced professionally.

47.7.3   The research

At the following Black History event I discussed the research findings with service users, their families, friends, carers, and professionals. It was a satisfying experience because this is where the research title was born. Many participants expressed an interest in the research findings and asked for a brief summary of the findings to be circulated.

I was also invited to talk about the research at the two WPF Therapy academic meetings and at Manchester Metropolitan University. I was so pleased with the response to my research that I decided to publish it.

CHAPTER FORTY EIGHT

Methodology evaluation

48.1 Involving work colleagues

In my culture we have a saying that a baby is yours only while it is in the womb: once born, it belongs to the whole community. Although I was prepared to let others influence the development of "my baby"—the research—I sometimes found it difficult to let go of my ideas and welcome other people's suggestions.

I found piloting the questionnaire with work colleagues quite helpful in predicting possible difficulties. It gave me the opportunity to iron them out or consider how to contain them. For example, I had not been aware of the impact of Questions 11a and 12a. My colleagues' reaction of rebelling and joking alerted me to the emotional impact of the research, so I added Question 1 to the interview schedule to give participants the opportunity to debrief as they talked about the impact of the research on them.

48.2 The equipment

I live in Surrey and the research was carried out in London, so I could not "pop" back if I forgot something or if anything went wrong. I also learnt how important it is to check equipment in advance: I assumed, for instance, that the new dictaphone tapes I had bought would work, but just prior to interviewing I found them incompatible with the dictaphone I had been given. Another problem was that I did not know that used tapes need cleaning, so lost an interview after it got mixed up with previous work on the tape. Fortunately the participant agreed to reschedule.

48.3   The video

The video achieved its purpose in raising racial self-awareness and improving the participants' responses to a "racist" client. Its poor quality became an unplanned source of rich material as participants reacted in various ways—some thought it was a trick and one switched off. For the purpose of this research it was successful but as a training video its poor quality would interfere with the training aims and objectives. It needed to be redone professionally.

48.4   The environment

I did not think enough about the environment, or take into account the heat wave we had that summer. WPF Therapy had two buildings and I chose the one I was familiar with, but as it backs onto a railway station and trains run past every five minutes, we could not open the windows. This, however, meant using fans, and the noise made it difficult to transcribe tapes of soft-spoken participants. Therefore I decided to move to the second building.

48.5   The participants

Due to various delays I started the research towards the end of term, when trainees were breaking for summer holiday. I believe that was one of the reasons why some participants failed to attend the group debriefing.

Initially some participants forgot to attend the video-watching sessions but when I started displaying the schedule on the notice board their attendance improved.

I had planned to carry out all the interviews a week after watching the video, but because most people were going on holiday we re-arranged and met sooner. I think this worked out better because I had not realized how emotionally provoking the video and the questionnaire had been. Most used the interview space for debriefing and exploring their reactions.

48.6   Group debriefing

Debriefing offers opportunity for feedback, helps participants to feel valued and presents a cathartic opportunity to reflect on how the inter-view went (Bowling, 2002).

After completing the research I invited the participants to a debrief-ing meeting. No-one attended. I believe I failed to use my knowledge of the trainees' fear of exposing themselves in a group. In suggesting self-exposure in a gathering of different year groups I was insensitive to that fear. I could have worded the invitation letter to the debriefing differently, using the same tone as in my first letter, which did not focus on personal experience. The second explanation is that since the partici-pants used the interview space for debriefing they did not see the need for further work. The last possible explanation is that most participants had gone on holiday.

48.7   The questionnaires

Five participants failed to return the second questionnaire, and even after sending them self-addressed stamped envelopes three still did not respond, which was disappointing. I wondered whether they found the questions difficult, however, I included them in the research because I felt they were part of the dynamic needing inter-pretation. From the exercise identifying who they spoke to about issues of skin colour, all three belonged to the group which did not speak to its therapist, and these (two of whom were first-years) found it difficult to respond to the "racist" client. I wondered whether the first years expected too much of themselves and did not believe they were doing well, yet the research showed that their group was the only one to choose being honest in supervision as one of the top six important qualities of a counsellor both times. Their contributions were helpful.

48.8   The vignette

All participants found the vignette the most challenging activity as it was emotionally provocative. Here are some of their comments:

Views on the vignette
• … I would have found it very offensive if I had to deal with somebody who was racist against me and that would be the kind of bottom line.
• I think you have to be able to follow your own feelings and deal with them, and recognise your own feelings and watch them … I've had an experience which feels a bit like that, with a nineteen year old … She absolutely terrified me, and I'm sure she felt that I was terrified and she never came back. Now, I would deal with it quite differently, because I'm more experienced … I don't think I would be as terrified. I would be able to reflect back … and I would be able to use my feelings to explore hers, like folding flour into a cake whereas then I was just terrified.
• For example, the immediate reaction to *"I hate all Blacks, not just you"* would have been *"If you hate me I hate you too, you know"* … he has his own roots, the hate did not start from today. … it could be something that happened before … so how can I be able to persuade someone who is telling me to my face *"I am not going to sit down because I hate you?"*
• … not to act out the projections. I think with some clients it could exacerbate the projection, and the counsellors pay lip service to what they think is politically correct … So yeah, it's difficult, very difficult.
• The man seemed incredibly defensive, strongly offensive, and obviously was pretty ambivalent about coming to counselling and was looking for an easy way out, maybe … he definitely scared me … I expect it is not about colour, after a certain point, it is about all sorts of vulnerabilities.
• … we talk about experiencing the nature of transference/countertransference, sitting with it, as repetition of something to do with client's internal world.
• I think it always helps if somebody has been through similar experiences but I think ultimately it is a level of empathy and emotional understanding and ability to connect with somebody and their experience and their pain.
• I need to be open to not knowing what it means to somebody and to listen and see and not be afraid to bring it up and talk about it if it feels like it needs to be talked about.
• One needs to be comfortable sitting in a room with difference. … one needs to acknowledge that the culture that I have grown up in has probably infused me with implicit racism and that I have absorbed that and that I am continually surrounded by that, and that's in me. … and be able to tolerate that in me but it can be uncomfortable to bring to one's

conscious mind, and by doing that hopefully seeing that much of it is
a defence, much of it is denial, much of it is a displacement of my own
stuff.
- Reflect on what has been brought up and relating it back to my own
internal relationships. Probably that would lead me to what it means
to be persecuted or happy, feeling guilty, issues of abandonment,
ambivalent attachment, splitting, projections—all those things. So, in
a sense it is about working through the more ugly parts of myself really.
- I think as you pointed out in the video that we are the same, that our deepest resistances and fears come from a very early time and that a skilled
counsellor can bring you to those which transcend colour. But there are
also real issues about being a minority race in any society; again a skilled
counsellor of any skin colour should have some sensitivity to that.

Most participants said they would not have changed the vignette as it felt
like a real life situation, and they talked about how, as counsellors, we
have to work with what is presented to us. However, those who suggested
changes tended to suggest removal of the frightening aspects, such as
stopping the counsellor from provoking the client by calling him by his
first name, removing the tattoos and one joked about changing "him"
altogether. There was a general wish for an "easier" client. Here are some
of the comments:

- It had a purpose and I think it does it very well, because it is raising all
these questions in my mind that I really don't know.
- … if she (the counsellor) is Black and she is living here maybe she is
used to not being treated fairly. I don't know I haven't done any survey
on Black therapists but I assume, all one assumes is there are very few
Blacks.

48.9   Can this research be reproduced?

It would be interesting to see if the findings from this research could
be duplicated if the same things were carried out by someone else.
I believe that would not be possible because the researcher's skin colour, gender, culture, training, and ability to facilitate an honest discussion all influence the research. I also think the poor quality of the video
provoked a specific discussion, something a professionally produced
video would not have done. The video provoked creative thinking
as some participants tried to outsmart what they thought was "the
researcher's tricks". Producing a similarly poor quality video that
showed "a black speaking blob" would be difficult to engineer if the
researcher is White.

CHAPTER FORTY NINE

The vignette: working with racism in therapy

49.1 Mr. Smith

This chapter discusses building working alliances with the client in the research vignette who expressed racist views. Using this vignette I demonstrate how theory influences my practice and how I make use of transference and countertransference.

Winnicott (1986, p. 94) states: "... the child (client) absolutely requires an environment that is indestructible in certain respects". Therefore, my initial dynamic administration task is to create a psychologically safe environment by establishing clear boundaries and protecting the client's space and time.

I define confidentiality and explain that it can be broken—after discussion with the client—if concerned for their safety or that of others. While regular attendance and punctuality are essential in developing trust and intimacy, it is more important to explore the meaning of their lateness and absence.

I actively listen to verbal and non-verbal communication, aware that when overwhelmed with distress or anxiety the client's ego will engage defence mechanisms in order to cope. For example:

On seeing me, Mr. Smith stated, "I do not see the point of sitting down because I am a racist and you are Black. This is not going to work. I hate Blacks". However, his aggressive outburst evoked maternal feelings in me. Bateman, Brown, and Pedder (2000, p. 62) explain countertransference as the therapist's feelings towards the client and how a therapist can use these feelings to attune to the client's unexpressed feelings. Bollas (1987, p. 202) states that, "In order to find the patient we must look for him within ourselves". Foukles (1964, p. 179) states that "The capacity of the therapist to observe what happens in the patient's mind, to comprehend it, rests on his own empathy ... he must be free enough from personal problems not to be drawn into the emotional whirlpools of his patients".

Racism can draw one into these "whirlpools" but my training and personal therapy enabled me to stand back and attune to my countertransference feelings. I responded empathetically, encouraging reflective thinking: "I appreciate your honesty and directness, but can you tell me more about what you mean by being a racist?"

"My father fought for this country. Look at what is happening! Right now I am thinking, couldn't they find me a White therapist?"

I said honesty is good in therapy, then proceeded to set boundaries. As the session progressed it became clear that Mr. Smith used projective identification to defend against his own vulnerability. He was born with a distinctive bright strawberry birthmark that covered most of his face (it is now hardly noticeable) and his father would not touch him. At four years of age his father abandoned the family. Mr. Smith felt rejected because of his skin condition. My surname, Maher, is Irish, therefore Mr. Smith had expected to see an Irish woman, not a Black therapist. My skin colour triggered off these painful memories about being judged because of his own skin condition. He wanted to get rid of the pain by getting rid of me—a reminder that one can be judged by one's skin. So, like his father—the internalized critical, rejecting father— he rejected me. I understood Mr. Smith's behaviour as transference reaction in the here-and-now of these past painful experiences. I did not give this interpretation because we needed to built a therapeutic alliance first.

Winnicott (1984, pp. 176–177) says "antisocial acts ... indicate that at any rate momentarily there can be hope—hope of rediscovering a good-enough mother, a good-enough inter-parental relationship. Even anger may indicate that there is hope ...".

Therefore, Mr. Smith's attack held some hope and I knew that "good-enough" mothering would allow him to work through these internal conflicts and pain.

Mr. Smith accepted the offer for therapy, adding that he had expected me to turn him down. I wondered whether he normally rejects before he is rejected. He recognized this as a pattern he needed to change. I believe Mr. Smith felt held and accepted having exposed himself "warts and all". I had contained his distress, anxiety, fear of rejection and fear of being judged. As a therapist I contain unwanted and disowned feelings and process them, sometimes in supervision. I then give them back to the client, like a mother giving the *ruzoka*, as interpretations sensitively timed so that the client is ready to hear, chew, and digest.

CHAPTER FIFTY

Reflections

The research supports the hypothesis that if we become more aware and accepting of our unconscious racism we will be more effective in working with difference and in penetrating beyond skin colour. We become more able to bond with our clients. Gorman (2006) states that the therapist/patient bond is the foundation to the patient improving. However, he acknowledges "some degree of mistrust" due to "historical factors" and that the therapist needs to develop skills to deal with this so as to build trust and develop a therapeutic alliance. The patient needs to feel held (Bion) and contained (Winnicott). The trainee also needs to feel held and contained by his/her training institution through training (theory), supervision (practice) and personal therapy (personal development).

The training video was effective in raising racial self-awareness and bringing together Black and White experiences. Its poor picture provided unexpected data which could not have been produced had it been professionally done.

Sharing experiences about skin colour with others, as shown by the research, builds one's confidence in working with someone of different skin colour. Participants who did not talk about skin colour with their therapists struggled most to respond to a "racist" client and they found participating in the research difficult.

This research could be repeated but my prediction is that if carried out by a White person it would produce different data because, as the research proved, Whites and Blacks react differently and another person's skin colour does influence their reactions.

The research was productive because it attended to trainees' different learning styles: internalization, reflective practice, and self-evaluation. Here are some of their comments:

Trainees' different learning styles

1. **Internalization**
   - "I don't know really where this research is going inside me yet as I'm still kind of in it. ... probably you have confirmed things to me that were embryonic or beginning to be understood inside".
2. **Thinking/reflecting**
   - "It heightened my awareness, I suppose, in terms of thinking about client work". Recalling an experience with a client, "I think something else that happened outside in the world made me include the capacity to be neutral ... because if the client sees me smiling, they might think I'm mocking them".
   - Reflecting on her first sessions with her own therapist "... we actually had to work through these issues before I felt secure in the therapeutic alliance really and I suppose this is partly what I reflected on in my answers without realizing it. I didn't realize until talking to you that actually that is my experience as well".
3. **Evidence based**
   - "I found your presentation really helpful. I'm not aware of things having changed, you might see a difference in the way I filled in the second questionnaire".
4. **Self evaluation**
   - "It made me realise ... how much my views have changed since my twenties for instance".
5. **Playing with new ideas**
   - "Your first question, What do you see? I thought Black, then I thought Black woman. What is the dominant thing that I see when I look at you? And I thought probably Black. When I came out I was wandering the streets looking at people thinking—black, tall, fat, stupid, etc".
6. **Aha! Experience—when the penny drops**
   - "... what was really interesting was that the morning I came to see your video, ... after I filled in the form, I had been talking about race,

colour and class and so on in my own therapy ... we talked about an experience that I talked to my therapist about a couple of times before and he had not recognised until that moment that the woman who took care of me when I was younger was Black".

- The video "... I hadn't thought about race and skin colour and difference in the way that you presented it in the video and attaching it very closely to stages of development. I found that very helpful and I actually found that it was very similar to what I think, I already thought, about but I didn't think it in quite that way ... that would have influenced the change in the second questionnaire".

7. Connectedness

- "But I actually went to see six people [in search of a therapist] ... it was about an intuitive feel .... She was the last person I saw, and I just thought I want to work with her. She was able to access something about me ... and I thought, this is somebody who can know me and who I will be able to be emotionally very in tune with. There were issues around race that came up straight away, culture that came straight away in the work with her ... So we talked about culture and race in the first session actually".

8. Use of metaphors/stories

- One participant spoke about the aggression in the vignette and how when it's expressed verbally it is less likely to be acted out. He told a story about a young kite/hawk that was sent by his mother to catch a meal. He returned with a duckling. Mother Hawk wanted to know whether Mother Duck was angry about the loss of her duckling. When the young one said that Mother Duck did not complain Mother Hawk explained that a silent mother is a dangerous mother and that she would definitely come after them. The young one was sent back to return the duckling and look for something else. He went and caught a chick. Mother Hen flapped and clucked about. On hearing about Mother Hen's big fuss Mother Hawk settled to eat the chick stating that it was safe to eat because Mother Hen had exhausted herself and was less dangerous and unlikely to come and attack them.

9. Self awareness

- I think counsellors need to have explored their own feelings and attitudes to difference and to skin colour. I think that they really need to have taken the opportunity to think about their prejudices.

10. Sharing the experience

- The vignette ... it was very thought-provoking, very good. I even read it to my thirteen-year-old daughter this morning, and asked her how she would answer it. She said *"Maybe he should go to another counsellor"*.

PART IV

PERSONAL DEVELOPMENT

INTRODUCTION

In Part Four I reflect on the process I went through while working on my research *Can psychotherapy penetrate beyond skin colour?* I chose the design of a bamboo because it is an appropriate symbol for me, capturing how I perceive myself and my personal development.

The bamboo was commonly seen as an outdoor plant—for example, *Phylostachys nigra*, the black hardy bamboo that can survive bitter winters, symbolizing my determination through various life struggles. This bamboo has become a popular indoor plant, representing my tranfer from my homeland and my struggle to establish myself in a country that can be challenging because of its racial hostility.

Like the bamboo, sometimes I get cut, but I do not die: I send out a new shoot in a different direction, beating the odds to flourish. When obstacles are placed in my way I see them as challenges to my creativity, and the curly branch demonstrates how I go around them, creating a unique design that draws attention and admiration to my spirit. Although I carry the scars of my struggles I still remain elegant, because I have no space for bitterness.

My experience at Manchester Metropolitan University (MMU) and my relationship with others who helped me work on my research is reflected in the healthy look of this well cared-for bamboo. Being an indoor plant, the bamboo is dependent on its relationship with others, and my success is a reflection of the secure relationships that water and feed me. In this analysis I reflect on these interactions.

CHAPTER FIFTY ONE

What I brought to the personal development group

51.1   Attitude

When I enrolled I was expecting two of my friends because we had planned to join the programme together, but they had withdrawn without telling me. So, when I joined the Personal Development (PD) group my attitude was negative because I displaced my disappointment and irritation with my friends onto those joining the programme. My friends would have been more or less my age, unlike those enrolling. I felt as if I had walked into a kindergarten as most of the students were young enough to be my children. Of course my attitude was also influenced by my stereotypical assumptions about young people, such as that they cannot be serious about their studies.

Being aware of my negative attitude and of my ability to sabotage myself, I knew I had to deal with this before I became destructive: for example, dropping out and using distance as an excuse, even though I had travelled to and from Manchester for five years when I trained to be a group analyst. I started to question my motivation.

How much did I really want to be on this programme? To answer this vital question I recalled an experience of sleeping on the coach station bench.

I had come to enroll. Since I had to be at the university for 9.30 a.m. I boarded the midnight coach from Victoria, arriving in Manchester at 5.30 a.m. It was too dark to venture out and I was very tired, so seeing some men sleeping on the benches I stretched myself across one of the benches. I was woken up hours later by the station staff shouting at the men that they could not sleep there. I felt like a tramp on a park bench. That is how desperate I was to be on this programme.

Having established my level of motivation my attitude towards my PD group changed. I was also impressed by how motivated and focused these young people were. They were confident and clear about what they wanted to do and also accommodated my needs. For instance, everyone wanted to meet at 11 a.m. but this was changed to 11.15 a.m. to accommodate my travelling time from the station. I felt included and cared for and I happily ate the humble pie because I was pleased I had found a group that was willing to work as a team. I developed a sense of belonging and committed myself to the group.

51.2   Knowledge

I like working in groups because I come from a group-orientated family: I grew up with my five brothers and sisters plus five of my cousins whose parents had died, and now my family consists of my five children and their two cousins, my late brother Obediah's children. We are a very close family and supportive of each other.

When I joined the Manchester Metropolitan University I was a group analyst working at an NHS Resource Centre and also facilitated NHS staff support groups. I worked part time at WPF Therapy, where I facilitated therapy groups and an experiential group for trainee counsellors. My NHS employer, Manchester Metropolitan University and WPF Therapy supported me in preparing and carrying out my research.

I brought my knowledge of group processes and group dynamics to influence positive working within my PD group. Here is a sample of the feedback from a colleague:

Feedback from another student

Hi MJ,

Just a quick note to say what a pleasure it was working with you. You struck me as very reflective, and skilled at managing group dynamics. You brought appropriate material to the group to discuss, and when others were struggling to understand concepts you were patient and adept at explaining ideas without sounding like you were being a teacher!

I was always impressed by your commitment to the group—all that travelling from London!

I'm sorry you won't still be in the group this year. Good luck with your writing up.

Best Wishes,
Alex

My psychiatric knowledge came in handy when our group was discussing their experiences in working with the elderly and with people with a Borderline Personality Disorder diagnosis. I enjoyed participating because I knew what I was talking about when we discussed diagnosis and treatment.

51.3 Skills

I brought teaching and editing skills with me from my previous jobs. For example, when I planned my teaching sessions I focused on the objectives, ensuring they suited the needs of the audience I was presenting to. I enjoyed writing reports and carrying out market researches. I am skilled in building and maintaining relationships because of my effective communication skills. As an active listener I am interested in what others have to say. Although I enjoy playing the devil's advocate I still take other people's points of view seriously. I believe my research has made me more appreciative of other people's opinions and has also improved my ability to analyse responses, looking at things from various angles and accepting constructive criticism. Sometimes the criticism was given in a hurtful manner and that made me more sensitive to how I offer others criticism—it needs to be constructive, enabling and encouraging the receiver to digest it without choking on it. That has been an important skill to acquire.

I am a good observer and quite skilled at making connections. This skill proved essential for the work I did in my research, which needed a good eye to spot any inconsistency and change. By the end of the research I was better at analysing data and became more patient and thorough at double-checking till I was satisfied.

I am skilled at defending my corner and do not like people taking me for a ride. As a child I always argued with my father, and he taught me how to present my arguments so that I could be heard. However, this skill often causes me problems because I argue with people in authority, who then perceive me as disrespectful and undermining of their authority. The other problem is that I enjoy arguing, which sometimes irritates others. On the other hand, I found this skill helpful in setting boundaries around my work.

During the research I became engaged in the third Employment Tribunal case. I felt pressurized, being involved in yet another case of victimization at work while working on integrating racial differences. The quality of the work I did in my PD group showed how much better I have become at managing racism so that it does not affect my relationships with a different group of Whites. I found the first Employment Tribunal difficult because I could not separate the racism at work from my training experience with White tutors, supervisors, and other trainees. My training with the Institute of Group Analysis taught me how to deal with unfairness more constructively.

CHAPTER FIFTY TWO

Learning styles

D uring my study at Manchester Metropolitan University I found identifying the learning styles I find effective very useful. Here are my learning styles.

52.1 Participative

I believe I learn best by engaging and participating: for instance, presenting papers, working on projects, holding discussions and debates. I have used a number of other platforms for presenting; at the yearly Black History event I presented the following papers—*Psychotherapy penetrates beyond skin colour; What makes an effective counsellor/therapist when working with difference?; Belonging to two cultures: is it a blessing, mixed blessings or a curse? Assimilation: What does it take to fit in?* Presenting my research to academics was a great challenge as I find academics scary and I do not classify myself as one. I am a clinician.

The reason I enjoy presenting is that it offers an opportunity for feedback that can be encouraging and challenging, and it enables me to look at things from various perspectives I might not have considered before. It also gives me a chance to feel proud of my work, as the feedback massages my confidence.

52.2   Learning through folk stories and metaphors

Most of my childhood involved listening and learning from my grandmother's folk stories and the family's use of proverbs, therefore I enjoy stories and metaphors. It is easier to remember something attached to a story, a metaphor or a proverb. However, during my research an interest in stories proved to be a disadvantage because it left me feeling overwhelmed as I became seduced by the stories I was listening to and found it difficult to stay focused. It was painful to leave out interesting findings that were not relevant to the research. In some ways this experience taught me how to let go and stay focused—at first it was hard and I hated it.

By the way, did you work out—*Rakazvirova rikazhamba?*—what bird beats itself and then cries loudly? *Jongwe!* A cock! When a cock crows it flaps its wings first then goes "Cock-a-doddle-doo!" What about the proverb, *Azvuva sanzu azvuva nemashizha aro*—the translation is "he who decided to drag a branch drags with its leaves". It means that if you decide to take on someone you have to accept them, warts and all; for example, if you fall in love with a father you have to accept his children too.

52.3   Learning from mistakes

This is an effective method of learning which I hate because of the shame, fear, embarrassment, and humiliation attached to the experience. As an example, my stereotypical belief that young people do not take studying seriously—I was proved wrong and received more support than I expected. I felt ashamed and embarrassed. I will not forget this lesson. On the other hand, I enjoy learning from other people's mistakes, learning by proxy, because some of the experiences can be funny and I do not suffer the embarrassment or humiliation personally. I enjoy it more if the mistake does not have serious consequences and if it involves people I get on well with and who have enjoyed my humiliation in the past. We can then have a good laugh together.

52.4   Self-directed learning

I enjoy formal learning, private studying, reading, and e-learning. Living far from Manchester, I could not attend the local lectures, so decided to set up my own learning programme. I looked for lectures and conferences taking place in London and Surrey, and selected those relevant to my study. The following diary covers my training, conferences, meetings, appointments, and other events significant to my research:

Personal development diary
1. 27th September—Enrolment & induction
2. 28th September—Induction
3. 4th October—PD meeting
4. 22nd October—PD meeting/AJ's (grandson) birth
5. 27th October—Black History presentation
6. 12th November—Study day: Hate & containment
7. 25th November—Study day: Internalizing the history past: Issues for separation and moving on
8. 10th December—PD meeting
9. 28th January—Study day: Groups on the Edge
10. 11th February—PD meeting
11. 25th February—Study day: Cult, attachment, and religion
12. 28th February—Black ethnic minority conference: Winning with quality
13. 1st March—Tutorial
14. 11th March—PD meeting
15. 2nd May—Tutorial
16. 13th May—Study day: Desire and sexuality in group psychotherapy
17. 18th May—Meeting with WPF Therapy training management
18. 19th May—Foukles annual lecture: Group analysis & spirituality: Continuing the dialogue
19. 20th May—PD meeting
20. 23rd May—WPF Therapy meeting with training programme managers
21. 30th May—Tutorial
22. 1st June—Video shooting
23. 7th June—Study day: Attachment and religion
24. 15th June—Tutorial
25. 16th June—Meeting with WPF Therapy student representative
26. 16th June—Ethan's (grandson) birth
27. 17th June—PD meeting
28. 20th June—Manchester Pre-conference workshop
29. 21st June—Video presentation
30. 30th June—Video presentation/Research
31. 3rd June—Manchester Annual Conference Research/tutorial
32. 5th July—Research field work

33. 6th July—Research Open Day at a London College
34. 11th July—Study day: Disability, Gender, and Race
35. 12th July—Video viewing
36. 18th July—Video viewing/research interviews
37. 19th July—Research interviews
38. 20th July—Research interviews
39. 21st July—Research interviews
40. 26th July—Research interviews
41. 27th July—Video viewing/research interviews
42. 2nd August—Video viewing/research interviews
43. 9th August—Research interviews
44. 10th August—Working on graphs with Fran
45. 14th August—Employment Tribunal Hearing
46. 15th August—Employment Tribunal Hearing
47. 22nd August—Dissertation presentation & Tutorial
48. 29th August—Presenting at WPF Therapy
49. 2nd November—Professional video shooting
50. 7th November—Tutorial
51. 9th November—Presenting at the WPF Therapy
52. 9th November—Weekend conference on trauma in organizations
53. 25th November—Submission of the Dissertation

52.5   Experiential learning

My other favourite learning style is experiential or situational learning because it is not pre-planned, thus adding to the excitement of learning. Like learning from mistakes it can be a painful experience. This learning style includes debriefing after a significant incident.

52.6   Discussions/debates

I have a wide range of experience which makes it easy to engage in discussions. I learn a lot from these because they give me a chance to reflect on past experiences and hear other people's views. For example, when a PD group member presented on Adult learning methods I found the discussion useful and it generated new ideas that made me reflect on my own learning methods. Another presented on the elderly and dementia. His discussion took me back to when I was training to be a nurse on an elderly ward. It reminded me of the lack of proper assessment and lack of other treatment choices for the elderly, such as alternative therapy besides medication. Their enthusiasm reminded me of mine when I was a trainee before I became disillusioned by the realization of the gap between the theory in our classrooms and the practice on the wards, where we were crippled by the realities of staff shortages, limited resources, and chipped budgets.

52.7 Psycho-social learning

In our PD group we also used psycho-social learning. On Saturdays, after the formal meetings we went to the local pub for lunch and got to know each other in a relaxed social atmosphere. We got excited about each others' news/stories, like the time my daughter went into labour while I was at a PD meeting. We also shared sad moments: when one group member left to live abroad. I missed her because she was quite active and interesting.

To understand how different my relationship with my PD group was I will discuss my husband's response to a time he came to Manchester with me. I took him round the university campus so that he could share my Manchester Metropolitan University experience with me. I later took him to our pub for lunch. As I sat explaining the pleasures of being a student discussing matters over a pub lunch he sat there shocked that I had been frequenting the pub because in the twenty-three years we had been together he failed to get me into a pub! Only his parents managed it a few times. In my culture a married woman does not go into pubs, an idea I like because I do not drink alcohol. Unfortunately that discovery took away my liberty not to go into pubs because if Manchester students can get me in there so can the family. Thanks guys!

52.8 Supportive learning

Besides my PD group meetings I had regular meetings and e-mail contact with my supervisor and occasional contact with the PD tutors. They were my campus and helped in clarifying my direction during the foggy moments, and that kept me on course.

52.9 Reflective learning

My other favourite learning style is reflective practice. I learn not to sit with what seems obvious at first sight because on reflection it might take on a different meaning. I wrote reflective notes on various experiences and events. I reflected on my feelings, thoughts and behaviour. I am always fascinated by how my unconscious mind influences my present feelings and behaviour, and my feelings influence my thoughts and behaviour, and my behaviour influences my feelings and thoughts. I realized that I was not making many new discoveries—just repeating the same old behaviours. By reflecting on events I became more aware of patterns of behaviours that I needed to change, as they happened more often than I had been aware of. A parallel process happened with the participants on the research who, on reflection, discovered that what they had written was different from what they thought they did. Here are samples of my reflective notes:

Personal development record		Date: 26th September	
Event	Planned objective what happened?	Personal objectives	Previous experience/thoughts/feelings prior the event
Personal experience	To get to Manchester by coach.	1. To reclaim my territory and show hat I was not intimidated by him.	1. I will fight to make a point regardless of the consequences of my action.
	I got on the coach at 23:30 hrs from Victoria. I sat opposite an ethnic minority man in his late 60s. He decided to sleep with his feet stretched cross to my seat sometimes resting his feet on mine. I felt intruded upon.		2. His culture, which is different from mine, is stereotyped as a culture that allows men to dominate their women, so I was not going to let this man dominate or intimidate me, I would teach him a lesson. 3. I knew I was being unreasonable but it felt good. 4. I hate losing an argument.

What happened. An analysis of the event	I hated feeling the feet of a stranger on mine but I was not going to move away, who is the idiot here? I could not just step down so I had to rationalize in order to make the stepping down more acceptable. Thinking of it as a power struggle each time he rubbed his feet on mine enabled me to withstand the revolt of strange feet on mine. What germs am I catching? I questioned myself but that did not bother me enough to remove my feet. Is it possible that he just lacks manners rather than that he is trying to intimidate me? That did not make me move my feet away either. Maybe he is just an old man who is tired and just wants to rest his feet—with that I moved my feet. Respect for the elders always works with me. It is a cultural conditioning I will always respond to and in this situation it made me feel ashamed of myself.
What I learnt from it	Nothing new, I already knew that I can be unreasonable when I have a point to make. My attitude was influenced by my own prejudices and the media that portrays his race as disrespectful and demeaning of its women. The reality of the matter is that I paid for one seat—the one I was sitting on. He had stretched his feet across three seats— the third we were "fighting" over was next to me but it did not belong to either of us, it was just a spare seat. I was surprised that I had not even considered that it was not my seat.
Any further learning? (*Priorities*)	I need to have more respect for myself rather than my principles—most of my troubles stem from fighting for my principles at a cost to my good health including the stress generated during the fighting. Do I have issues around power? I will monitor how many issues of power I get involved in and see if being aware of it reduces the number of incidents. This made me think about my driving. I will check my response to other drivers when they suddenly pull in front of me or take away my right of way.

Personal development record		Date:	8th October
Event	Planned objectives	Personal objectives	Previous experience/ thoughts/feelings prior the event
The first Personal Develop- ment Group meeting.	1. To decide on the structure of the meeting. 2. To work on the contract. 3. To clarify about the format of the journal. 4. To discuss how market visits are arranged. 5. To discuss personal goals.	1. To establish a working relationship with others. 2. To participate in the discussion.	1. I felt negative about joining a group of young people. 2. I felt anxious and unsure of what was expected of me.
What happened: an analysis of the event	1. Only four people attended and my heart sank. This is what I expected to happen with young people who are out to have fun. Initially I felt that it was a wasted journey. 2. I was quiet at first then became more involved. We worked on the contract. I contributed with ideas from my experience of writing learning contracts with student nurses I mentored. I found myself enjoying the experience. 3. I showed the notes I had already started writing, others were impressed by my enthusiasm as I was the only one who had started—for once. 4. We went out for pub lunch and talked some more. I had received text messages that my daughter was in labour. I was surprised by how excited everyone else became, crossing fingers with me that the baby does not come before I get back.		

| What I learnt from it | 1. I learnt that stereotyping can cause unnecessary worry and that by allowing my stereotypical beliefs to be challenged I became less anxious and more excited.
2. I left feeling more positive and sure that I would enjoy my group experience. I felt quite motivated and clear about what I wanted to do with my research. We had set group goals for the following meeting and I felt contained within the structure we had set for our group. |
| Any further learning? (*Priorities*) | 1. To write down my learning objectives and information about what I can offer the group.
2. To sort out who will pick up the people coming to the Black History presentation.
3. To finish off my preparations for the presentation. Although I felt excited about others coming from Manchester I felt a bit of pressure to impress. |

Personal development record Date: 25th November			
Event	Planned objective	Personal objectives	Previous experience/ thoughts/feelings prior the event
Conference Internalizing the historical past: Issues for separation and moving on.	To learn about a historical perspective of the impact of slavery.	1. To learn more about slavery and its impact on the present generation.	1. I do not relate to the history of slavery with the same passion as those whose ancestors were taken into slavery but I relate more passionately to the issues of colonization.
		2.To join an art group and see if I can learn anything new about myself.	2. I usually go for popular speakers but today I decided to join the least attended workshop because I was getting cynical about how effective art therapy is.

What happened. An analysis of the event

1. It was the first time I had been to a gathering in United Kingdom with over 60 Blacks and a handful of Whites. The atmosphere was quite anti-White in the language used by some passionate people who related angrily to the slavery history. During the art session we were asked to draw our families. When I started to talk about my work I realized, to my horror, that I had left out my husband and my in-laws (all White) who are important members of my family. I was shocked by that and I fedback this observation to the whole group. I linked my wiping out of my White family to how I had felt that there seemed to be no space for Whites here and wondered how the White participants felt about being there. I thought I would be attacked but the audience started clapping

saying how well I spoke and suggested that the theme for the following year would be on mixed race marriages. One elderly Zimbabwean woman asked for my totem and started thanking me in Shona using my totem. She spoke about how proud she was of me, speaking as if she was my mother. I was deeply touched.

What I learnt from it	1. I used to believe that psychodynamic/psychoanalytic therapies were the best forms of treatment and any other methods are second rated. However, this experience really arrested my attention. Maybe it is about seeing other forms of treatment as just different, just like skin colour is different and not a defining factor of who is better than the other.
	2. I was struck by the impact of mob mentality, how could I wipe out the important people in my life just because they are White and I am in an environment that felt hostile towards Whites? But that is the reality for some of us. I then remembered how my brother, Obediah, who was a major in the Zimbabwean army kept giving my husband and I excuses for not inviting my husband to his house in the army barracks in Kwekwe yet he invited us to stay with him at his home in Harare. After Obediah died my sister and I went to sort out his possessions. As we went through the manned gate into the barracks we overheard some Black soldiers talk about their disgust that a White man had visited their camp and how they would have killed him had they found out sooner. I was shocked and shaken by the venom in their voices. I then understood why my brother never wanted me to visit him at the barracks when I was with my husband—he feared for my husband's safety.
Any further learning? (*Priorities*)	1. I was left feeling quite disheartened, how can I contribute to changing people's opinions/attitudes if there is so much hostility and hatred between people of different skin colour? However, I reflected on the feedback from the people I had thought were hostile to Whites and I had expected them to attack me for stating the obvious. My despair turned into excitement because of

the hope that I left this conference with. I also understood their passion about slavery because of the changes taking place in Zimbabwe. I feel I have lost my home and my culture. The painful realization of never seeing my grandmother's homestead again, never having a country home where our roots were is hard to think about. At least those whose ancestors were forced to leave their country have the slave masters to blame whereas people like me who chose to leave our country only have ourselves to blame. My children will never know where they came from or experience my culture the way I did because all my siblings and most of my cousins left Zimbabwe leaving noone to maintain the village home. Therefore, engaging passionately with the slavery concept feels me with guilt about my own contribution to the destruction of my children's history.

Personal development record		Date: 10th May	
Event	Planned objective	Personal objectives	Previous experience/ thoughts/feelings prior the event
Shooting the training video	To shoot a 30 minute training video for my research	a. To look good in the video b. To put across my points about Attachment Theory, linking child development to possible racial experiences.	1. I felt very anxious and hated to think about shooting the video. I kept cancelling the shooting and tried to get someone else to do it for me but noone was prepared to do it.

    c. To motivate viewers to think about the Black and White relationships based on working with similarities rather than differences.

    d. To encourage self reflection in order to improve self awareness of racial prejudices, stereotypical beliefs/thoughts/behaviours/feelings.

2. I was worried about my appearance and bought an expensive lip stick in the hope of improving my confidence

3. I knew that I would hate every minute of doing it so I tried to focus on when it is finished and how satisfying it would be.

What happened. An analysis of the event

1. One of my colleagues, Stu, offered to shoot the video and edit it. I felt calm and comfortable with Stu and we refused to have an audience. He was encouraging and calming which helped to keep me focused.

2. When he brought the video it was of poor quality, my face could hardly be seen because the lighting was poor, my expensive lipstick could not be seen because I became just "a black blob". Stu had ideas of improving the lighting and he offered to shoot the video again. The first shoot had been such an ordeal for me and I was not prepared to go through it again. The power point presentation was clear and my voice was clear only that it was coming out of "a black blob"—so what? I decided that the video was good enough as it was.

3. This experience reminded me of a time when I was six and my dad had upset me so when a door-to-door photographer passed by I asked him to take many photos of me and my white doll. We spent a fortune for my father to pay and he was not impressed. In the photos I came out as "a black blob" but my doll was nice and clear. In the Black History video my demonstration with the white doll showed me as "a black blob" and the white doll was nice and clear, what do you make of it?

What I learnt from it?	1. I learnt that working with imperfections can be much more fun as it threw up more material to analyse.
	2. When I watched the video I realized that I had made two grammatical errors. I said describe me in one word then I repeated by saying describe me *with* one word. The other mistake was adding verbs as descriptive words. Those mistakes kept replaying in my head and nearly drove me to surrender and re-shoot the video but the fear of standing in front of a camera again won the day.
Any further learning? (*Priorities*)	1. Watching the video I decided to use the original Black History demonstration of the white doll because it had the audience's response and their reaction was thought provoking. What was your reaction to the cover picture?
	2. I was surprised that people were surprised to see me carry a white doll on my back because I have always had white dolls. When I was growing up there were no black dolls at all so the choice was a white doll or a dressed-up maize cob.
	3. Watching the video made me think that it would be good to add a question about early life experiences in the interview schedule.

Personal development record			Date: 3rd July
Event	Planned objective	Personal objectives	Previous experience/ thoughts/feelings prior the event
Presenting the research at Manchester Metropolitan University Open Day.	1. To give an overview of my research. 2. To encourage feedback on what I need to think about. 3. To network.	To test my ability to present to a gathering of academics.	1. I had attended a pre-conference on 20th June where we had practised how to present our researches. I had been advised to present an overview since I was still working on my research. We were given a five minute trial run and we offered each other feedback on how we presented. I had received good feedback on how I get people involved by asking reflective questions and that I use my experience as a way of getting people curious and interested to know more. I felt confident and ready.
What happened? An analysis of the event	1. My husband accompanied me to Manchester. When we got there I carried my doll on my back all the time and most people looked at me curiously because it had its head covered. I had decided to do this so that people get used to seeing me with the "baby" on my back. I met my supervisor and then Sam Ndoro, a member from my PD group. It was good to see familiar faces and later I met other students who had been to the pre-conference workshop. We were excited to see each other. It felt as if we had known each other for a long time.		

2. When it came to presenting I was very nervous but people seemed quite interested. The doll demonstration was a hit, some had believed that it was a real baby but had been puzzled by its good behaviour—no fidgeting and no crying.

3. I displayed my research poster that looked simple among sophisticated ones but I still felt proud of it because I had done my best with the little knowledge I had on how to do it.

What I learnt from it

1. I learnt that my research was interesting and many people wanted know about my findings. I got a good number asking for my details—the start of the net working process.

2. I was grateful that my supervisor had asked me to take part in this event. If it had been left to me I would have avoided it because I was scared, yet by doing it I gained more confidence in my work and belief in myself.

3. I had looked more confident when presenting than I actually felt within myself.

4. I learnt that it is all right to be proud of my work and that it is down to me to sell myself. It is difficult when I was taught to be modest and it felt like showing off/boasting, then I argued with myself that I deserve to show off because I had worked hard.

Any further learning?
(*Priorities*)

1. To plan further networking. This event left me thirsty for recognition and hungry for more feedback so I needed to distribute my work to a wider audience.

2. To find out where I can present my work when it is finished.

3. Attending the conference motivated me into thinking more about a future research I could do. I found myself thinking about coming back and researching on Zimbabweans who are leaving the country as refugees coming to live here in poverty working in jobs well below their normal standards. What happens to their spirit? The lost culture? What happens to the country that is being drained of its human resources? I had so many questions and felt a new research forming itself. I had to force myself to stay focused on what I am doing now. I hope to be able to come back to do this.

CHAPTER FIFTY THREE

Personal Development Group in action

53.1 Setting up the group

When I first joined the Personal Development Group (PD group) I felt quite uncooperative and angry because I thought it would be a waste of time. During enrolment we set up our PD groups. I joined a group of part-timers because we planned to meet on Saturdays, whereas the other group was meeting during the week and due to work commitments I would not be able to commit to regular weekday meetings. We set a date for our first Saturday meeting.

When I came to the first meeting there were only four of us. This irritated me but as the meeting progressed I was surprised by the enthusiasm of the other three members. Jill offered to chair and Leanne offered to be the secretary. We worked on the contract and agreed to circulate it, allowing enough time for others to contribute. The contract was finalized and passed through at the second meeting. Here is the sample of our contract:

Contract for the Personal Development group

Membership
Members;   Alex
                   Anna
                   Jill
                   Ken
                   Leanne
                   Louise
                   MJ
                   Caroline

Objectives:
The PD meetings aim:

- To help members to achieve personal goals however, it is the individual's responsibility to bring their personal goals to the meeting.
- To offer peer support to its members and constructive feedback on their progress, however it is the member's responsibility to ask for feedback and other members to make personal decisions on how they give it—orally or in writing.
- To provide a space for individuals to share their skills and knowledge. Members will be asked to provide a personal profile stating their goals, skills, interests and work backgrounds. This will be emailed to all other members.

Membership—The group consists of seven part time students and one full time student who will provide a link with the other students. The full time students from the other group will be welcomed to social events.

Member's responsibility: Each member will be expected:

- To be punctual as the meeting will start and end on time.
- To communicate their absence to the Chair more than a week before the meeting, if possible, to allow time to cancel the meeting should the attendance be too low to form a group.
- To take personal responsibility in bringing up topics of interest to them for group discussion.
- To take responsibility of letting the Chair know of their opinions about any issue planned for discussion at a meeting they are unable to attend.
- To offer their names for nomination for the Chair's and the Secretary's posts.

Confidentiality: Members' personal contact details will be kept confidential to the group. Personal information shared in the group must not be taken out of the group without the consent of the concerned member. It is important for members to state that the information they are about to share is confidential before disclosing it. Should confidentiality be broken the group will seek the tutors' advice on how to deal with the responsible group member.

Behaviour: Abusive language and behaviour will not be tolerated. Members are expected to respect each other's beliefs and opinions. During meetings members are expected to be free of any mind altering substances.

The Chair: The Chair will be by nomination and will serve a period of six months.

The Chair's role would be:

- To collect items for the agenda, plan, and send out the agenda at least a week before the meeting.
- To make contact with any new students and inform them about the PD group.
- To circulate the dates for important events, for example nominations, in advance to allow for maximum attendance as it is a decision-making meeting.
- To invite the tutors to a meeting agreed to by the members.
- To circulate any deadline dates to remind members.
- To ensure that all correspondence is distributed to all group members.

Secretary: Will be appointed at each meeting.
The secretary's role will be:

- To write minutes of the meeting and distribute them to all members.
- To liaise with the Chair in preparing the agenda and circulating it.

Number of meetings:
Students are expected to attend a minimum of four meetings per year however more meetings will be held to accommodate those needing eight meetings in order to complete their training in one year.

Web-based meetings will also occur to support students completing in one year.

Time and venue:
The meetings will be held in Manchester Metropolitan University Library on Saturdays from 11.15 p.m. to 1.00 p.m.

Name of member..

Signature of member..

Date..

CHAPTER FIFTY FOUR

Personal development meetings

Our PD meetings became our main source of inspiration and support and we always started on time and finished on time. At first we agreed on having a secretary writing the minutes and distributing them but after some reflection we agreed that each individual take their own minutes, because they might need to reflect on their minutes-taking skills in their personal development write up. Those who missed a meeting would take the responsibility of getting minutes from those who attended.

The meetings were quite lively and interesting. Generally attendance was good. When the group became too large with a membership of twelve we decided to split it into two. At the first meeting after splitting the group, only two of us from our half of the group turned up. The other half invited us to join them. After this the group became one again as the numbers dropped. Here are two samples of the content of the PD meetings:

Sample 1
Personal development group meeting

Meeting held on 8th October

Attendees: Jill—Acting Chair
Louise
MJ
Leanne—Secretary

Apologies: Alex
Anna
Caroline
Ken

- It was agreed that minutes would be distributed to all members.
- **Contract**—The contract was drafted and will be circulated to all members. The contract will be finalized at the next meeting on 22nd October and any alterations or suggestions to be forwarded to Chair.
- **Journal format**—It was suggested that members decide on a format that suits them. MJ shared her format with the group. Jill and Leanne would like to use a more structured format.
- **Market visits**—MJ invited members to her market visit. She is presenting a paper on *"Psychotherapy penetrates beyond skin deep"* at a Black History event. The event aims at increasing referrals of Black Ethnic Minority service users to psychotherapy. The presentation is on Thursday 27th October. Those interested to contact MJ or Leanne who has MJ's flyers which give more information about the event and the venue.
- **Personal goals**—It was agreed that members would share their personal goals at the next meeting. Leanne is unable to attend so she will pass hers onto the Chair. It was decided that all members should email their goals and personal profiles to the Chair before the next meeting.
- **The Chair**—It was agreed that Jill would be the acting Chair until nominations, which will be held on 22nd October. Those who cannot attend to email their nominations to the Chair before the meeting.
- **Tutor attendance**—Louise is to find out how many meetings tutors have to attend a year.
- **Membership**—Jill to invite Mary and Katie the new part time students seeking to join a PD group.
- **AOB**—Next meeting is 22nd October.
- The agenda for the next meeting:

Contract
Introductions from members: about themselves and their personal goals
Learning objectives
Reading lists

Sample 2
Personal development group minutes

Meeting held on 22nd October

Attendees:	9 members
Apologies:	3 members
Agenda:	1. Splitting the group
	2. Contract—to finalize and sign
	3. Introductions and personal goals
	4. Reading list—activity for next meeting
	5. Inviting tutor
	6. The Chair
	7. AOB
	8. Date of next meeting

Splitting the group

Members were made aware that the group had increased from 8 to 12 members since the last meeting. One suggestion was to split the group into two. Initially most group members were undecided about this. Three absent members had emailed their votes for the split. During the meeting it became clear that the group could not function effectively with a large membership so it was agreed to split it up into two, both groups had one male and five females.

Louise suggested that both groups meet on the same day and at the same time so that we could still attend social events together.

We went into our new groups to set the agenda for the following meeting. (I was in Group 2). Louise was chosen to be the Acting-Chair for Group 2 till election.

Contract

- Jill asked the group for their opinions on the draft contract.
- Ken noted that the meeting time needed to be changed to 11:15 a.m. to accommodate MJ who will be coming from Surrey.
- New members—Sam, Mary, Jo, and Katie need to be added onto the membership list.
- Some discussion about forming a closed group for fear of the numbers increasing again but no decision made as people need more time to reflect on the implications of this decision.
- Caroline suggested that the contract be reviewed at a later date, if and when circumstances within the group change.

Jo suggested further changes to the wording of the contract—all agreed with her.

Introductions and personal goals
A deadline of 29th October was set for all to email personal profiles and personal learning goals to the Chair. The personal profiles should include information such as one's areas of expertise, relevant employment history and hobbies.

Reading List
It was agreed that each member chooses a book from the reading list and presents something from it.

AOB

- Market visits—Ken, Jill, and Sam confirmed attending the Black History presentation. Anna will forward details about another market visit to all members.
- Jill will circulate the amended contract to all members and will send a copy to the course tutors.

Date of next meeting:
Saturday 10th December.

CHAPTER FIFTY FIVE

Reflecting on working on the research

55.1   The training video

Initially I had planned to use the video that was shot when I presented my paper: *Psychotherapy penetrates beyond skin colour* at a Black History event, but unfortunately the sound was terrible because the sensitive microphone had picked up the noise from the nearby construction work, destroying our video. I decided to shoot a thirty-minute video still using the same presentation. I roped in my family. My eldest daughter, Karen, was my make-up artist. My youngest daughter, Kiara, helped me rehearse the poem I was going to recite so she was my director and choreographer. The rest were cynics who thought they had found free entertainment. It was fun working with both supporters and cynics.

55.2   Grounding theories

Deciding on the grounding theory for my research was easy as I knew what theories are important when dealing with skin colour issues. However, I became interested in seeing how these theories were experienced within the PD group. For my research I chose Attachment Theory (Bowlby, 1973) as one of my grounding theories. I felt that in my PD

350

group we had grown a healthy attachment to each other and were able to support and hold each other in mind even when apart. Sometimes we emailed each other when anxious about our progress or to just catch up if the break between meetings was long, for example:

From: MJ

Sent: 13 June 16:38

To: Sam

Subject: Re: Greetings

Sam,
I have been busy digging and planting maize and pumpkins, so I am well behind schedule. I am hoping to carry out the field research in July. I need 16 participants and at the moment I only have one. So, I am a bit scared about not having enough people to interview.

I will try to start working on the paper next week. Are you coming on Saturday? Do you know where we are meeting on Monday 20th? I don't know whether to come to Manchester on Sunday or not.

MJ

From: Samuel

Sent: 14 June 14:49

To: MJ

Subject: Re: Greetings

Hie MJ,
It has been a pleasure reading your email after such a long time. *Sha*, I have been busy with my research and at last I have finished the ethic approval and I will hand it on Friday, after approval I will start. My target is to finish it in August.

How far are u with yours now? I will meet you on Monday the 20th for the pre-conference.

I am ok.

SEE U

In my research I explored Klein's concepts of the defence mechanisms when dealing with Black and White issues. In our PD group there was a Black/White split which resulted in two of us pairing up (Bion).

Sam and I were the only Black students and were both Zimbabweans, so we tended to split off by speaking in our home language, Shona, when others were not present. While I am aware of pairing as a defence mechanism that can be destructive, I felt that our pairing allowed for a different experience as we continued encouraging each other in working on our individual projects. At other times we reflected on the distress in our country and shared our concerns for its future. As a Zimbabwean, Sam could appreciate my news on my progress in farming at my allotment, which others would have found boring.

When the group stopped meeting in summer Sam and I kept contact and supported each other in presenting our researches at the Research Institute of Health and Social Change conference. We were the only ones from our PD group to present.

55.3   Impact of presenting the research

When presenting the research at the Research Institute of Health and Social Change Conference I was nervous and intimidated by so many academics. I felt I was offering a humble meal but was surprised by the interest shown in my research, and left the conference excited and rejuvenated. I had been feeling overwhelmed with my research but after presenting it that was replaced with clarity and enthusiasm. I suddenly knew what I needed to do and how to do it. I gained much confidence and became very proud of my work. The labour pains had disappeared as I proudly cuddled my bundle of joy.

After completing my research I was unable to present my findings to my PD group because by the time I had analysed the findings the group had stopped meeting. However, since presenting at the conference I became motivated and confident in presenting whenever I got the opportunity, for example at the WPF Therapy and at the following Black History event. My manager read my research and asked me to present it at our academic forum.

55.4   What was the cost of studying?

When we enroll for training or studying we tend to think about the financial cost and the blood, sweat, and tears that goes into studying, but we forget about the cost on those who love us and are affected by our decision. My poor family missed me even though we still lived under the same roof. I stopped enjoying them because I was consumed with my work.

My younger children and grandchildren tried all sorts of tricks to draw my attention away from the work: they kept coming in to ask for things when they knew where they were, they kept fighting and having accidents. Sometimes I responded by barking, but for them being barked at was better than no attention. At other times I felt guilty but soothed my conscience by reminding myself of the promise of good times to come. Wherever possible I included them in my work. Kim and Brendan were interested in the findings, but Bryan and Tayler-Ray were not at all amused by my absence and had a lot to say about it. Bryan spent more time with me at the allotment where he could have my total attention as we dug and planted the maize, corn, and pumpkins.

However, when it came to the graduation everyone was excited and everyone claimed the right to attend. I could only get two guest tickets for a dozen of my immediate family—children and grandchildren. When I pleaded with administration they gave me three more tickets. It was difficult to decide which five would go, so in the end everyone came and fortunately there were empty seats so everyone attended. The following day we toured the university site, then went to Blackpool to celebrate. Soaking in the pleasure on everyone's face was very rewarding. I was forgiven.

My family would agree that the cost was worth the outcome. Personally, I enjoyed being a student at Manchester Metropolitan University because of the support I got from my supervisor, my PD group, the programme management tutors and administration staff. I believe I have developed into an established flourishing bamboo that treasures constructive interactions with others and deals with challenges by being strong and creative and, most importantly, like the indoor bamboo, by being able to trust and accept help from other people.

I have seen myself grow from a sulking immature old woman to a content, confident, respected, respectful, and seasoned old woman. I will definitely come back for further studies.

CONCLUSION

Racism as a form of abuse

Racism, like any other form of abuse, does claim victims. The experience is often traumatic and can destroy one's self-esteem and confidence. It can cause mental and physical ill-health. Racism can also generate social problems as the burden of its consequences affect family and work relationships, not to mention employment prospects as victims fail, or no longer have the opportunity, to operate at their optimum. This in turn can be a great loss for a society.

The impact of racism, therefore, should never be underestimated, and recovery depends on how the person is supported in coping with their experiences. Whether one continues being caught in the web of racial victimization—or becomes a perpetrator in a tit-for-tat game—also depends on the support given in exploring alternative ways of coping. One of the most effective tools is psychotherapy, which can facilitate the separation of what might have been evoked from the past onto the present and make sense of it all.

The search for a caregiver

It is impossible to work with racism without some understanding of the important theories, such as Bowlby's Attachment Theory, Klein's defence mechanisms, Winnicott's Hate in Countertransference, Bollas's concept of extractive introjection and the Racial Identity Models—just to mention a few. These theories guide the counsellor/therapist while sailing in the whirlpool of complex emotions.

At the John Bowlby Twentieth Anniversary Conference (2010), Jude Cassidy spoke about the impact of a traumatic event on an individual. She said that if the individual has a secure attachment, their ability to empathize and explore is reduced drastically as the fear triggered by the trauma takes hold. They seek a caregiver to contain their fear, and if the caregiver proves to be available the individual is able to survive the experience because the fear is contained and reduced to a manageable level: and their ability to empathize and explore is restored. This is illustrated in Part One of this book, where I looked at how I sought a caregiver in the form of the Employment Tribunal. Since the first Employment Tribunal proved to be an available caregiver by creating enough time for my case and listening to what I had to say, I was able to stand up for myself at the hearing: on returning to work I was able to feel empathy for colleagues who had been unfair to me and I regained the capacity to explore and make sense of my experiences. I believe if I meet anyone who was involved with the first Employment Tribunal I will genuinely be pleased to see them again because what they did was not as deliberately cruel as those involved with the second tribunal who instisted that they banned the animal metaphors. However, Cassidy (2010) states that if the individual has an insecure attachment or fails to find an available caregiver, the fear is heightened and the individual does not recover from the event; their ability to show empathy and to explore remains reduced. I believe the Second Employment Tribunal, by not finding time to hear my case in full, was unavailable for me. Therefore, without the available caregiver, the fear was heightened and I regressed considerably. I could not restore my ability to show empathy and to explore. I had expected the Second Employment Tribunal to contain my distress and fear in the same way I had expected my father's best friend to contain my distress and fear: to be there for me, to make time to listen to me and be my secure base. When both failed me the fear I was experiencing was heightened and

I had to seek other caregivers (my distant cousin and my part-time employer).

Why that particular cousin? Because she had worked for my father, and she was one of the people who looked after me when I was young. She was my secondary secure base whom I sought when in distress after losing my primary caregiver.

Why my part-time employer? Because that was my training hospital, the first hospital I came to after arriving in the United Kingdom, and it took good care of me when I was new and vulnerable in a foreign country. It was my secure base. Thus, both my cousin and my part-time employer were able to contain my distress and the fear died down. I regained my capacity to explore and show empathy. I was ready to face the world again.

When victims of racism visit our consulting rooms they come in search of a secure base, a caregiver who is consistently available to make time to listen, to create a safe space to contain their fear and distress so that they can be assisted in moving on from the victim position to a position of strength. The ability to explore and show empathy can only be regained when the fear is contained.

Reconciliation between victim and perpetrator

Reconciliation between a victim and a perpetrator can be achieved by seeking a safe secure base to contain the individuals and to allow for exploration and make sense of the experience. Sometimes perpetrators end up feeling like victims or become victims of their victims, while victims may become perpetrators of their perpetrators. Sometimes racist experiences are like sitting on a see-saw—swapping the victim/perpetrator roles in an up-and-down movement. For example, being taken to an Employment Tribunal can be a traumatic experience for a person who is experienced as racist. My observation is that a small number of people are made responsible for institutional failings, a tall order for an individual or the few made to carry the can because they end up being the institution's scapegoats. The perpetrators follow the same cycle as victims, in search of a secure base, a calming caregiver to contain their fears and distress. Victims/perpetrators of racism are some of the people who might visit our consulting rooms: therefore, one of the therapist's tasks is to create a safe secure base for exploration.

The other task is in finding the victim in a perpetrator and the perpetrator in a victim as a way of moving on. Being a victim might earn some sympathy but it does not get one out of the hole of helplessness. Curling up like a millipede and hoping to die is not a solution.

The Black person as an organizational container

Historically, Blacks have contained negative projections of being ignorant, stupid, lazy, over-sexualized, murderous, mad, and so on. While the role of a scapegoat is essential in carrying the unwanted load, it is important to understand that being the carrier of unwanted projections is a heavy burden for an individual. On the other hand, disowned projections can leave the organization impoverished, because it loses part of its function that allows for effective working.

The Black junior clinician, who was fired for being incompetent even though the problem of patients absconding from hospital was a long-standing one, is an example of an individual being made to carry the responsibility of an organization's failings. The organization decided not to investigate the incident and so lost the opportunity to explore what the Black junior clinician was made to carry for it. Firing her did not solve the problem. If the organization had owned up to the incompetence and taken responsibility for sorting out the abscond problem by investigating the incident, it would have learnt that in order to function more effectively it needed to ensure that security checks were being carried out regularly; that all windows were on the check list and that the appropriateness of treating people with Borderline Personality Disorder on an open acute admission ward needed to be reviewed. That would have led the organization to consider offering psychotherapy, but this opportunity was lost and one of the consequences of sacrificing the Black junior clinician was that the organization was in the local paper being taken to task over its ineffectiveness in treating people who needed psychological therapy. Projecting onto an individual is destructive to both the individual and the organization.

When I carried projections for my organization I could not function effectively. At first I did not mind because I understood the concept of being made the container of unwanted projections, but when I could not give them back it became very difficult because I felt burdened. Had the internal investigation accepted that some of the things happening to me were because of my race I would have felt understood and contained, and had the organization accepted some responsibility for what was going on I would not have sought outside help, but denying my claims made me more determined to prove the reality of my experiences. When an organization refuses to take back its projections it leaves itself vulnerable, as an individual is likely to take legal action against it rather than carry the burden of negative projections and suffer the consequences.

Institutional racism needs to be challenged, but this is not easy for the individual or the witnesses because of the fear of isolation and further victimization. In this book I have shown how both Blacks and Whites share the fear of victimization. The reality of this fear is serious: because of my personal experience of the cost of daring to challenge racism, I now understand and appreciate why it is difficult for witnesses to challenge any racism they might observe. However, I still think it is worth doing something about what we witness, otherwise we become part of the machinery that perpetuates racism. I could not live with witnessing individuals suffer without doing anything to support them—they would sit heavily on my conscience.

The racist register and early life/traumatic experiences

Mr Smith's vignette demonstrates how one can use a racist register as a way of defending against feeling vulnerable and against fear of rejection. By being racist Mr Smith was trying to get some control over a situation he felt was out of his control. Looking at the child development stages discussed in the video presentation, the first few stages are when children are most vulnerable because they have not developed a language to articulate feelings they might be experiencing. The most difficult early life experiences are within one's family—first with the attachment figure and then gradually with the growing family; after that come school relationships, then society at large. It was during these early stages that Mr Smith experienced his father's rejection because of his skin condition, which left him feeling unwanted and unloved by his father.

At this tender age children do not pick on the difference of skin colour: they classify people by the roles the individuals play in their lives. For example, a four year old whose mother was White got upset that her mixed-race father was being called black, stating, "He is not Black. He is my dad".

By the time children begin to understand treatment based on skin colour difference they would have developed enough language to articulate their experiences—for example, my son at five years of age coming home upset because he was called "poo-poo colour"—and families can help their children in dealing with such experiences.

Mr Smith became aware of the skin colour difference and the rejection of Blacks by his society in his late teens, and when he saw his Black therapist his immediate reaction was to use racist language to defend against his vulnerability and fear of rejection. The most traumatic rejection he had experienced was by his father because of his skin condition, and he was now rejecting the therapist, whom he identified with, for her skin colour. The therapist's task is to contain and hold on to the racist behaviour, then later work on finding and understanding its meaning for the individual. Mr Smith was able to make the link between his racist outburst and the rejection by his father and could mourn the parent he never had. The racist register helped him find words for the internal pain he was previously unable to articulate.

It would be interesting to research the background of racists to try and understand why A and not B reacts in a racist register. My belief is that those who use racist language are trying to tell us something about their internal pain—early childhood wounds that have nothing to do with race. Being racist gives them the strength needed to release that pain, which has more to do with their own early family experiences rather than solely with people of a different skin colour.

My own experience must also say something about the kind of people who complain about racism. I was brought up in a Black community having hardly any contact with Whites and I came from a very affluent family, so I was not used to being perceived as inferior, being discriminated against or being made to feel like a second-class citizen because of my skin colour. However, as a child I always felt that I was discriminated against and treated like a second-class citizen by my extended family because they were angry with my mother who left their son/brother to look after six children. I think their anger with my mother was displaced on me as the eldest daughter; fortunately my father picked this up and protected me by refusing to let someone else take us to look after. The common practice was that when a mother was absent the children were looked after by a grandmother, but my father chose to keep us and employed nannies and house maids.

However, we occasionally still visited our grandmother in the countryside. I loved my grandmother—not only was she was the best story teller I have ever known, but she often saved me from my father's wrath. For example, if I had done something wrong I would not tell until my grandmother was visiting us. That was a good time to confess because I could then *potera* behind my grandmother (seek refuge behind her). No parent could beat his child in front of his mother, no matter what, and once I *potera* my father could not punish me for that crime ever again. So, my grandmother was a great source of comfort and refuge.

However, she was also my source of pain, because she was one of the very few people who made me miss my mother. The one thing she did which pierced right into my heart was favouring some of her grandchildren. I remember from a very young age being filled with rage for grandmother for always favouring my cousins—the children by her daughters. In Shona culture the children belong to the father, therefore the children of a daughter belonged to their father, *mukwasha*, son-in-law. Therefore *vana vemukwasha* (children of a son-in-law) were treated well. Since I was her grandchild by her son I was her family and did not matter as much as my cousins. If I got hurt while in my grandmother's care it was said *ihuku yadya mazai ayo*, meaning, it is a hen which has eaten its own eggs so it does not matter. On the other hand, if my cousin was hurt my grandmother would run around like a headless chicken, clapping her hands in despair trying to make it better, chanting "*Nhasi hangu nemwana wemukwasha!*" which is equivalent to "Oh, today I am in trouble with the son-in-law's child!"

The only time I felt proud of my grandmother treating me better than my cousin was when she gave us maize cobs to share. She always gave me and my sister a cob each, then asked us to give a piece to her favourite granddaughter. My sister and I felt proud to own a cob each and happily broke half of it to give to our "poor cousin", who had none. However, as I grew older and began to understand fractions I realized that while my sister and I had half a cob each our cousin had two halves, making it a full cob. I felt angry and stupid; to this day I react angrily when I feel I am being treated unfairly, like an idiot. So, my experience of racism gets connected to this experience of unfairness and of yearning for a mother to take care of me. I end up feeling the burning urge to prove that I am not an idiot and can look after myself.

My awareness of racism was in my teens, when I became conscious of the racial segregation. Unlike my family experiences, which happened when I was young and vulnerable, the racial discrimination was when I was old enough to articulate, so I had the language to fight back. Had I been brought up in a multi-racial society I might have learnt better ways of dealing with racism, or acquired the learned helplessness of accepting that "racism happens, so what?", but with my background racism was just unacceptable. Growing up in a society that fought for its liberation, raised by a father who encouraged a fighting spirit from a very young age, set me up to combat racism—a repetitive attempt to correct the unfairness I experienced at an age when I could not articulate.

The fact that I represented myself three times may indicate that I have an avoidant attachment, not trusting anyone to do any important job for me because of my upbringing with an absent mother. I had to step in and step up as a mother to my younger siblings. They could rely on me but I could not allow myself to rely on them. My family would say I was a problem child because I stood my ground. Again, it would be interesting to research what kind of people complain about racism when others can ignore the unfairness. Why would B complain about racism and not A?

The fact that I have been to three Employment Tribunals can make me appear like someone with a chip on her shoulder, and if I play with that idea there might be something in it, because racist experiences are only a vehicle of the more raw family early-life experiences for both perpetrators and victims of racism. I believe that for the victims, some of these unfair experiences (for example, the unfair treatment by my grandmother) are easier to deal with if we see them as racism (for example, the unfairness of institutional racism) because our experiences of racism happen at a time when we are able to speak for ourselves.

In fighting racism, if one does not get drawn back into early life traumas or unfairness one is able to remain in control of articulating oneself. For example, I was able to deal with racism during the first Employment Tribunal because the tribunal was available to me and we stayed focused on exploring the racism. On the other hand, when the second Employment Tribunal proved to be unavailable to me, that triggered off the pain of the unfairness of not having my own mother to take care of me like my cousins and friends had, and this was compounded by my feelings of betrayal by colleagues I identified with: that sense of betrayal got entangled with my traumatic family early life experiences—the betrayal by my own people at my most vulnerable time—when my mother left us and when my father died. The case stopped being about my complaints as the fear around feelings of betrayal by my father's best friend was brought back to life during the second Employment Tribunal. I regressed and relived my fears. Therefore, it is easier to deal with racism than with issues connected to one's earlier traumatic life experiences.

When working with racism it is import to think about child developmental stages because they set the therapist and the individual to start from a point of connection: they are on common ground because, whether Black or White, they know what it feels like to be ignored, discriminated against and excluded. The research showed that dwelling on difference, especially during the initial sessions, may make a client or counsellor/therapist more anxious with the possibility of falling into the paranoid–schizoid position, a position that defends against connecting with the other person, and the client is in danger of being lost.

Containing the destruction

In Part Two I looked at how feelings around racial experiences can spread to other relationships, for example, my relationships with Whites on my training course, where I perceived the help I was offered as racism. I became the perpetrator attacking my supervision space, but my supervisor was robust enough to withstand the attack and we were able to make sense of the dynamics evoked. Supervision is a very valuable space for containing and making sense of the dynamics in action, as they can be re-enacted between supervisor and supervisee. The research showed that it is no use knowing the theory—for instance, transference and countertransference—without the ability to identify the dynamic when it is in operation. Racism is a complicated dynamic and can only be worked through if the counsellor/therapist is willing to be honest and is prepared to improve his or her own racial self-awareness. Sometimes the counsellor's/therapist's own personal dynamics interfere with therapy, but if one is honest in supervision then one could be assisted in working out what needs to be taken to one's own personal therapy for further exploration, leaving the counsellor/therapist in a position to make sense of the transference and countertransference.

Training in a White-dominated institution proved that Whites can work with racism and contain the individual, but it calls for the container to be firm and unafraid. Political correctness does not help, because valuable information is not challenged and worked with. On the other hand, just because someone is Black does not necessarily mean they can contain feelings evoked by racist experiences, nor does it mean that the Black client would be better understood. However, the betrayal which can be experienced between Blacks can be devastating for the client. As role models, responsibilities are placed on us, and the solution is not in avoiding letting someone down, but in helping them face up to the reality of their situation, which might include failing to live up to their phantasy. Therefore, the work would be in supporting them to survive and to work through their disillusionment.

It is easier to work on racial experiences when one has worked through one's own feelings of racial shame and guilt—often felt by Whites because of the history of slavery, and by Blacks for being silent witnesses to racism. Sometimes the stories are so awful that it is a struggle to remain untouched, and to not want to make it better, justify or deny the reality of the story, because one cannot withstand the awfulness of the experience. Such interventions would be unhelpful. It is important to work with the emotions evoked, make sense of the experience and explore the client's options. Sometimes moving away from the situation is a better option and should not be seen as defeat—it is taking care of oneself.

Feelings of abandonment, separation, and loss often come into play when working with racism, and we need to understand when someone is regressing in order to catch and contain them. These feelings have a wildfire effect, and can spread to other relationships if not contained.

Internalized racism

My research has had a powerful impact on me, making me more tolerant of others and more aware of my own unconscious racism. I now speak with confidence, authority and clarity. In the past, if someone attacked me or racially discriminated against me I took it personally—I would get angry and respond by saying something clever but hurtful and sarcastic, then walk off to organize a counter-attack. Now I go for resolution or choose my fights more carefully, which means letting go of most insults: I prefer to use my energy in engaging in constructive work. That is what I have gained from this research and from studying and working with racism and cultural diversity.

However, I do not think one can ever be totally free of internalized racism. For example, just when I thought I had figured out all my racial stereotypic assumptions and believed they no longer influenced my actions, I found myself in court because someone drove into the back of my car. At the time of the accident I was quite dazed, disorientated and in pain, but my internalized racial stereotypic thinking told me to be grateful that the other driver was an old White man and therefore in the category I considered to be the safest group of people. He told me not to worry, but left immediately because he was late for a meeting. I let him go without getting any witnesses because I was confident that I could trust a stranger simply because he was White and old.

Imagine my shock when I received legal papers demanding over a thousand pounds for the cost of the accident and personal losses! He said that if I failed to pay he would take me to court somewhere up north in a town I thought only existed in Lenny Henry's comedy (Dudley), and that it would cost me even more if I did not pay within two weeks. I could have been intimidated into paying, and my insurance was willing to pay, but he had picked the wrong person to try this on. We ended up in our local court, where I was quite prepared to defend myself but in the end did not have to—we won the case hands down, and he had to pay more than ten times what he had demanded from me.

The point here is that I trusted a stranger because my stereotypic thinking controlled my judgement of the situation. I relaxed and trusted a stranger simply because he was a White old man. This event awakened me from my internalized racism slumber. Do you have your own people you consider a safe category or a threat just because of their skin colour, age, or both?

At one of the Black History events I organized, the theme was *Belonging to two cultures, is it a blessing, mixed blessings or a curse?* When I decided on the date my priority was to have the event at the beginning of October so that I would have enough time to write up a report about it. To my disgrace, however, I realized that I had not considered the people who were fasting during Ramadan. In my group I had Muslim patients who had been talking about fasting yet I failed to note that the date I had chosen was inconvenient for them; maybe a week later would have been better. They attended the event but decided to arrive after lunch so they would not be tempted to eat. I like my food and felt punished with them as I imagined what it must be like to have Caribbean cuisine teasing your nostrils all afternoon without a bite. One of them talked about how much he loved jerk chicken. I had unintentionally discriminated against this group of people.

Added to this, some of the White participants were disappointed because we did not serve sandwiches. It never occurred to me that anyone would prefer sandwiches to jerk chicken, plantains, curry goat, chicken rice and peas. I had organized the event like a Black African and had discriminated against two groups of people. It might not have been intentional, but ignorance is no excuse.

Embracing other people's diversity

Thinking about how residents embraced the use of my cultural diversity, the animal metaphors in their therapy, made me think of others who embrace cultural diversity with a similar level of enthusiasm—Mother Nature and her wild life. While I was suffering racism and racial discrimination at work I felt angry that at my allotment I was not suffering any of it at all. When I grew African crops, the British wild life, which I assumed to be White, did not discriminate against my crops and think *This is a bit inferior and primitive, let's go for the British brand.* No, not the wild life.

Planting sweet potatoes is not an easy task, because one has to dig deep and make moulds bigger than for ordinary potatoes, a bit like a long fresh grave. I toiled on the land and with the hosepipe ban carried gallons of water in buckets to and fro a bit of a distance. I sweated and suffered and sweated some more, but the vision of a basketful of sweet potatoes kept me going. How many baskets did I harvest, you may well ask? None. Not a single sweet potato, because while I was slaving away above ground, basking at the promising sweet potato greenery crawling around on the surface (it is a climber), the British slugs underground were having a field-day partying as they munched and chewed through all my sweet potatoes. Who told British slugs about sweet potatoes?

I gave up sweet potatoes and moved on to maize. Because maize needs a longer warm season, I decided to grow them in small pots in the greenhouse first, with the plan of transferring them to the allotment three weeks later. Then one sunny morning I decided to leave the greenhouse door open. When I came back the squirrels had been. They dug up every single pot and ate the seeds, leaving the seedlings to die. I spoke to my White neighbour expecting some sympathy, but she told me it was my fault: if I had left some seeds for the squirrels they would not have been hungry! Not many Blacks would think of feeding a wild animal!

Anyway, I became better at growing maize. Brixton is a wonderful place for getting anything to experiment with, so initially I grew Ghanaian maize, but only for one season because the British weasels found the seeds I had reserved for the following season and turned them to powder. I now grow English sweet-corn, maroon pop-corn, Jamaican corn, and Zimbabwean maize. My favourite is Jamaican corn, which is multi-coloured and very sweet ... but the word was out. The British birds landed. They selectively went for the sweet Jamaican corn. How did they know? How can they tell a Jamaican stalk from the rest when they all look the same except for a light red tint on the Jamaican stalk and comb? But the British birds knew.

If you look at the front cover again, can you pick out the Jamaican corn? In the *rusero she is carrying there* are three types of corn,. Looking at the naked cobs you might be able to tell the difference but can you tell the difference among the three different crops behind her? The British birds can tell. Just to help you, in the *rusero* the woman is carrying, the yellow corn at the top is the English sweet corn, the multi-coloured cobs in the middle are Jamaican corn, and the white cobs are Zimbabwean maize. Looking at the ones with the leaves in the *rusero*, can you tell which is which? I can assure you there is a bit of red tint on the Jamaican. crop That is the defining difference. You might not notice it but the British birds worked it all out: they will only eat Jamaican corn. They made their preference known ... to my annoyance.

I will leave you to work out what we could learn from Mother Nature and her wild life about embracing other people's culture.

Society without therapy: the England riots of 2011

In previous chapters I discussed Winnicott's (1984) belief that antisocial behaviour shows that there is hope, hope of rediscovering a good enough mother/caregiver. So, even in the scenes of England consumed by tongues of fire there was hope, if only we could listen for it and nurture it to good health instead of drowning ourselves in self pity and worrying about what our global neighbours would say or think.

The 2011 England riots have given us a large and severe headache. It takes me back to the description of feeling Mama Elephant, a metaphor I used to discuss what happens when conflict kicks off in a therapeutic community. Where there is conflict there is splitting, a defence mechanism that splits things into Black/White, good/bad, in-group/ out-group, rich/poor, have lots/have nots; as a way of cutting off the undesirable and preserving what is perceived to be precious to an individual, a group or a nation. It is also a way of coping with what feels too shaming and too painful to stay with. We need to stay with it because shouting without listening to one another will bring chaos and divisions. There are divisions being played out, for example politicians/police. When divided we will definitely fall. This is not the time or place to fight about who got it right and who could have done better. Our children need to be contained.

For example, when my children shame me I will listen to their views, then draw a line with them about what is right or wrong, but I will not disown them. They will always be mine even though there are times I wish I could pass them on to someone else. But then, I was brought up in a culture which says "*Ane benzi ndeanerake, rikadzana anopuru-rudza.*" Translating this is a challenge because there is no translation for *pururudza*—the noise women make with their fingers tapping over their mouths during celebrations. However, basically it means that he who has a mad relative, it's his, and when the mad one dances he joins in making the celebrating noise. It is about accepting the relatives one has and making the best of them rather than being ashamed of them. It is also about normalizing the abnormal. Therefore, even the rioters need help in reflecting and understanding the impact of their behaviour.

The rioters frightened us and got us all hugging Mama Elephant, everyone shouting out what feels close to their hearts, but are we listening to each other? To get the full picture of what Mama looks like we have to rely on each other in building up the picture, so to be able to contain our children and grow as a nation from the experience we need to listen, especially to those who hold opinions different to ours, including the rioters. Obviously those holding Mama's trunk and those holding her bottom will have different views to offer, but neither is right or wrong—just different. The police, politicians, media, youth workers, former criminals/looters and rioters and so on will have a different opinion depending on what they specialize in. However, in all the coverage in the first week after the events there were two missing voices— the rioters and the therapists. There was plenty of coverage on what will be done to the rioters/looters but no-one offered them a platform to debate the simple question—What was that about?

Professor Gus John of University of London suggested an inquiry led by the youth after the murder of London teenager Yemurai Kanyangarara. John believes that such an inquiry would be more effective because "disaffected young people" are more likely to find solutions to the violence that erupted across the country and it would give them a chance to dispel myths about causes of youth crime (Williams, 2011).

I was interested in hearing the psychotherapists' voice because these are the people we work with daily and we are able to hold onto their other side, the side which whispering family members, friends, colleagues and neighbours tried to voice in their shock, "I can't believe she/he was involved in this." But this side that holds hope for the future is stifled, as we need to project the all-bad image on all looters and rioters.

Therefore, my focus is going to be on the young adults and the vulnerable adults who were caught up in this, because I do not believe that they deserve simply punishment without support to make sense of all this. I will not talk about those who committed murder or those who set fire to buildings with flats above them because they should have known that some people would be home. Human life is precious and if they cannot understand this then they need more than I can offer.

The history between Black youth and White police officers

Bollas talks about theft of self, that when elements of one's psyche are extracted and one's sense of identity destroyed, then feelings of primary injustice may be experienced and the desire to seek revenge. The law of talion is an unconscious act intended to recover by "violent intrusion into the other to recover what has been stolen from oneself." Therefore, we cannot afford to look at this national acting-out in isolation from its history. We need to understand what justified this behaviour. We need to listen to the history and identify the repeated patterns.

1981 Brixton riots

There is a history between the White police officers and the Black youth. The Brixton riots of 1981 were triggered off by the mistrust of the police by the Black community. The Black community felt that the police had delayed in taking a seriously injured boy to hospital; the police's view was that it would be too dangerous to move the boy so they decided to wait for an ambulance. A group of Blacks forcefully took the boy away from the police to hospital. This incident provoked the Brixton riots of 1981. There was looting and burning of buildings and vehicles. An inquiry was led by Lord Scarman.

1985 Brixton riots

The September 1985 riots were triggered off by an incident in which a black woman was shot during a police search. Cherry Groce was paralysed from the waist down. Black people rioted and set fire to buildings and cars, looted from shops, and a journalist, David Hodge, was attacked and killed. Ms Janet Boateng, a Labour councillor, said that "the real lack of accountability of the police" was demonstrated when Mr. Alec Marnoch, the local police commander, refused their request to meet with him to discuss the shooting of Mrs Groce and the consequent problems facing the community. Mr Marnoch's view was that the community leaders had convinced him that the riot had been the work of "a criminal and hooligan element" which is swiftly being "excluded" from the rest of Brixton. He denied that the riot had shown a widespread hatred of the police (Rose, 1985). Douglas Lovelock, the police officer who shot Cherry Groce, was acquitted of malicious wounding.

1985 Tottenham riots/Broadwater Farm riots

In October 1985, there remained a tense atmosphere between the Black community and White police officers because of the Brixton events. Then another death occurred in Tottenham, a week after the Brixton riots. Cynthia Jarrett, an African-Caribbean woman, collapsed during a police search of her home and died. This resulted in another riot. Again there was looting and burning of property and cars. Constable Keith Blakelock was killed when he went into the estate with a group of officers (Policing London, 1986).

1999 Tottenham riots

In January 1999, Roger Sylvester, another Tottenham resident, died after being restrained by eight policemen. The officers were suspended following an unlawful killing verdict but were reinstated when this verdict was challenged and overturned. No police officer was prosecuted for his death.

There was a belief in the Black community that the police were racist in the way they dealt with Black youth, and the Scarman report into Brixton riots of 1981 had criticized the police. Years later another inquiry, the MacPherson Inquiry into the death of Stephen Lawrence, accused police of institutional racism.

Therefore, the history of the tension between the Black community and White police officers has its roots deeply embedded in their lack of trust, and even though the riots were triggered by a death of a Black person after police involvement, no officer was held responsible.

Philip Larkin's poem warns us of passing misery from generation to generation. We need to study our history and see where the problem lies in order to make sense of what needs to be different, otherwise history will keep on repeating itself.

2011 England riots

The August 2011 England riots were sparked off by the death of a young man of mixed heritage, Mark Duggan (twenty-nine) who was shot by the police trying to arrest him. The Tottenham community staged a peaceful demonstration requesting an investigation into his death but this was high-jacked by rioters and looters in Tottenham, with disturbances then spreading to Hackney, Enfield, Lewisham, Clapham, Brixton, Croydon, Catford, Ealing, and so on. The ripple then moved out to other cities and towns outside London: for example, Birmingham, Liverpool, Manchester, and Nottingham. Buildings and vehicles were set on fire and looting took place everywhere. In Birmingham three Asian men were run over and killed while protecting their community.

Why are the youth so angry?

I believe that we need to understand why the youth are angry even to the point of self destruction. I am sure people do not want to hear what they have to say, in the same way that people did not want to hear my stories of racism. I will discuss one of these in order to illustrate the intense feelings around Blacks being targeted for stop and search.

My nineteen year old nephew, Tafadzwa, my late brother Obediah's son, worked hard in two jobs while attending college, and after years of saving he decided to surprise me by buying himself a car. He thought that he could first buy the car, then get the insurance. This was an easy assumption because he had seen us buy cars from a private car dealer friend and get the insurance afterwards, but what he did not know was that our dealer had the car insured until we got our own insurance. Unlike us, however, he bought his Ford Focus hatchback at a Croydon garage, but five minutes after driving out of the garage he was stopped and searched. Being nineteen and Black, driving a white car with tinted windows is as good as waving a red rag to a bull. He was charged with driving without insurance and advised to correct this as soon as possible.

When he got home we were all pleased for him, and poured beer over the car and danced around, which is our tradition. I was very proud of him and wished my brother, his father, could witness this. It was an historical moment, the guy works hard and is well disciplined. My husband sorted out the insurance for him and also registered himself so that he could drive the car too, but my nephew did not tell us he was going to court for driving without insurance. He later said he felt too embarrassed and was confident that he would manage because he assumed he would be fined and given some points. A police officer had told him that if he pleaded guilty he would just get a fine.

But that is not what happened. I wondered at how fair the court had been to this Black young man who drove a car with tinted windows. There are cars a Black young man should never drive and that was one of them.

"Hutchinson-Reis, describing his work as a social worker on the Broadwater Farm Estate, depicts the difficulties his team had in protecting the rights of young black people charged with offences following the 'uprising' there. He makes it clear that young blacks needed social work intervention aimed at securing justice from both the police and courts" (Dominelli, 1988, p. 115).

The court disqualified him. He lost his driving license. He was in shock because it never occurred to him that this might happen. All he could think about was what to do with the car, whether to keep it or not. As he drove home he was stopped and searched again, and after checks he was charged with driving without a driving licence. The car was impounded and sent to Perivale.

When he told us what had happened we wished he had told us before: we could have looked for a lawyer, could have gone with him, but my brother's son never asks for help unless he is desperate. It annoys me and he knows that. Most of the time my children tell me what he needs, but not him. Anyway, my husband went to get the car but was told that he needed to bring a copy of the insurance, which he had paid for on line but not printed out. When he got home he phoned the insurance company, only to be told that the police had been in touch and informed them that the owner of the car was disqualified, and therefore to cancel the policy. My husband argued that he was also on the policy, and asked why they cancelled him too. The man said the police told him to.

We were running out of time. I contacted my car dealer friend and asked him to get the car and sell it. He contacted Perivale but was told that they do not accept car dealers. They also wanted insurance with my nephew's name. It was clear that they would not get a new insurance before the date Tafadzwa was given as the last day to collect his car, so he phoned the police and explained about the difficulties he was having and asked for more days to sort this out. My husband phoned too, just to make sure. A few days later they got the insurance and went to get the car after phoning ahead to say they were on their way, but when they got there they were told that the car had been destroyed. His beautiful white Ford Focus with tinted windows was crushed. His pride and joy ... crushed. I never knew that I could hate a uniform to the depth I felt. Crushed his car. The car he had just bought! Years of slaving away and saving ... crushed. How is a nineteen-year old supposed to handle this? As a young Black man in the United Kingdom, he will have to learn to suck it? What does not kill him makes him stronger, eeh?

So when people talk to me about the rioters' lack of respect for other people's property I just can't help but think of the double standards. Is it all right for the White policeman to destroy Tafadwza's pride and joy because it is their duty? It broke my heart. Crushed his dream. Crushed his sense of achievement. Crushed him. The pain of what he could be going through was just unbearable. This is my little brother's son. He came to the United Kingdom barely ten years old, to live with people he had only met twice, but he settled. He has grown into a fine young man of whom I am very proud, and this was his first achievement, something he could hold onto as his own. His pride and joy. Tafadzwa spent more time in his car than in the house. It was the cleanest car in the neighbourhood. Yet, Mr White Policeman just crushed it. It was too cruel. How do people who do this sleep at night? I offered to buy Tafadzwa another car when he gets his driving licence, but it would not be the same. For the next few months he worked hard to clear the bill he got from the police.

Tafadzwa's loss of his car was quite traumatic. I have discussed how trauma can cause the past and the present to collide, resulting in serious mental anguish and regression, back in time to another most traumatic experience—mine is the time my father died, and my nephew's loss would have sent him to the most significant loss in his life—his parents. Being aware of this I kept an eagle's eye on him.

There is something cruel and rubbishing about destroying someone's car. It was not an old banger but a beautiful well looked after car. They could have sent it to the auction and offered the money to treatment centres that deal with traumatized Black youth.

With this in mind I wonder how many of the rioters were actually regressed, frightened, vulnerable people enacting what was done to them? Were they using Bollas' law of talion to violently reclaim what was taken from them? Victims becoming perpetrators? In that case would we dare listen to their horrors and help them break the cycle of abuse by working on what their destruction is about? Some arrive at our consulting rooms but does the government want to know and help? That level of anger needs a safe place to be processed. What does one do with all this anger? With my nephew we shared the outrage, the injustice, the lack of respect for his property. I understand my husband lost his rag and my nephew was more concerned that he would be arrested because he expressed how we all felt. He told the officer that he could not talk to Tafadzwa with such total disregard. It was good to have someone express the rage he felt, thus acknowledging and validating his emotions for him, because otherwise he might have felt he was going mad. Maybe that is what helped him not to join the rioters. His anger was processed.

My anger, on the other hand, took longer to process—over two weeks of waking up in a cold sweat, hoping that it was a nightmare, only to remember that it actually happened. I cried. I cried for him. I cried for my brother for not protecting him. Not protecting his pride and joy. Yes, my nephew should not have driven his car without insurance, but couldn't the garage have explained this to him? I guess they just wanted his money. After being disqualified he should not have driven, he should have phoned home for one of us to drive the car back. It is not that far, I guess he was in a state of shock and not thinking straight but what is the police's excuse or justification for this cruelty? I know, Tafadzwa broke the law, but did he deserve to have his car destroyed? Does the punishment fit the crime, or is it a case of using a sledge hammer to crack a nut? Does whatever Duggan did or did not do deserve his death? Leaving his three minor children without a father?

Having someone you know get killed by the police for no reason must be really tough to bear. If I could experience such pain for my nephew over a minor thing like his loss of a car which can be replaced what more do those who have to bury their loved ones feel? We were all able to recover and while I hate the way my nephew was treated I do not hate all the police and I felt sorrow watching them being attacked by rioters, that was not necessary, but how does one restore trust in the police following a death of a loved one? When Murphy, Davidson, and Hall (1985) interviewed Mr. Charles Hanson, the neighbour of Mrs Grove he said, "… When she came out of the bedroom she was shot. Cherry, who always sleeps with her children, looked very weak when I saw her. I feel terrible. Very bitter about what happened. From now on I hate every policeman."

These are the experiences of some young Blacks. Most of them have White friends who witness their suffering. From the research we learnt that Whites who have not suffered racism themselves, but have witnessed their Black friends being treated unjustly, carry the guilt and try to make up for it. One participant explained that her motivation to join the research was so that she could support the Black trainee in her year group. This togetherness of Blacks and Whites was well portrayed during the riots.

More police or more therapy?

Twilight Bey of Hogarth Blake education consultants and a former gang member, said, "It costs something like £54,000 a year to keep someone in prison, but you could take just £1,500 of that from your law and order budget and invest it into social intervention which has more positive results" (Pears, 2011). Watching the shocking images, I could not help but think that most rioters could benefit from therapy and it would be cheaper than keeping them in prison. We know that being able to express how one feels is more likely to stop acting out behaviour. For example, the local commanding officer, Chief Superintendent Colin Couch, made a clear tactical decision to allow the demonstrators to "vent their anger" in the wide road outside the station, where the police had the initiative. Eventually the demonstrators disperse on their own (Policing London, 1986). On the other hand, it is reported that the violence of 1981 which were triggered by the attempt by two plain clothes policemen to arrest a black cab driver for no apparent reason would not have happened "if the police had not been there in such large numbers in the first place, the confrontation would not have occurred" (Langley, 1981).

Therefore, I do not believe that increasing police numbers and giving them more power (which can be misused) is the solution. The call for more police is understandable considering the scary scenes we saw. However, there is an outrage reaction to the fire-setting and looting, as if it is the first time it has happened. Look at all riots in the

United Kingdom and other countries. For example, during the 1981 riots it was reported:

"Nobody could deny the seriousness of what occurred. It is difficult to recall a worse example of street rioting outside of Northern Ireland. Houses, shops and pubs have been gutted by fire over a wide area. Shops have been looted ..." (Langley, 1981).

Setting fire and looting are what separate a riot from a peaceful protest. While I do not condone what happened I believe in facing reality, no matter how ugly it looks. Those youth and vulnerable adults were exhibiting the normal behaviour of a rioter and the people who are shocked are either naive or have been there, got the T-shirt, burnt it and now pretend that it does not happen in a civilized society.

Since people who are not able to express how they feel are likely to make others experience how they feel, what feelings did we experience watching all this unfold? Mine was fear, frustration, hatred of the injustice towards the owners of the properties which were destroyed. I live in Croydon borough. My sister lives near West Croydon, a few minutes from where the woman jumped out of the window of a burning building. As the carnage continued we kept ringing each other to make sure we were all right. At the time of writing, Croydon looks like a ghost town. Most shops are boarded up and there are no buses from Croydon to my sister's home, so we have to walk from Croydon. I am unable to get a reference because my work colleagues are not allowed into their offices, which are a few minutes from the furniture shop that was torched. My heart goes to those who suffered personal losses. However, I feel I am also in the thick of it to a significant degree and believe strongly that something should be done to listen and make sense of this, otherwise it will happen again. We cannot expect our young and vulnerable to become our scapegoats, carrying the burden of society. They have spoken about their fear, frustration and hatred by acting it out and making us feel it for them, therefore it is our duty to help them decode their destructive behaviour and put it into words. There is no point in dropping a prickly pear after you have caught it, because once held, you already have the prickly stuff on you. You might as well persist in cleaning it, and then eat it.

Double standard

We are outraged that the youth have no respect for life, but what triggered the riots off? A death by police. The history of Tottenham shows a lack of respect of Black people's lives and yet no police officer is held accountable for it. Let us not ask our youth to do what we are failing to do. Whose children are they? They are the children of a society devoid of respect for rules, and some of our role models are politicians who were sucking the coffers dry. Were they asked to give up their second homes? No, yet for these youths and vulnerable adults, we are considering tossing them onto the streets. It was reported that Wandsworth Council has already applied to evict eighteen-year-old Daniel Sartain-Clarke, his mother Maite de la Calva, and her eight-year-old daughter Rebecca. Sartain-Clarke is charged with violent disorder and burglary (Pears, 2011). What happened to our mission statement that "children's needs are paramount?" Does Rebecca's needs for home and warmth not count? She is a child and her needs should be the focus above those of a young adult. Are we not in danger of becoming perpetrators of our youth while they become victims of their victims in the see-saw game of abuse?

We complain about their lack of education, yet we are closing libraries where a lot of youth hang, especially those without computers at home. We are increasing university fees so that it is next to impossible for the poor to catch up. In The Times (1981) it was reported:

"... Young blacks have been particularly badly hit [by recession] more than half the 16–19 year olds unemployed in the area are black. And it is the fate of this 'second generation'—the blacks born and educated here—which is potentially the most explosive for future race relations. Their parents have mostly been content with relatively menial jobs, but the new generation will not be so easily satisfied. Often they have exam qualifications to buttress their sense of injustice." Then we ask, whose children are they? We pathologize them, then close down the therapeutic communities for severe Personality Disorder and Drug and Alcohol Rehabilitation units. The money saved from this betrayal? We pay for more police?

Dominelli (1983) states, "Youth in general and black youth in particular currently has few opportunities for contributing to society in significant ways and acquiring a sense of belonging to it. Society's major concern with youth has been to control the rebellious elements threatening its fragile stability ... Because white people pathologize blacks by treating them rather than racism as the problem, black people's activities resisting racism receive similar treatment" (Dominelli, 1988, p. 113). Is it not time to change the record?

What was striking about the England riots is that what started off as a peaceful race protest quickly stopped being about Black/

White because a significant number of Whites joined the Blacks. The research I carried out showed that participants who socialized with Blacks adopted the Black culture—the language, food, music and sport. I had an emotional connection with them. Pears (2011) reports on David Starkey's controversial comments on BBC's Newsnight programme in which he appeared to support aspects of Enoch Powell's *Rivers of Blood* speech and also said that the riots reflected the fact that "whites have become black. A particular sort of violent destructive, nihilistic gangster culture has become the fashion." Starkey got over 700 complaints over the language he used. However, his observations confirmed the change I had noticed in youths which marked the difference between the England riots and those in the past. Although some of the past riots were joined by a few Whites, the 2011 riots included a significant number of Whites and there was a connectedness between Blacks and Whites. This connectedness of the Black/White youth was also demonstrated in Emily's language, which the nation was not prepared for coming from a White woman. It was considered to be racist and she was asked to leave the Big Brother programme for using Black in-language. I believe the reaction to Whites "becoming black" is negative because of the stereotypical belief that Blacks want to be White. This is captured in a Newsweek report (1981). It is reported that, "Mr. Charley Stacey, a white clothing store manager, surveyed his looted shop. 'I think most colored people were born with chips on their shoulders', he said within earshot of two black employees. 'Till they find something that will turn a black man white, there isn't going to be a solution." These youth showed that they are coming together as equals, crossing race barriers that have been there for generations.

Here are some of the dynamics I observed as the riots progressed:

Paranoid–schizoid position

There was an initial Black/White split which marked the history of Tottenham—a young Black man was shot dead by a White police officer. When the riots started I was conscious of this split, with each race looking at what the other was doing. I felt compassion for the Duggan family, which is of mixed heritage. Being Black with some White family members, I know how tough it is when the environment is anti-White. Bereavement can cause guilt feelings and the Black/White split would have made their situation worse. I recalled when I went to a conference where I felt the anti-White atmosphere and during an Art Therapy session I drew my Black family, leaving out the White members. It is hard to be in such a situation.

It is important to hold onto that initial split and try to find its meaning. Thinking of the badly produced video some were able to withstand its bad production, however, the participant who could not tolerate it, like our Black youth, made us stop to pause and a different view which would have been lost came to light. That is the pause I hope would be taken to give Black youths a voice. Let us not quickly dismiss the racial element and, like the past riots, insist that it was not about racism, because I believe that it started being about racism and a history of White police being involved in the death of Black person. That still needs addressing. The 2011 riots showed great solidarity with the police and hopefully that paves the way for honest discussions which aim in making sure that history does not keep repeating itself. Life is precious.

My initial reaction to seeing an older Black woman looting was one of shock and shame. I wished she was White. The shame was intolerable and her skin colour and age brought it closer to me. I did not like that.

Unable to withstand the shame, some found comfort in blaming the parents. Some parents come from a culture that believes in spare the rod and spoil the child, and the child sometimes ends up in prison, or is sent back home to their country of origin for disciplining. Either way, it's a no-win situation. These parents don't need blame, but support in adapting to the new culture of disciplining their children. In any case, the child development discussed in the presentation shows how a child is influenced outside the family. Parents cannot be our scapegoats for what we witnessed.

Others blamed the riots on poverty, but the looter who happened to be a millionaire's daughter challenged this stereotypic thinking. In my mixed community we started counting how many Blacks and Whites were involved in the looting, and realized that we were all well represented. Somehow the shame became bearable in the knowledge that we were in it together. Years of Blacks carrying the shame seem to peel off. This was no longer about racism but about togetherness, and the solidarity between Black and White youth filled me with hope for the future. Maybe the issues the Black community was raising in various riots might be taken seriously. Remember, my first case was only taken seriously after a White colleague complained about something which was similar to my complaints. It might have hurt that my judgement was not trusted but the Black/White solidarity gave the needed push. The solidarity seen during the England riots mean that no one race was going to carry the burden of the mess created. Without the Black/White split hopefully focus will go to what the youth are really angry about. It will be a shared task. It is an interesting paradox: the rioters were engaged in destructive activities and yet they brought together different races, united in destruction.

Depressive position

In the previous chapters I looked at how Mr. Smith's engagement in therapy started off from a racist point. By staying with him and making sense of his attack we were able to work on the underlying vulnerability to do with his father's rejection. Mr. Smith showed that sometimes racism is used to create a barrier, but if that barrier is crossed then an intimate relationship which allows for creativity can be achieved. The rioting youth showed this connectedness which allowed for the community to come together and reflect together, because no-one was preoccupied with issues of racial difference. There was no room for splitting. As the realization of what had happened hit home, some looters turned themselves in, some parents frog-marched their children to the police stations and others grassed them up over the phone, but most parents did not disown their children. Instead, they nailed the boundaries of what is right and wrong firmly. What needed to follow was work on trying to understand what all this was about and dealing with the underlining issues. If politicians, police and the know-it-all could stop and listen they might find that there is a lot to learn from this community of youth and their parents.

As discussed before, Bollas (1987) asks the therapists that in order to find the patient we must look for him within ourselves. The same applies to these youth. We cannot afford not to recognize our children. We need to identify with them in order to help and contain them. We have all done daft things we are ashamed of, and maybe we were lucky that we did not end up on the front page of several national newspapers, in the same boat with those accused of murder. That is a burden looters should not be made to carry.

As the communities came together, they adopted a depressive position of feeling sad about what had happened and took responsibility for clearing up the mess in their streets. Everyone, Black and White, young and old, men and women, worked together. Identified victims were looked after. Those who lost their homes were offered shelter, food and clothes; Asyraf Haziq, a Malaysian youth who was mugged by the people who seemed to be helping him after he had been attacked, was offered comfort and financial help. That was a proud moment for England. I was proud to be British.

The Black/Asian conflict contained

In Birmingham, three Asian men, Haroon Jahan (twenty-one), Shazad Hussain (thirty), and Mustafa Hussain (thirty-one) were killed in a hit and drive by men who are believed to be Black. They were in a group that was protecting their community's properties and the mosque from rioters and looters. Following their deaths there was fear that this could develop into a serious racial war between Asians and Blacks. Birmingham has a history of such racial unrest and the Asians were expected to retaliate. Taylor (2011) reported:

"Police in Birmingham were struggling to contain swelling anger within the Asian community after a hit-and-run by suspected rioters killed three young men. Despite appeals for calm from senior officers, young Asian men vowed to defend their streets." The history of the Black/Asian conflict is well known. Taylor reports that six years ago the racially mixed inner city suburb of Lozells exploded in two days of running battles between blacks and Asians, "… sparked by the rumour that a black woman had been raped by an Asian man." Therefore the fear that this might explode again was very real but Tariq Jahan, father of Haroon, stood up and pleaded with everyone to stop. He asked people to remain calm and go home; not to turn this into a race war but to stand united; to respect his son's death. "This is not a race issue," he said. "The family has received messages of sympathy and support from all parts of society. Blacks, Asians, Whites—we all live in the same community."

The youth listened. The politicians listened. Everyone listened, because in that moment not only was Jahan the father of his son, but also the father of the nation. I believe his intervention was what calmed the country down. Seeing a grieving man making such a heartfelt plea touched many hearts. He spoke with such dignity and humility. One could feel his pain, yet he had the strength to care about his community at a difficult time of great personal loss. He was experienced as a containing father, reminding me of Winnicott's view that antisocial behaviour holds the hope of finding a good enough mother/carer, and Jahan is the treasure the nation found. I think other fathers of this nation could learn from him about how to deal with a distressed nation: no threats, no rejection, because disowning our children never works, but holding them firmly to our bosom and saying, "It will be all right, we are in it together," is likely to get better results.

Scapegoats

Behr and Hearst (2005) say the attack on a scapegoat may revolve around disowned guilt and shame and lack of mutual identification, reflective empathy. What is challenging about the England riots is that one can identify with some of them and it feels uncomfortable. The temptation is to use projective identification by getting angry with those we identify with and look for ways of getting rid of them, such as locking them up for life. It seems impossible to consider that some looters are good people who were caught in the adrenaline rush of the moment. For example, is it possible that the guy who looted bottled water, the assistant teacher, the eleven-year-old boy, Olympic ambassador, social worker, the sons of the missionary, and so on are good people who made bad choices? Can there be more people who were just caught in the moment of madness? I suppose accepting that possibility would mean taking them off the hook, which would mean reflecting on our identification with them. I believe good people caught in this can be seen looting without even covering their faces. We should not underestimate the power of mob psychology. When I suffered institutional racism the people involved were good people as individuals but as a group they seem to have lost their sense of compassion. I believe that we should not destroy good people who made bad choices by treating them unfairly. I struggle to count on one hand people who have not stolen something in their lives. Check where you stand on this and use that experience of shame and guilt to reflect and to help you show some empathy for people who joined on impulse. I suspect the seasoned criminals were operating from the sidelines far from anyone's gaze and their immediate commanders were totally covered, and will not smell the inside of a prison because no-one can prove it was them. They knew how to play the game. I also believe that it is the small fish who know very little about crime, hence smiling into the camera, who will be paraded before going down in total humiliation. Their only hope is for a fair trial.

Withholding benefits

Littelwood and Lipsedge (1989) warn us that children brought up with guilt-inducing techniques have a higher number of depressed people than those who use shame-inducing techniques. The name-and-shame the looter will hit home for most. They will live with this stigma on them. However, the threat to make families homeless goes towards inducing guilt, and too much guilt is likely to seek the help of defence mechanisms, thus sending one into the paranoid schizoid position where there is a lack of concern for others and an inability to take responsibility for the consequences of one's actions.

One debate about the riots suggested making rioters who live in state homes, homeless. I can understand people's frustration in signing this petition, but Bion warns us about the unconscious destructiveness. He looks at the connection between the container and the contained and how thoughts may become progressively depleted: there is greedy or destructive interaction coming together in a mutually destructive way. These are our children, whether we like it or not. Most of them have traumatic backgrounds and they need help, not punishment. Making families homeless when we know they cannot manage is engaging in mutual destructiveness. It will boomerang.

I find Winnicott's concept of Hate in Countertransference very helpful when flooded with negative feelings such as rage. It is alright to feel the rage about the riots, and being aware that this is how one feels will help in making better decisions rather than acting out this hatred. I think all those making decisions about what to do next need debriefing exercises to ensure they are not acting out their anger. Individuals cannot carry the aches and pains of a nation.

Having spent years working with challenging people I know that most of them are very intelligent but use it in destructive ways because no-one has shown any interest in them. Being destructive gives them attention, as this event has arrested our attention. However, if they are listened to and encouraged and helped to find their own sense of direction all that destructive energy can be spent in more creative ways. If you think about how all this was organized one has to admire the energy and strategy used. There is a thread of hope here which needs to be grabbed. If the energy used to torch England was used to building it we would see amazing results. Let us not give up on our children. They are our future.

Stephen Lawrence

The murder of Stephen Lawrence is a notable murder case surrounding the killing of an eighteen-year-old student. The black British teenager from Eltham, South-East London named Stephen Lawrence (13 September 1974–22 April 1993) was stabbed to death while waiting for a bus on the evening of 22 April 1993.

After the initial investigation five suspects were arrested but never convicted. It was suggested during the course of investigation that the murder was racially motivated and that Lawrence was killed because he was black, and that the handling of the case by the police and Crown Prosecution Service was affected by issues of race leading to an inquiry.

In 1999, an inquiry headed by Sir William Macpherson examined the original Metropolitan police investigation and concluded that the force was "institutionally racist". This was termed "one of the most important moments in the modern history of criminal justice in Britain".

APPENDIX II

The video presentation

Slide 1

Black History Event

Psychotherapy penetrates beyond skin colour

By
MJ Maher
Adult Group Analyst

Slide 2

Group work

1. Can you describe me in one word?
2. What words came to your mind and what word did you choose to write down?
3. Is it the same word?

Slide 3

Words used to describe me

Sensational	bold	vivacious
great insight	open minded	energetic
scatty	confident	poetic
very helpful	bossy	mysterious
a professional woman	nurturer	relaxed
persistent	unexpected	happy
approachable	outrageous	scary but v. professional
very helpful	warm	

Slide 4

Words avoided, why?

- No one wrote black, short or fat.
- Many admitted to having thought about black but had felt too uncomfortable to say it.
- What do you think about your response?
- Are you aware that you censor your responses? Why?

Slide 5

When you look at me

When you look at me,
What do you see?
Do you see me,
Or do you see what you think there is to see?
Do you see what you see?
Or do you see beyond me?
Through me?
Around …
But me?
Do you see what I want to see
Or do you see what you want to see ?
Do you see what you don't want to see,
Or do you see what I don't want you to see?
Do you see what you think I want you to see,
Or do you see what we both feel comfortable to see?
When you look at me,
What do you see?
What do you really see?

MJ

Slide 6

The Black History

PSYCHOTHERAPY PENETRATES BEYOND SKIN COLOUR

Slide 7

Assumptions are not always correct

The above design of a sheep in a lion's skin draws attention to the fact that assumptions can be misleading:

- **Wolf in a sheep's skin**—my culture is not familiar with wolves, they look like dogs therefore might be mistaken for the faithful friend, so I chose a sheep in a lion's skin to make things simple and clear.
- **A lion in a sheep's skin**—being a victim is a popular position; White like sheep stands for purity and innocence yet commanding the power of oppression and racism. Aggression hidden in weakness, tears that induce guilty feelings in others (powerful).
- **A sheep in a lion's skin**—vulnerability is hidden behind anger and aggression. Black like a lion is associated with anger, aggression, powerful sexuality, yet vulnerable to oppression and racism. (powerful)

Skin colour does not determine one's culture. For example, a Black child brought up by a White family will identify with a White culture and vice versa. Therefore to know someone one has to go beyond their skin colour.

Slide 8

Kitten/lion in the mirror?

I showed them a picture of a kitten looking into the mirror and seeing a lion.

Slide 9

What do you think of the kitten/lion picture?

- This picture warns us against relying solemnly on external appearances and it also alerts us to the possible internal/external conflicts that might be experienced by the client, e.g., a Black child brought up by a White family who gets labelled "coconut/bounty" (brown on the outside but white on the inside), for acting like a White person when that is the culture he or she was brought up in. If you call someone a coconut it is just a reflection of your own ignorance. How one sees themselves or feels inside might be different from how they present themselves to others.
- In the world of political correctness are you able to explore your observations without worrying about litigation? Can you stay with a client experiencing you as racist long enough to make sense of it? Can you stay with the uncomfortable feelings and encourage explorations of their significance?
- How we feel might be different from how others think we feel, for example laugh when you want to cry, appear strong when you feel vulnerable, attack when feeling scared.
- Are you able to explore different views, listen and learn about other people's cultures?

Slide 10

Child development

- **First community (family)**—colour binding. Children do not notice the significance of different skin colour, they define relatives by the roles individuals play in their lives, e.g., a child crying because someone said his father was Black, *"He is not Black, he is my dad!"*
- **Second community (school)**—Colour conscious. At school colour becomes an issue, e.g., of bullying and being bullied about. They become colour conscious, e.g., *"You are poo-poo colour."*
- **Adult community (society at large)**—becomes colour-blind. It is polite not to mention Black, e.g., *"I do not notice that you are Black/ Your skin colour means nothing to me because it makes no difference/As far as I am concerned people are people whether green, yellow, purple."*

Slide 11

First community—Influences how we react today

Stage 1 Me—The baby

- Feeds   Burps
- Vomits   Pees
- Poos   Coos
- Giggles   Sleeps
- Cries   Screams
- Engages   Farts
- Demands attention   Smiles

Do you recognize any of these dynamics during a therapy session?

Slide 12

Whether the baby is Black or White:

The baby believes in magic—that the world rotates around it and that it controls everyone/everything.

- It feels adored, loved.
- Obeyed and attended to.
- It feels powerful.

yet it can also feel

- Neglected, ignored.
- Abused, Abandoned.
- Powerless and frightened.

So a White adult in the group does not need to be Black to know how it feels to be abused, ignored, abandoned. A Black adult knows how it feels to be loved, adored, listened to and respected.

Slide 13

Stage 2—Me and my first love

- Have you heard of the saying—"You marry your mother/father?"
- What happens to White children brought up by Black nannies and Black children adopted by White couples?
- What is the impact on the baby when it feels loved, nurtured, telepathically understood and protected on its sense of security, safety, and self worthy?

Slide 14

Stage 2—Continued

However, first love will disappoint the baby, for example:

- making it wait so as to help it survive the frustration of not being in total control and it learns to love and hate.

Therefore, whether Black or White one is capable of:

- Loving and hating.
- Feeling frustrated and surviving frustrations and disappointments.
- Being misunderstood and feeling ignored.
- Feeling insecure, frightened, and not important enough.

Slide 15

Problems that may result from this stage of development:

- **Perfect parenting**—fear of making mistakes.
- **Deprivation**—inability to feel satisfied.
- **Separation/Abandonment**—poor attachment.

Clingy or detached

- **Abuse**—lack of trust.
- **Neglect**—feeling not good enough/does not deserve anything good.

Slide 16

First community: Stage 3—Me and my first love and the partner

Whether Black or White one learns about:

- Inclusion/exclusion.
- Splitting.
- Jealousy.
- Being visible/invisible.
- Competition.
- Being the favoured.
- Being the neglected.
- Oedipus complex—Managing a triangle.

Have you heard about *"Two is company and three is a crowd?"*

Slide 17

First community: Stage 4—Siblings

Whether Black or White, one learns about:

- Rivalry from within the family.
- Sharing.
- Discrimination.
- Favoured child.
- First child.
- Middle child.
- Last child.
- Only child.

Slide 18

Possible questions to ask

1. We are the same but are we treated the same?
2. While it is OK not to treat children the same, are the differences acknowledged and explained?
3. Are the parents being fair?
4. Feelings of unfairness, discrimination, exclusion, rivalry, competition, neglect, and being ignored can be experienced in early childhood, whether one is White or Black. However, in adulthood these feelings can be re-experienced in racism but their roots can be traced back to these stages of development—experienced by all—Black and White.
5. So, can racism be understood by those who have never experienced it?

Note: Not all Black people have experienced racism and some White people have experienced racism.

Slide 19

Second community: Stage 5—The school

Whether Black or White, one learns about:

- Peer pressure/solidarity.
- Competition within difference.
- Inclusion/exclusion.
- Fairness/Unfairness.
- Belonging or not.
- Bullying/being bullied.

Relationships with authority are replayed.

Slide 20

Third community: Stage 6—Society

All the issues from the different stages of the first and second communities are brought into play in different categories:

Cultural	Social	Class
Political	Racial	Religious
Gender	Economical	

Discuss the impact of the following events on individuals and what feelings might be leaking from childhood:

1. **Racial**—Positive discrimination—it's impact on a White person who had to live with a favoured/disabled sibling all his childhood.
2. **Political**—An immigrant, whose father was a notorious criminal, lies about coming from South Africa and talks of his pride in Nelson Mandela—actually his country of origin is ruled by a dictator.
3. **Religious**—A Christian, who witnessed sexual abuse at 5 years of age, decides to give up his/her faith because their local priest has been arrested for sexually abusing children.

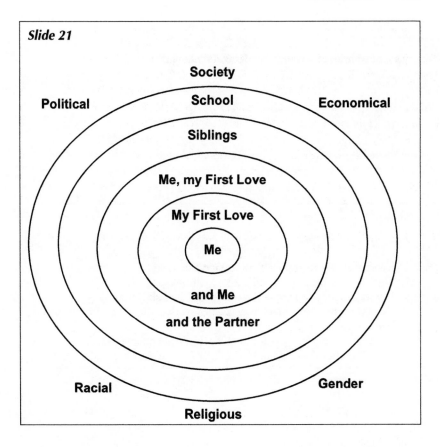

Slide 22

Let's mend bridges, avoid using derogatory language

- Coconut/Bounty
- Chalky
- Wigger
- Mongrel
- Slave baby
- Fanta face & Coca cola body

Slide 23

Conclusion: Discuss

1. Can psychotherapy penetrate beyond skin colour?
2. Do you treat Black and White people the same?
3. Is your reaction to people dependent on their skin colour?
4. Does it matter for a Black therapist to work with a White client or vice versa?
5. Does it matter if you do not treat Black/White people the same?
6. Does it matter if you do not treat Black/White people equally/fairly?

Slide 24

MWANA ASINGACHEME ANOFIRA MUMBEREKO (a child who does not cry will die on its mother's back)

What possible dynamics could take place between the following:

- a Black therapist and a Black service user who hates being Black
- a Black therapist and a White service user whose father is racist
- two Black service users, one believes that the other is too White

We all have a history, but don't let that turn you into a Black or White slave of history—**Learn from it.**

Research questionnaire

Thank you for volunteering to participate in this research. You are encouraged to write as much as you would like in order to express or reflect on your thinking about the questions asked. Please feel free to use the back of the sheets if necessary. Your contributions are well appreciated.

1. Number & Module: 2. Gender:

3. Age: 4. Ethnicity:

5. Country of birth: 6. Religion:

7. Parents' country of origin:

8a. Have you ever discussed issues of skin colour?

           Yes ☐   No ☐

b. If yes, with whom and how often? *Please indicate below and also tick to show if the people you are referring to are of the same or different skin colour to yours.*

| | Skin colour | | | | |
	Same	Different	Often	Sometimes	Never
a. Friends					
b. Family					
c. Neighbours					
d. Your patients					
e. Work colleagues					
f. Your therapist					
g. Your training body					
h. Other (specify please)					
i.					
j.					
k.					

9. Do you think it is important for a client to been seen by a counsellor of the same skin colour as themselves?

        Yes □   No □

Please explain your answer:

10. In a therapeutic relationship, do you think the counsellor and client of different skin colour can achieve a deep understanding of the issues they are working on?

        Yes □   No □

Please briefly comment on your answer:

11a. Choose 6 qualities you think are most important in a therapist working with someone of a different colour from himself or herself?
Please number them from 1–6 starting with 1 as the most important.

	Number here 1–6
1. Knowledge of the client's culture	
2. Having the same skin colour as the client	
3. Having a different skin colour from the client	
4. Ability to tolerate not knowing	
5. Sensitivity to cultural variations	
6. Ability to establish boundaries while aware of the power issues within the counsellor/client relationship	
7. Capacity to separate own issues from the client's	
8. Ability to be honest in supervision.	
9. Willingness to learn about the client's culture	
10. Being non-judgmental	
11. Ability to make use of the transference and counter-transference	
12. Capacity to be neutral	
13. Ability to convey empathic understanding	
14. Having worked on one's own feelings around separation, abandonment, alienation, loss, rejection	
15. Having trained on race, culture, and ethnicity	

11b. Any comments on the above activity?

12a. Choose awareness qualities you think are necessary to work on when working with someone of a different colour from you? *Please number them from 1–6 starting with 1 as the most important.*

	Number here 1–6
1. An awareness of Attachment Theory	
2. An awareness of the impact of "culture shock", "survivor's guilt"	
3. An awareness of the impact of loss on depression, formation of conscience, and development of empathy	

4. An awareness of the impact of the processes of immigration, racism, discrimination, and harassment on mental health	
5. An awareness that one treats everyone the same	
6. An awareness that skin colour and culture are not the same	
7. An awareness of the importance of family structures/ beliefs/values and their impact on the individual	
8. An awareness of the impact of family reunions	
9. An awareness of family histories repeating themselves	
10. An awareness of the impact of cultural practices, traditions, customs, beliefs, values, on one's identity	
11. An awareness of one's own prejudices about people of a different colour	
12. An awareness of stereotypical beliefs around different cultures	
13. An awareness of one's blind spots/weaknesses	
14. An awareness of the importance of family history to one's identity	
15. An awareness of the various transitions a client is having to make	

12b. Any comments on the above activity?

13. What anxieties would you have when you are about to meet a client of a different skin colour to yourself?

14. Please read this vignette carefully and then answer the following questions:

A 25 year old counsellor walked into the waiting room and called out:

"James!"
A big, tall bald-headed man stood up dwarfing the counsellor. He looked about 55 years of age. The counsellor smiled at him.

"My name is Bobby, please come with me," she said.

They walked a few doors down the corridor to a consulting room. Bobby indicated a chair for James to sit but he remained standing arms folded across his chest exposing the skull and crossed bones tattoo on his left arm. The left knuckles were tattooed HATE while the right knuckles had matching LOVE tattoo across them, and a serpent tattoo resting along the right arm.

"My name is Mr Smith and I would rather call you Mrs Andrews. Only my best friends call me James or Jim. Eh ... I do not see the point of sitting down because I am a racist and you are black."

a. Can you list possible issues to consider in this vignette?

b. How would you have responded?

c. Do you think Bobby should consider working with Mr Smith?

                    Yes ☐   No ☐

    Please explain your answer.

REFERENCES

Allen, J. (2005). *Apartheid South Africa: An Insider's Overview of the Origin and Effects of Separate Development.* USA: iUniverse.

American Psychiatric Association. (2006). Position statement. Resolution Against Racism and Racial Discrimination and Their Adverse Impacts on Mental Health, July 2006.

American Psychiatric Glossary. (2003). *American Psychiatric Glossary* (8th ed.). Washington DC; American Psychiatric Press, Inc., p. 120.

Ashmore, R. D. & Del Boca, F. K. (1981). Conceptual approaches to stereotypes and stereotyping. In: D. L. Hamilton (Ed.), *Cognitive Processes in Stereotyping and Intergroup Behaviour* (pp. 1–35). Hillsdale, NJ: Erlbaum.

Atkinson, D. R., Morten, G. & Sue, D. W. (1989). *Counselling American Minorities: A Cross-Cultural Perspective* (3rd ed.). Dubuque, IA: W. C. Brown.

Banister, P., Burman, E., Parker, I., Taylor, M. & Tindall, C. (1994). *Qualitative Methods in Psychology: A Research Guide.* Berkshire: Open University Press.

Bateman, A. & Holmes, J. (1995). *Introduction to Psychoanalysis: Contemporary Theory and Practice.* London: Routledge.

Bateman, A., Brown, D. & Pedder, J. (2000). *Introduction to Psychotherapy: An Outline of Psychodynamic Principles and Practice* (3rd ed.). London: Routledge.

413

Baxter, L., Hughes, C. & Tight, M. (2000). *How to Research* (2nd ed.). USA: Open University Press.

Behr, H. & Hearst, L. (2005). *Group-Analytic Psychotherapy: A Meeting of Minds*. London: Whurr Publishers.

Bollas, C. (1987). *The Shadow of the Object: Psychoanalysis of the Unthought Known*. London: Free Association Books.

Bowlby, J. (1973). *Attachment and Loss: Volume 2; Separation: Anxiety and Anger*. London: Penguin Books.

Bowling, A. (2002). *Research Methods in Health: Investigating Health and Health Services* (2nd ed.). USA: Open University Press.

Boyer, L. B. (1998). (Ed.). Dotty, L. L. *Countertransference and Regression*. Northvale, NJ: Jason Aronson.

Bretherton, I. (1992). The origins of attachment theory: John Bowlby and Mary Ainsworth. *Development Psychology, 28*: 759–775.

Burman, E. (1994). In Banister, P., Burman, E., Parker, I., Taylor, M. & Tindall, C. (1994). *Qualitative Methods in Psychology: A Research Guide*. Berkshire: Open University Press.

Callaway, H. (1981). Women's perspectives: Research as revision. In P. Reason and J. Rowan (Eds.), *Human Inquiry: A Sourcebook of New Paradigm*. Chichester: Wiley.

Cassidy, J. (2010). Bowlby's concept of the therapist as a secure base: exploring the psychological territory of pain. *The John Bowlby Memorial Lecture 2010 given on 27th March 2010*.

Clark, K. B. & Clark, M. P. (1939). The development of consciousness of self and the emergence of racial identification in negro pre-school children. *Journal of Social Psychology, 10*: 591–599.

Coles, R. (1989). *The Call of Stories*. Boston: Houghton Mifflin.

Constantine, M. G. (1997). Facilitating multicultural competency in counseling supervision: Operationalizing a practical framework. In D. B. Pope-Davis & H. L. Coleman (Eds.), *Multicultural Counseling Competencies: Assessment, Education and Training, and Supervising* (pp. 310–324). Thousand Oaks, CA: Sage.

Constantine, M. G., Juby, H. L. & Liang, J. J. (2001). Examining multicultural counselling competence and race-related attitudes among white marital and family therapists. *Journal of Marital and Family Therapy, 27*(3): 353–362.

Constantine, M. G., Warren, A. K. & Miville, M. L. (2005). White Racial Identity Dyadic Interactions in Supervision: Implications for Supervisees' Multicultural Counseling Competence. *Journal of Counseling Psychology, 52*(4): 490–496.

Corvin, S. & Wiggins, F. (1989). An antiracism training model for white professionals. *Journal of Multicultural Counseling and Development, 17*: 105–114.

Cross, W. E. (1978). The Cross and Thomas models of psychological Nigrescence. *Journal of Black Psychology, 5*: 13–19.

Cross, W. E., Jr. (1971). The Negro-to-Black conversion experience: Towards a psychology of Black liberation. *Black World, 20*: 13–27.

Cross, W. E., Jr. (1991). *Shades of Black: Diversity in Africa-American Identity.* Philadelphia: Temple University Press.

Cross, W. E., Jr. (1995). Oppositional identity and African-American youth: Issues and prospects. In W. D. Hawley & A. W. Jackson (Eds.), *Towards a Common Destiny* (pp. 185–204) San Francisco: Jossey-Bass.

D'Andrade, R. G. (1984). Cultural meaning systems. In R. A. Schweder & R. A. LeVine (Eds.), *Cultural Theory: Essays on Mind, Self and Emotion.* (pp. 88–119). Cambridge University Press.

Dalal, F. (1997). A Transcultural Perspective on Psychodynamic Psychotherapy: Addressing Internal and External Realities: Group Analysis, *Volume 30* (pp. 203–215). London: SAGE Publications.

Denzin, N. K. & Lincoln, Y. (2000). *Handbook of Qualitative Research* (2nd ed.). USA: Sage Publications Inc.

Dominelli, L. (1983). *Women in Focus: Community Service Orders and Female Offenders.* Warwick University, Nuffield Foundation Research Report.

Dominelli, L. (1988). *Anti-Racist Social Work: A Challenge for White Practitioners and Educators.* London: Macmillan Education Ltd.

Dovidio, J. F. & Gaertner, S. L. (1986). *Prejudice, Discrimination, and Racism.* London: Academic Press. Inc.

Falicov, C. J. (Ed.). (1983). *Cultural Perspectives in Family Therapy.* Rockville, MD: Aspen.

Falicov, C. J. (1988). Learning culturally in family therapy. In H. A. Liddle, D. C. Breunlin & R. C. Schwartz (Eds.), *Handbook of Family Therapy and Training and Supervision* (pp. 335–357). New York: Guilford.

Falicov, C. J. (1995). Training to think culturally: A multidimensional comparative frame. *Family Process, 34*: 373–388.

Fanon, F. (1952). *Peau Noire, Masques Blanc* (Paris Editions de Seuil transl.) C. L. Markmann, Black Skin, White Masks. New York: Grove Press. 1967.

Fanon, F. (1986). *Black Skin White Masks.* London: Pluto Press (original work published in 1952).

Fernando, S. (1991). *Mental Health, Race & Culture: Issues In Mental Health.* London: MacMillan Education Ltd.

Foukles, S. H. (1964). *Therapeutic Group Analysis.* London: George Allen & Unwin.

Foulkes, S. H. (1966). Some basic concepts in group psychotherapy. In E. Foulkes (Ed.), *S. H. Foulkes, Selected Papers* (p. 152). London: Karnac Books, 1990.

Foulkes, S. H. (1983). *Introduction to Group Analytic Psychotherapy.* London: Marefield Library.

Foulkes, S. H. & Anthony, E. J. (1973). *Group Psychotherapy: The Psychoanalytical Approach*. London: Karnac (Books).

Frederickson, G. (1995). *Black Liberation: A Comparative History of Black Ideologies in the United States and South Africa*. New York: Oxford Press.

Freud, S. (1950). *Totem and Taboo*. London: Routledge & Kegan Paul.

Freud, S. (2002). *Totem and Taboo: Some Points of Agreement between the Mental Lives of Savages and Neurotics*. London: Routledge (Classics English ed. first published 1913).

Fromm, E. (1956). *The Art of Loving*. New York:Harper & Row.

Frosh, S. (1991). *Identity Crisis: Modernity, Psychoanalysis and The Self*. London: MacMillan Press.

Gainor, K. A. & Constantine, M. G. (2002). *Multicultural counselling group supervision: A comparison of in-person versus Web-based formats*. Professional School Counseling, 6: 104–111.

Gersie, A. (1997). *Reflections on Therapeutic Storymaking: The Use of Stories in Groups*. London: Jessica Kingsley Publishers.

Gorman, D. (2006). *Imperial Citizenship: Empire and the Question of Belonging*. Manchester & New York: Manchester University Press.

Greenberg, J. R. & Mitchell, S. A. (1983). *Object Relations in Psychoanalytic Theory*. London: Harvard University Press.

Halevy, J. (1998). A genogram with an attitude. *Journal of Marital and Family Therapy*, 24: 233–242.

Harrison, D. K. (1975). Race as a counsellor-client variable in counselling and psychotherapy: A review of the research. *Counselling Psychologist*, 5: 124–133.

Helms, J. E. (1984). Toward a theoretical explanation of effects of race on counseling: A black and white model. *The Counselling Psychologist*, 12: 153–165.

Helms, J. E. (Ed.). (1990). *Black and White Identity: Theory, Research, and Practice*. Westport, CT: Greenwood Press.

Helms, J. E. & Parham, T. A. (1991). The development of Racial Identity Attitude Scale. In R. L. Jones (Ed.), *Handbook of Tests and Measurements for Black Populations (Vols. 1–2.)* Berkeley, CA: Cobb & Henry.

Hinshelwood, R. D. (1994). *Clinical Klein*. London: Free Association Books.

Holloway, W. (1989). *Subjectivity and Method in Psychology*. London: Sage.

Holmes, J. (1993). *John Bowlby & Attachement Theory*. London: Routledge.

hooks, b. (1992). *Black Looks: Race & Representation*. Brooklyn, NY: South End Press.

Hopper, E. (2003). *The Social Unconscious: Selected Papers*. London: Jessica Kingsley Publishers.

Hutchinson-Reis, M. (1986). "After the Uprising—Social work on the Broadwater Estate". In *Critical Social Policy*, no 17, Autumn, pp. 701–780.

Jackson, A. M. (2000). Shadeism: The Psychological Hangover of Slavery. *Counselling, November*, 546–550.

Jacobs, M. (1998). *The Presenting Past: The Core of Psychodynamic Counseling and Therapy* (2nd ed.). Buckingham: Open University Press.

Jones, J. M. (1972). *Prejudice and Racism*. Reading, MA: Addison-Wesley.

Kelly, G. A. (1955). *The Psychology of Personal Constructs, Volume 1*. New York: Norton (Reprinted by Rouledge, 1991).

Kernahan, C. & Wolfgram, H. (2003). Racial Identity and Attitude Development Among White Undergraduates: The Effects of a Diversity Course. *Kaleidoscope 11, Winter 2003*.

Kernberg, O. F. (1975). *Borderline Conditions and Pathological Narcissis*. New York: Jason Aronson.

Kitzinger, C. (1987). *The Social Construction of Lesbianism*. London: Sage.

Kitzinger, C. & Perkins, R. (1993). *Changing Our Minds: Lesbianism, Feminism and Psychology*. London: Only Women Press.

Klein, M. (1946). "Notes on Some Schizoid Mechanisms". In M. Klein, *Envy and Gratitude and Other Works*. New York: Delta, 1975.

Klein, M. (1959). Our adult world and its roots in infancy. In: *The Writings of Melanie Klein, Volume 3* (pp. 247–263). London: Hogarth Press, 1975, and Virago Press, 1997.

Klein, M. (1975). *The Writings of Melanie Klein, 4 vols. Vol. 1: Love, Guilt and Reparation and Other Works 1921–1945. Vol. II: The Psychoanalysis of Children. Vol. III: Envy and Gratitude and Other Works 1946–1963. Vol. IV: Narrative of a Child Analysis. The Conduct of Psycho-Analysis of Children as Seen in the Treatment of Ten-year-old Boy*. London: Hogarth Press and the Institute of Psychoanalysis.

Knox, R. (1950). *The Races of Men: A Fragment*. (London: Renshaw) cited by Bonton (1987).

Kohut, H. (1971). *Analysis of the self*. New York: International Universities Press.

Kovel, J. (1984). *White Racism*. London: Free Association Books, 1988.

Krause, I. (1998). *Therapy Across Culture*. London: SAGE Publications.

Lacan, J. (1977). *Ecritis: A Selection*. New York: W. W. Norton.

Lago, C. & Thompson, J. (1996). *Race, Culture and Counselling*. USA: Open University Press.

Langley, S. (1981). *Police to Blame for Brixton Confrontation*. Tribune 17 April, p. 1.

Larkin, P. (2003). *Collected Poems*. London: Faber and Faber.

Littlewood, R. & Lipsedge, M. (1989). *Aliens and Alienists: Ethnic Minority and Psychiatry*. London: Unwin Hyman Ltd.

Lord Scarman (1986). *The Scarman Report: The Brixton Disorders 10–12 April 1981*. London: Penguin Books, first printed by Her Majesty's Stationery Office, London 1981.

Lorenz, K. Z. (1952). *King Solomon's Ring*. New York: Cromwell.

MacPherson, W. (1999). The Stephen Lawrence Enquiry, London: The Stationery Office.

Mahler, M., Pine, F. & Bergman, A. (1975). *The Psychological Birth of the Human Infant*. New York: Basic Books.

Marris, P. (1991). The social construction of uncertainty. In: C. M. Parkes, J. Stevenson-Hinde & P. Marris (Eds.), *Attachment across the Life Cycle*. London: Routledge.

Marshall, J. (1984). *Women Managers: Travellers in a Male World*. Chichester: Wiley.

Maslow, A. H. (1968). Towards a Psychology of Being, (2nd ed.) Princeton, NJ: :Van Nostrand.

May, R. (1983). *The Discovery of Being: Writings in Existential Psychology*. New York: W. W. Norton.

McGoldrick, M., Giordano, J. & Pearce, J. K. (1996). *Ethnicity and Family Therapy* (2nd ed.). New York: Guilford.

Murphy, C., Davidson, P. & Hall, P. (1985). Brixton Ablaze! Petrol bombers' revenge for mum shot by police. In *Sunday People*, 29 September, p. 1.

Nelson, C. & Altorki, S. (Eds.). (1997). Arab Regional Women's Studies Workshop [Special issue]. *Cairo Papers in Social Science, 20(3)*.

Neville, H., Spanierman, L. & Doan, B. (2006). Exploring the association between color-blind racial ideology and multicultural counseling competencies, cultural diversity and ethnic minority. *Psychology*, 12(2): 275–290.

Newsweek (1981). *A race war in Brixton. One family's anguish*, 27 April, pp. 24–25.

Nitsun, M. (1996). The Anti-Group: Destructive forces in the group and their creative potential. London & New York: Routledge.

Oakley, A. (1985). *The Sociology of Housework*. Oxford: Blackwell (first published by Martin Robertson, 1974).

Obholzer, A. & Roberts, V. Z. (1994). *The Unconscious at Work: Individual and Organizational Stress in the Human Service*. London: Routledge.

Okun, B. F. (1996). *Understanding Diverse Families: What Practitionsers Need to Know*. New York: Guilford.

Oldham, J. M., Skodol, A. E. & Bender, D. S. (2005). *Textbook of Personality Disorders*. USA: American Psychiatric Publishing, Inc. Open University Press.

Palmer, S. & Laungani, P. D. (1999). *Counselling in a Multicultural Society*. London: SAGE.

Paniagua, F. A. (2001). *Diagnosis in a Multicultural Context: A Casebook for Mental Health Professionals*. UK: SAGE Publishers.

Parker, I. (1994). In Banister, P., Burman, E., Parker, I., Taylor, M. & Tindall, C. (1994). *Qualitative Methods in Psychology: A Research Guide*. Berkshire: Open University Press.

Parker, I. (2005). *Qualitative Psychology: Introducing Radical Research*. Buckingham: Open University.

Pears, E. (2001). The fight begins: Government increases police powers, threatens families of looters with eviction and benefits cuts and cracks down on social media as part of a tough response to last week's riots. In *The Voice*, August 18–24, p. 6.

Pine, M. (1979). "How a group develops over time." *Group Analysis* August, *12(2)* pp. 109–113 London: SAGE Publications.

Policing London. (1986). Vol 38, Feb-March pp. 108–110. Police tactics in Brixton and Tottenham.

Ponterotto, J. G. (1988). Racial consciousness development among white counselors' trainees: A stage model. *Journal of Multicultural Counseling and Development, 66*: 237–245.

Race Relations Act (1976). London: Her Majesty's Stationery Office (HMSO).

Rack, E. (1982). *Race and Culture and Mental Disorder*. London: Tavistock Publications.

Raphael, B. (1984). *The Anatomy of Bereavement: A Handbook for The Caring Professions*. London: Routledge.

Rapoport, R. N. (1960). *Community as Doctor: New Perspectives on A Therapeutic Community*. London: Tavistock Publications.

Reason, P. & Rowan, J. (Eds.) (1981). *Human Inquiry: A Sourcebook of New Paradigm Research*. Chichester: Wiley.

Rose, D. (1985). Police "window dressing" failed to mask the tension. *The Guardian* September 30, p. 2.

Rose, E. (1997). Daring to Work with Internalized Racism. *Counselling* pp. 92–94. Routledge.

Sagar, H. A. & Schofield, J. W. (1980). Racial and behavioral cues in black and white children's perceptions of ambiguously aggressive acts. *Journal of Personality and Social Psychology, 39*: 590–598.

Sayce, K. (Ed.). (1987). *Tabex Encyclopedia Zimbabwe*, Harare: Zimbabwe Quest Publishing (PVT) Ltd.

Segal, J. (1992). *Melanie Klein*. London: SAGE Publications.

Simpson, I. (1995). "Group therapy within the NHS 1. We all know about 'good enough' but is it safe enough?", Group Analysis, London: SAGE Publications Vol 28 (pp. 225–237).

Stern, D. N. (1985). *The Interpersonal World of the Infant: A View from Psychoanalysis and Developmental Psychology*. USA: BasicBooks.

Stoltenberg, C. D. (1998). A social cognitive—and developmental—model of counselor training. *Counseling Psychologist*, 26, 317–323.

Sue, D. W., Carter, R. T., Casas, J. M., Fouad, N. A., Ivey, A. E., Jensen, M., LaFromboise, T., Manese, J. E., Ponterotto, J. G. & Vasquez—Nuttall, E. (1998). *Multicultural Counseling Competencies: Individual and Organizational Development*. Thousand Oaks, CA: Sage Productions.

Sue, D. W. & Sue, D. (1990). *Counselling the Culturally Different: Theory and Practice*. Canada: John Wiley & Sons, Inc.

Sue, S., Allen, D. & Conaway, L. (1975). The responsiveness and equality of mental health care to Chicanos and Native Americans. *American Journal of Community Psychology*, 45: 111–118.

Sue, S. & McKinney, H. (1974). Delivery of community health services to black and white clients. *Journal of Consulting and Clinical Psychology*, 42: 794–801.

Sue, S., McKinney, H., Allen, D. & Hall, J. (1974). Delivery of community health services to black and white clients. *Journal of Consulting Psychology*, 42: 794–801.

Sullivan, M. A., Harris, E., Collado, C. & Chen, T. (2006). Noways tired: Perspectives of clinicians of color on cultural competent crisis intervention. *Journal of Clinical Psychology: In Session*, 62(8): 987–999.

Suman, F. (1991). *Mental Health, Race & Culture: Issues in Mental Health*. London: MacMillan Education Ltd.

Symington, J. & Symington, N. (1996). *The Clinical Thinking of Wilfred Bion*. London : Routledge Taylor & Francis Group.

Tatum, B. D. (1997). Why Are All the Black Kids Sitting Together in the Cafeteria? And Other Conversations About Race. New York, NY: Basic Books.

Taylor, J. (2011). Race relations' on knife edge after three Asian men were killed in a hit-and run. *The Independent*, 11 August 2011, p. 4.

Tindall (1994). In Banister, P., Burman, E., Parker, I., Taylor, M. & Tindall, C. (1994). *Qualitative Methods in Psychology: A Research Guide*. Berkshire: Open University Press.

The BAC Code of Ethics and Practice for the Supervision of Counsellors, British Association for Counselling 1987.

Thomas, C. W. (1969). Black-white campus and the function of counselling. *Counselling Psychologist*, 1: 70–73.

Thorndycraft, B. (2000). The Colditz Syndrome: The Need to Escape from Group Therapy *Group Analysis, Volume 34* (pp. 273–286). London: SAGE Publications.

Trade Union Congress (July 2000). Report of the TUC's "Root Out Racism" hotline- Exposing racism at work. TUC's Campaigns and Communication Department.

Troyna, B. (1993). *Racism and Education: Research Perspectives*. Buckingham: Open University.

Turquet, P. (1974). Leadership: The individual and the group, in A. D. Colman and M. H. Geller (Eds.), *Group Relations Reader 2*, A. K. Rice Institute Series (Washington, DC), 1985.

Vandiver, B. J., Fhagen-Smith, P. E., Cokley, K. O., Cross, Jr., W. E. & Worrell, F. C. (2001). Cross's nigrescence model: From theory to scale to theory. *Journal of Multicultural Counseling and Development*, 29(3): ProQuest Psychology Journals, pp. 174–200.

Vespia, K. M., Heckman-Stone, C. & Delworth, U. (2002). Describing and facilitating effective supervision behavior in counseling trainees. *Psychotherapy: Theory /Practice Training*, 39(1): 56–65.

Wallis, K. C. & Poulton, J. L. (2001). *Internalization: The Origins and Construction of Internal Reality* (ed. Jacobs, M.). Buckingham: Open University Press.

Walrond-Skinner, S. (1986). *A Dictionary of Psychotherapy*. London: Routledge & Kegan Paul.

Waska, R. T. (2002). *Primitive Experiences of Loss: Working with The Paranoid–Schizoid Patient*. London: Karnac (Books) Ltd.

Wheeler, S. (2000). What makes a good counsellor? an analysis of ways in which counsellor trainers construe good and bad counselling trainees. *Counselling Psychology Quarterly*, 13(1): 65–83.

White, J. (1989). Racism and Psychosis: Whose Madness Is It Anyway?, paper presented at "Psychoanalysis and the Public Sphere" conference. University of East London, September 1989.

Williams, H. (2011). Top black professor calls for "people's" inquiry following riots, *The Voice*, August 18–24, p. 4.

Willie, C. V., Kramer, B. M. & Brown, B. S. (1973). *Racism and Mental Health*. Pittsburgh: University of Pittsburgh Press.

Winnicott, D. W. (1947). Hate in the countertransference'. In: Winnicot (1958) *Collected Papers: Through Paediatrics to Psycho-Analysis* (pp. 194–203). London: Hogarth.

Winnicott, D. W. ([1949] 1958). Mind and its relation to the psyche-soma. In *Collected Papers: Through Paediatrics to Psycho-analysis*. New York: Basic Books.

Winnicott, D. W. ([1950] 1958). Aggression in relation to emotional development, in *Collected Papers: Through Paediatrics to Psycho-analysis*. New York: Basic Books.

Winnicot, D. W. (1950). Aggresion in Relation to Emotional Development'. In D. W. Winnicott, *Through Paediatrics to Psychoanalysis,* London: Hogarth Press, 1958.

Winnicott, D. W. (1984). *Deprivation and Delinquency.* London: Tavistock Publications.

Winnicott, D. W. (1986). *Home is Where We Start From.* London: Penguin.

Wise, S. (1987). "A Framework for Discussing Ethical Issues in Feminist Rsesearch", *in Writing Feminist Biography,* 2: Using Life Histories, Studies in Sexual Politics *no. 19. Manchester: Department of Sociology, University of Manchester.*

INDEX

424   INDEX